HARUKAZE BITTER★BOP

Volume 2
Created by Court Betten

HAMBURG // LONDON // LOS ANGELES // TOKYO

Harukaze Bitter Bop Volume 2
Created by Court Betten

Translation - Christine Schilling
English Adaptation - Kereth Cowe-Spigai
Retouch and Lettering - Star Print Brokers
Copy Editor - Shannon Watters
Production Artist - Courtney Geter
Graphic Designer - James Lee

Editor - Alexis Kirsch
Digital Imaging Manager - Chris Buford
Pre-Production Supervisor - Erika Terriquez
Production Manager - Elisabeth Brizzi
Managing Editor - Vy Nguyen
Creative Director - Anne Marie Horne
Editor-in-Chief - Rob Tokar
Publisher - Mike Kiley
President and C.O.O. - John Parker
C.E.O. and Chief Creative Officer - Stu Levy

A 🐢 **TOKYOPOP** Manga

TOKYOPOP Inc.
5900 Wilshire Blvd. Suite 2000
Los Angeles, CA 90036

E-mail: info@TOKYOPOP.com
Come visit us online at www.TOKYOPOP.com

ISBN: 978-1-4278-0329-0

First TOKYOPOP printing: May 2008
10 9 8 7 6 5 4 3 2 1
Printed in the USA

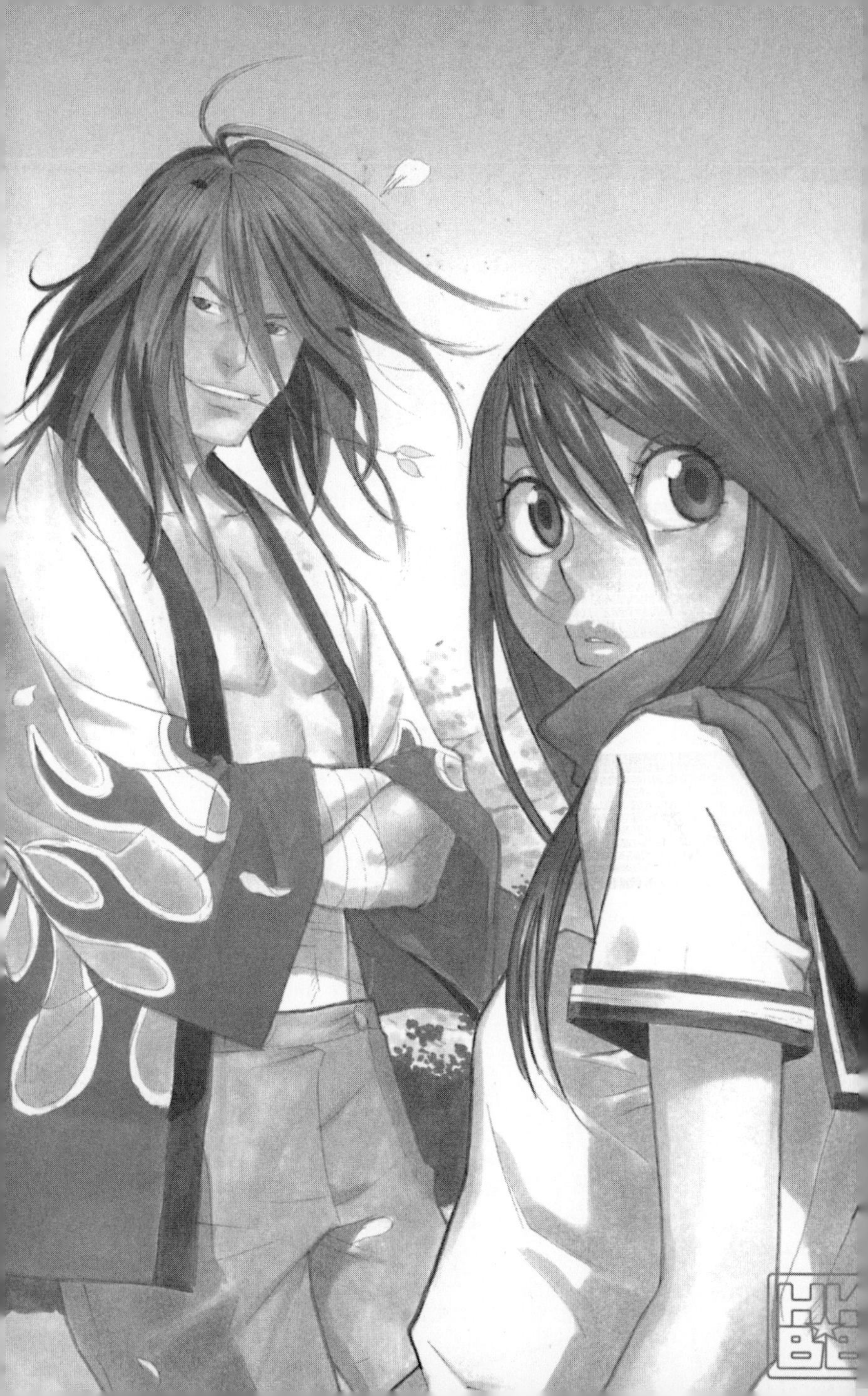

HARUKAZE BITTER★BOP

Character Bios

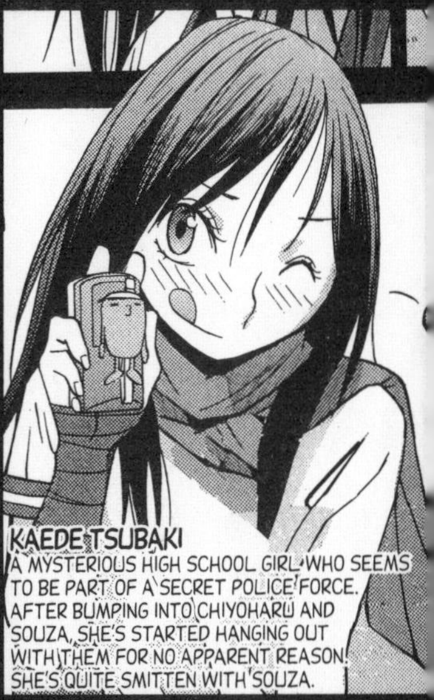
KAEDE TSUBAKI
A MYSTERIOUS HIGH SCHOOL GIRL WHO SEEMS TO BE PART OF A SECRET POLICE FORCE. AFTER BUMPING INTO CHIYOHARU AND SOUZA, SHE'S STARTED HANGING OUT WITH THEM FOR NO APPARENT REASON. SHE'S QUITE SMITTEN WITH SOUZA.

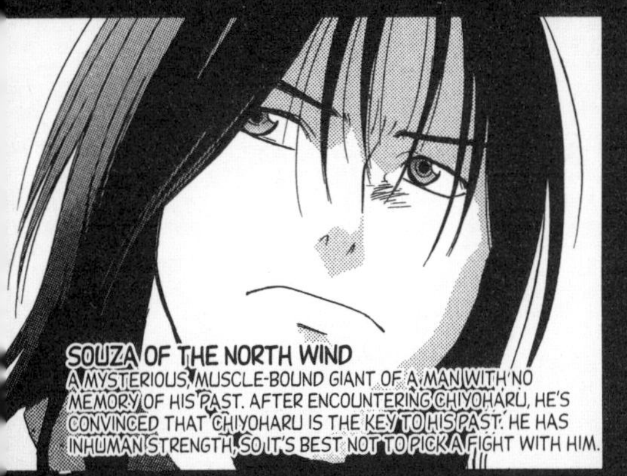
SOUZA OF THE NORTH WIND
A MYSTERIOUS, MUSCLE-BOUND GIANT OF A MAN WITH NO MEMORY OF HIS PAST. AFTER ENCOUNTERING CHIYOHARU, HE'S CONVINCED THAT CHIYOHARU IS THE KEY TO HIS PAST. HE HAS INHUMAN STRENGTH, SO IT'S BEST NOT TO PICK A FIGHT WITH HIM.

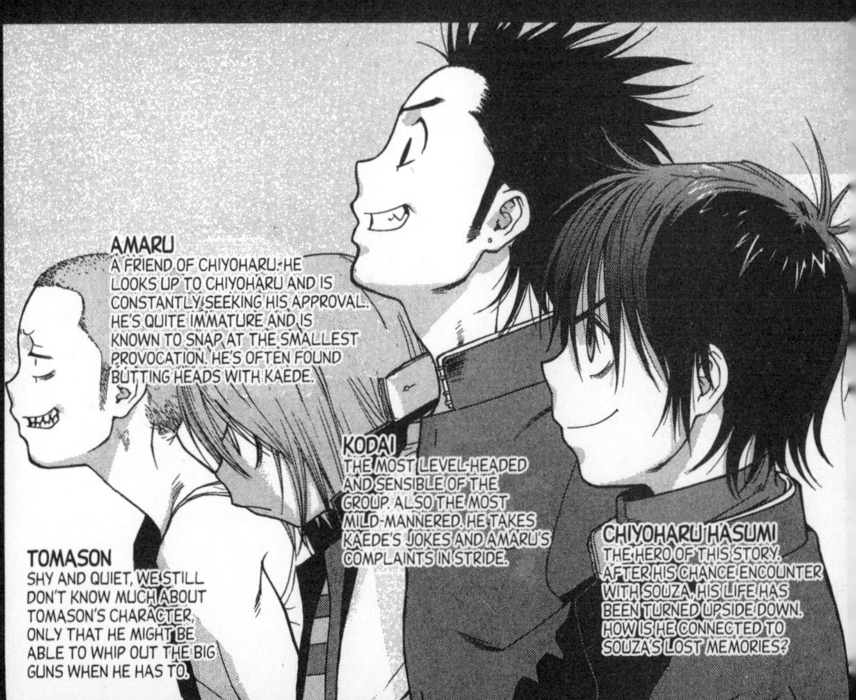
AMARU
A FRIEND OF CHIYOHARU. HE LOOKS UP TO CHIYOHARU AND IS CONSTANTLY SEEKING HIS APPROVAL. HE'S QUITE IMMATURE AND IS KNOWN TO SNAP AT THE SMALLEST PROVOCATION. HE'S OFTEN FOUND BUTTING HEADS WITH KAEDE.
KODAI
THE MOST LEVEL-HEADED AND SENSIBLE OF THE GROUP. ALSO THE MOST MILD-MANNERED. HE TAKES KAEDE'S JOKES AND AMARU'S COMPLAINTS IN STRIDE.
CHIYOHARU HASUMI
THE HERO OF THIS STORY. AFTER HIS CHANCE ENCOUNTER WITH SOUZA, HIS LIFE HAS BEEN TURNED UPSIDE DOWN. HOW IS HE CONNECTED TO SOUZA'S LOST MEMORIES?
TOMASON
SHY AND QUIET, WE STILL DON'T KNOW MUCH ABOUT TOMASON'S CHARACTER, ONLY THAT HE MIGHT BE ABLE TO WHIP OUT THE BIG GUNS WHEN HE HAS TO.

HARUKAZE BITTER★BOP

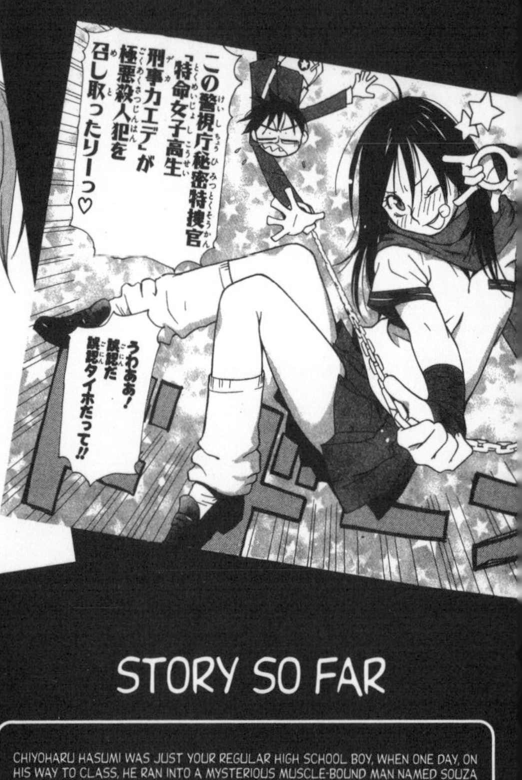
この警視庁秘密特捜官「特命女子高生刑事カエデ」が極悪殺人犯を召し取ったりーっ♡
うわああ! 誤認だ 誤認タイホだって!!

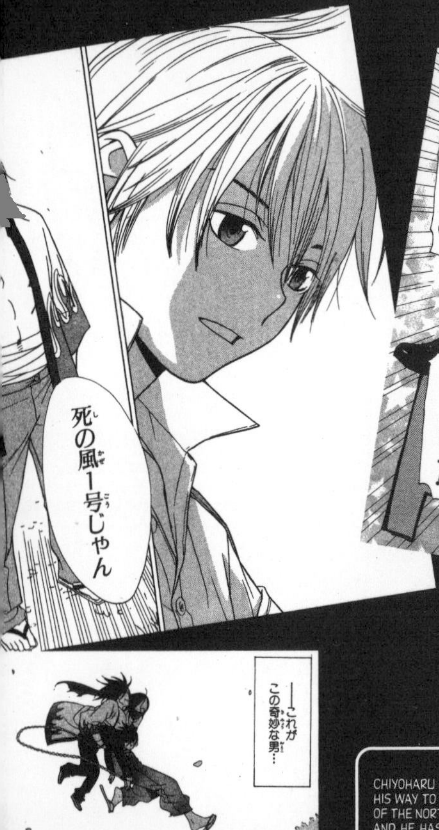
死の風1号じゃん

STORY SO FAR

CHIYOHARU HASUMI WAS JUST YOUR REGULAR HIGH SCHOOL BOY, WHEN ONE DAY, ON HIS WAY TO CLASS, HE RAN INTO A MYSTERIOUS MUSCLE-BOUND MAN NAMED SOUZA OF THE NORTH WIND. SOUZA HAD LOST ALL OF HIS MEMORIES EXCEPT FOR HIS NAME, AND HE HAS AN ALMOST UNEARTHLY AMOUNT OF STRENGTH. CHIYOHARU WANTED NOTHING TO DO WITH HIM AND WAS JUST CONTINUING ON HIS WAY TO SCHOOL, WHEN HE WAS SUDDENLY APPREHENDED BY A PRETTY, BUT CRAZY, YOUNG GIRL, KAEDE, WHO CLAIMED TO BE A SPECIAL HIGH SCHOOL STUDENT FEMALE DETECTIVE.

SHE SLAPPED ON A PAIR OF HANDCUFFS ONTO CHIYOHARU AND SOUZA, SO THEY HAD NO CHOICE BUT TO GO TO SCHOOL TOGETHER. AT FIRST, CHIYOHARU DIDN'T KNOW WHAT TO MAKE OF SOUZA. BUT ONCE SOUZA WENT TO THE MAT FOR HIM, HE COULDN'T HELP BUT LET SOUZA MOVE INTO HIS APARTMENT WHILE HE TRIED TO REMEMBER HIS PAST. FOR NO APPARENT REASON, KAEDE BEGAN HANGING OUT WITH THEM, AND SO THE THREE OF THEM BECAME A TEAM.

SOON AFTER, CHIYOHARU'S OLD FRIENDS KODAI, AMARU AND TOMASON JOINED UP TO TRY AND HELP SOUZA REGAIN HIS LOST MEMORIES. THEY TRIED ALL SORTS OF METHODS, BUT NOTHING WORKED. THEN ONE DAY, WHILE THE GANG WAS AT THE SCHOOL LATE AT NIGHT, ANOTHER MYSTERIOUS BOY, AYAME, WHO HAD A CONNECTION TO CHIYOHARU IN THE PAST, APPEARED. BESIDE HIM STOOD A LARGE MAN NAMED KURUSU OF THE SUN. HE SEEMED TO BE ACTING AS AYAME'S BODYGUARD, BUT IMPLIED HE HAD SOME CONNECTION TO SOUZA, AS WELL. AFTER QUICKLY DISPOSING OF A BATCH OF YAKUZA WHO WERE AFTER AYAME, HE TURNED HIS ATTENTION TO SOUZA. ONCE ALONE, KURUSU THEN REVEALED THAT SOUZA WAS ACTUALLY A REMODELED HUMAN WHO'D SHIRKED THE ORGANIZATION WHO'D CREATED HIM, AND THAT HE WAS THERE AS AN ASSASSIN TO DISPOSE OF SOUZA.
SOUZA WAS TOO STUNNED TO REACT AS KURUSU PLUNGED HIS FIST RIGHT INTO HIS CHEST, AND SOUZA FELL...

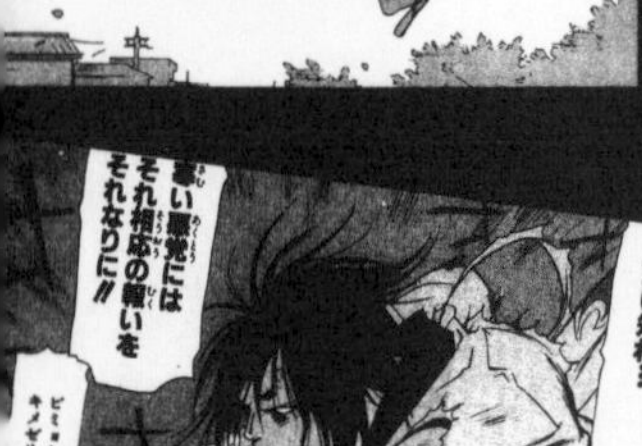
――これが この奇妙な男…

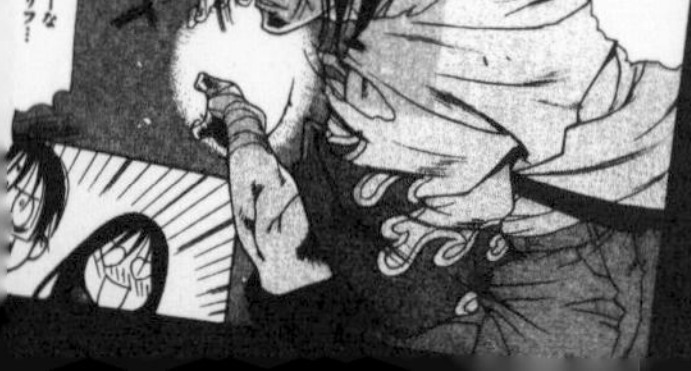
キサマの方こそ思い知れ…
悪い悪党にはそれ相応の報いをそれなりに!!
ビミョーなキメゼリフ…

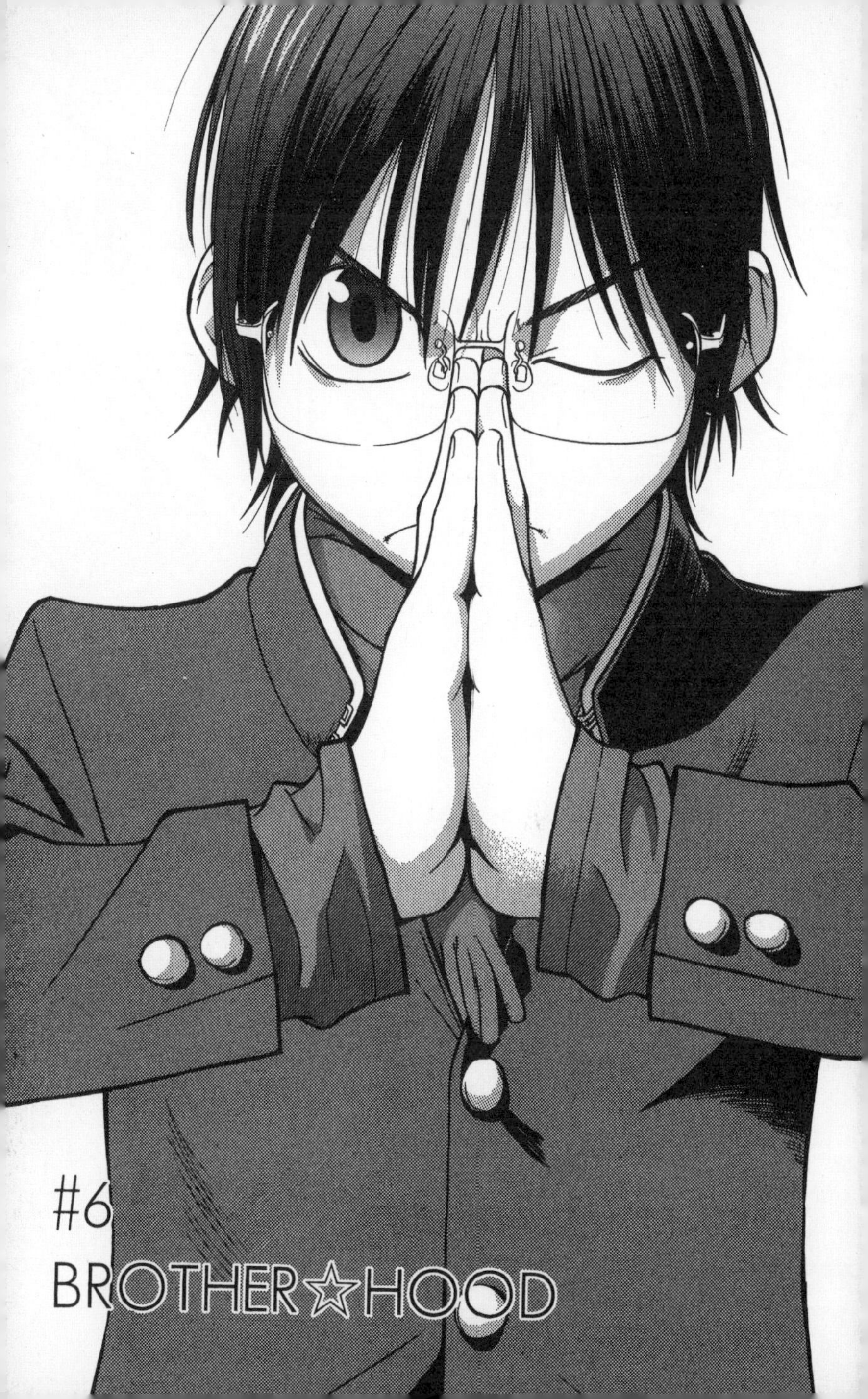
#6
BROTHER☆HOOD

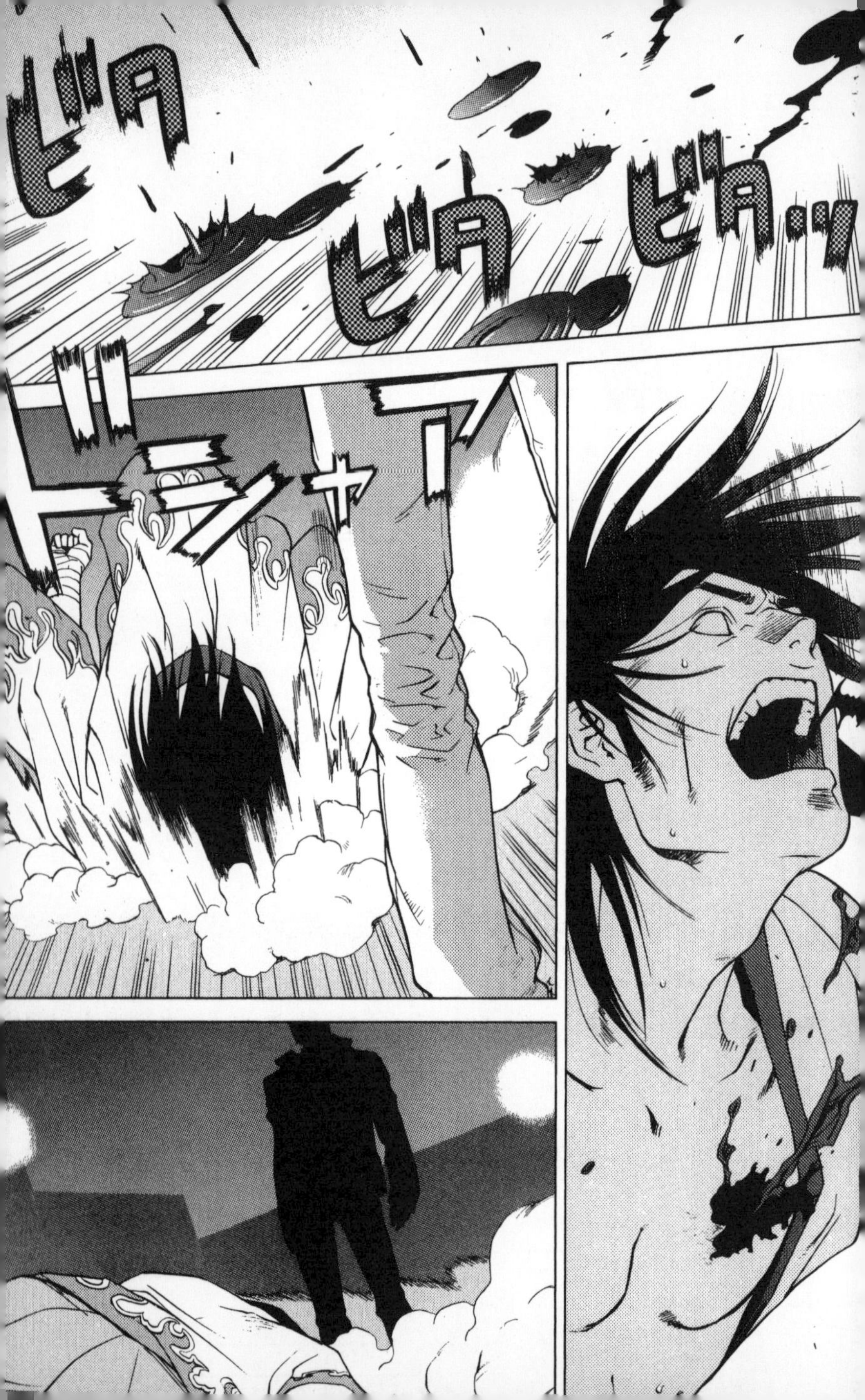

ビタ ビタ ビタ…ッ
ドシャア

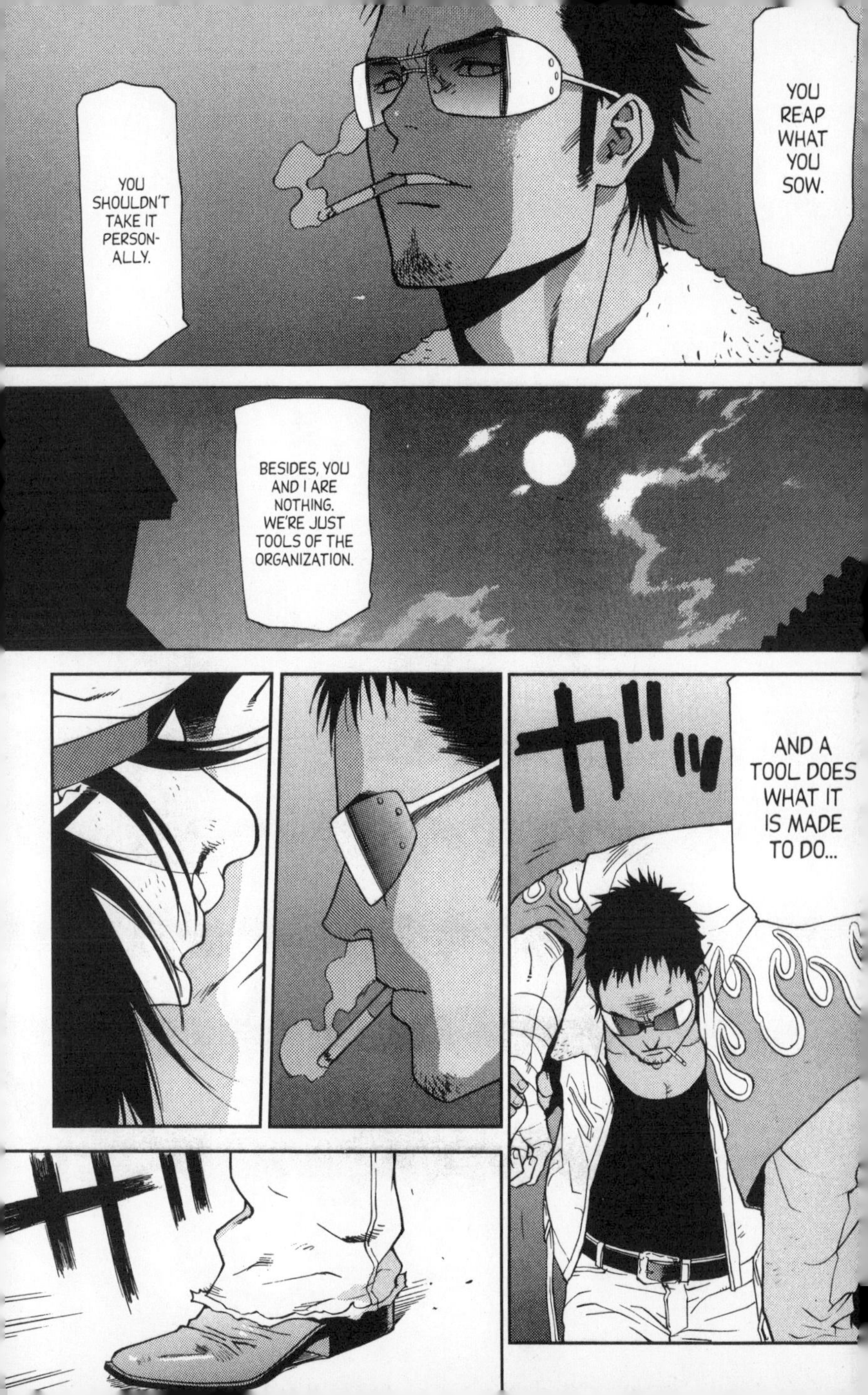
YOU REAP WHAT YOU SOW.
YOU SHOULDN'T TAKE IT PERSON-ALLY.
BESIDES, YOU AND I ARE NOTHING. WE'RE JUST TOOLS OF THE ORGANIZATION.
AND A TOOL DOES WHAT IT IS MADE TO DO...
ガッ
ガッ

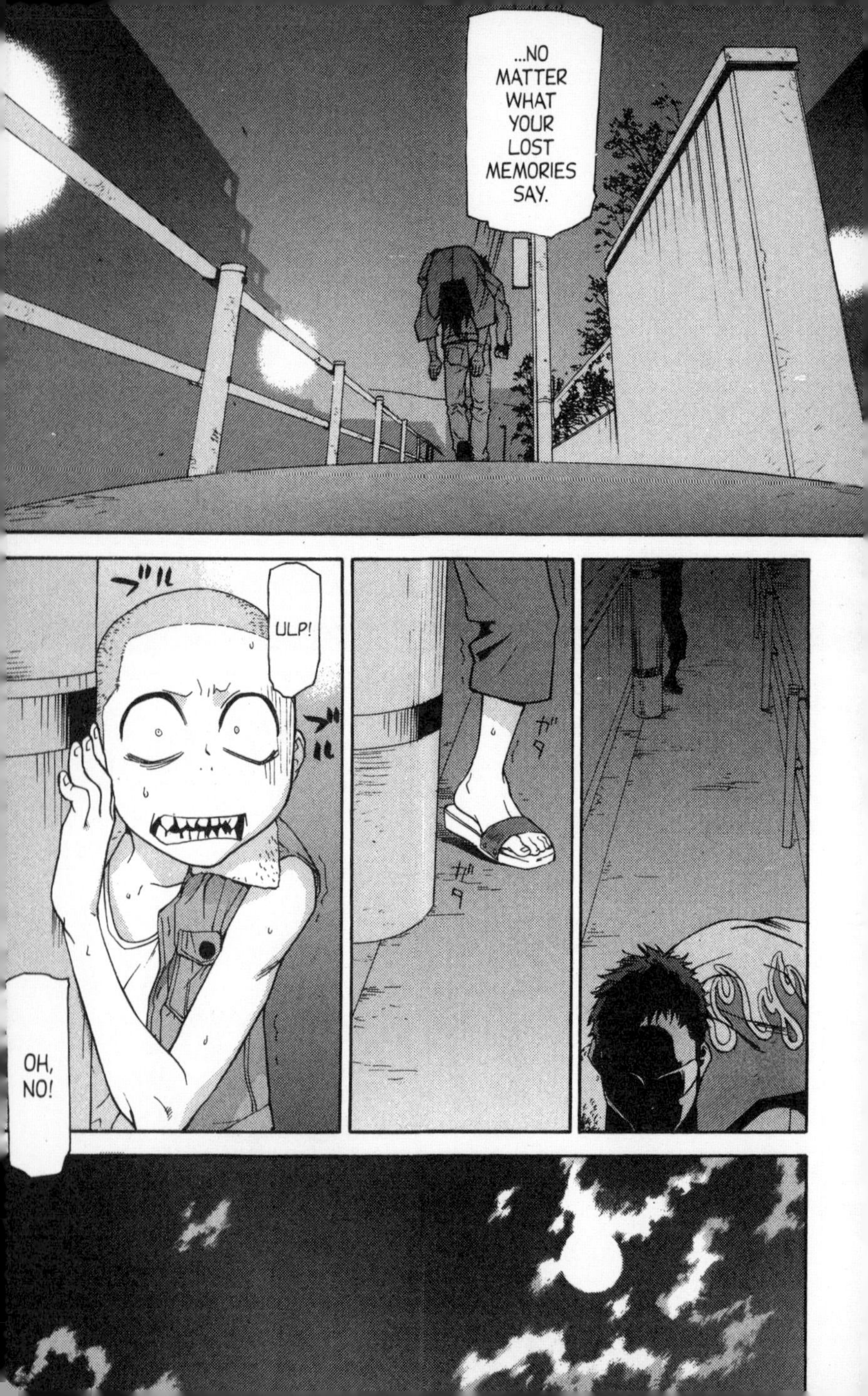
...NO MATTER WHAT YOUR LOST MEMORIES SAY.
ULP!
OH, NO!

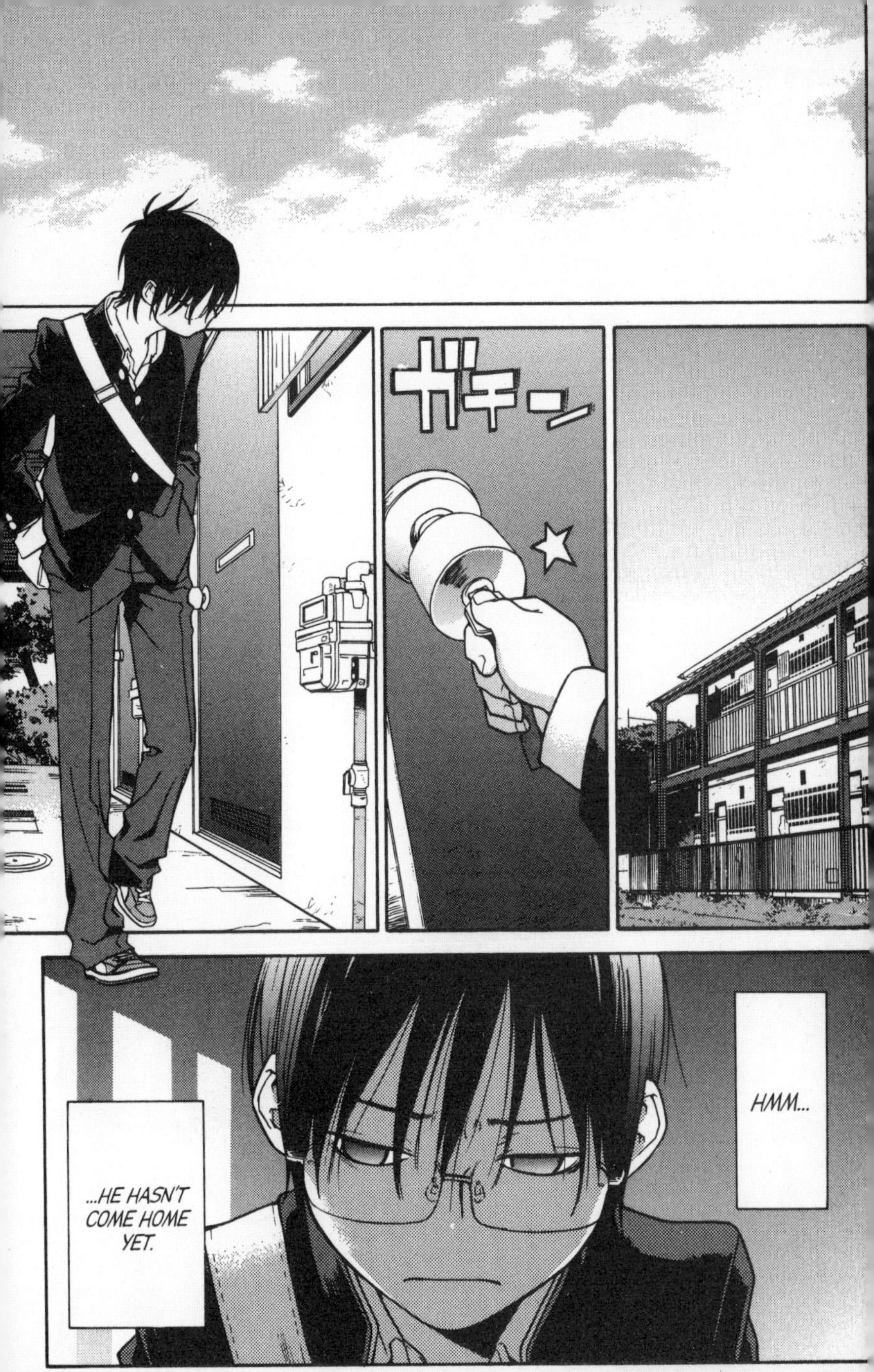
ガチーン
HMM...
...HE HASN'T COME HOME YET.

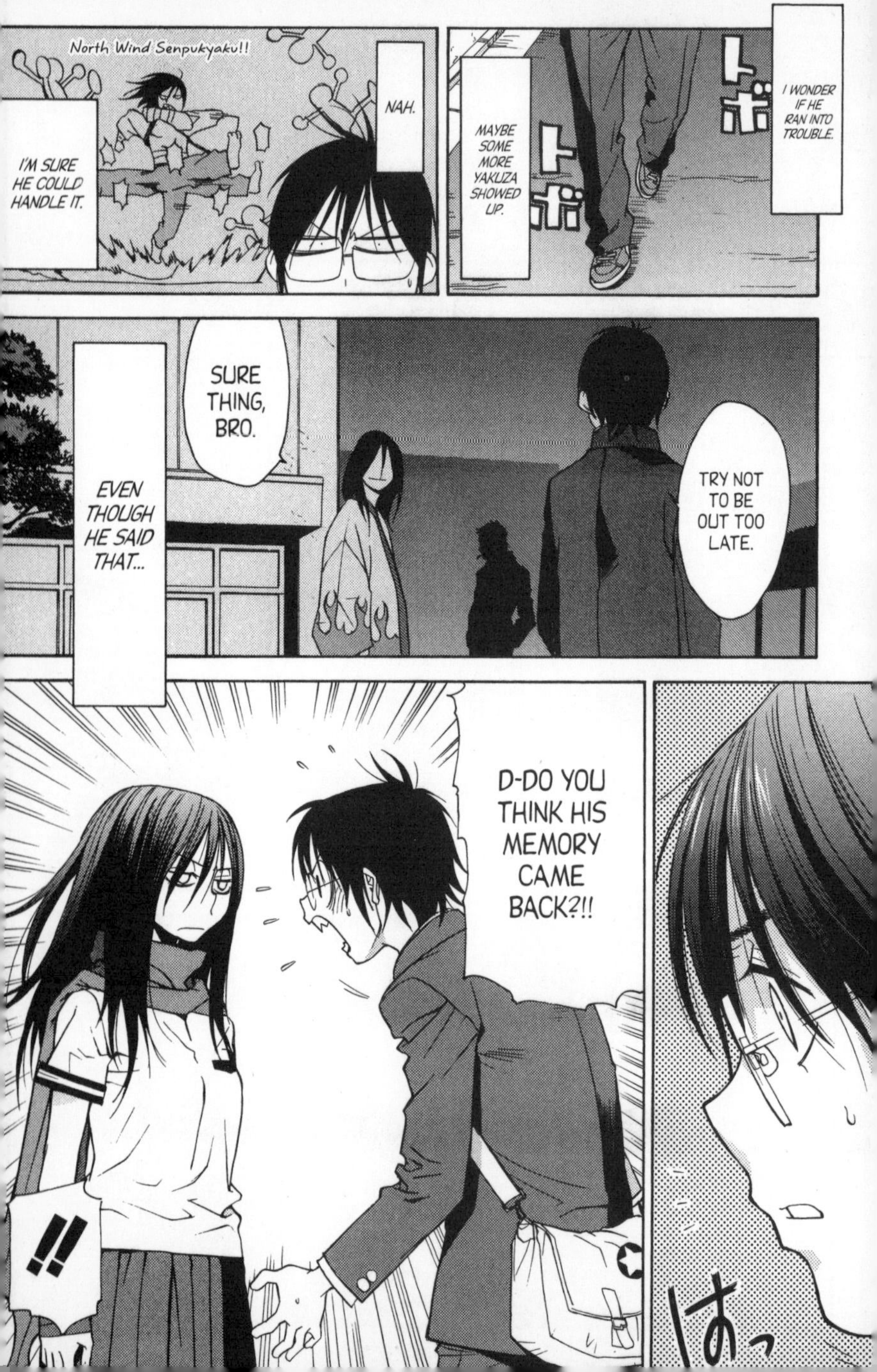
I WONDER IF HE RAN INTO TROUBLE.
トボ
トボ
MAYBE SOME MORE YAKUZA SHOWED UP.
NAH.
I'M SURE HE COULD HANDLE IT.
North Wind Senpukyaku!!
TRY NOT TO BE OUT TOO LATE.
SURE THING, BRO.
EVEN THOUGH HE SAID THAT...
はっ
D-DO YOU THINK HIS MEMORY CAME BACK?!!
!!

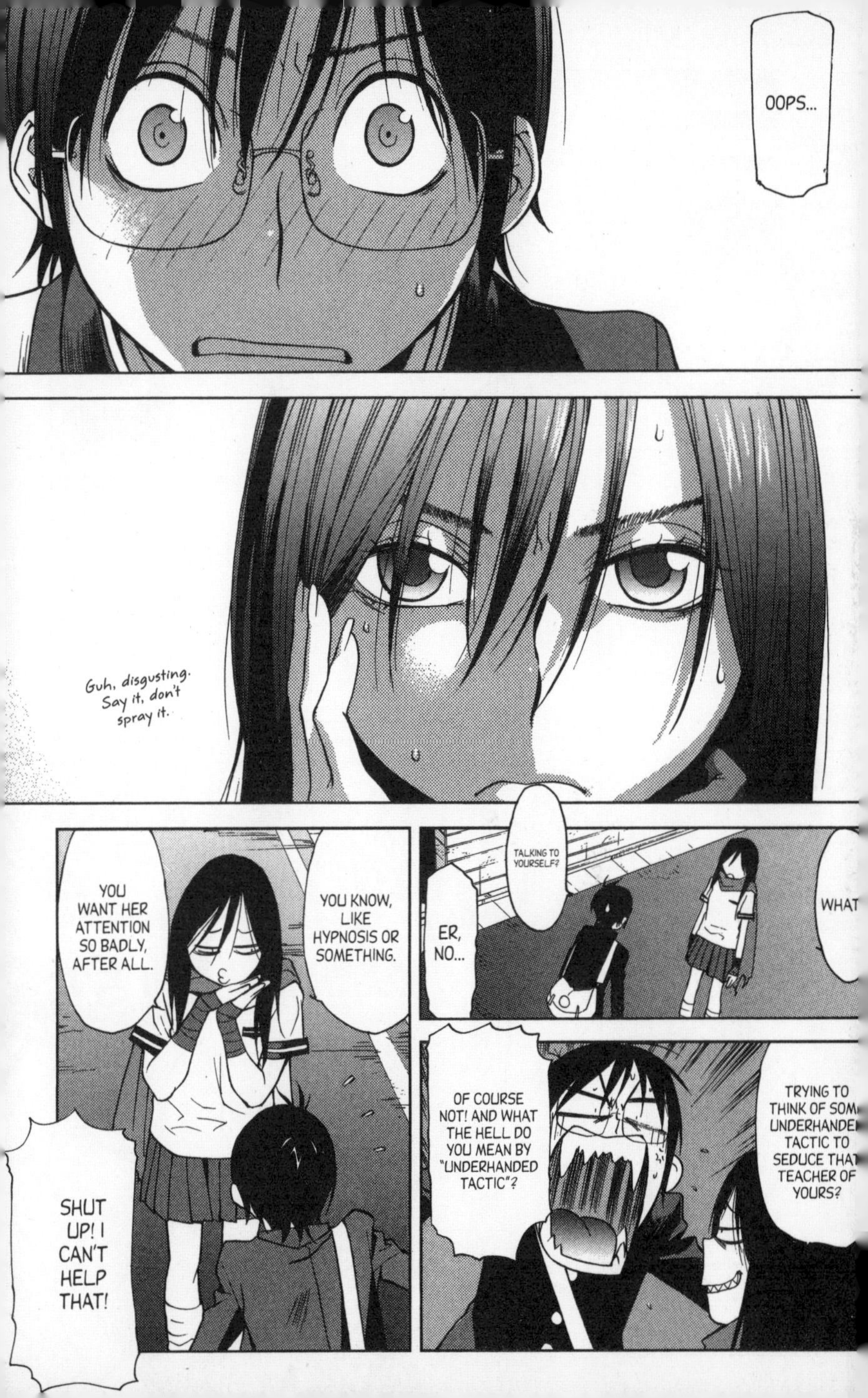
OOPS...
Guh, disgusting. Say it, don't spray it.
WHAT
TALKING TO YOURSELF?
ER, NO...
TRYING TO THINK OF SOM UNDERHANDE TACTIC TO SEDUCE THAT TEACHER OF YOURS?
OF COURSE NOT! AND WHAT THE HELL DO YOU MEAN BY "UNDERHANDED TACTIC"?
YOU KNOW, LIKE HYPNOSIS OR SOMETHING.
YOU WANT HER ATTENTION SO BADLY, AFTER ALL.
SHUT UP! I CAN'T HELP THAT!

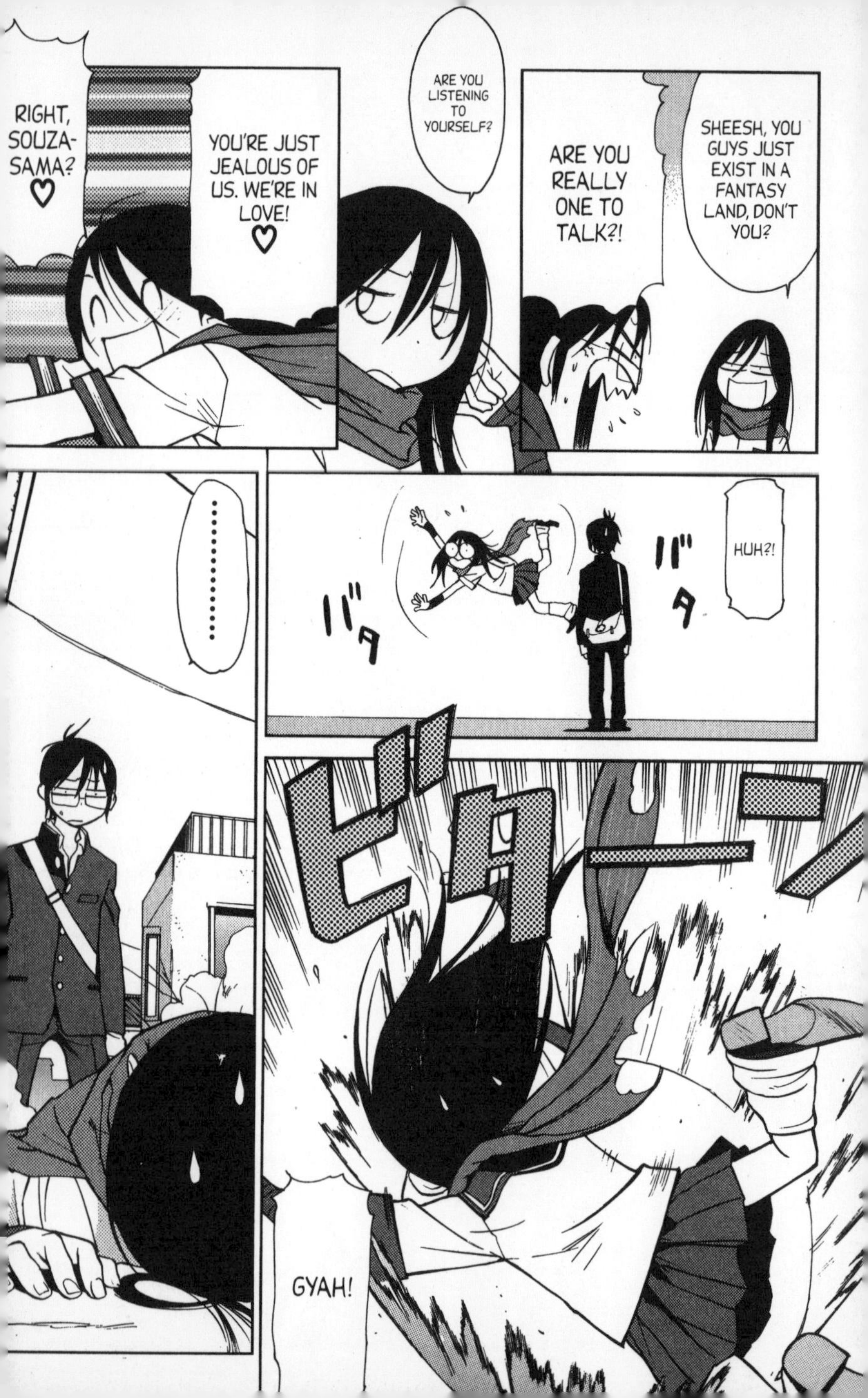
SHEESH, YOU GUYS JUST EXIST IN A FANTASY LAND, DON'T YOU?
ARE YOU REALLY ONE TO TALK?!
ARE YOU LISTENING TO YOURSELF?
YOU'RE JUST JEALOUS OF US. WE'RE IN LOVE! ♡
RIGHT, SOUZA-SAMA? ♡
HUH?!
バタ
バタ
……
ビターン
GYAH!

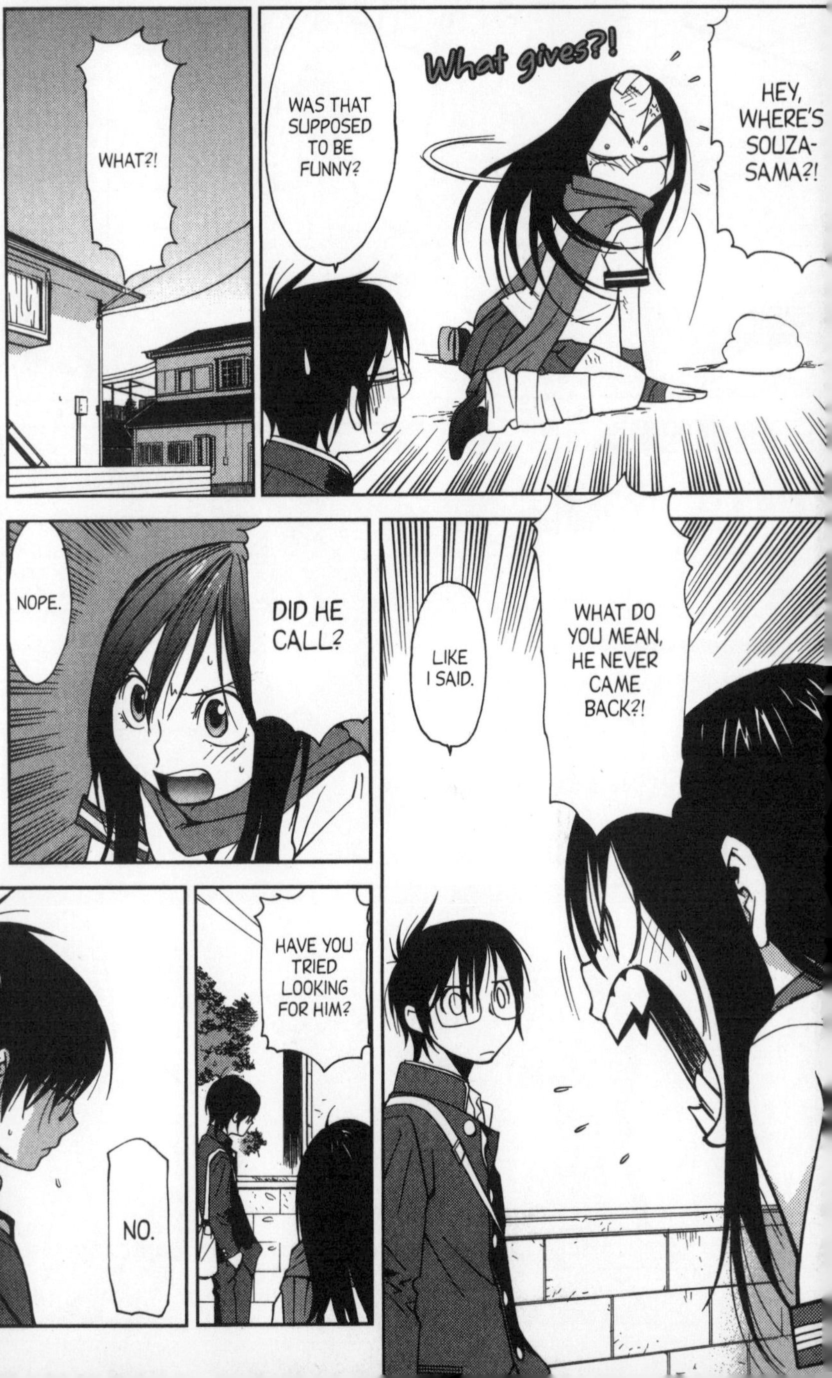

HEY, WHERE'S SOUZA-SAMA?!
What gives?!
WAS THAT SUPPOSED TO BE FUNNY?
WHAT?!
WHAT DO YOU MEAN, HE NEVER CAME BACK?!
LIKE I SAID.
DID HE CALL?
NOPE.
HAVE YOU TRIED LOOKING FOR HIM?
NO.

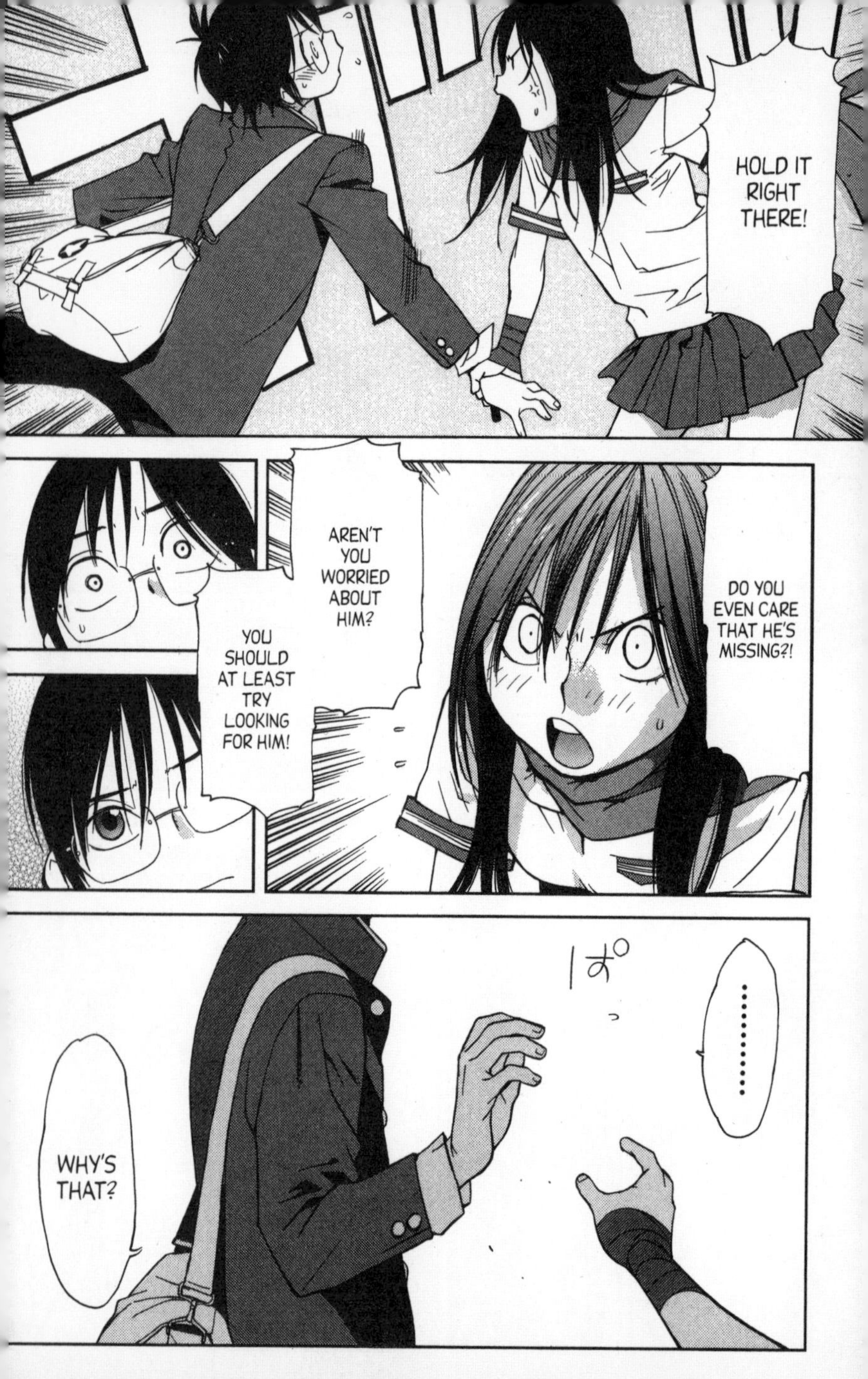
HOLD IT RIGHT THERE!
DO YOU EVEN CARE THAT HE'S MISSING?!
AREN'T YOU WORRIED ABOUT HIM?
YOU SHOULD AT LEAST TRY LOOKING FOR HIM!
……
ぱっ
WHY'S THAT?

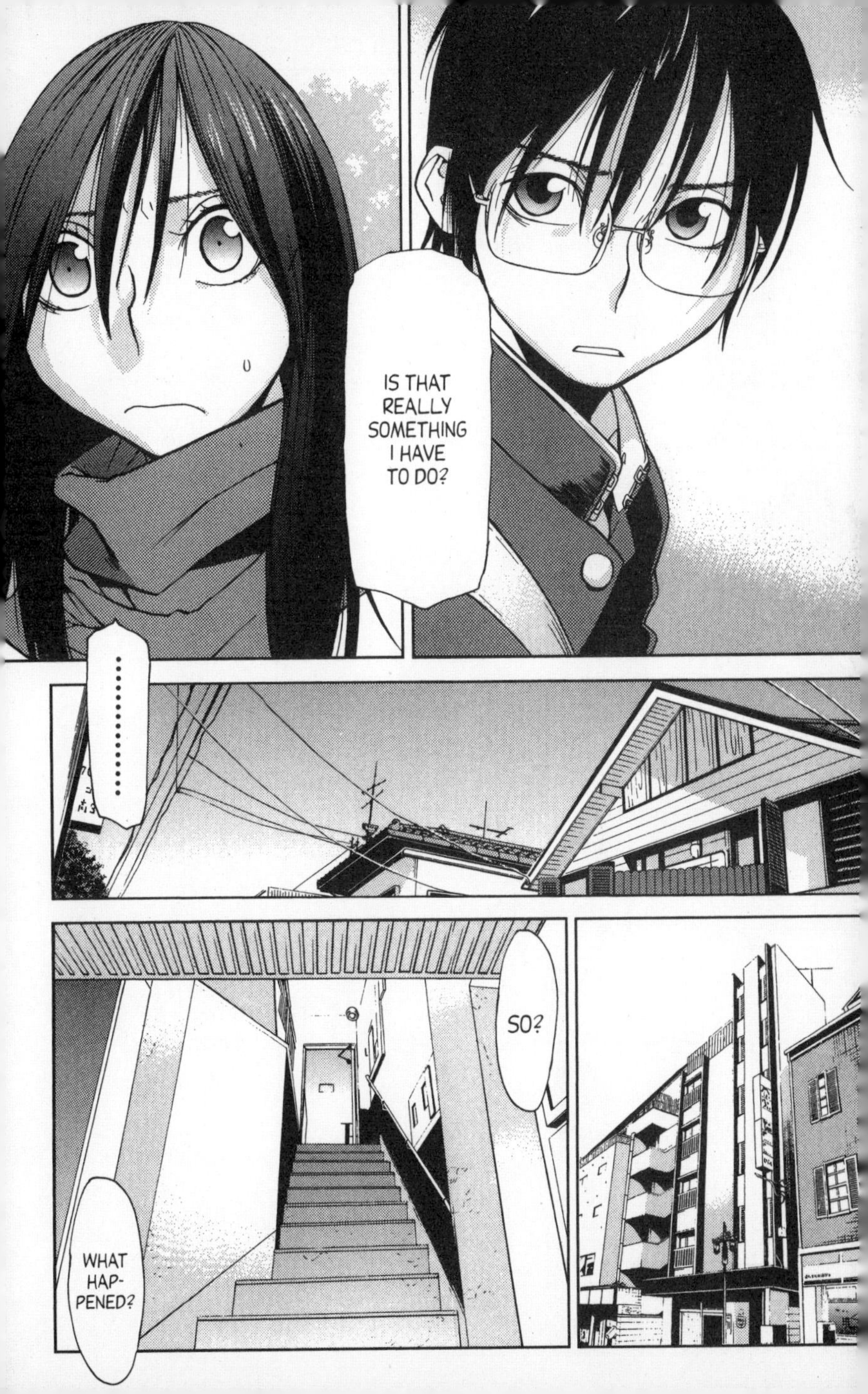
IS THAT REALLY SOMETHING I HAVE TO DO?
……
SO?
WHAT HAP-PENED?

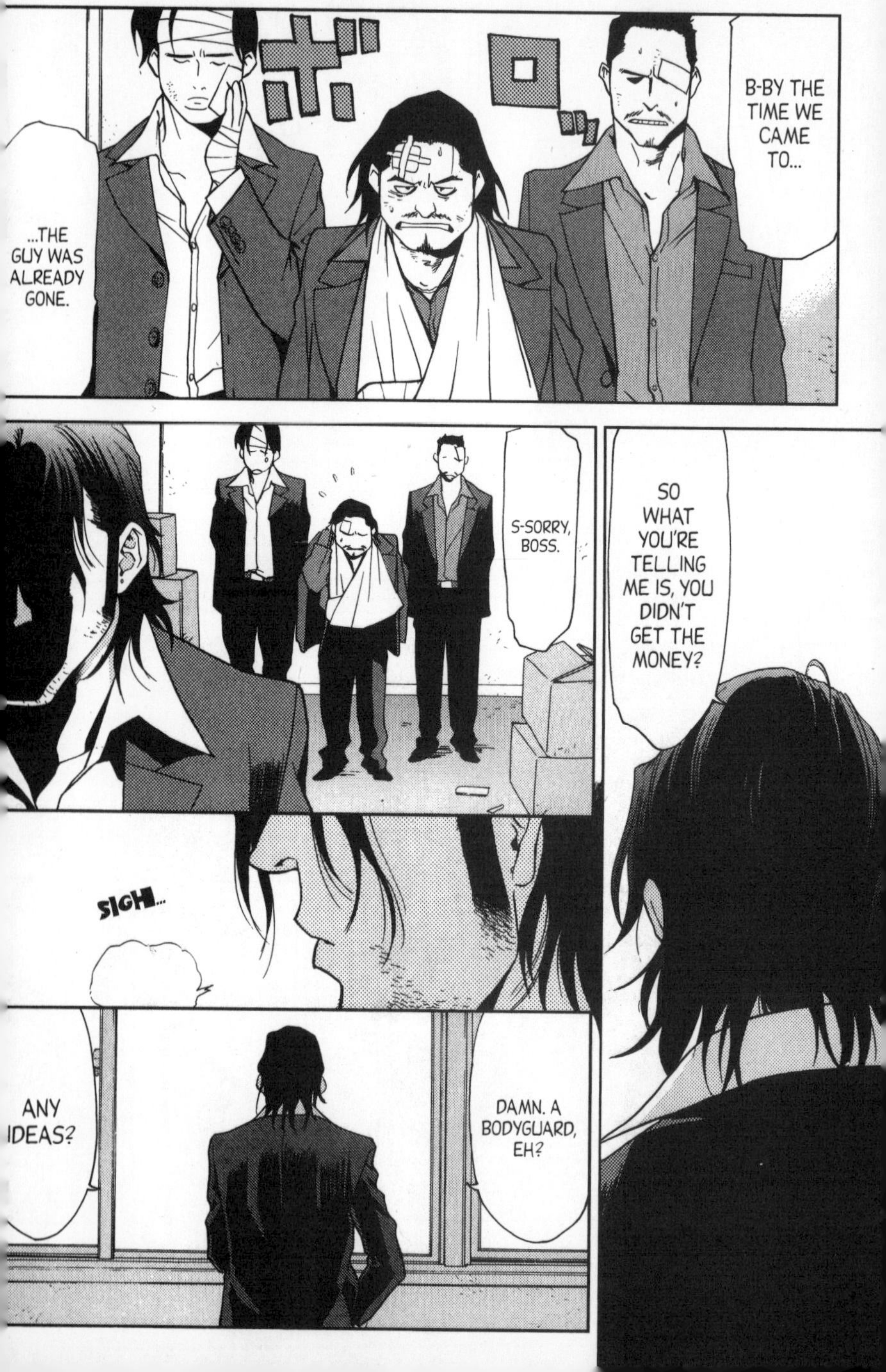

B-BY THE TIME WE CAME TO...
ボロッ
...THE GUY WAS ALREADY GONE.
SO WHAT YOU'RE TELLING ME IS, YOU DIDN'T GET THE MONEY?
S-SORRY, BOSS.
SIGH...
DAMN. A BODYGUARD, EH?
ANY IDEAS?

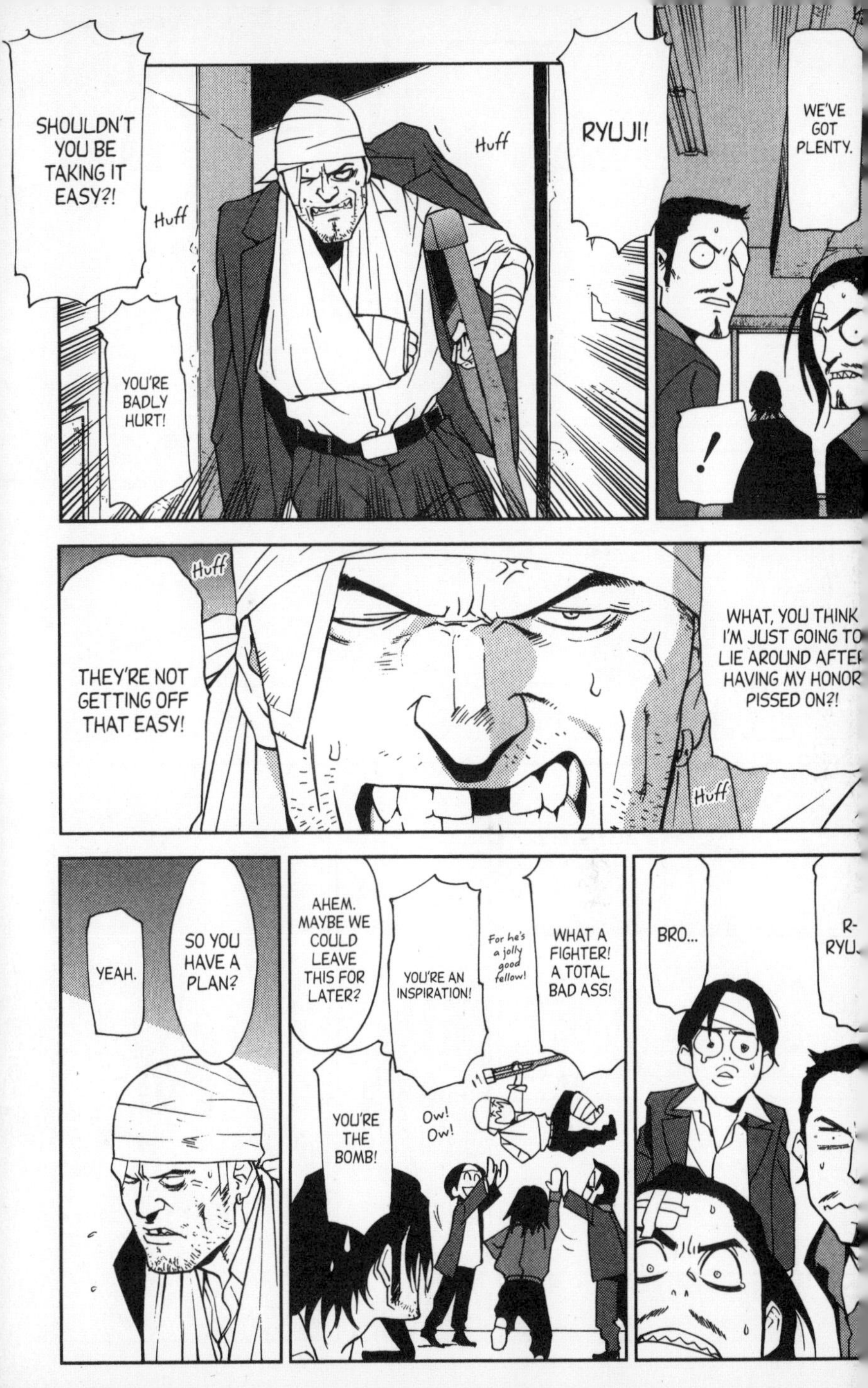
WE'VE GOT PLENTY.
!
RYUJI!
Huff
SHOULDN'T YOU BE TAKING IT EASY?!
Huff
YOU'RE BADLY HURT!
WHAT, YOU THINK I'M JUST GOING TO LIE AROUND AFTER HAVING MY HONOR PISSED ON?!
Huff
Huff
THEY'RE NOT GETTING OFF THAT EASY!
R-RYU
BRO...
WHAT A FIGHTER! A TOTAL BAD ASS!
For he's a jolly good fellow!
YOU'RE AN INSPIRATION!
AHEM. MAYBE WE COULD LEAVE THIS FOR LATER?
YOU'RE THE BOMB!
Ow! Ow!
SO YOU HAVE A PLAN?
YEAH.

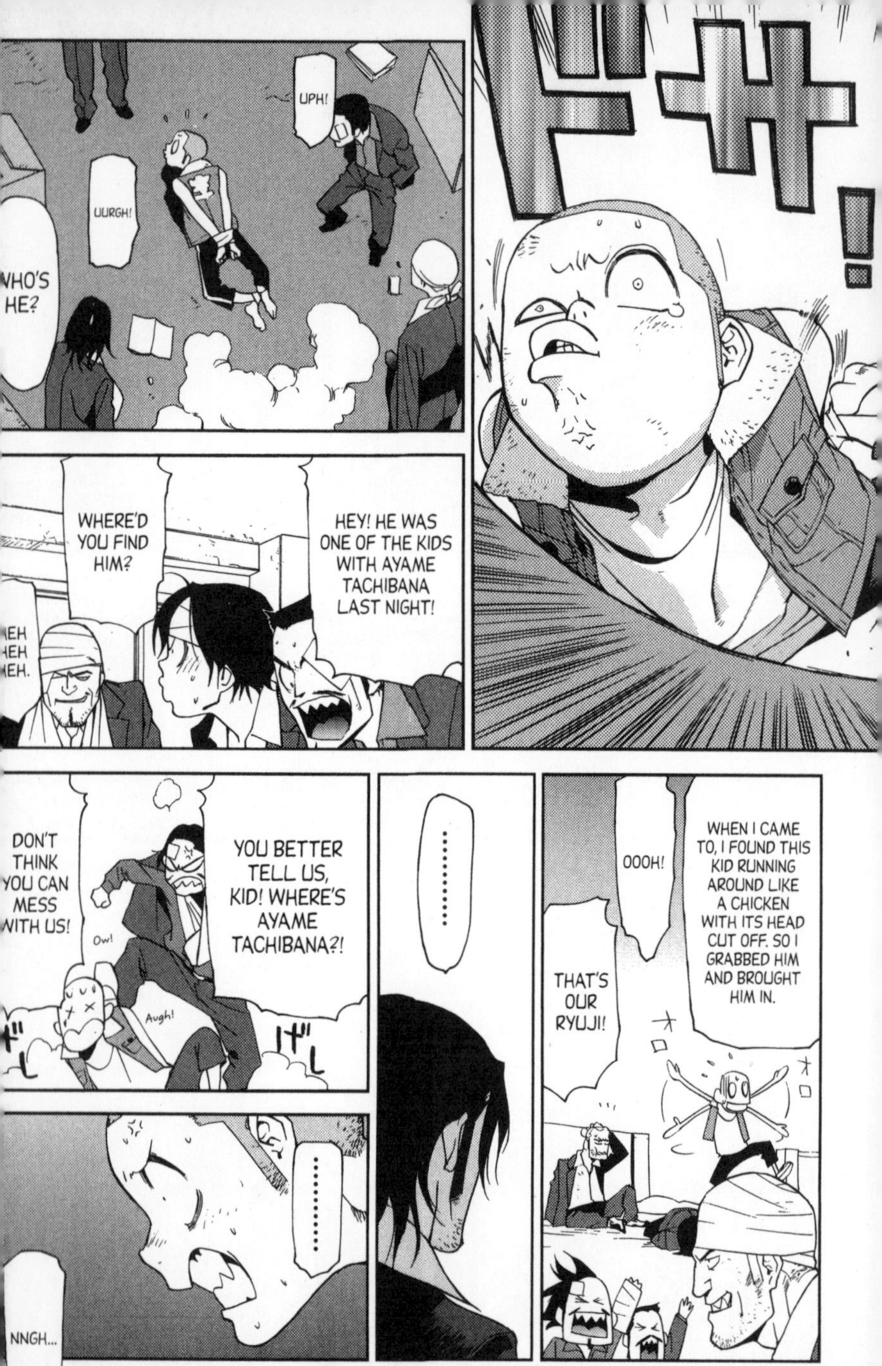

ドサ!
UPH!
UURGH!
WHO'S HE?
HEY! HE WAS ONE OF THE KIDS WITH AYAME TACHIBANA LAST NIGHT!
WHERE'D YOU FIND HIM?
HEH HEH HEH.
WHEN I CAME TO, I FOUND THIS KID RUNNING AROUND LIKE A CHICKEN WITH ITS HEAD CUT OFF. SO I GRABBED HIM AND BROUGHT HIM IN.
OOOH!
THAT'S OUR RYUJI!
....
YOU BETTER TELL US, KID! WHERE'S AYAME TACHIBANA?!
DON'T THINK YOU CAN MESS WITH US!
Ow!
Augh!
げし
....
NNGH...

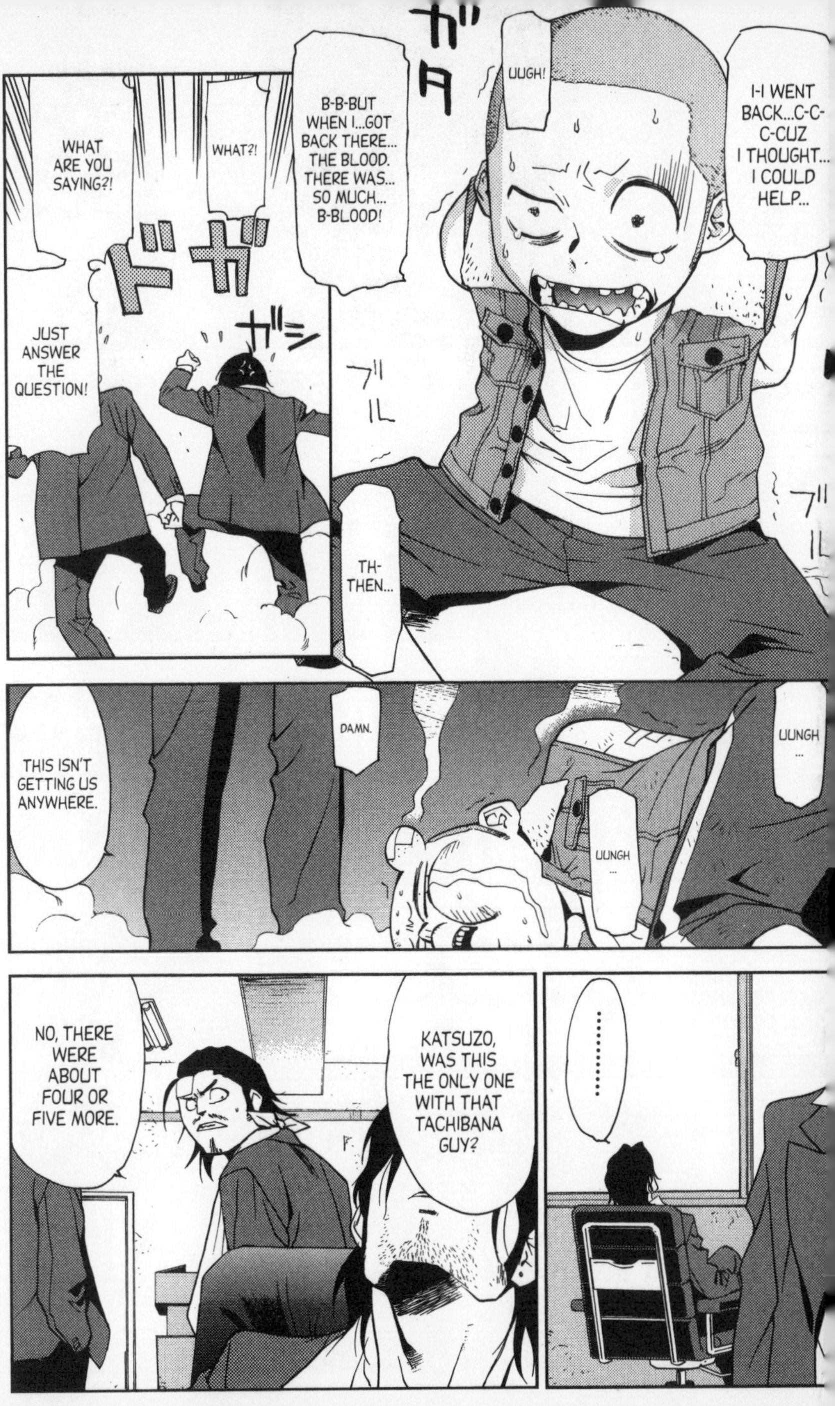
ガタ
UUGH!
I-I WENT BACK...C-C-C-CUZ I THOUGHT... I COULD HELP...
B-B-BUT WHEN I...GOT BACK THERE... THE BLOOD. THERE WAS... SO MUCH... B-BLOOD!
ブル
ブル
TH-THEN...
WHAT?!
WHAT ARE YOU SAYING?!
ドガ
ガシ
JUST ANSWER THE QUESTION!
UUNGH ...
UUNGH ...
DAMN.
THIS ISN'T GETTING US ANYWHERE.
....
KATSUZO, WAS THIS THE ONLY ONE WITH THAT TACHIBANA GUY?
NO, THERE WERE ABOUT FOUR OR FIVE MORE.

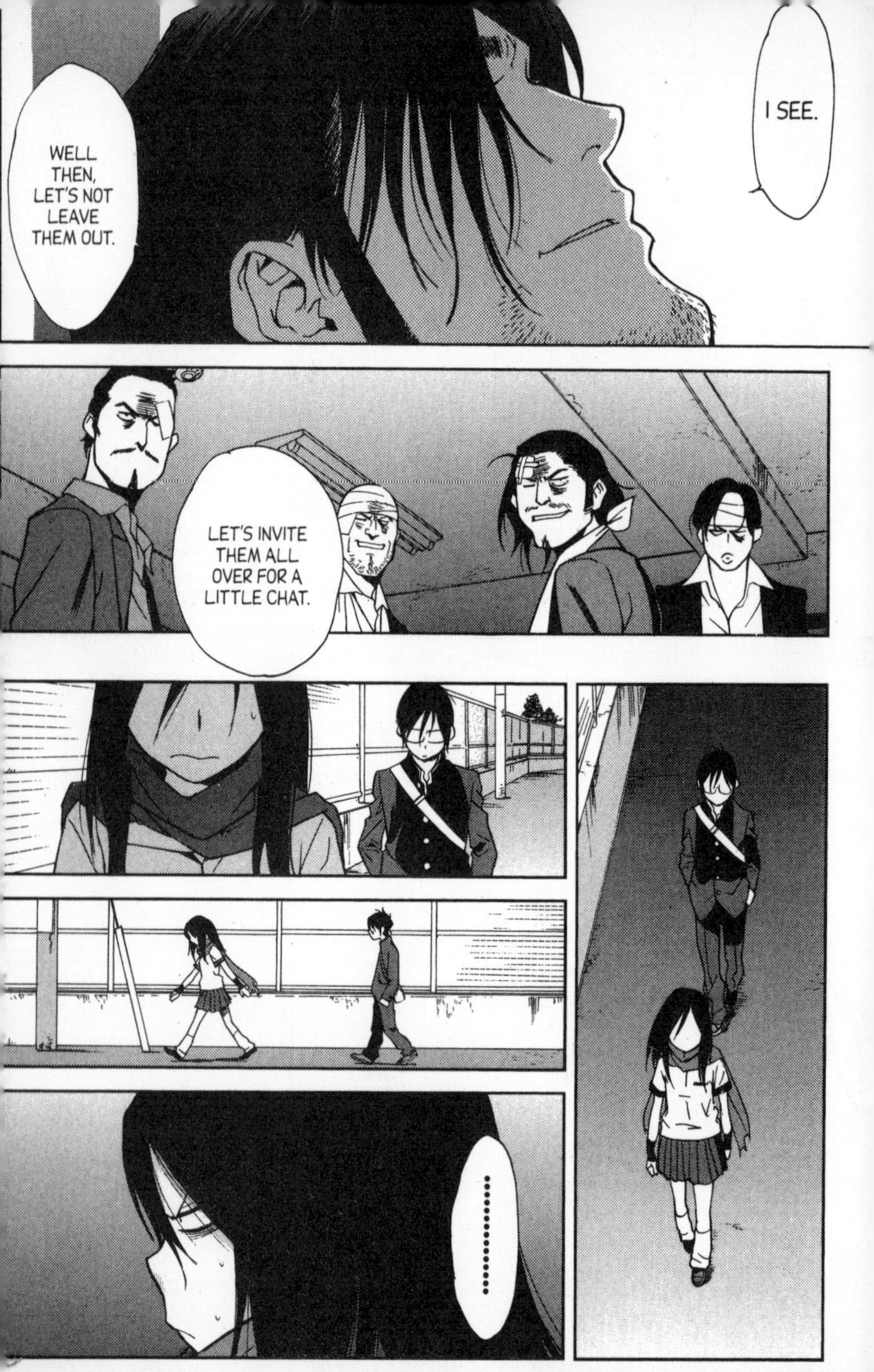
I SEE.
WELL THEN, LET'S NOT LEAVE THEM OUT.
LET'S INVITE THEM ALL OVER FOR A LITTLE CHAT.
……

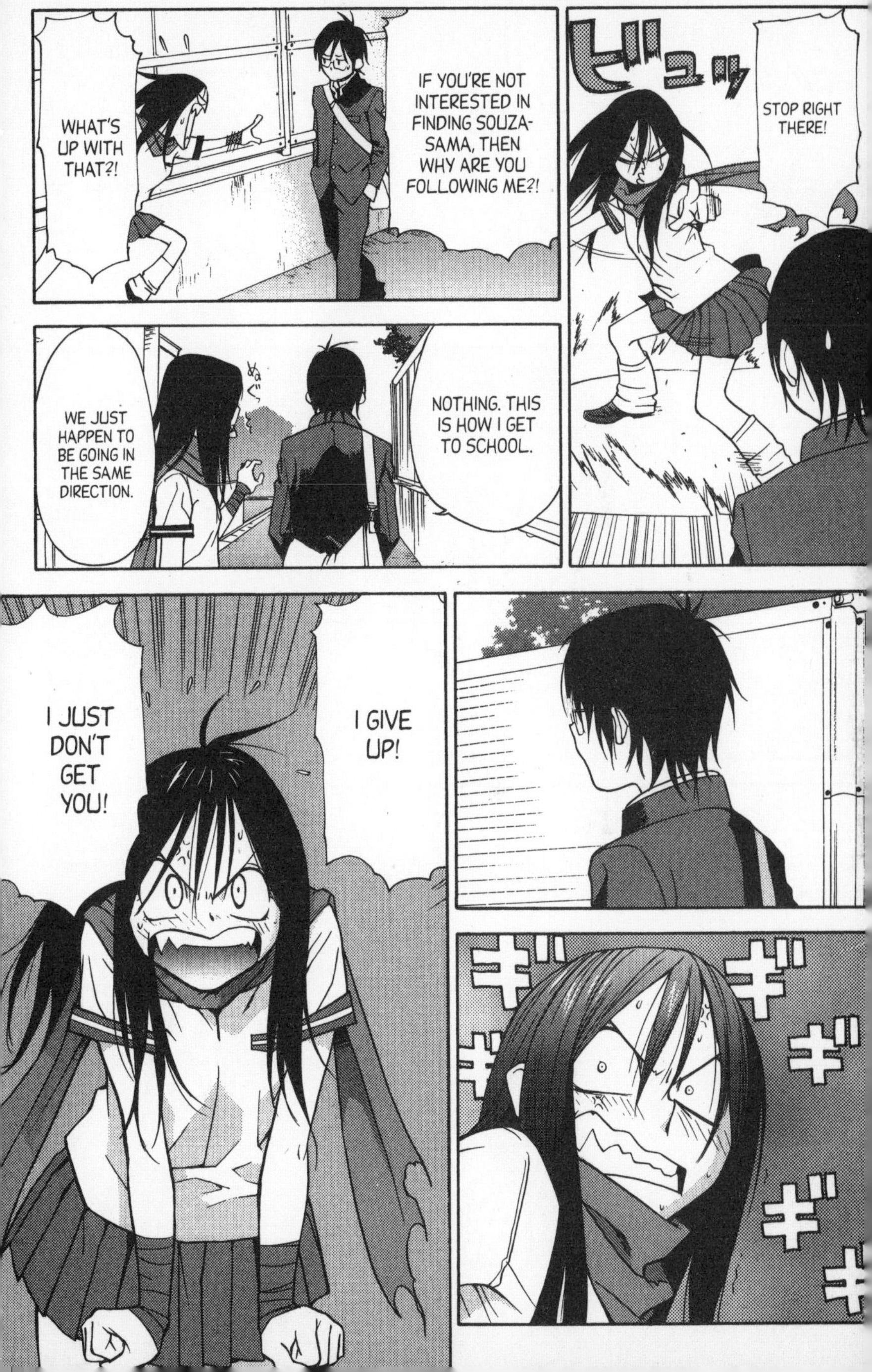
ビュッ
STOP RIGHT THERE!
IF YOU'RE NOT INTERESTED IN FINDING SOUZA-SAMA, THEN WHY ARE YOU FOLLOWING ME?!
WHAT'S UP WITH THAT?!
NOTHING. THIS IS HOW I GET TO SCHOOL.
WE JUST HAPPEN TO BE GOING IN THE SAME DIRECTION.
ギギギギギギ
I GIVE UP!
I JUST DON'T GET YOU!

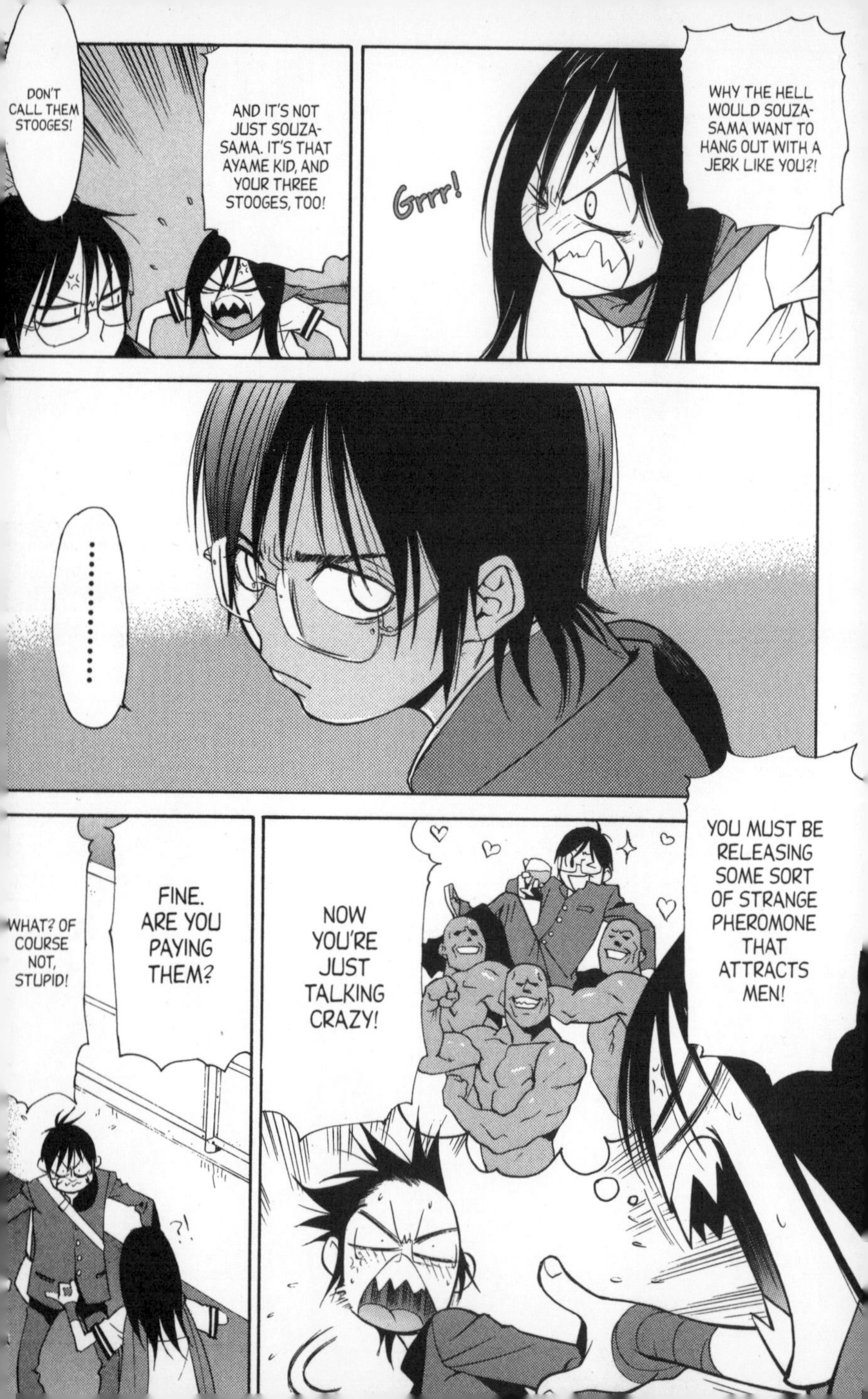
WHY THE HELL WOULD SOUZA-SAMA WANT TO HANG OUT WITH A JERK LIKE YOU?!
Grrr!
AND IT'S NOT JUST SOUZA-SAMA. IT'S THAT AYAME KID, AND YOUR THREE STOOGES, TOO!
DON'T CALL THEM STOOGES!
....
YOU MUST BE RELEASING SOME SORT OF STRANGE PHEROMONE THAT ATTRACTS MEN!
NOW YOU'RE JUST TALKING CRAZY!
FINE. ARE YOU PAYING THEM?
WHAT? OF COURSE NOT, STUPID!
?!

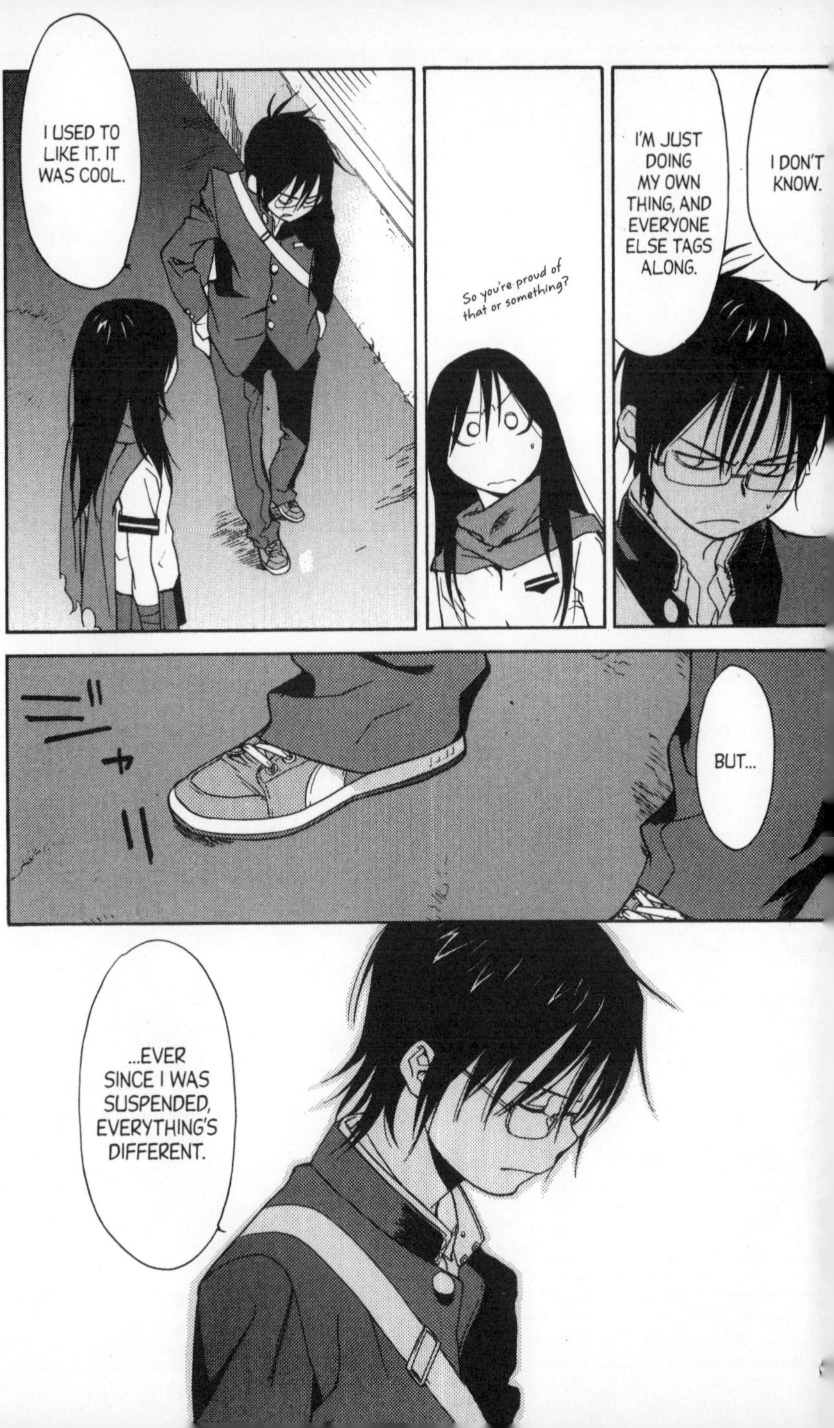
I DON'T KNOW.
I'M JUST DOING MY OWN THING, AND EVERYONE ELSE TAGS ALONG.
So you're proud of that or something?
I USED TO LIKE IT. IT WAS COOL.
BUT...
...EVER SINCE I WAS SUSPENDED, EVERYTHING'S DIFFERENT.

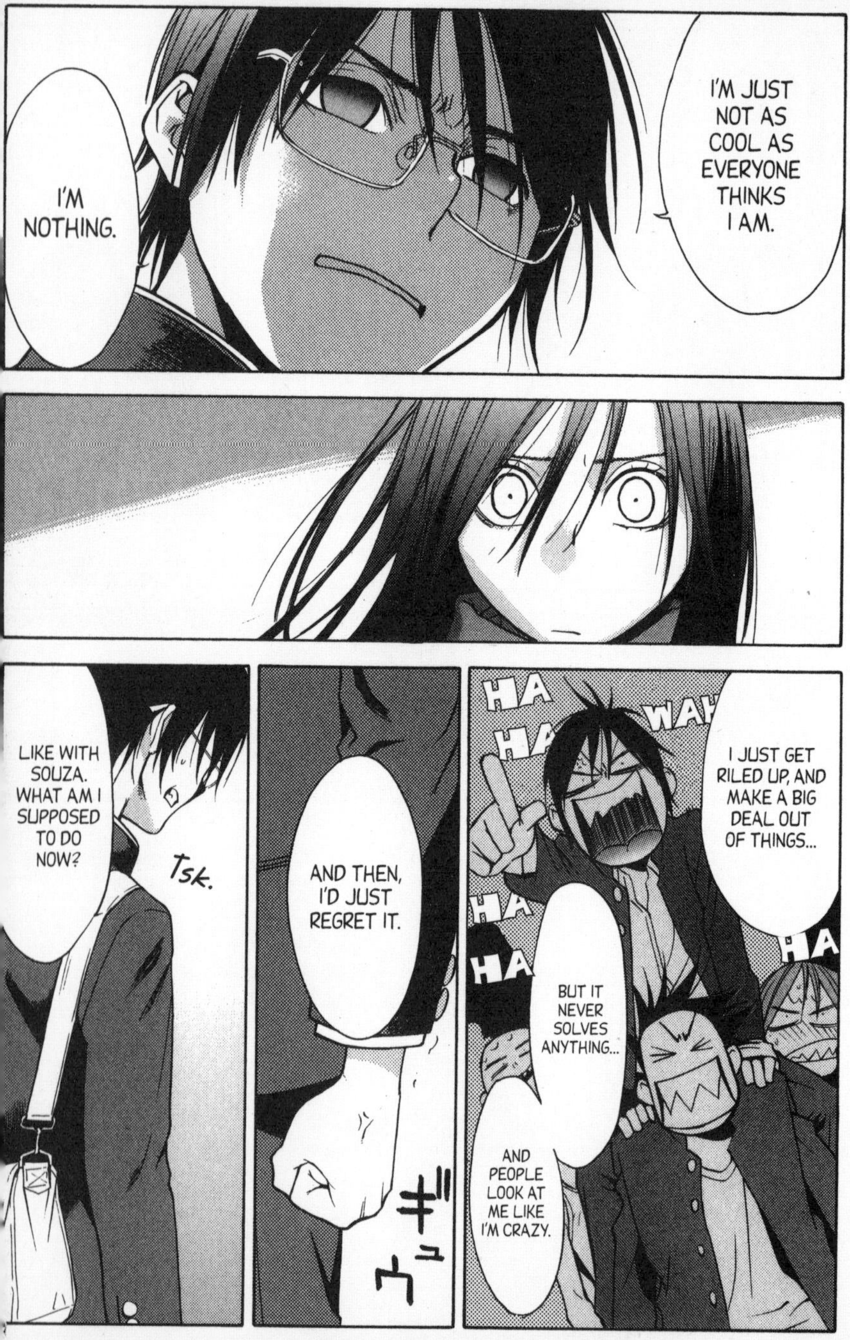
I'M JUST NOT AS COOL AS EVERYONE THINKS I AM.
I'M NOTHING.
HA HA
WAH
I JUST GET RILED UP, AND MAKE A BIG DEAL OUT OF THINGS...
HA
HA
HA
BUT IT NEVER SOLVES ANYTHING...
AND PEOPLE LOOK AT ME LIKE I'M CRAZY.
AND THEN, I'D JUST REGRET IT.
ギュウ
LIKE WITH SOUZA. WHAT AM I SUPPOSED TO DO NOW?
Tsk.

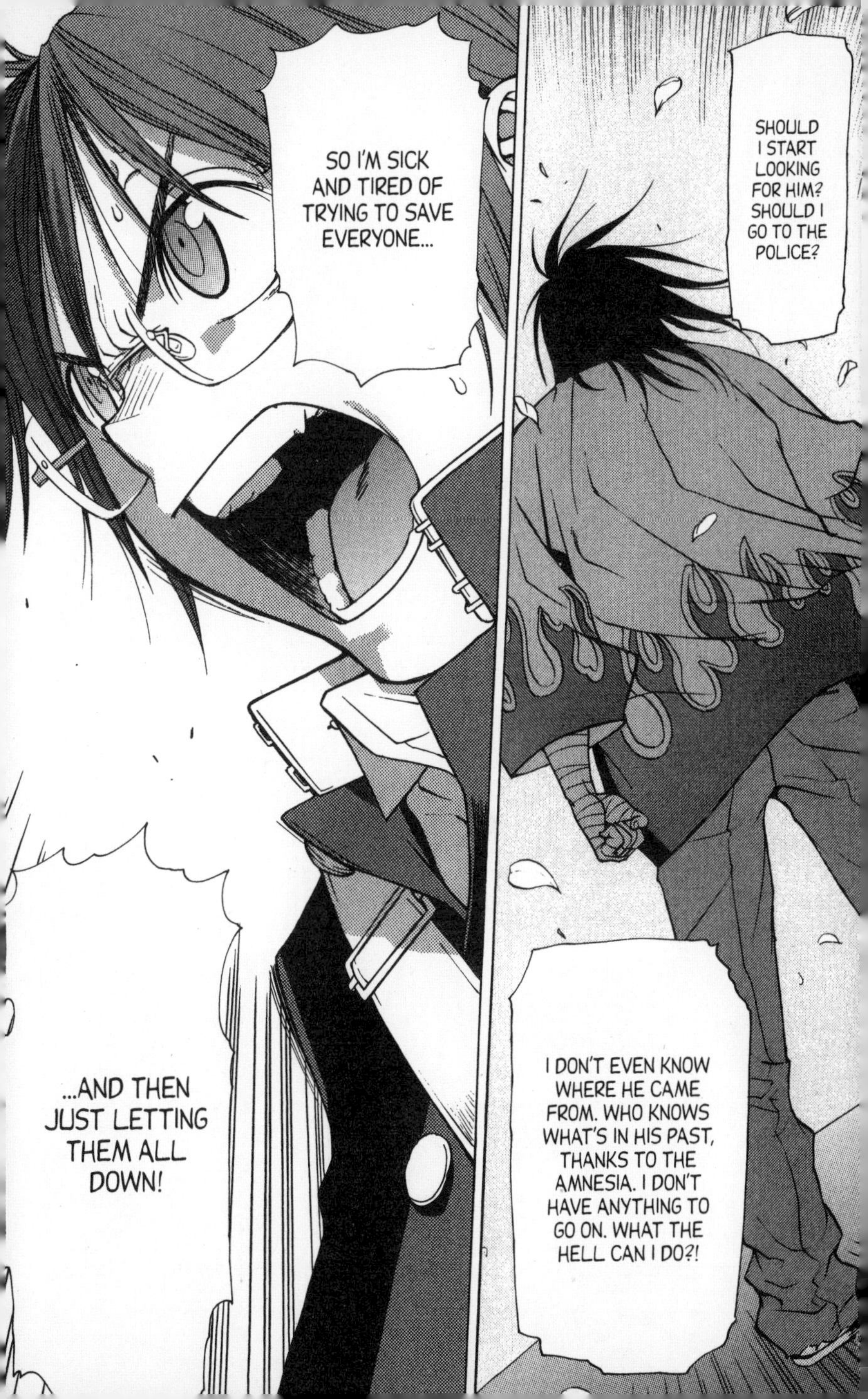
SHOULD I START LOOKING FOR HIM? SHOULD I GO TO THE POLICE?
I DON'T EVEN KNOW WHERE HE CAME FROM. WHO KNOWS WHAT'S IN HIS PAST, THANKS TO THE AMNESIA. I DON'T HAVE ANYTHING TO GO ON. WHAT THE HELL CAN I DO?!
SO I'M SICK AND TIRED OF TRYING TO SAVE EVERYONE...
...AND THEN JUST LETTING THEM ALL DOWN!

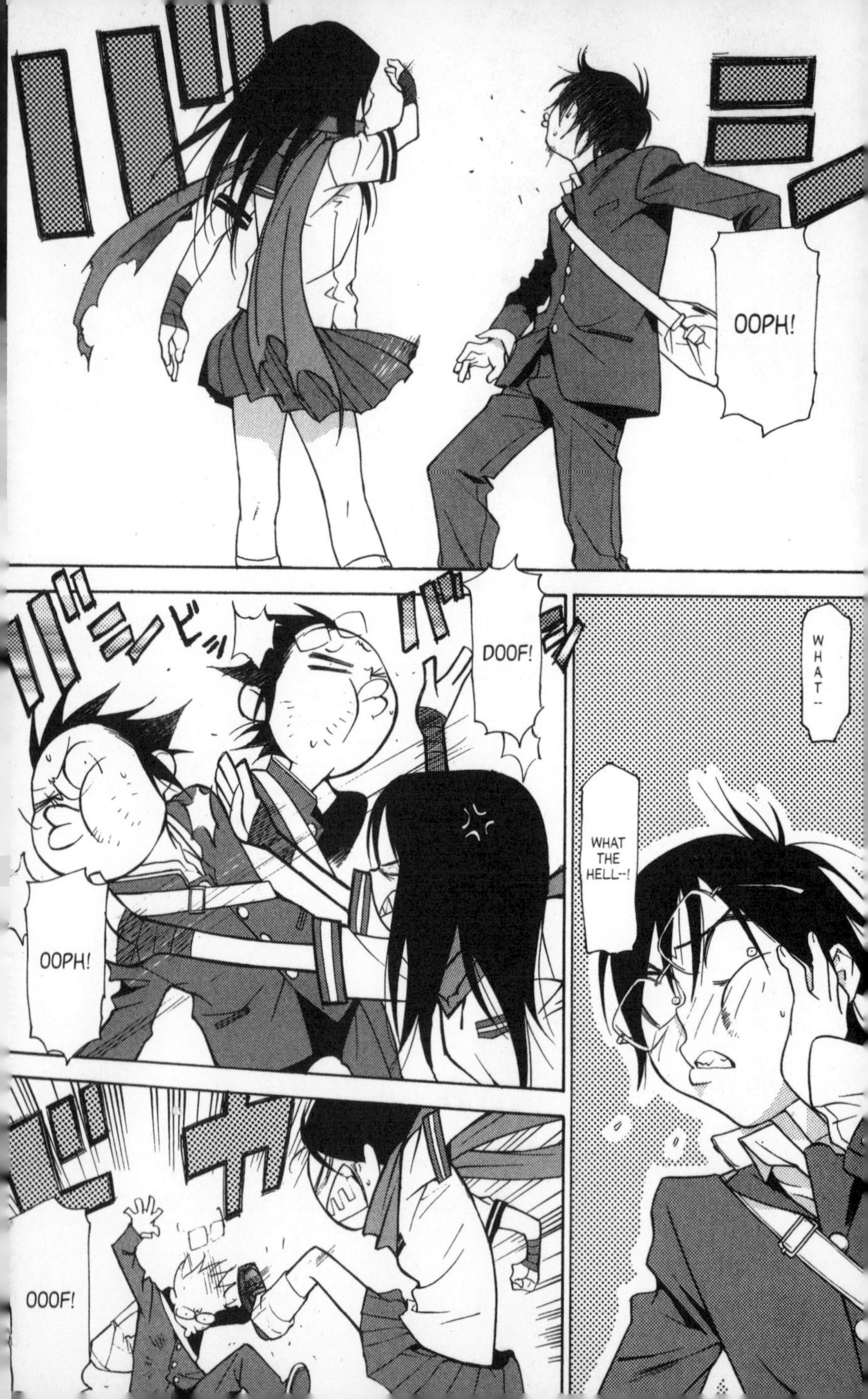
OOPH!
WHAT--
WHAT THE HELL--!
DOOF!
OOPH!
OOOF!

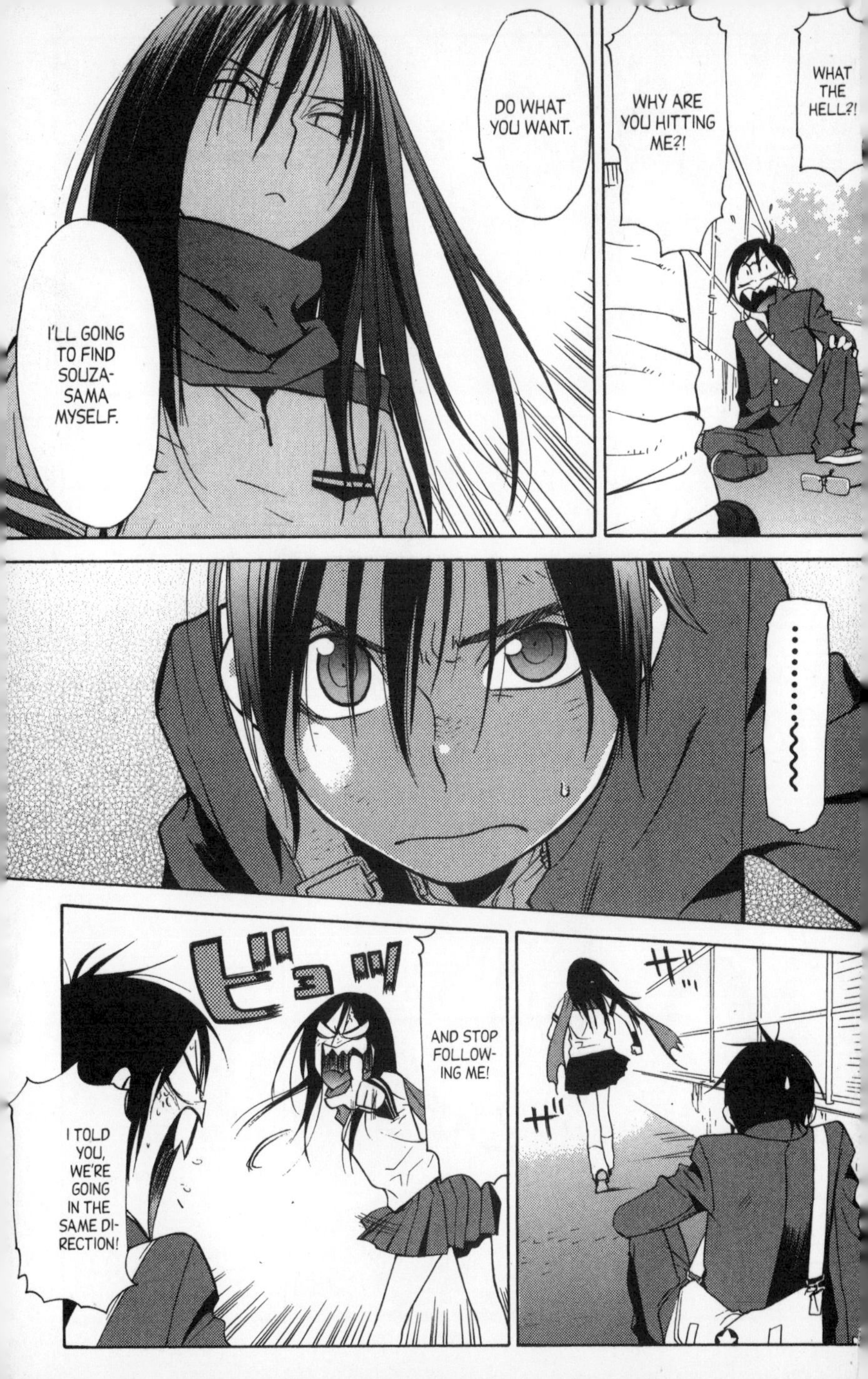
WHAT THE HELL?!
WHY ARE YOU HITTING ME?!
DO WHAT YOU WANT.
I'LL GOING TO FIND SOUZA-SAMA MYSELF.
......~
ザッ
ザッ
AND STOP FOLLOW-ING ME!
ビュッ
I TOLD YOU, WE'RE GOING IN THE SAME DI-RECTION!

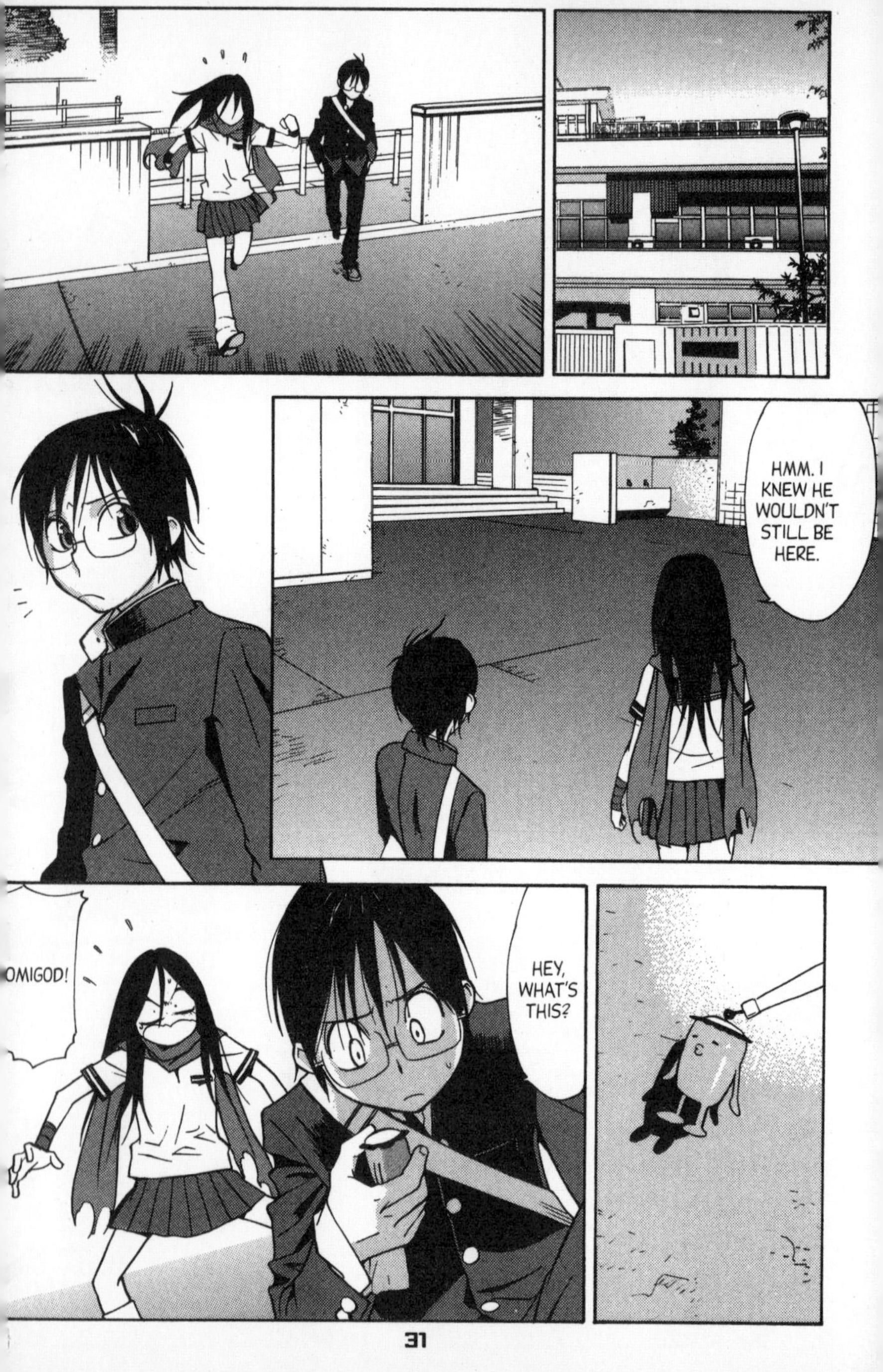
HMM. I KNEW HE WOULDN'T STILL BE HERE.
HEY, WHAT'S THIS?
OMIGOD!

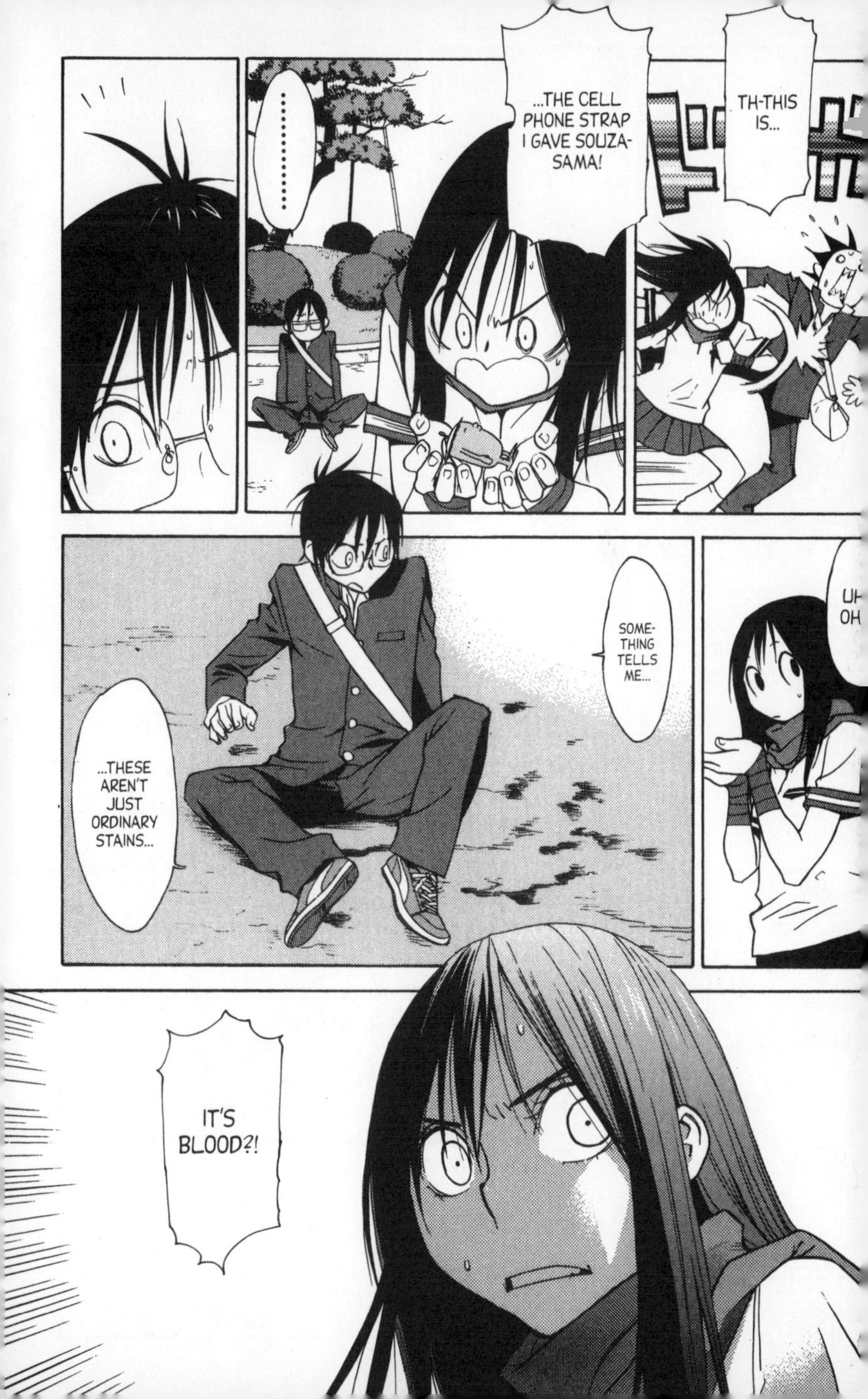
TH-THIS IS...
...THE CELL PHONE STRAP I GAVE SOUZA-SAMA!
....
UH OH
SOME-THING TELLS ME...
...THESE AREN'T JUST ORDINARY STAINS...
IT'S BLOOD?!

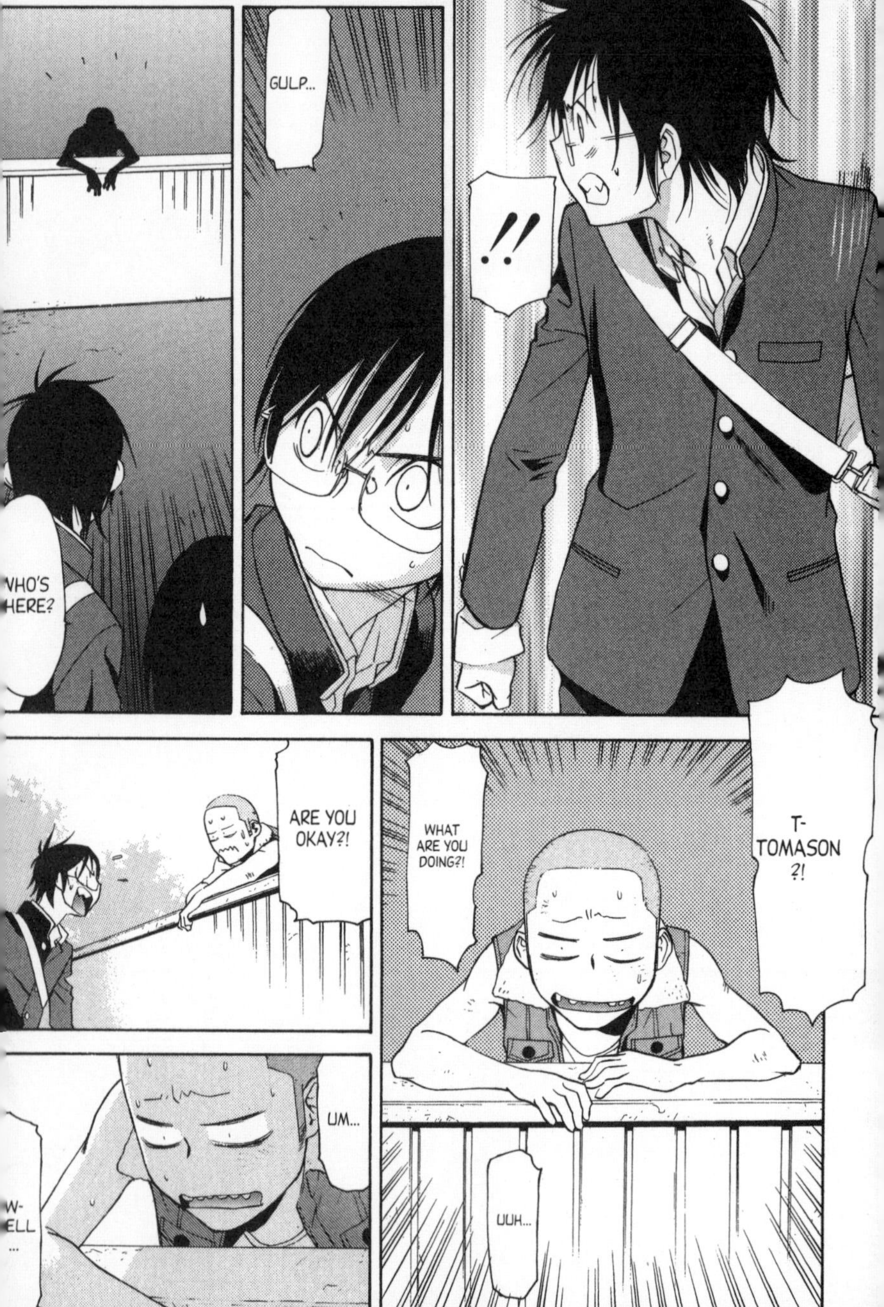
!!
GULP...
WHO'S HERE?
T-TOMASON?!
WHAT ARE YOU DOING?!
UUH...
ARE YOU OKAY?!
UM...
W-ELL...

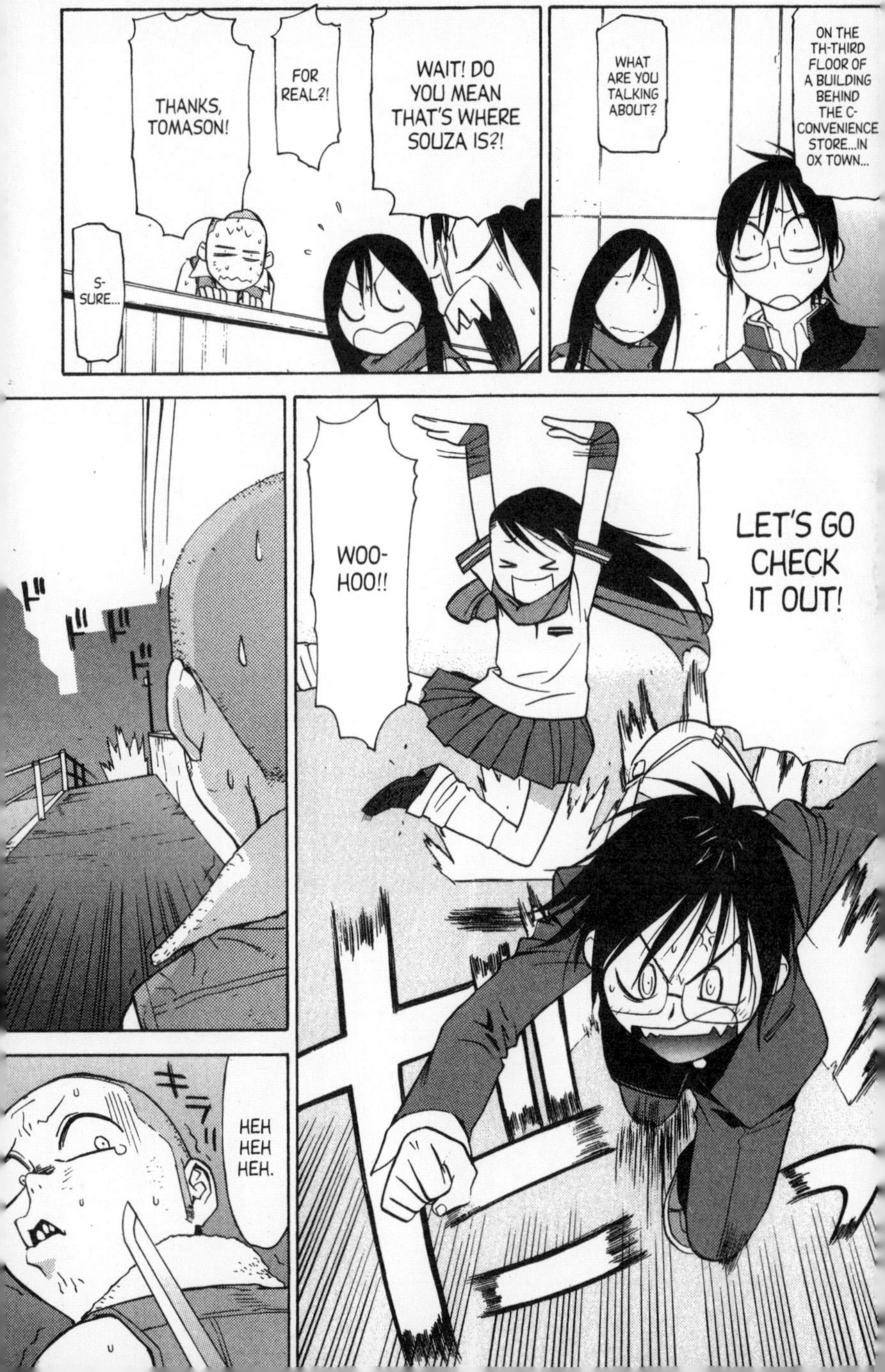
ON THE TH-THIRD FLOOR OF A BUILDING BEHIND THE C-CONVENIENCE STORE...IN OX TOWN...
WHAT ARE YOU TALKING ABOUT?
WAIT! DO YOU MEAN THAT'S WHERE SOUZA IS?!
FOR REAL?!
THANKS, TOMASON!
S-SURE...
LET'S GO CHECK IT OUT!
WOO-HOO!!
ドドドド
HEH HEH HEH.

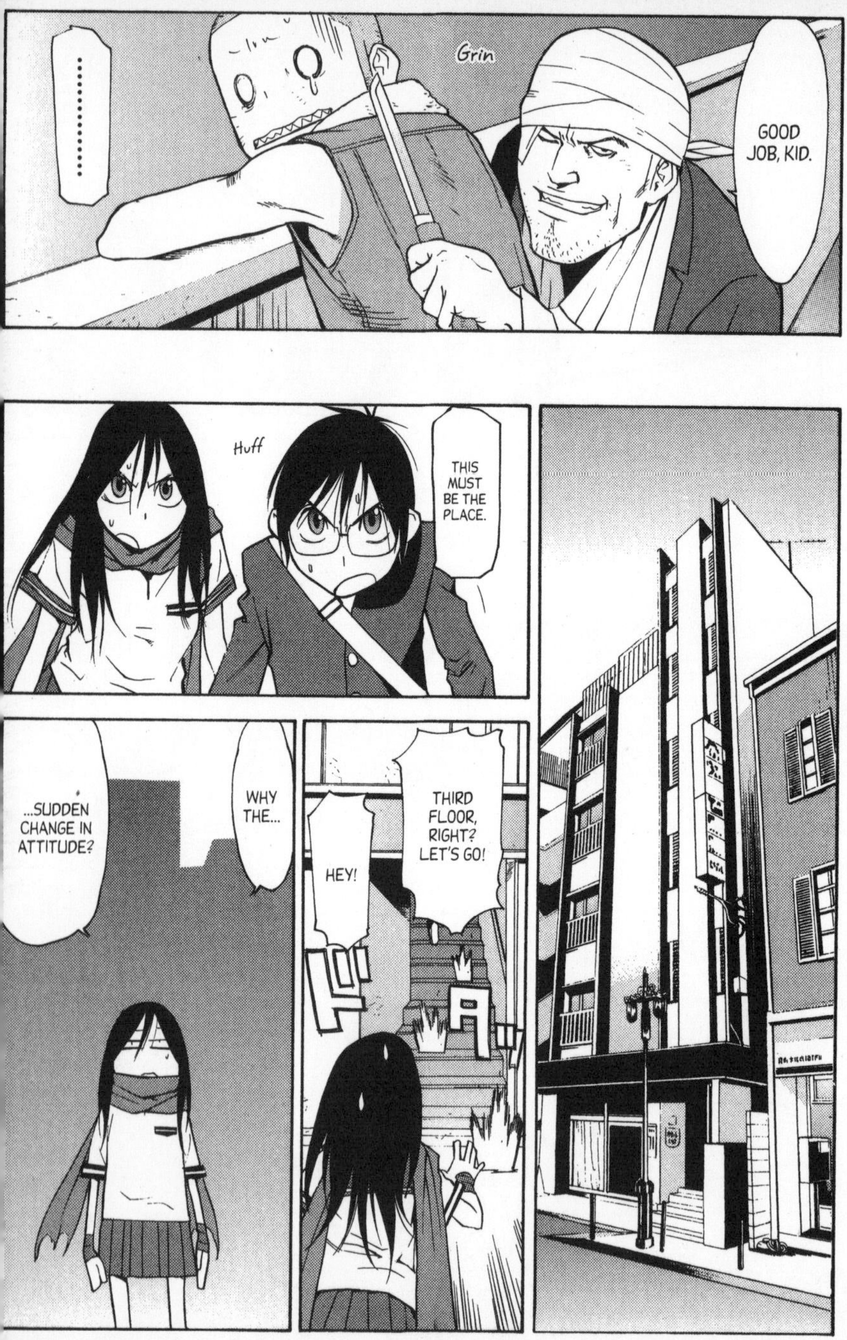
GOOD JOB, KID.
Grin
......
THIS MUST BE THE PLACE.
Huff
THIRD FLOOR, RIGHT? LET'S GO!
HEY!
WHY THE...
...SUDDEN CHANGE IN ATTITUDE?

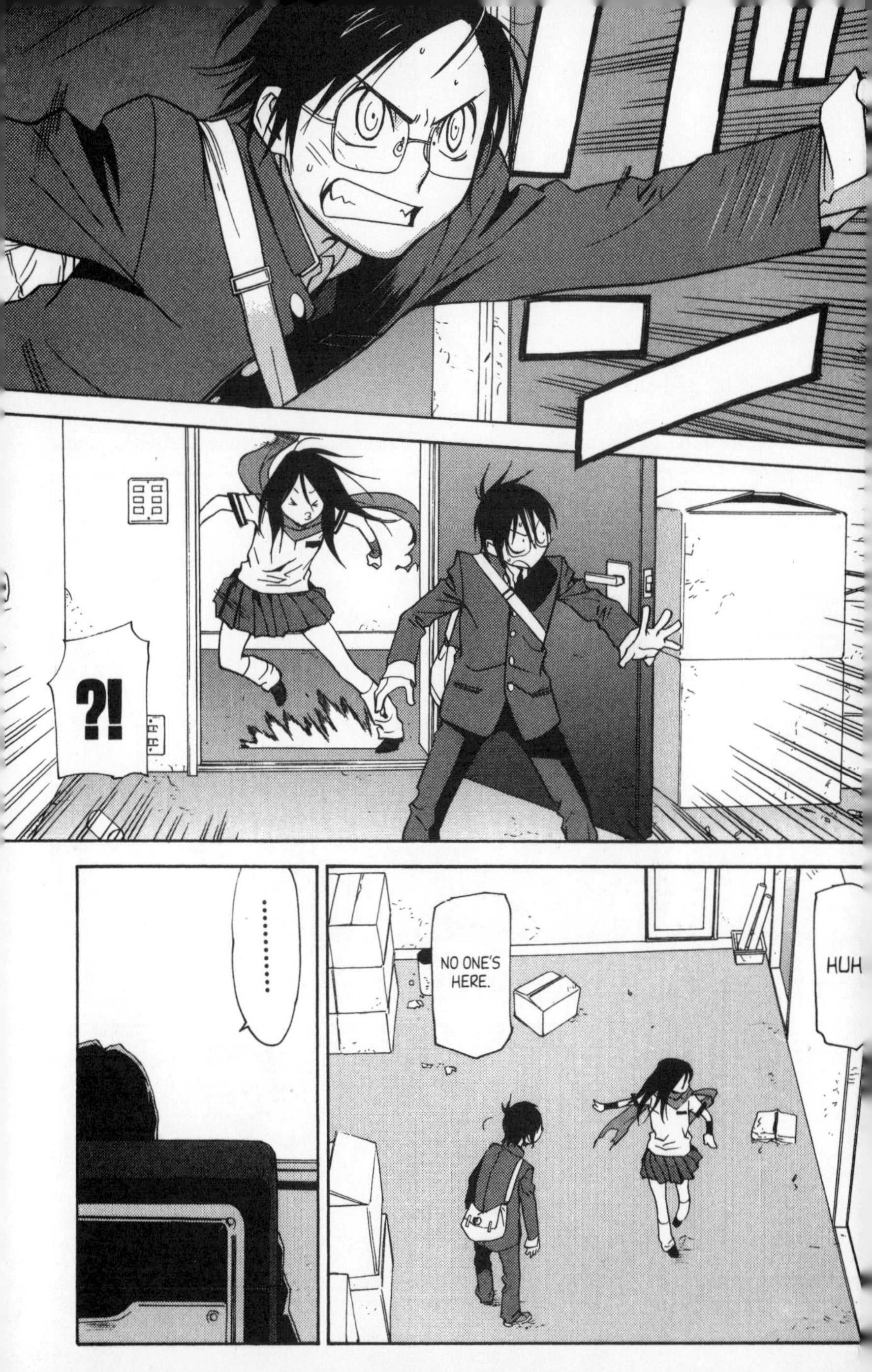
?!
HUH
NO ONE'S HERE.
....

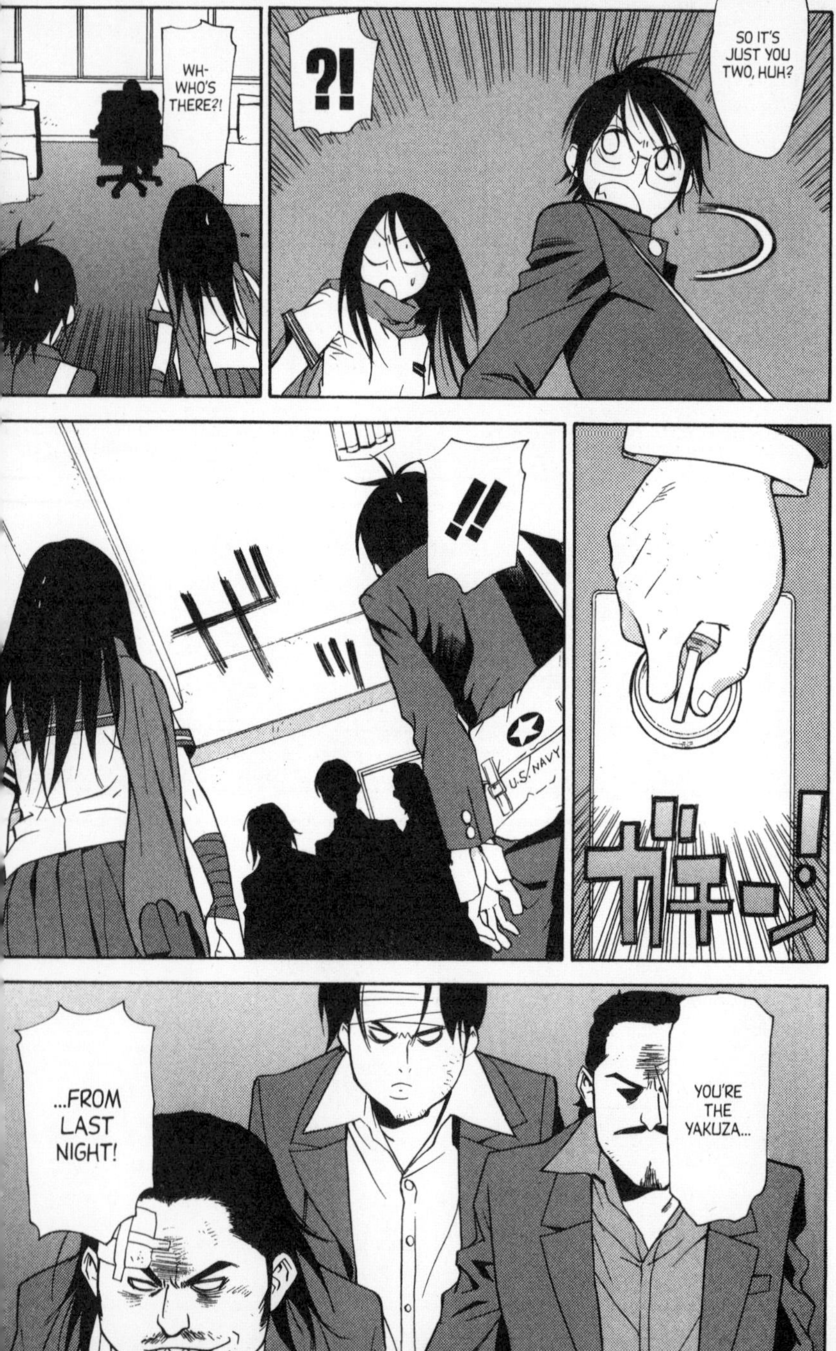
SO IT'S JUST YOU TWO, HUH?
?!
WH- WHO'S THERE?!
!!
ザザッ
YOU'RE THE YAKUZA...
...FROM LAST NIGHT!

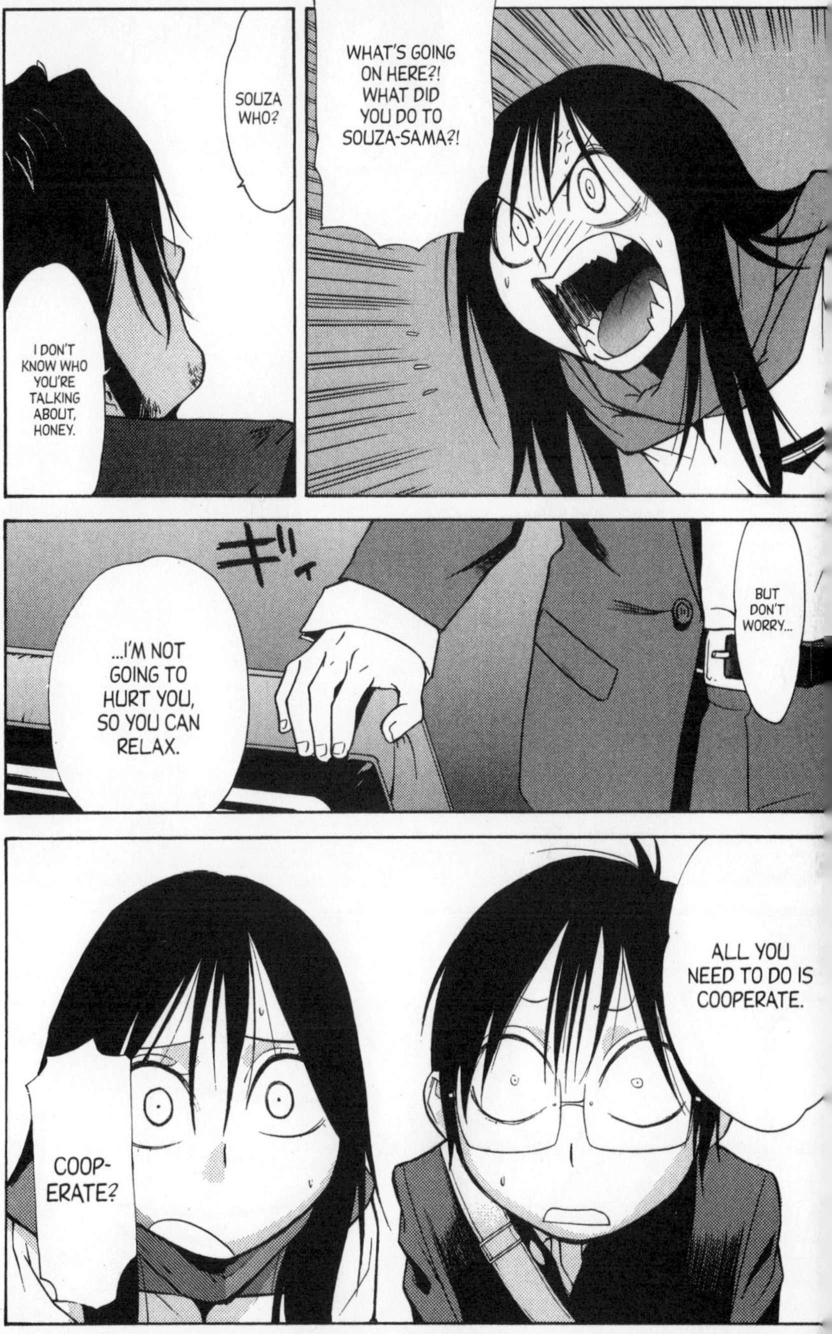
WHAT'S GOING ON HERE?! WHAT DID YOU DO TO SOUZA-SAMA?!
SOUZA WHO?
I DON'T KNOW WHO YOU'RE TALKING ABOUT, HONEY.
BUT DON'T WORRY...
ギィ
...I'M NOT GOING TO HURT YOU, SO YOU CAN RELAX.
ALL YOU NEED TO DO IS COOPERATE.
COOP- ERATE?

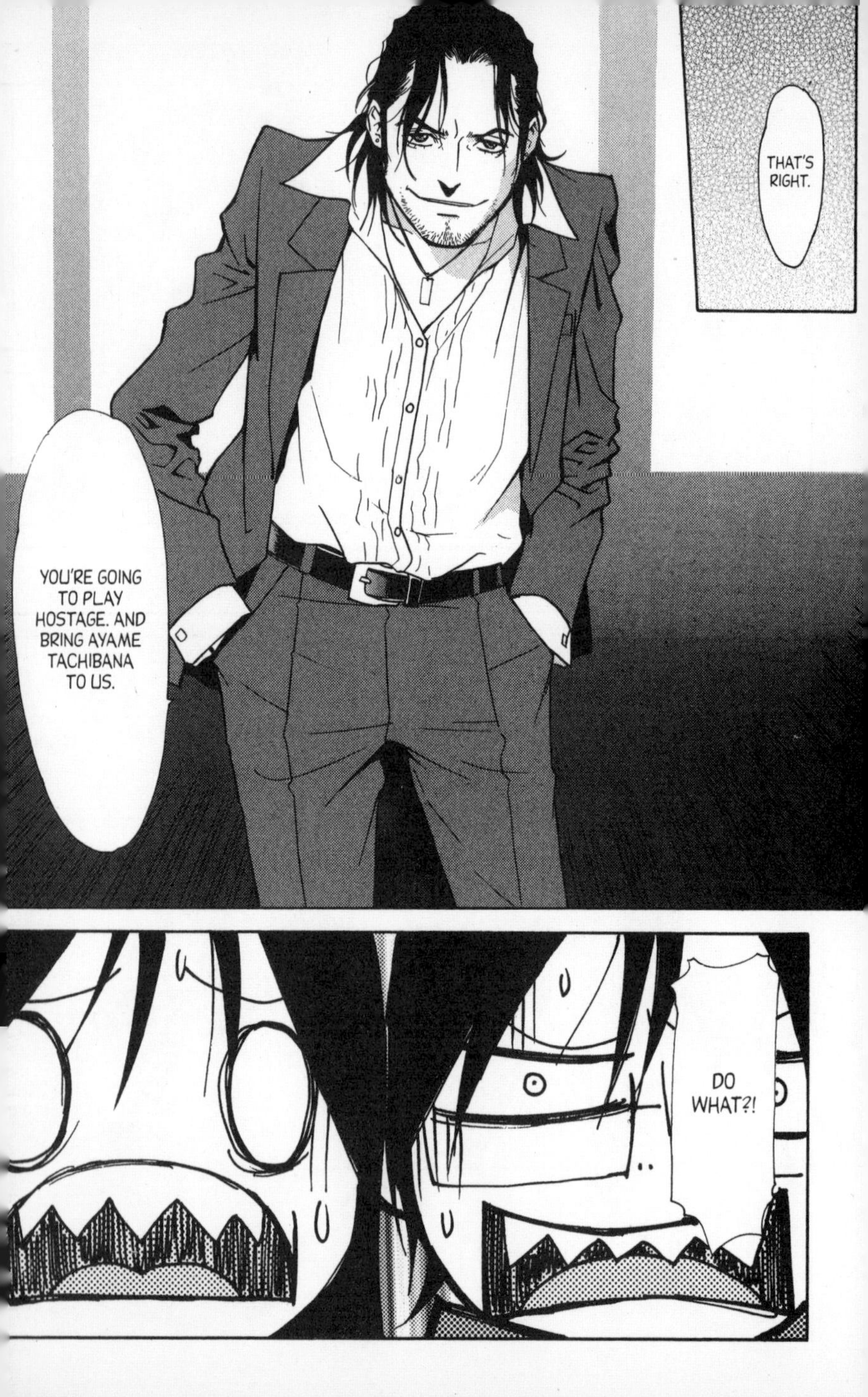
THAT'S RIGHT.
YOU'RE GOING TO PLAY HOSTAGE. AND BRING AYAME TACHIBANA TO US.
DO WHAT?!

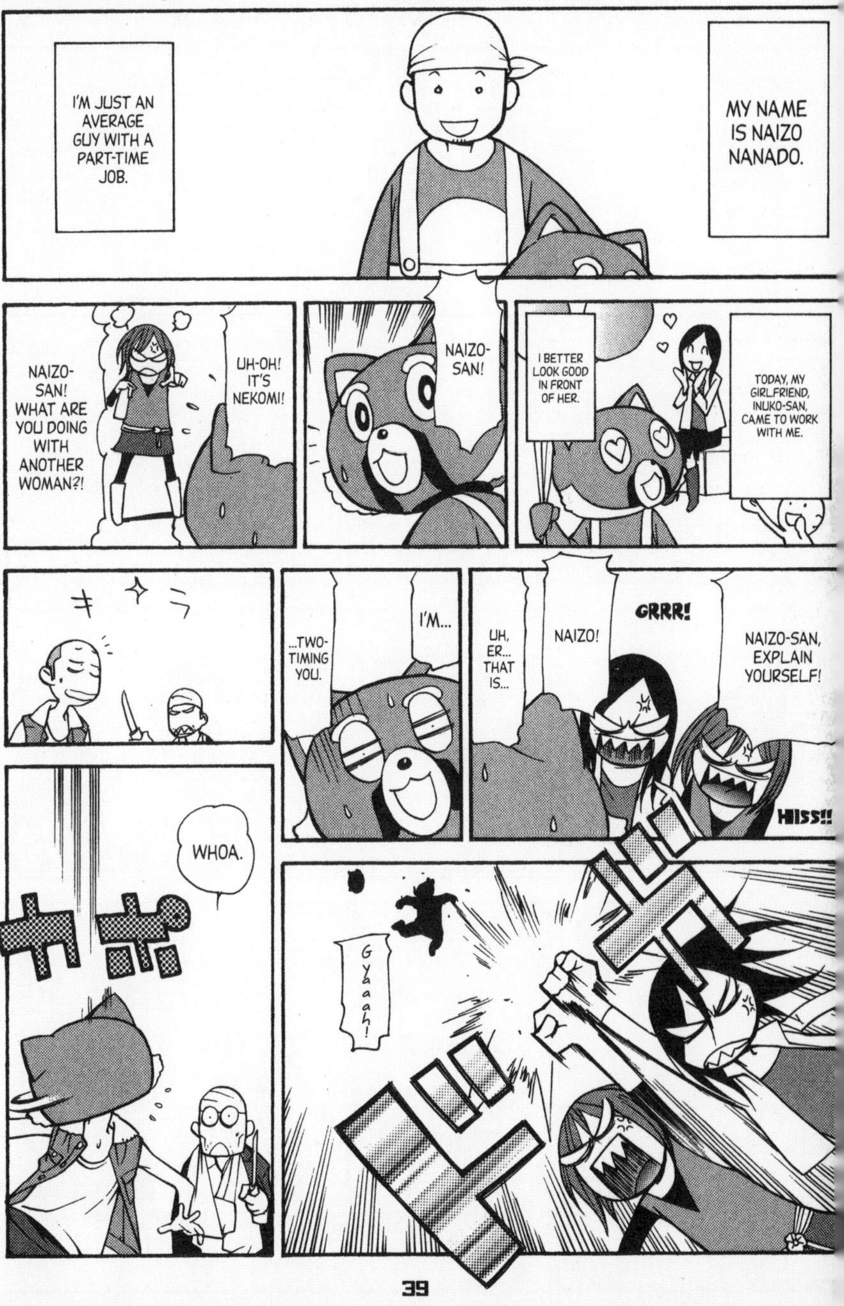
MY NAME IS NAIZO NANADO.
I'M JUST AN AVERAGE GUY WITH A PART-TIME JOB.
TODAY, MY GIRLFRIEND, INUKO-SAN, CAME TO WORK WITH ME.
I BETTER LOOK GOOD IN FRONT OF HER.
NAIZO-SAN!
UH-OH! IT'S NEKOMI!
NAIZO-SAN! WHAT ARE YOU DOING WITH ANOTHER WOMAN?!
NAIZO-SAN, EXPLAIN YOURSELF!
GRRR!
NAIZO!
UH, ER... THAT IS...
HISS!!
I'M...
...TWO-TIMING YOU.
キラ
Gyaaah!
WHOA.

Bonus Manga (2)

Whatever Theater

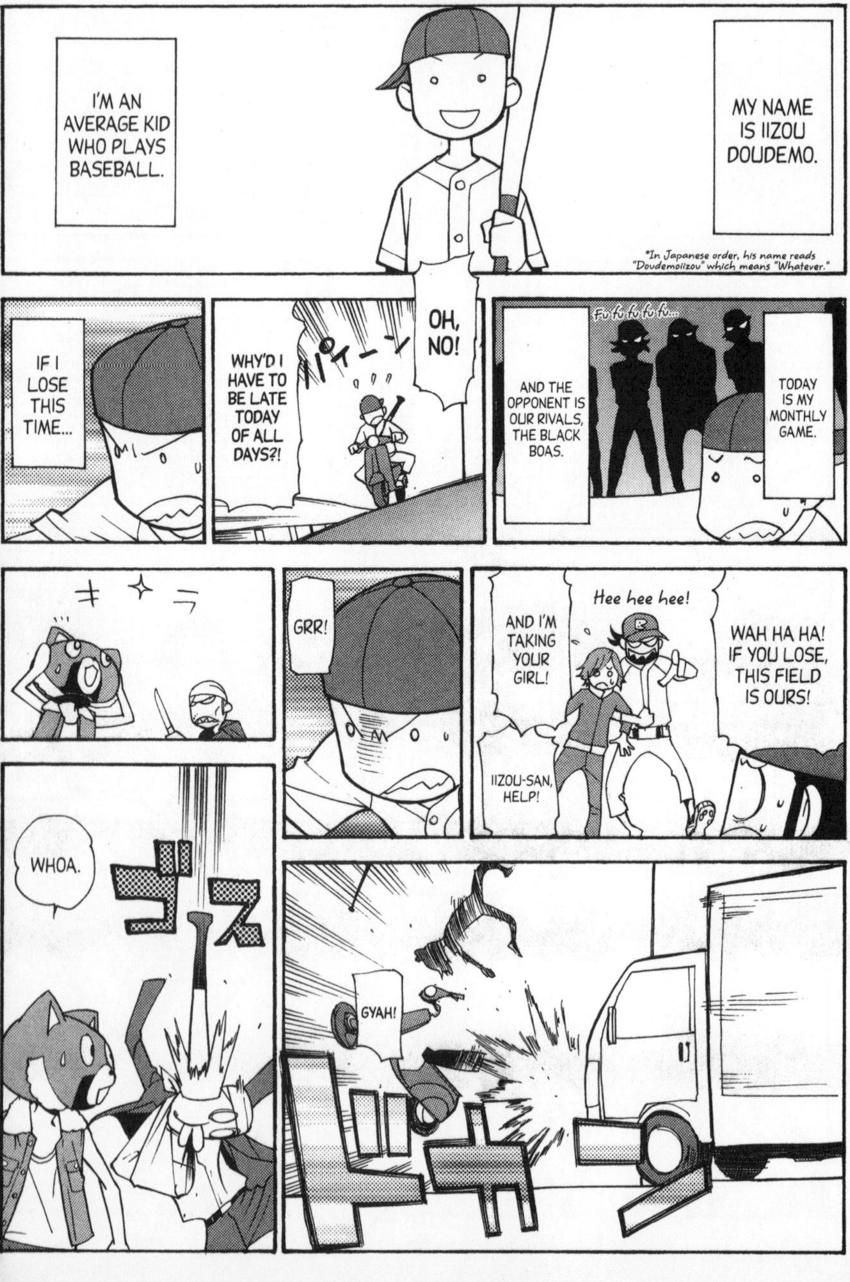
MY NAME IS IIZOU DOUDEMO.
I'M AN AVERAGE KID WHO PLAYS BASEBALL.
*In Japanese order, his name reads "Doudemoiizou" which means "Whatever."
TODAY IS MY MONTHLY GAME.
Fu fu fu fu fu...
AND THE OPPONENT IS OUR RIVALS, THE BLACK BOAS.
OH, NO!
WHY'D I HAVE TO BE LATE TODAY OF ALL DAYS?!
IF I LOSE THIS TIME...
WAH HA HA! IF YOU LOSE, THIS FIELD IS OURS!
Hee hee hee!
AND I'M TAKING YOUR GIRL!
IIZOU-SAN, HELP!
GRR!
キラ
GYAH!
WHOA.
ゴス

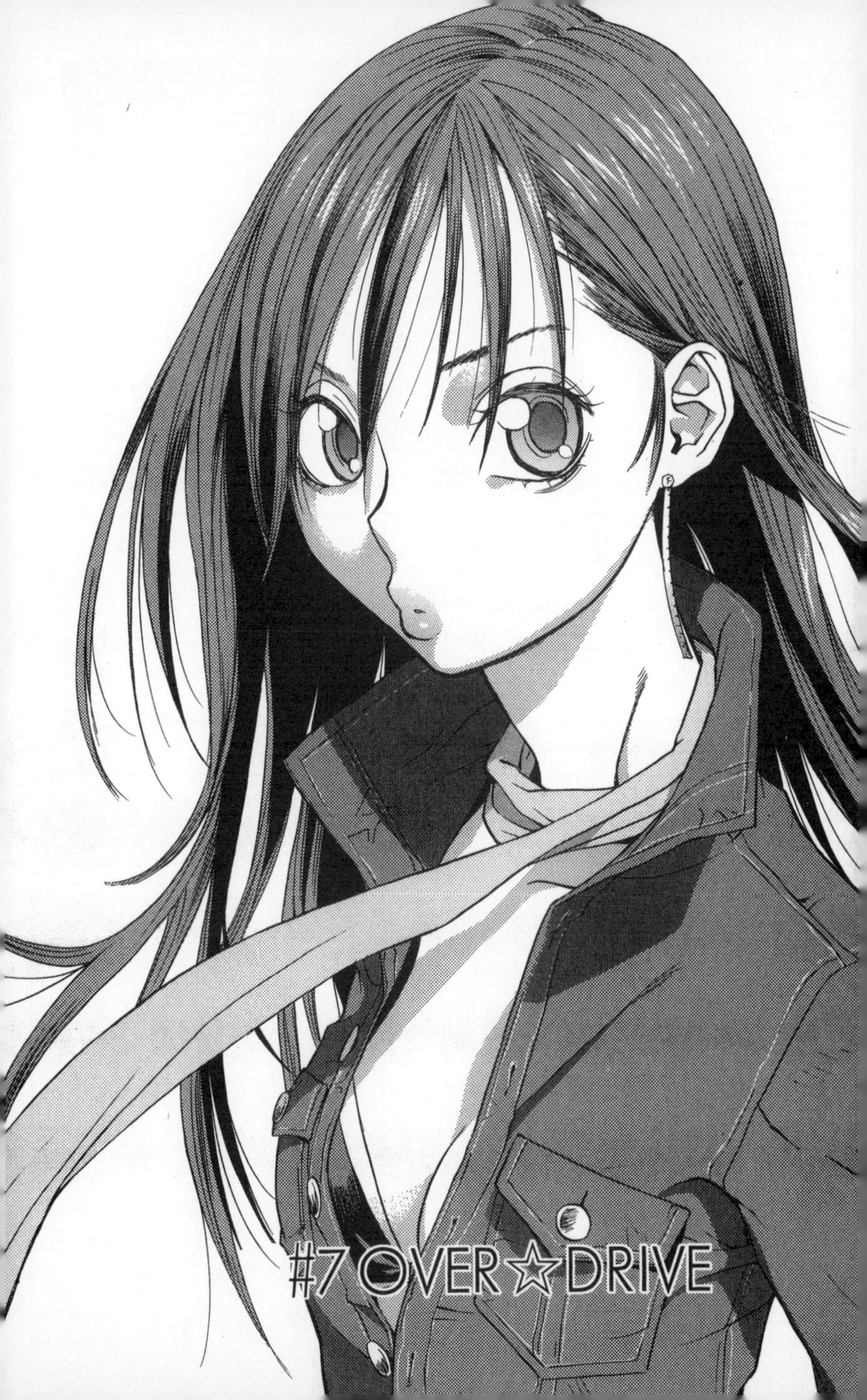
#7 OVER☆DRIVE

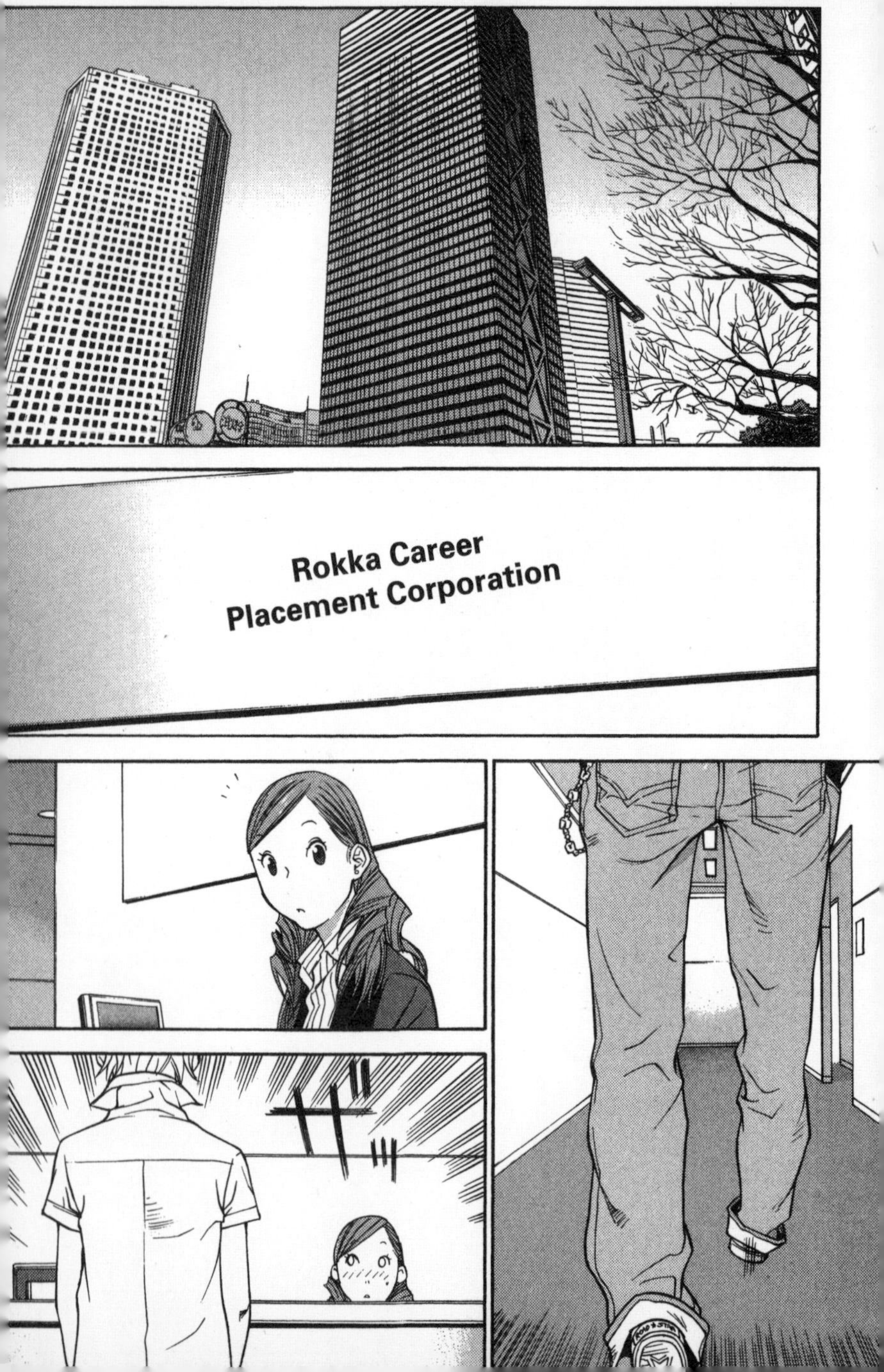
Rokka Career
Placement Corporation

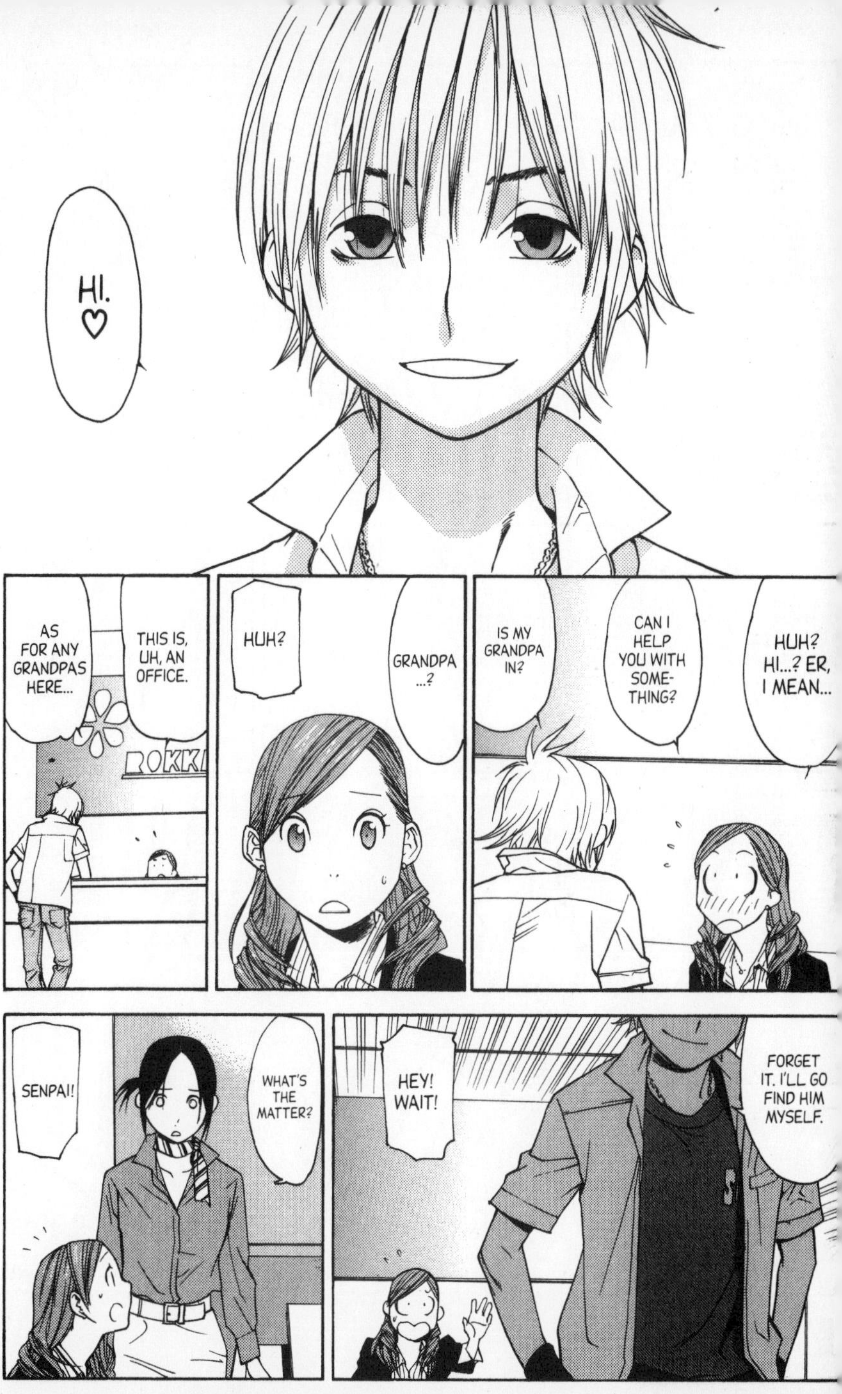
HI. ♡
HUH? HI...? ER, I MEAN...
CAN I HELP YOU WITH SOME-THING?
IS MY GRANDPA IN?
GRANDPA ...?
HUH?
THIS IS, UH, AN OFFICE.
AS FOR ANY GRANDPAS HERE...
FORGET IT. I'LL GO FIND HIM MYSELF.
HEY! WAIT!
WHAT'S THE MATTER?
SENPAI!

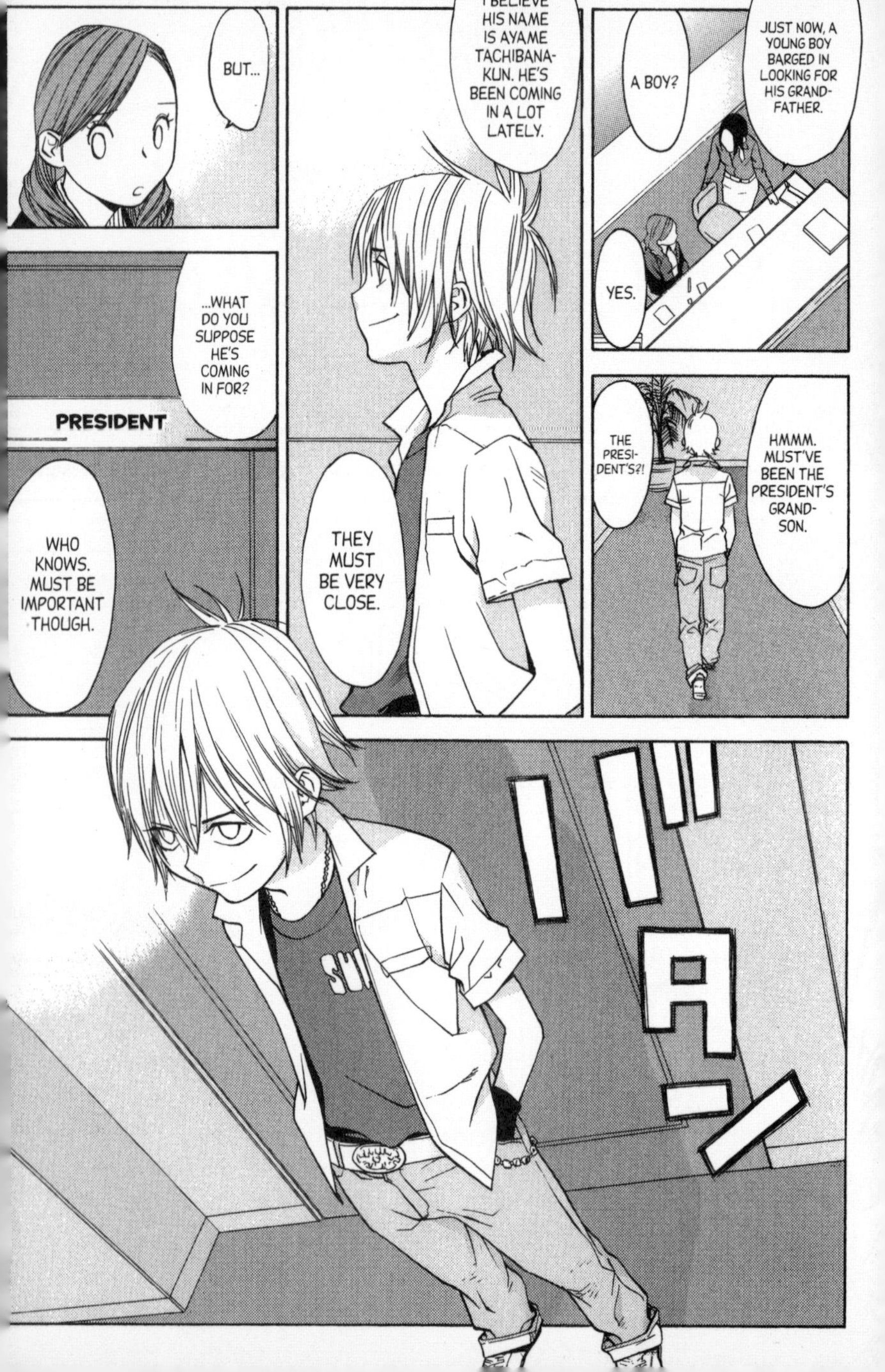
JUST NOW, A YOUNG BOY BARGED IN LOOKING FOR HIS GRAND-FATHER.
A BOY?
YES.
HMMM. MUST'VE BEEN THE PRESIDENT'S GRAND-SON.
THE PRESI-DENT'S?!
I BELIEVE HIS NAME IS AYAME TACHIBANA-KUN. HE'S BEEN COMING IN A LOT LATELY.
THEY MUST BE VERY CLOSE.
BUT...
...WHAT DO YOU SUPPOSE HE'S COMING IN FOR?
PRESIDENT
WHO KNOWS. MUST BE IMPORTANT THOUGH.

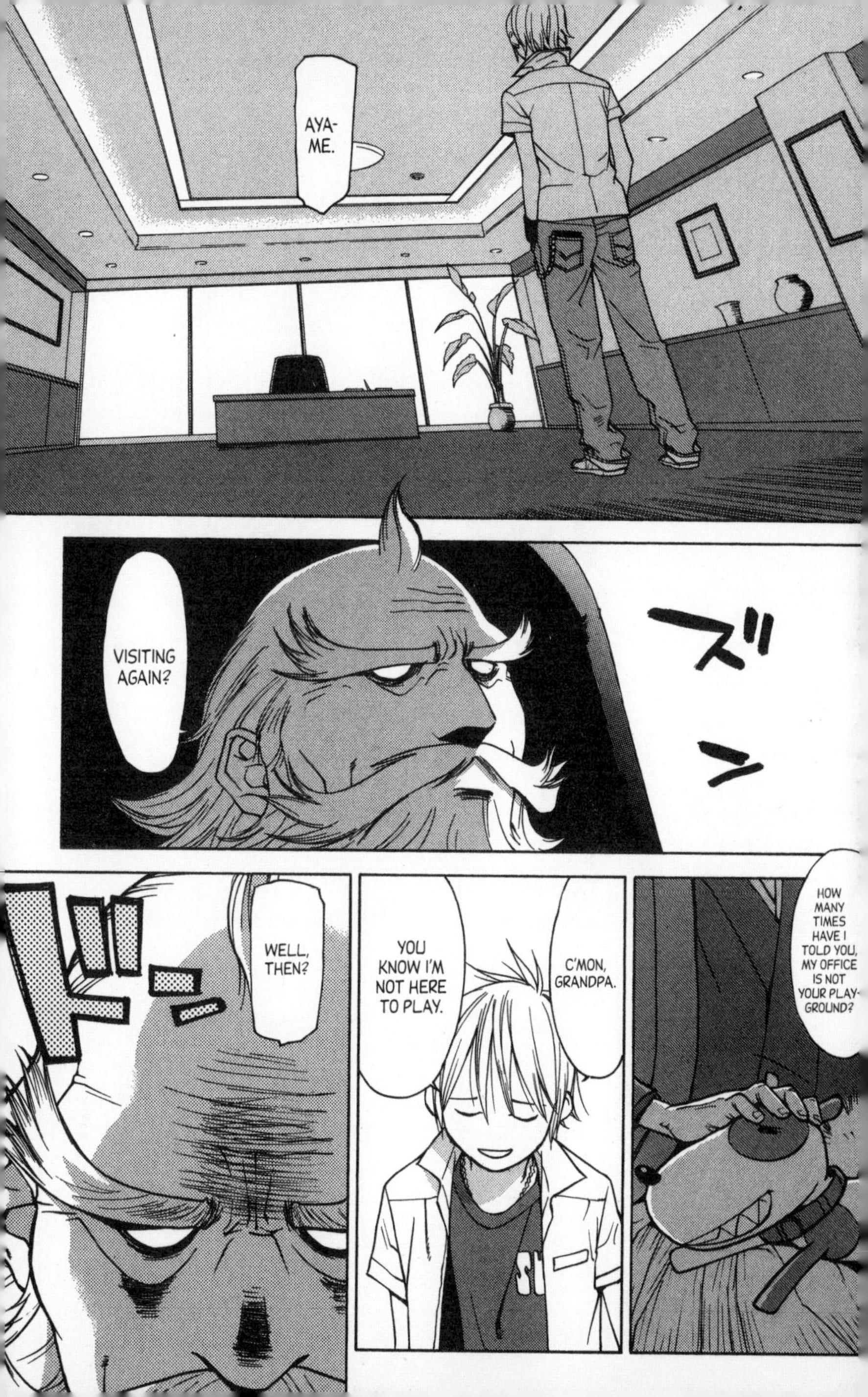
AYA-
ME.
ズン
VISITING AGAIN?
HOW MANY TIMES HAVE I TOLD YOU, MY OFFICE IS NOT YOUR PLAY-GROUND?
C'MON, GRANDPA.
YOU KNOW I'M NOT HERE TO PLAY.
WELL, THEN?

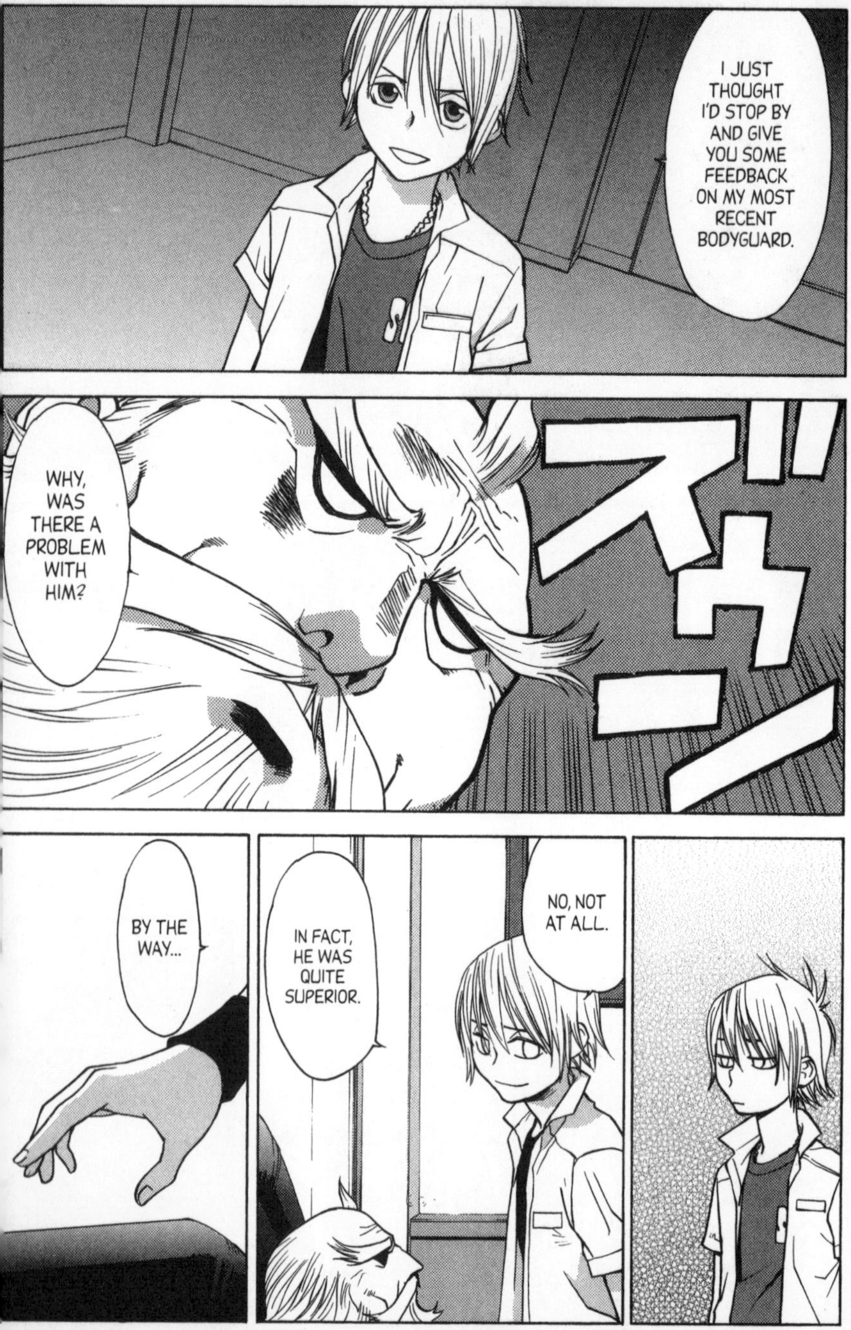
I JUST THOUGHT I'D STOP BY AND GIVE YOU SOME FEEDBACK ON MY MOST RECENT BODYGUARD.
ズウーン
WHY, WAS THERE A PROBLEM WITH HIM?
NO, NOT AT ALL.
IN FACT, HE WAS QUITE SUPERIOR.
BY THE WAY...

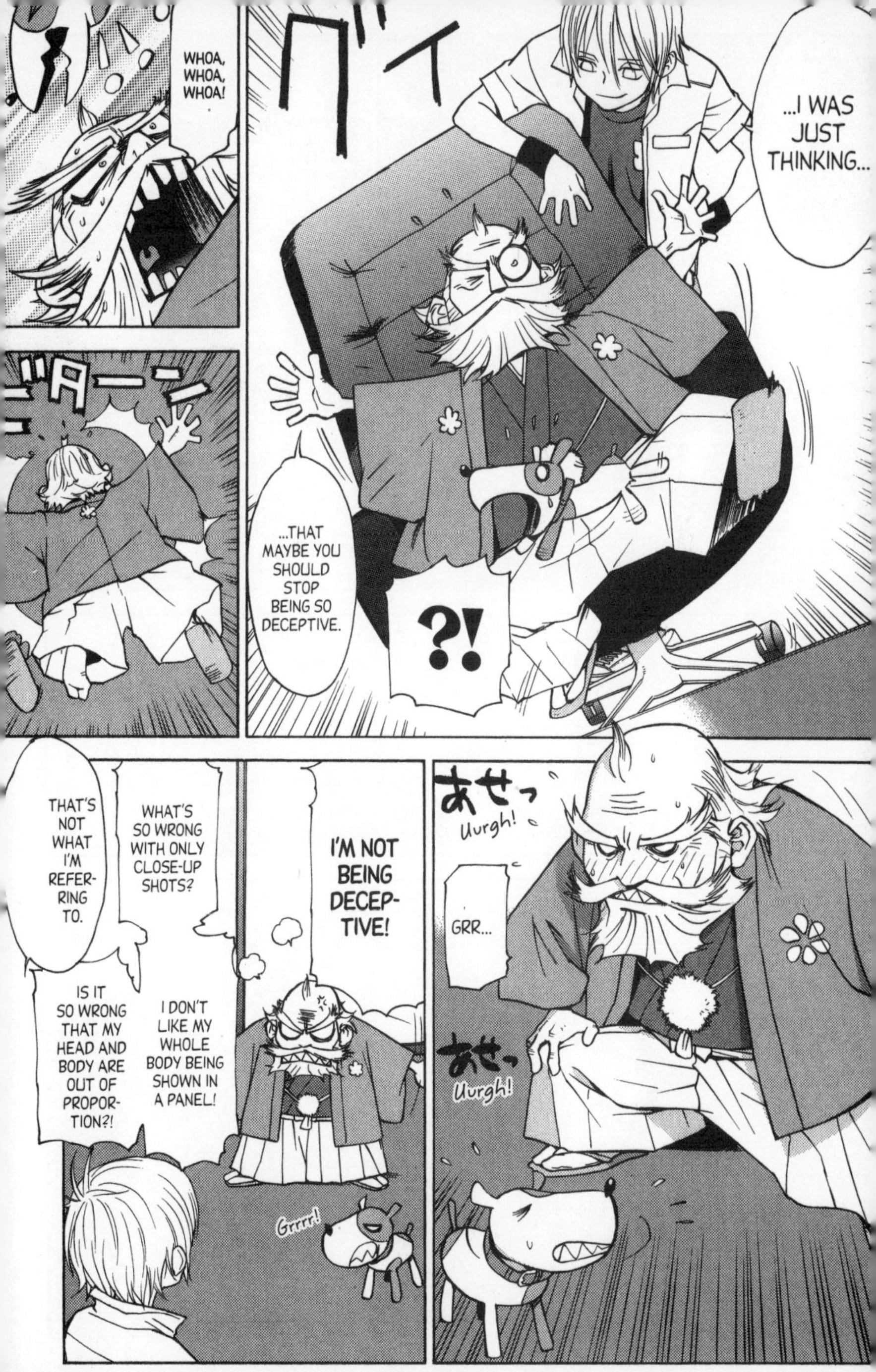
...I WAS JUST THINKING...
...THAT MAYBE YOU SHOULD STOP BEING SO DECEPTIVE.
?!
WHOA, WHOA, WHOA!
あせっ
Uurgh!
GRR...
あせっ
Uurgh!
I'M NOT BEING DECEPTIVE!
WHAT'S SO WRONG WITH ONLY CLOSE-UP SHOTS?
THAT'S NOT WHAT I'M REFERRING TO.
I DON'T LIKE MY WHOLE BODY BEING SHOWN IN A PANEL!
IS IT SO WRONG THAT MY HEAD AND BODY ARE OUT OF PROPORTION?!
Grrrr!

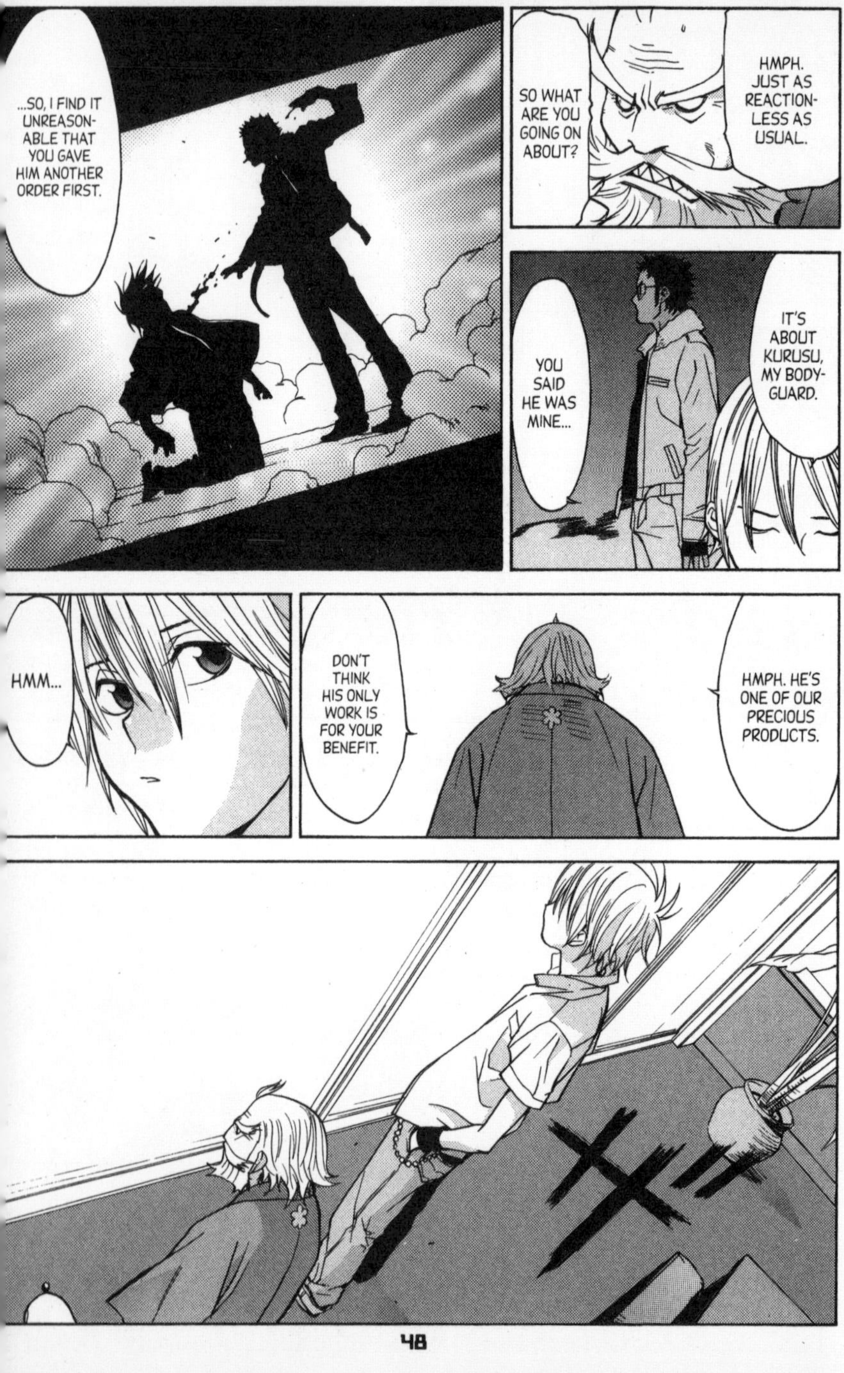
HMPH. JUST AS REACTIONLESS AS USUAL.
SO WHAT ARE YOU GOING ON ABOUT?
IT'S ABOUT KURUSU, MY BODYGUARD.
YOU SAID HE WAS MINE...
...SO, I FIND IT UNREASONABLE THAT YOU GAVE HIM ANOTHER ORDER FIRST.
HMPH. HE'S ONE OF OUR PRECIOUS PRODUCTS.
DON'T THINK HIS ONLY WORK IS FOR YOUR BENEFIT.
HMM...

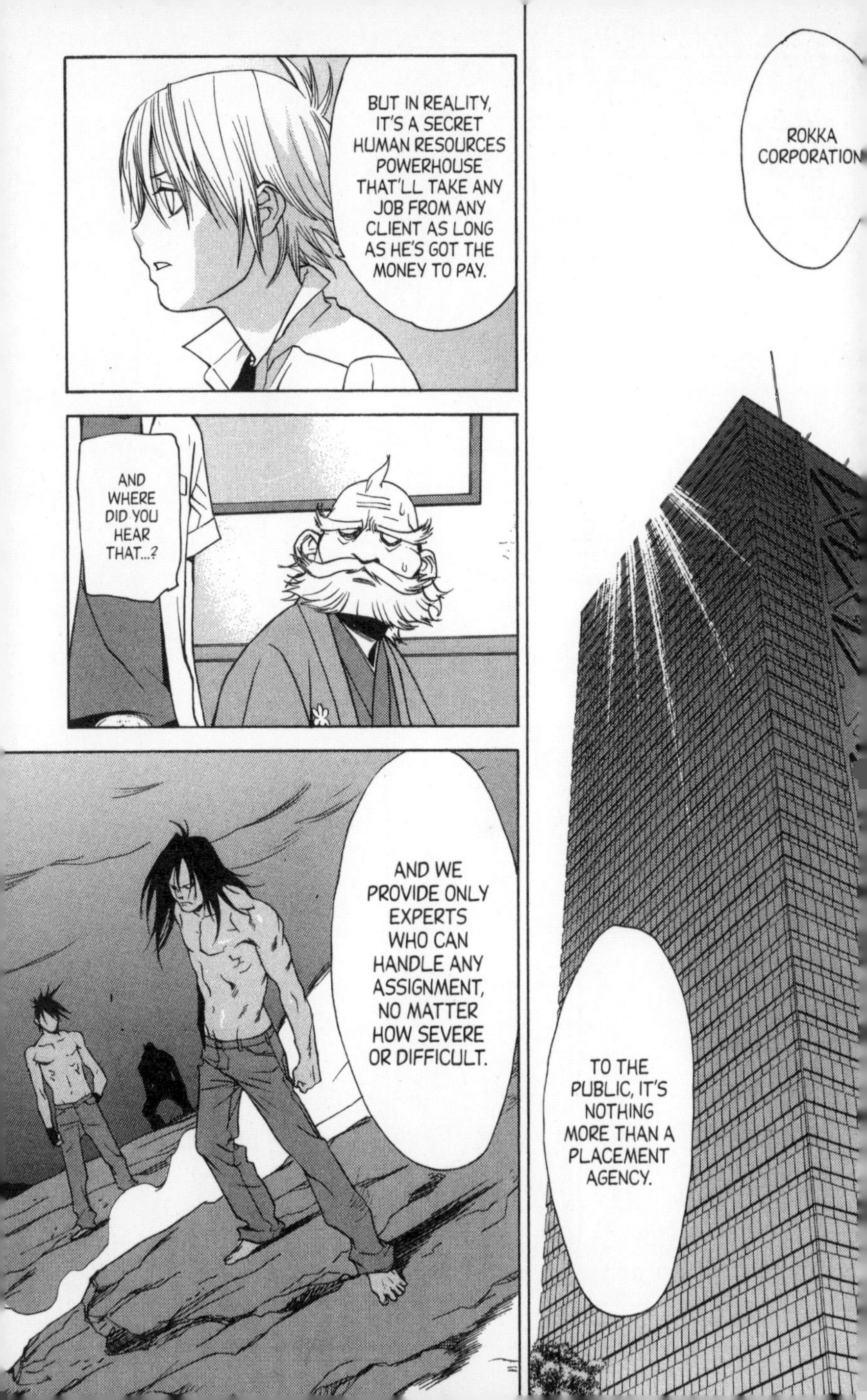
ROKKA CORPORATION
TO THE PUBLIC, IT'S NOTHING MORE THAN A PLACEMENT AGENCY.
BUT IN REALITY, IT'S A SECRET HUMAN RESOURCES POWERHOUSE THAT'LL TAKE ANY JOB FROM ANY CLIENT AS LONG AS HE'S GOT THE MONEY TO PAY.
AND WHERE DID YOU HEAR THAT...?
AND WE PROVIDE ONLY EXPERTS WHO CAN HANDLE ANY ASSIGNMENT, NO MATTER HOW SEVERE OR DIFFICULT.

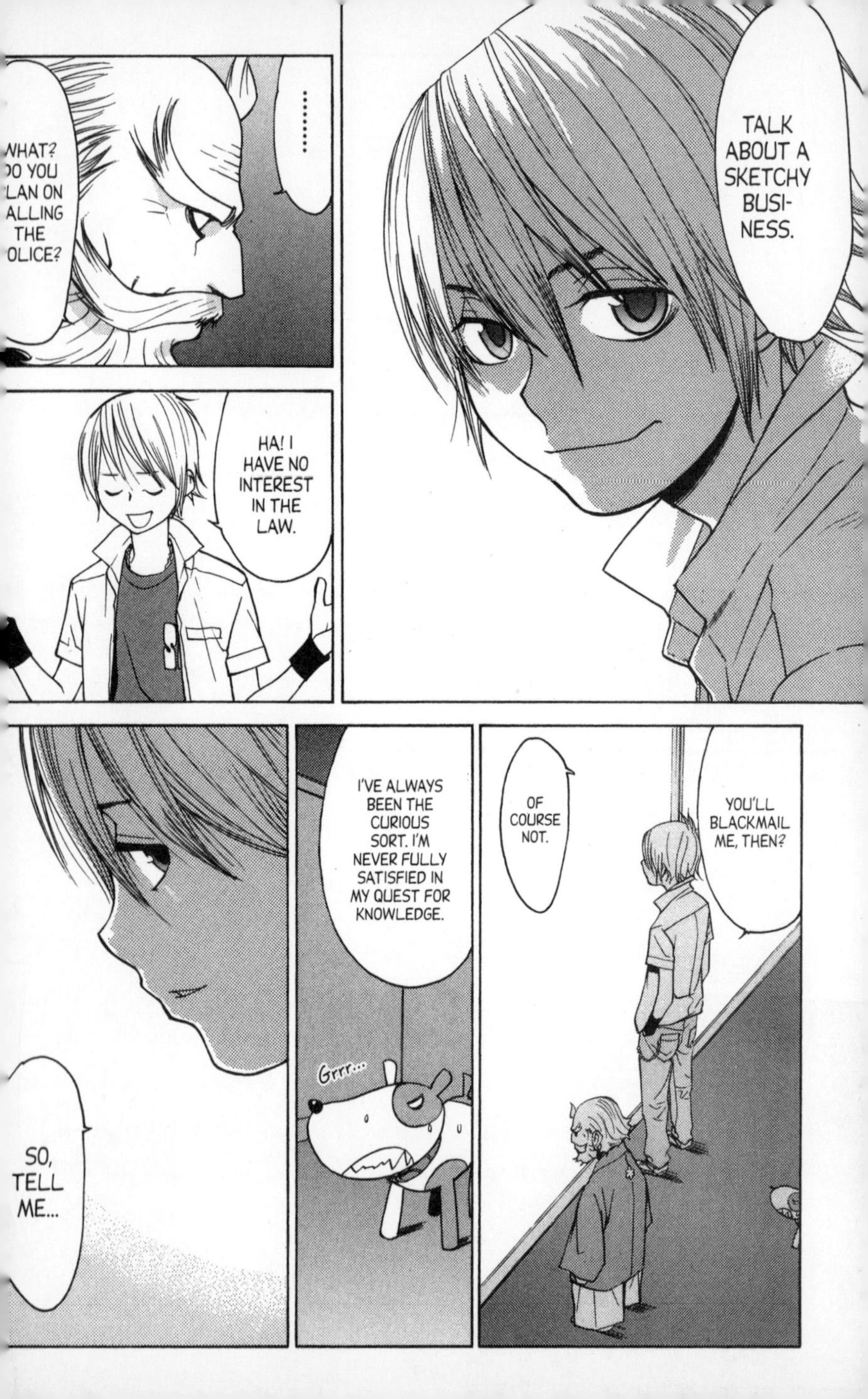
TALK ABOUT A SKETCHY BUSI-NESS.
......
WHAT? DO YOU LAN ON ALLING THE OLICE?
HA! I HAVE NO INTEREST IN THE LAW.
YOU'LL BLACKMAIL ME, THEN?
OF COURSE NOT.
I'VE ALWAYS BEEN THE CURIOUS SORT. I'M NEVER FULLY SATISFIED IN MY QUEST FOR KNOWLEDGE.
Grrr...
SO, TELL ME...

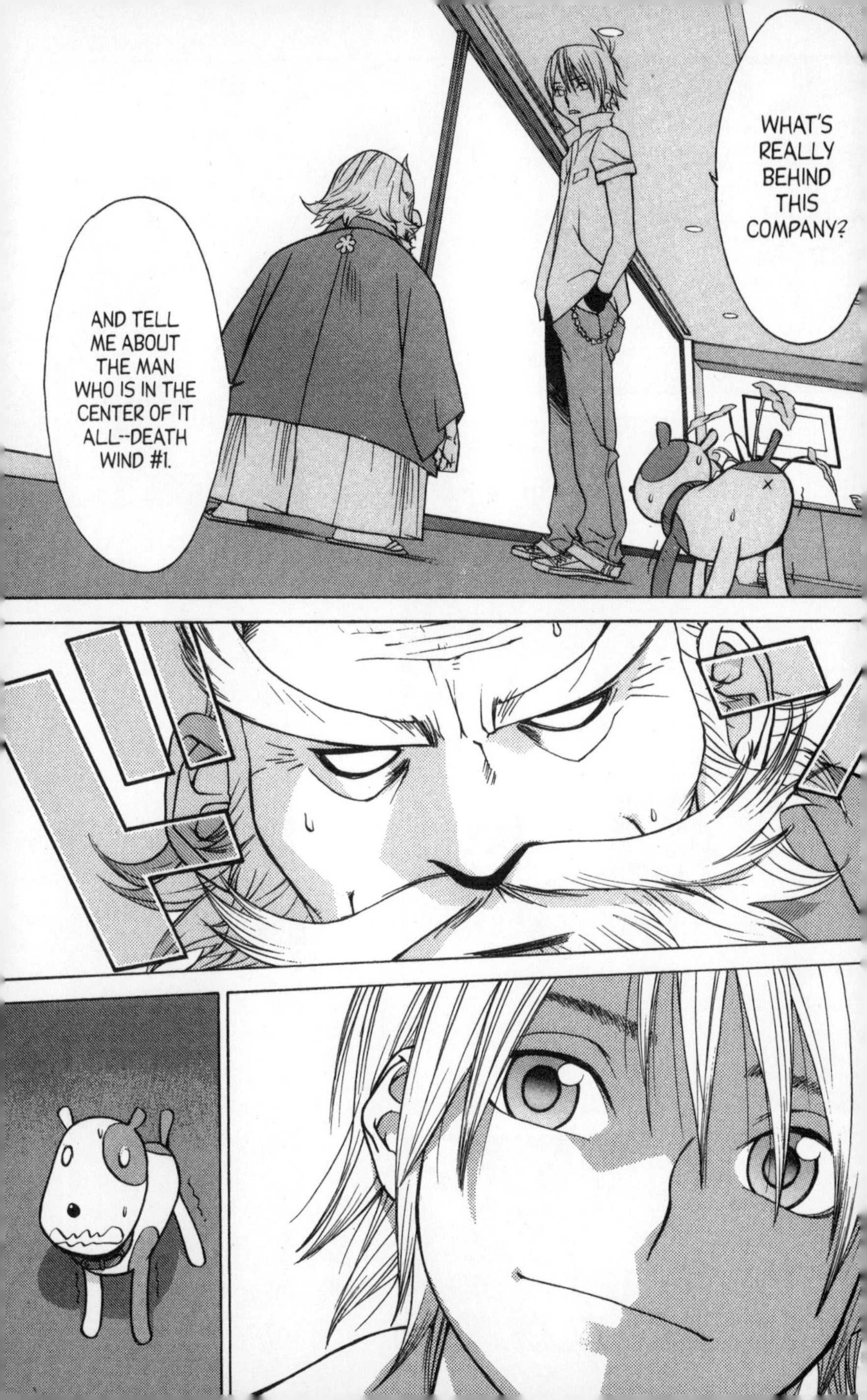
WHAT'S REALLY BEHIND THIS COMPANY?
AND TELL ME ABOUT THE MAN WHO IS IN THE CENTER OF IT ALL--DEATH WIND #1.

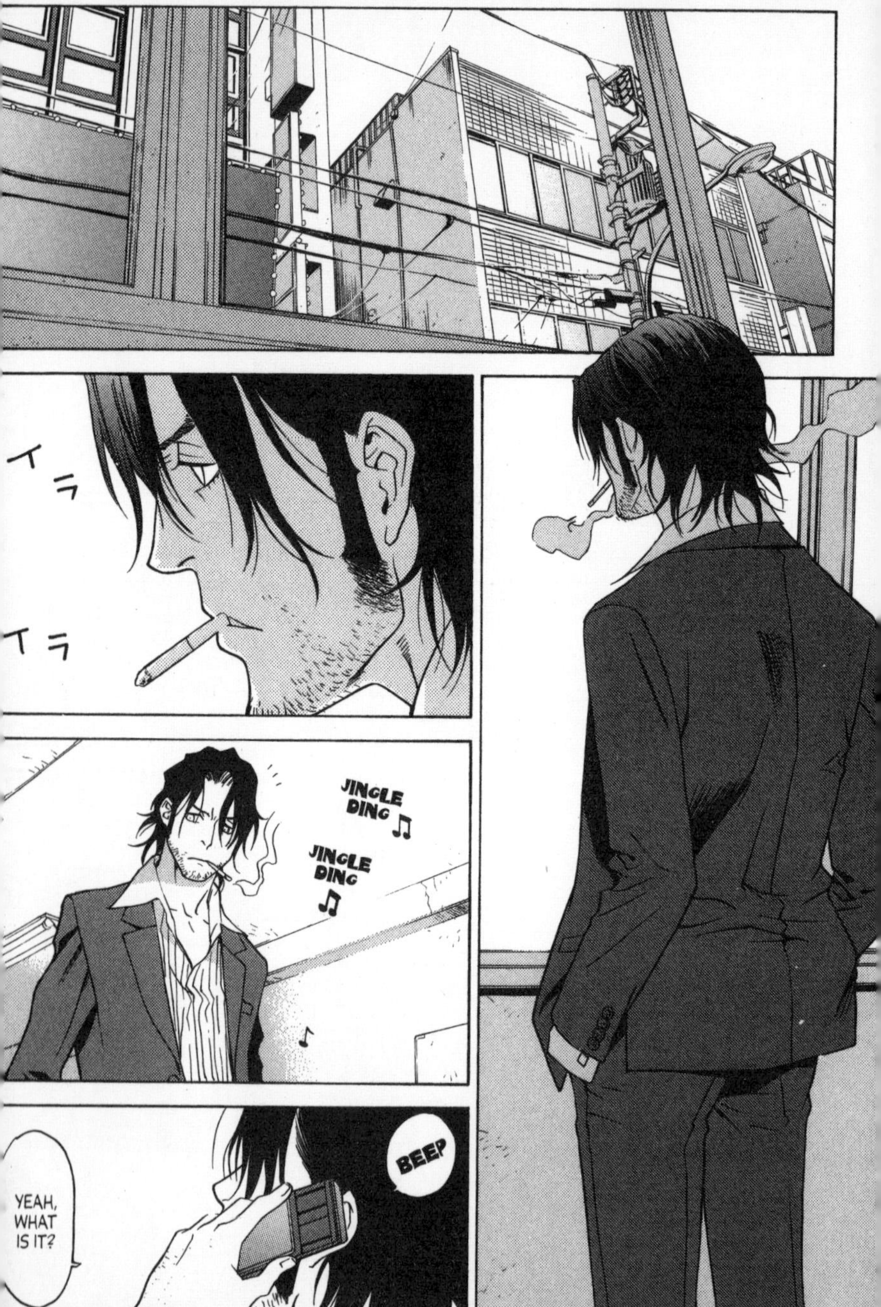
イラ
イラ
JINGLE DING ♫
JINGLE DING ♫
BEEP
YEAH, WHAT IS IT?

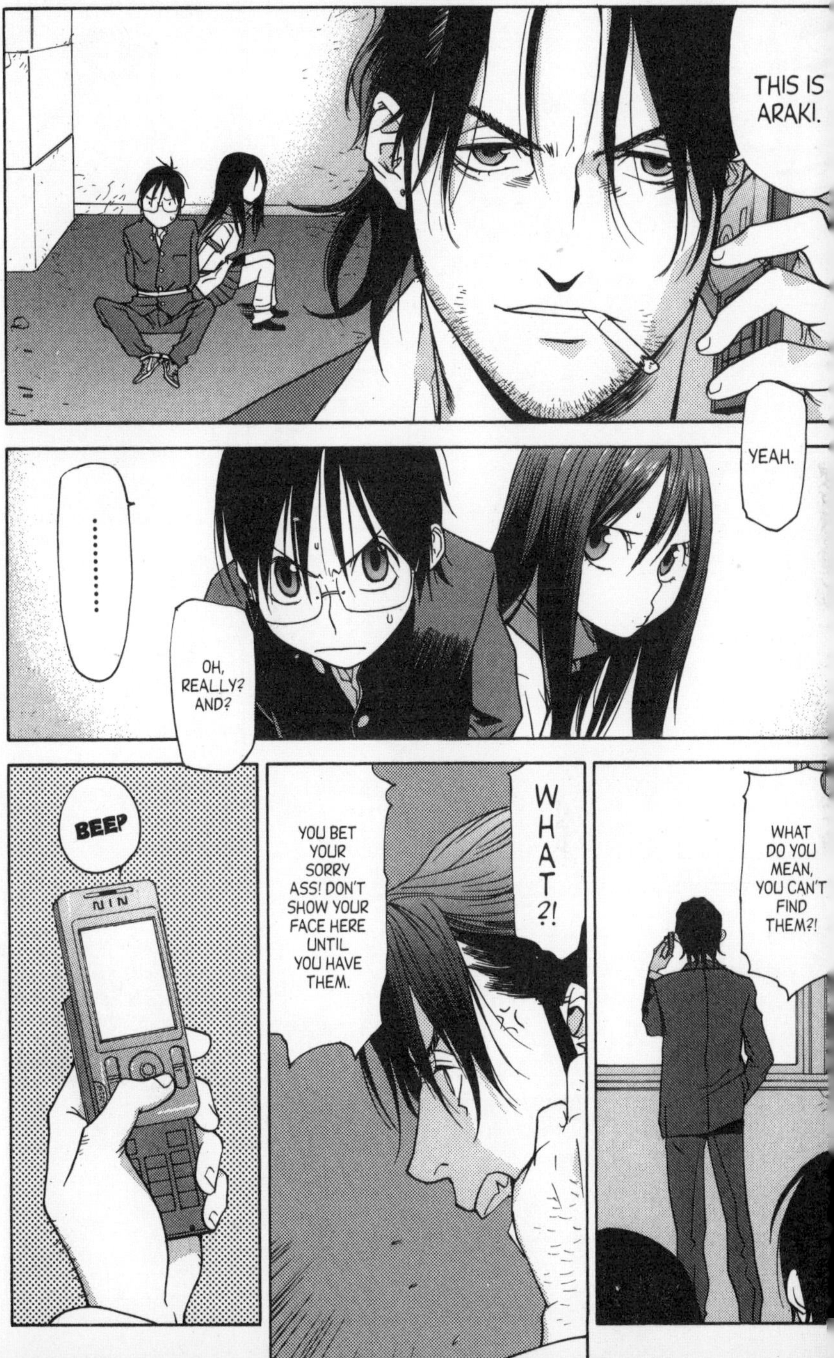
THIS IS ARAKI.
YEAH.
......
OH, REALLY? AND?
WHAT DO YOU MEAN, YOU CAN'T FIND THEM?!
WHAT?!
YOU BET YOUR SORRY ASS! DON'T SHOW YOUR FACE HERE UNTIL YOU HAVE THEM.
BEEP
NIN

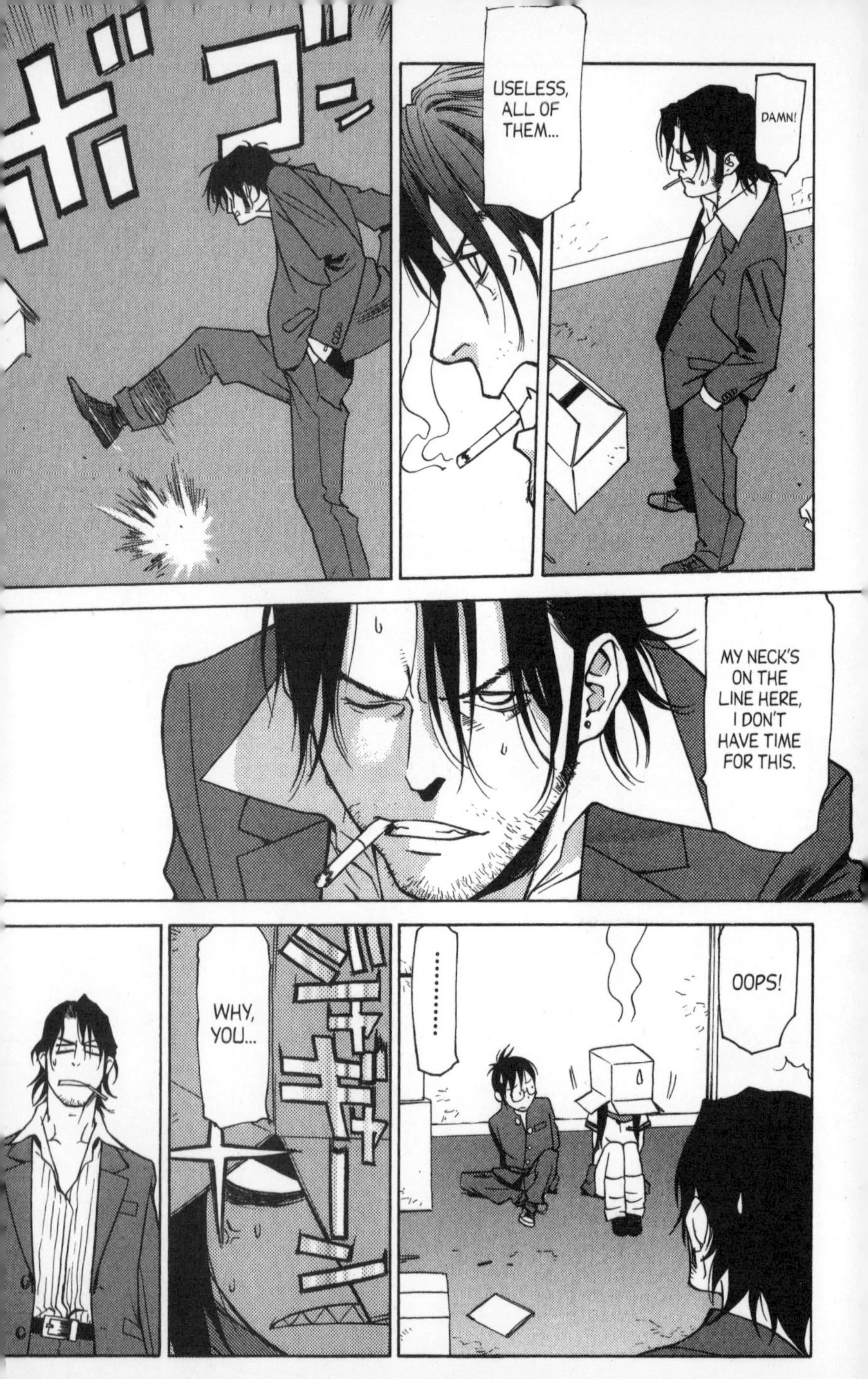
DAMN!
USELESS, ALL OF THEM...
MY NECK'S ON THE LINE HERE, I DON'T HAVE TIME FOR THIS.
OOPS!
....
WHY, YOU...

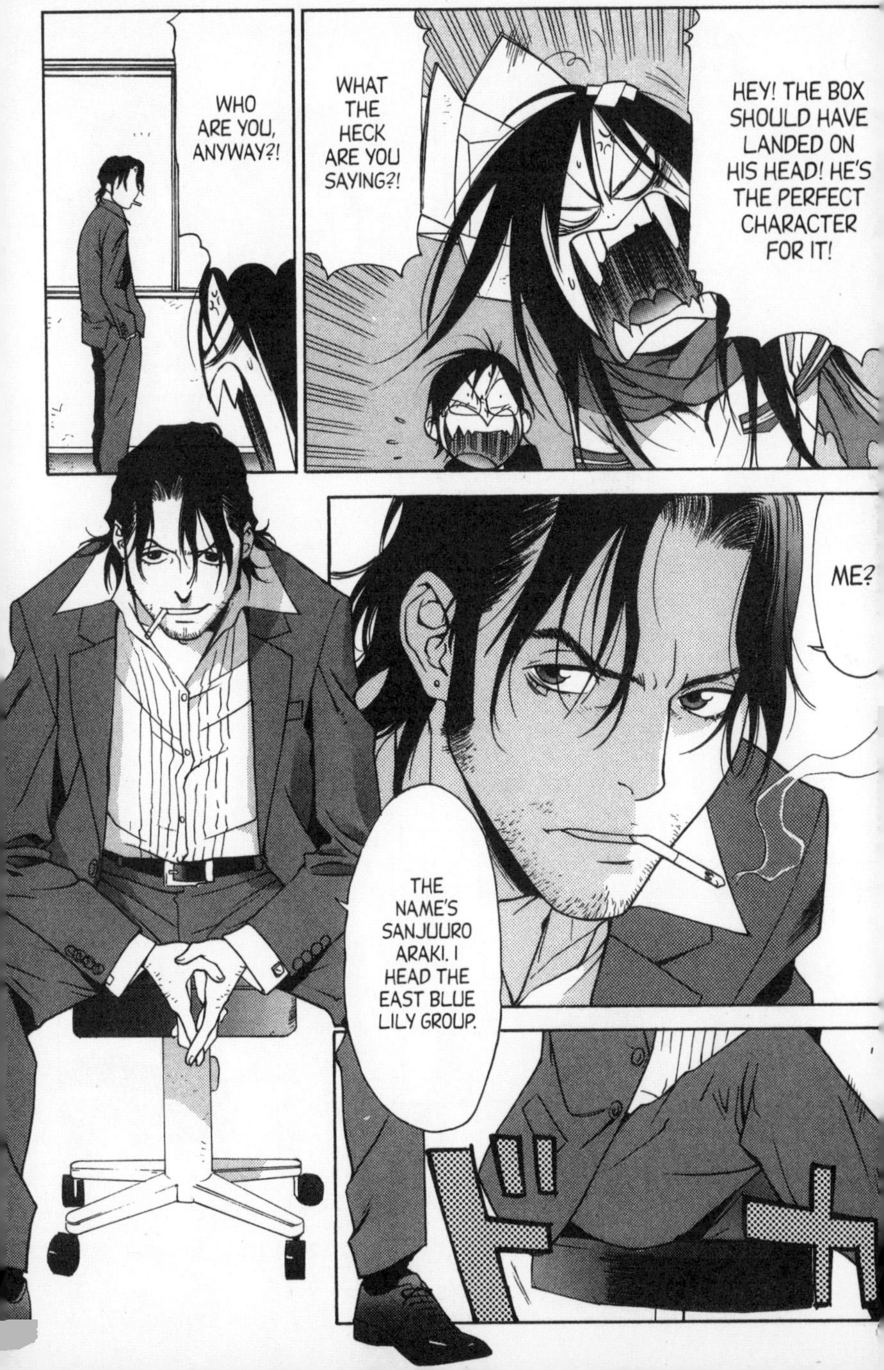
HEY! THE BOX SHOULD HAVE LANDED ON HIS HEAD! HE'S THE PERFECT CHARACTER FOR IT!
WHAT THE HECK ARE YOU SAYING?!
WHO ARE YOU, ANYWAY?!
ME?
THE NAME'S SANJUURO ARAKI. I HEAD THE EAST BLUE LILY GROUP.

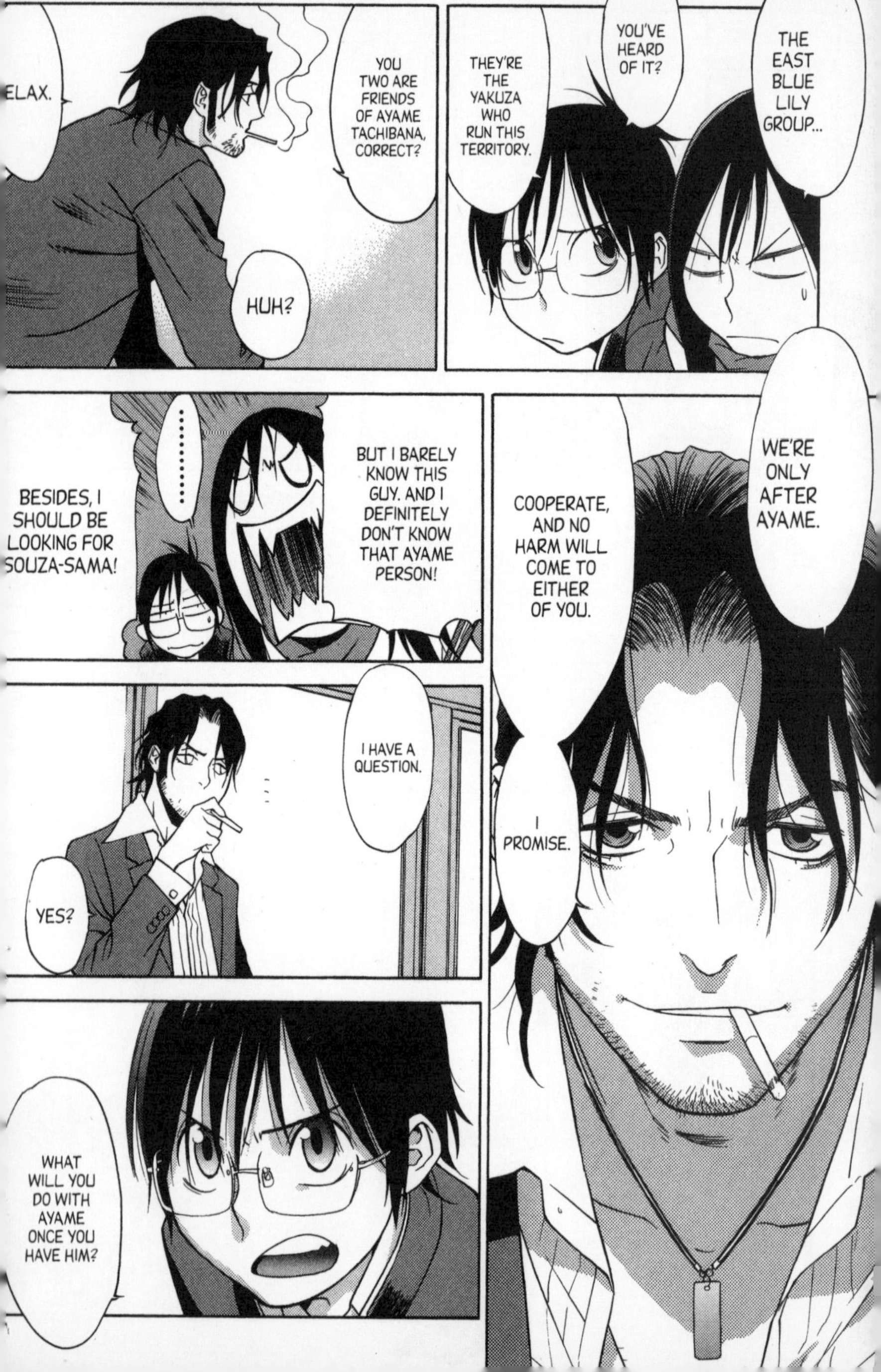

THE EAST BLUE LILY GROUP...
YOU'VE HEARD OF IT?
THEY'RE THE YAKUZA WHO RUN THIS TERRITORY.
YOU TWO ARE FRIENDS OF AYAME TACHIBANA, CORRECT?
HUH?
ELAX.
WE'RE ONLY AFTER AYAME.
COOPERATE, AND NO HARM WILL COME TO EITHER OF YOU.
I PROMISE.
BUT I BARELY KNOW THIS GUY. AND I DEFINITELY DON'T KNOW THAT AYAME PERSON!
....
BESIDES, I SHOULD BE LOOKING FOR SOUZA-SAMA!
I HAVE A QUESTION.
YES?
WHAT WILL YOU DO WITH AYAME ONCE YOU HAVE HIM?

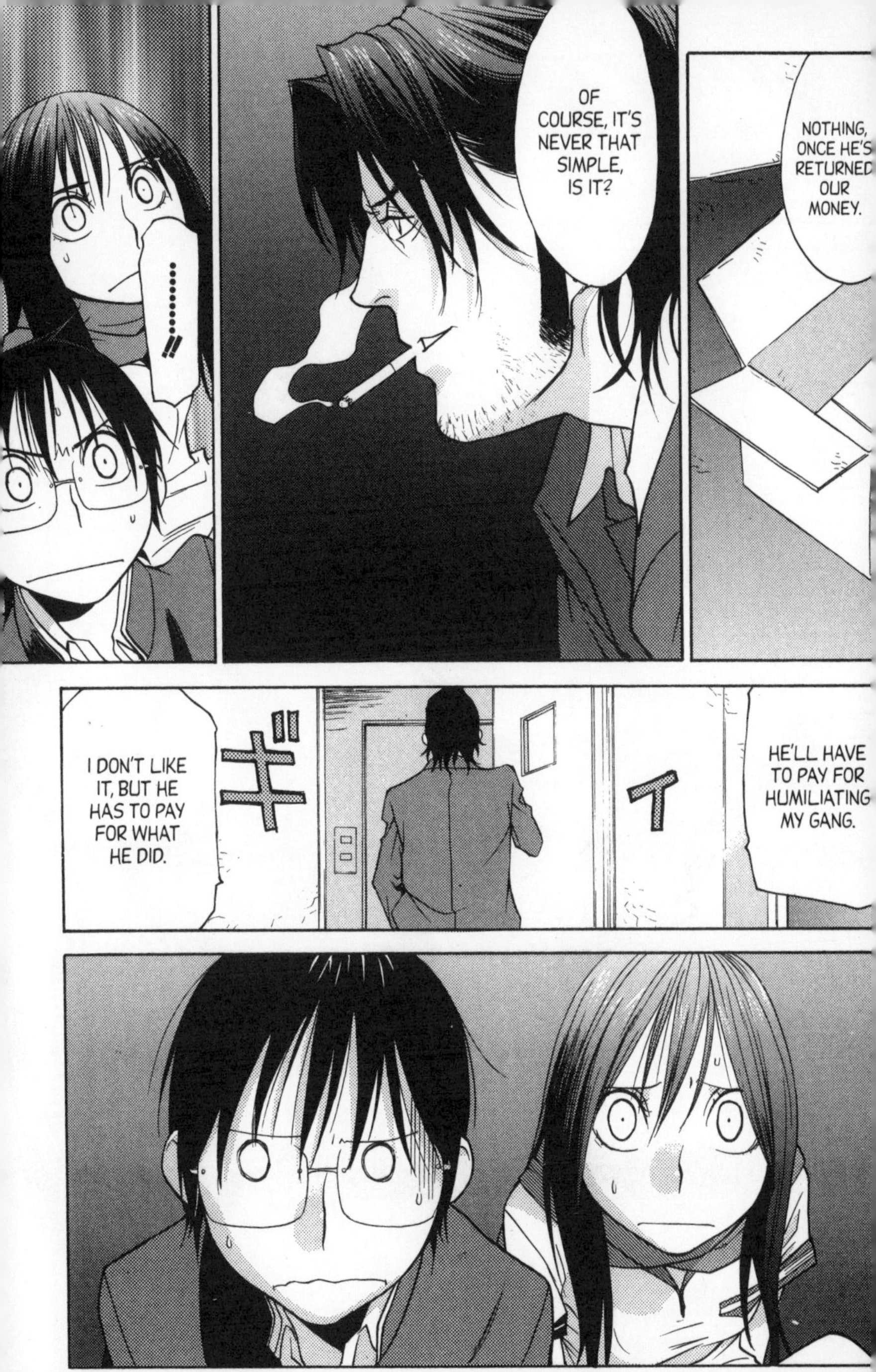
NOTHING, ONCE HE'S RETURNED OUR MONEY.
OF COURSE, IT'S NEVER THAT SIMPLE, IS IT?
......!!
HE'LL HAVE TO PAY FOR HUMILIATING MY GANG.
ギイ
I DON'T LIKE IT, BUT HE HAS TO PAY FOR WHAT HE DID.

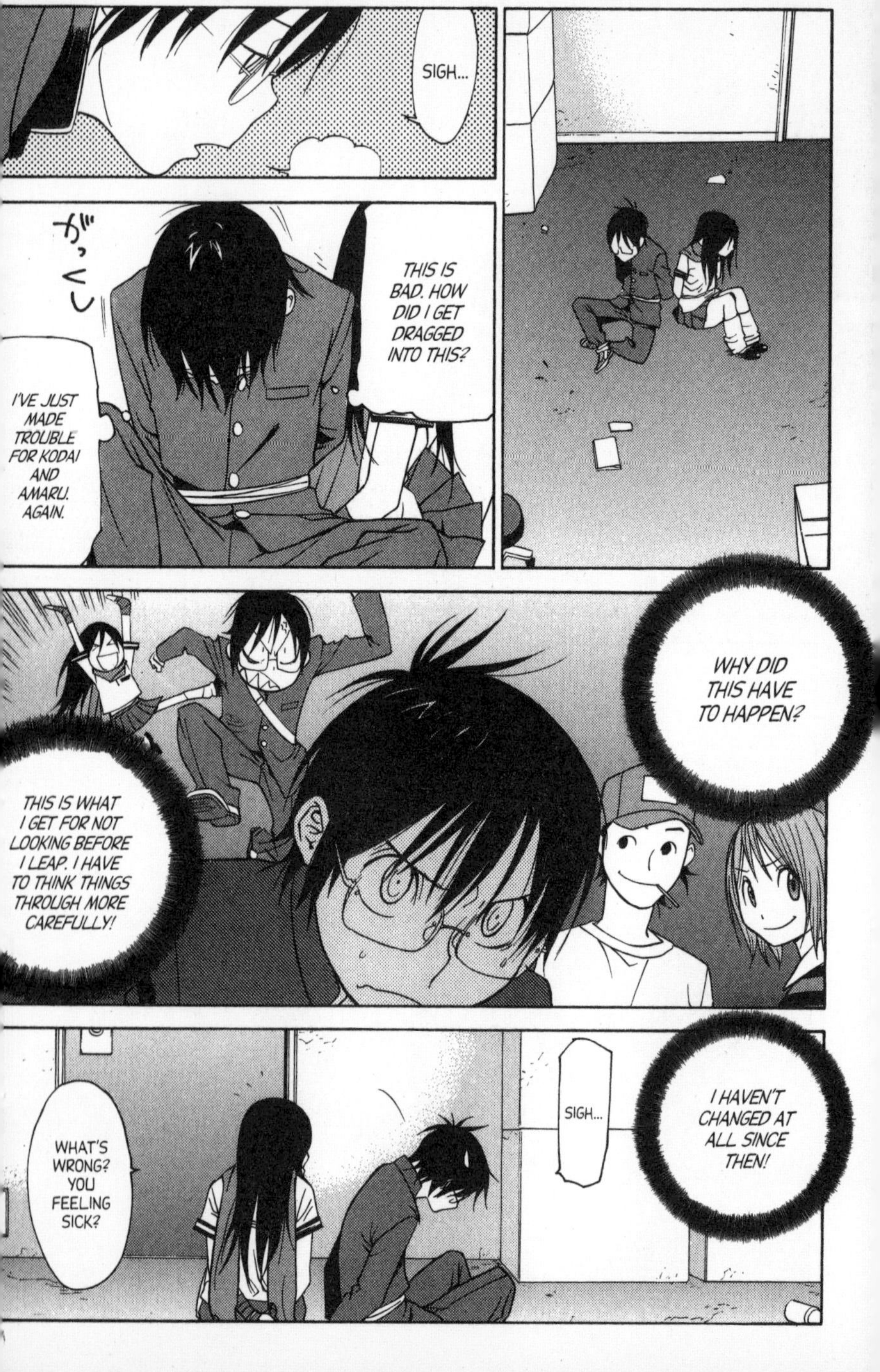
SIGH...
THIS IS BAD. HOW DID I GET DRAGGED INTO THIS?
がっくし
I'VE JUST MADE TROUBLE FOR KODAI AND AMARU. AGAIN.
WHY DID THIS HAVE TO HAPPEN?
THIS IS WHAT I GET FOR NOT LOOKING BEFORE I LEAP. I HAVE TO THINK THINGS THROUGH MORE CAREFULLY!
I HAVEN'T CHANGED AT ALL SINCE THEN!
SIGH...
WHAT'S WRONG? YOU FEELING SICK?

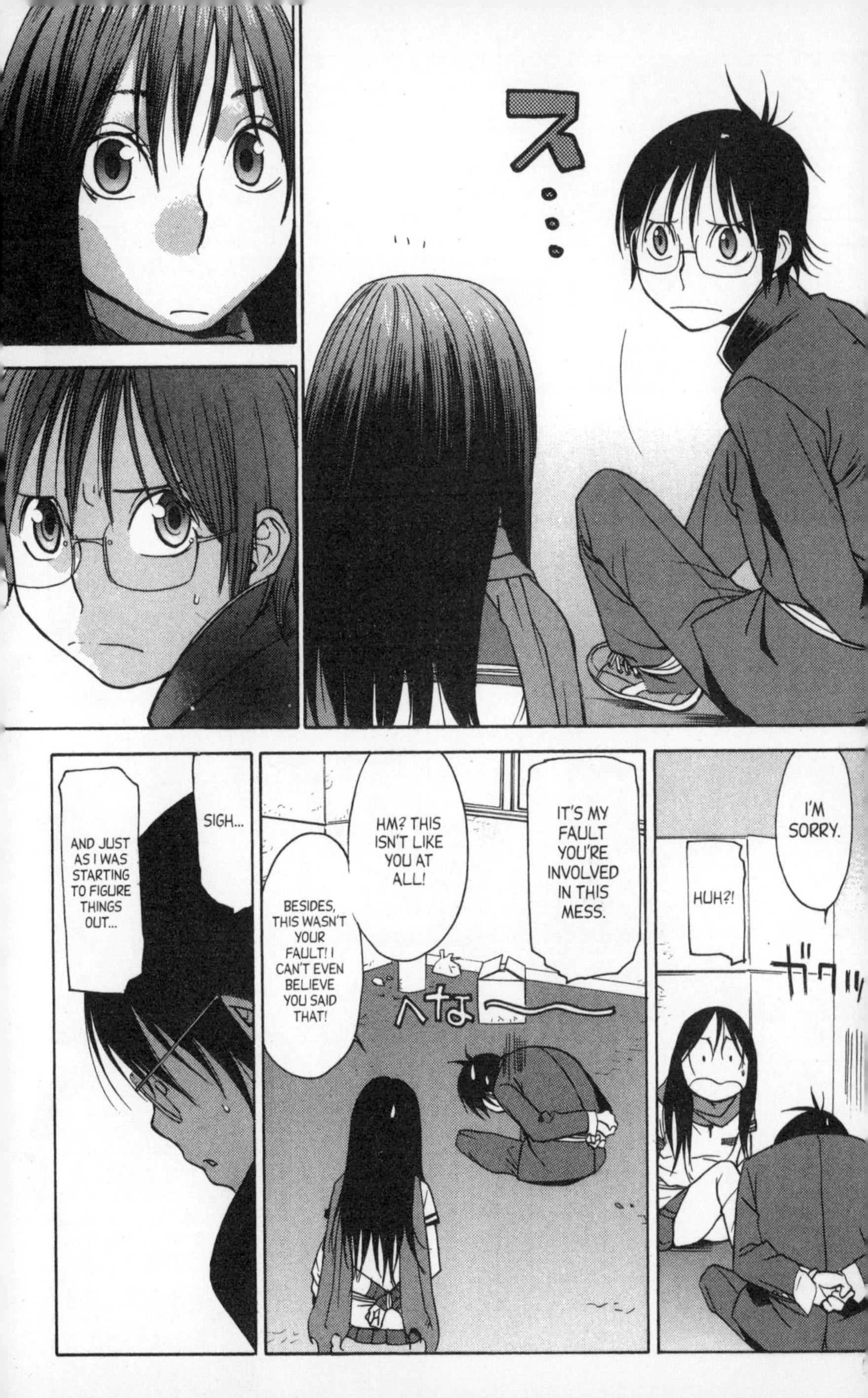

ス…
I'M SORRY.
HUH?!
ガークッ
IT'S MY FAULT YOU'RE INVOLVED IN THIS MESS.
HM? THIS ISN'T LIKE YOU AT ALL!
BESIDES, THIS WASN'T YOUR FAULT! I CAN'T EVEN BELIEVE YOU SAID THAT!
へな〜〜
SIGH...
AND JUST AS I WAS STARTING TO FIGURE THINGS OUT...

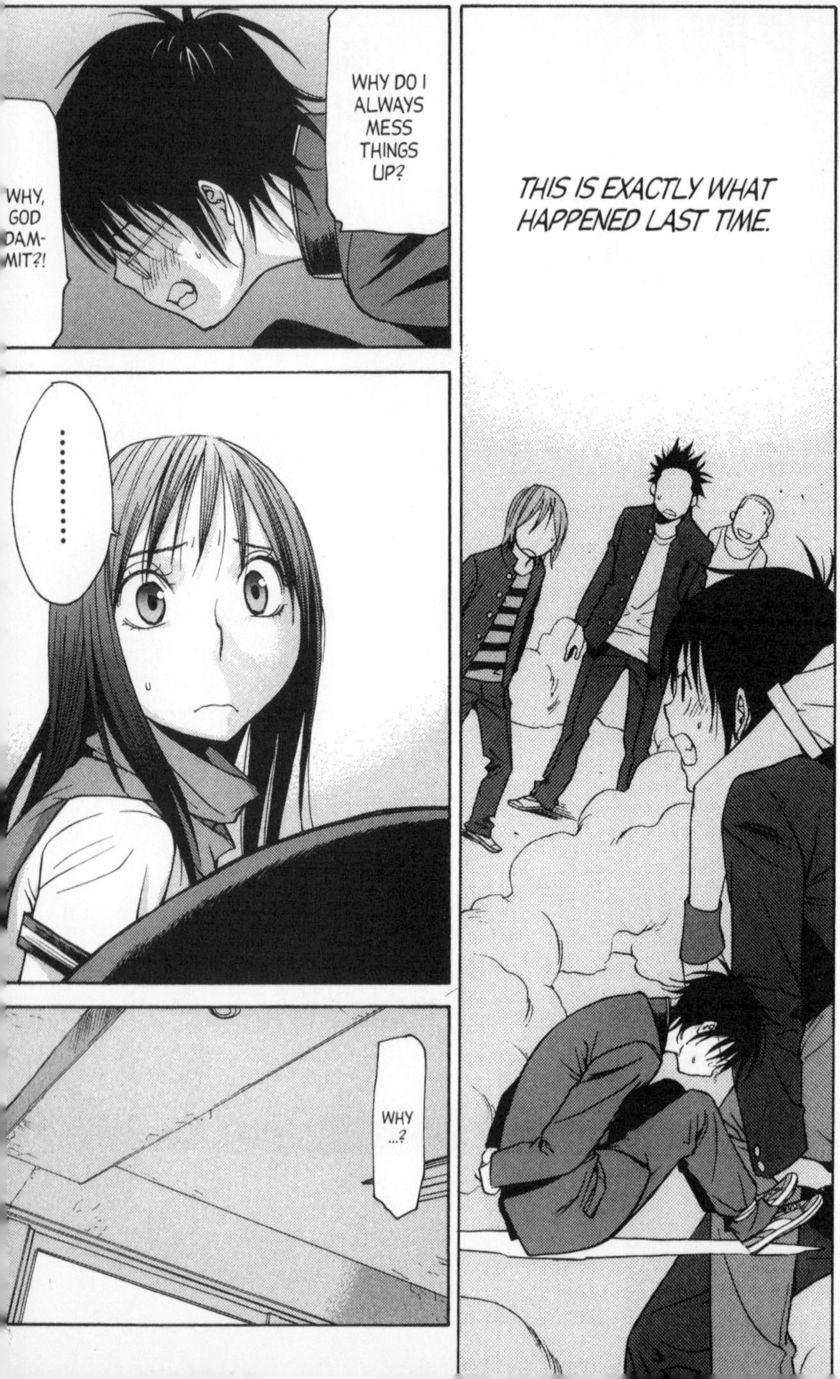
THIS IS EXACTLY WHAT HAPPENED LAST TIME.
WHY DO I ALWAYS MESS THINGS UP?
WHY, GOD DAM-MIT?!
....
WHY ...?

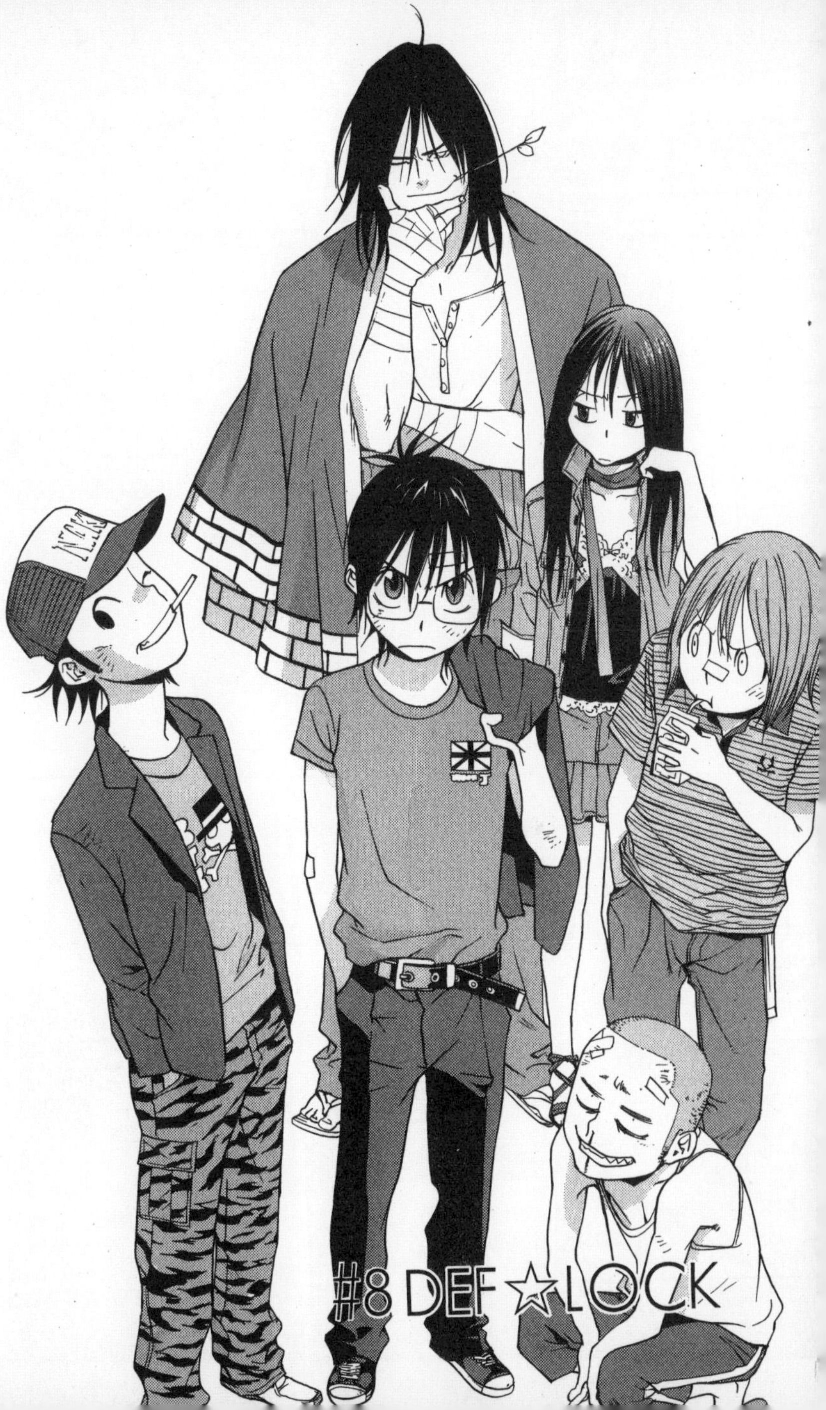
#8 DEF☆LOCK

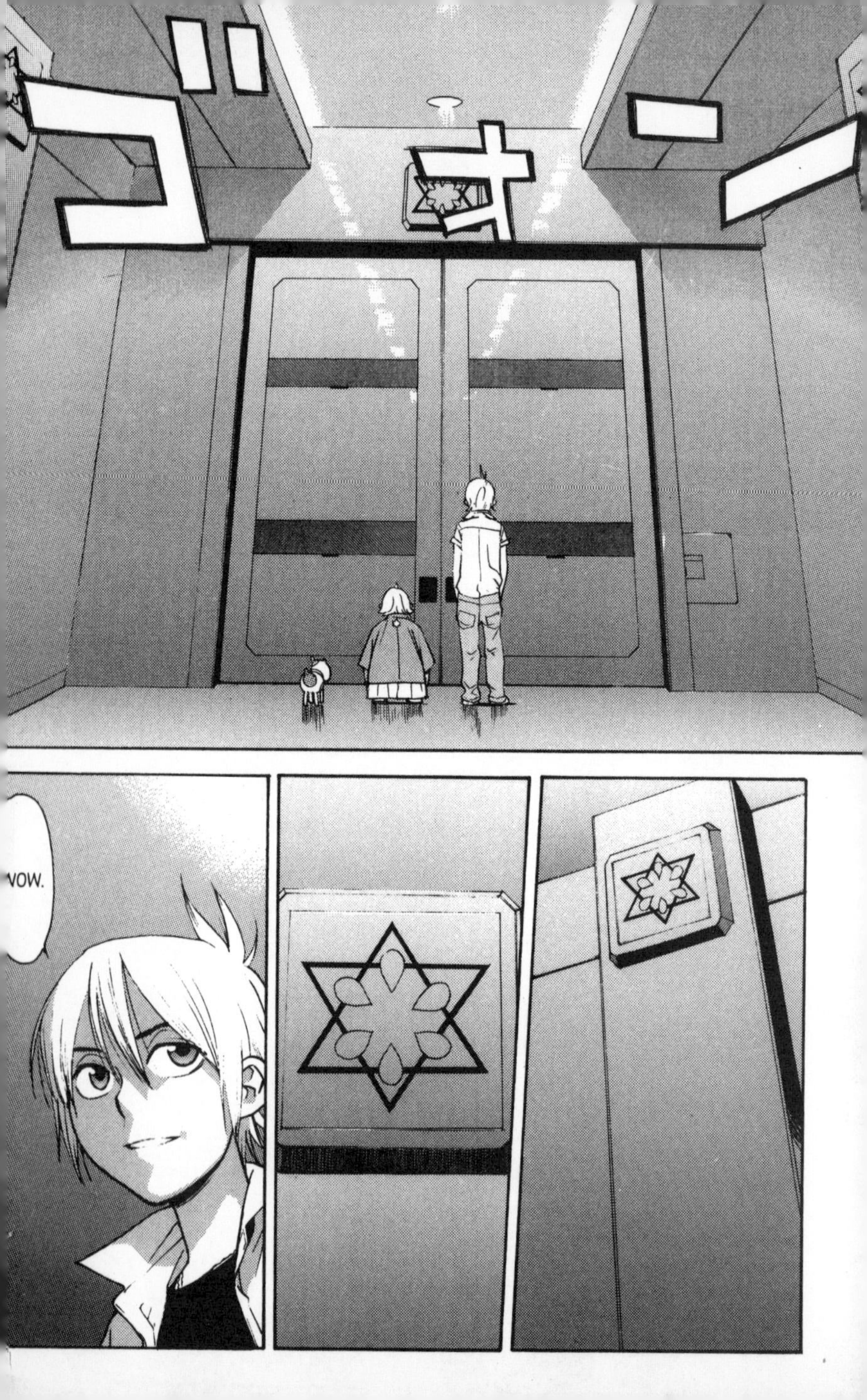
ゴオー
WOW.

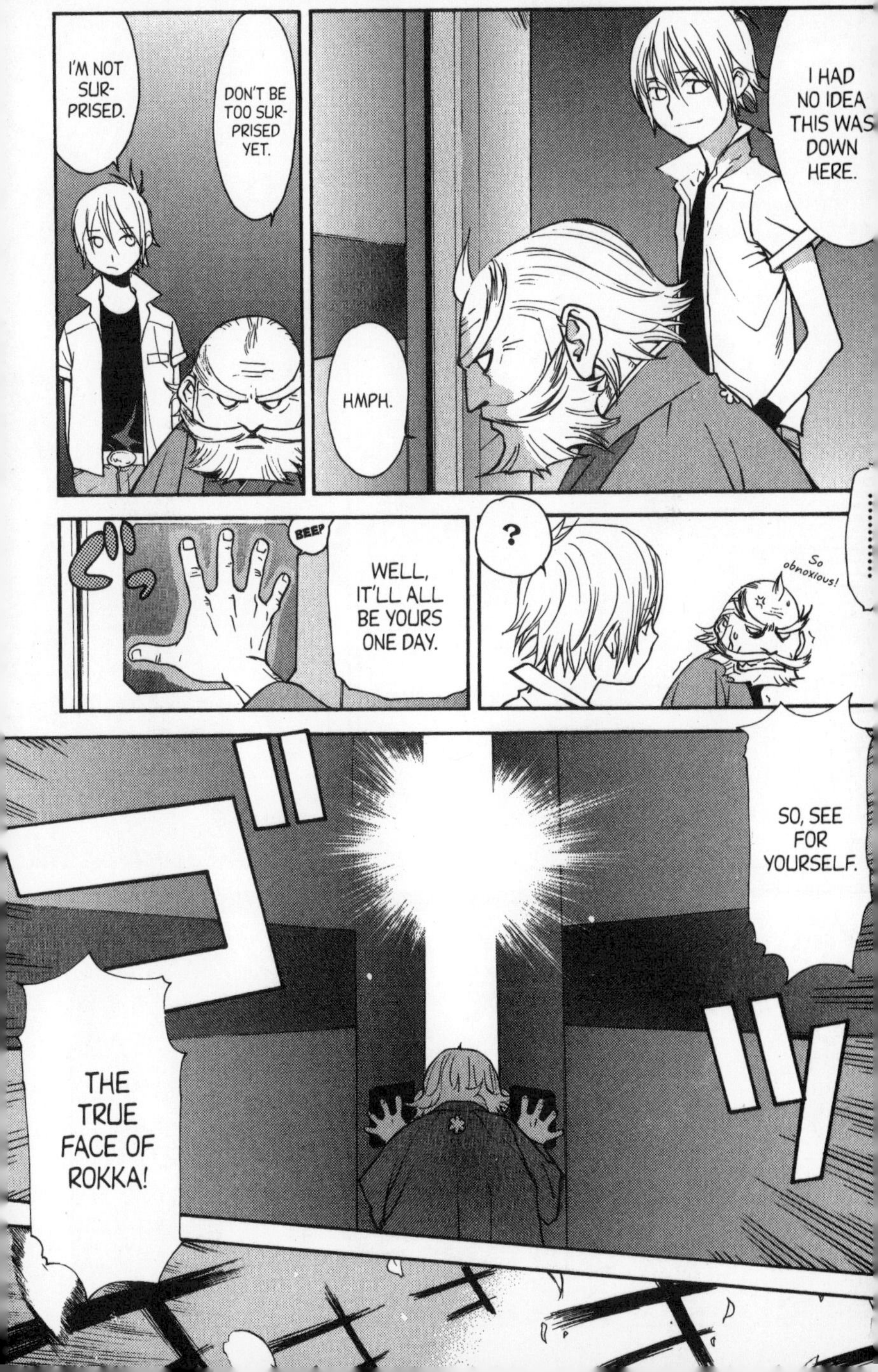
I HAD NO IDEA THIS WAS DOWN HERE.
HMPH.
DON'T BE TOO SUR-PRISED YET.
I'M NOT SUR-PRISED.
......
?
So obnoxious!
WELL, IT'LL ALL BE YOURS ONE DAY.
BEEP
SO, SEE FOR YOURSELF.
THE TRUE FACE OF ROKKA!

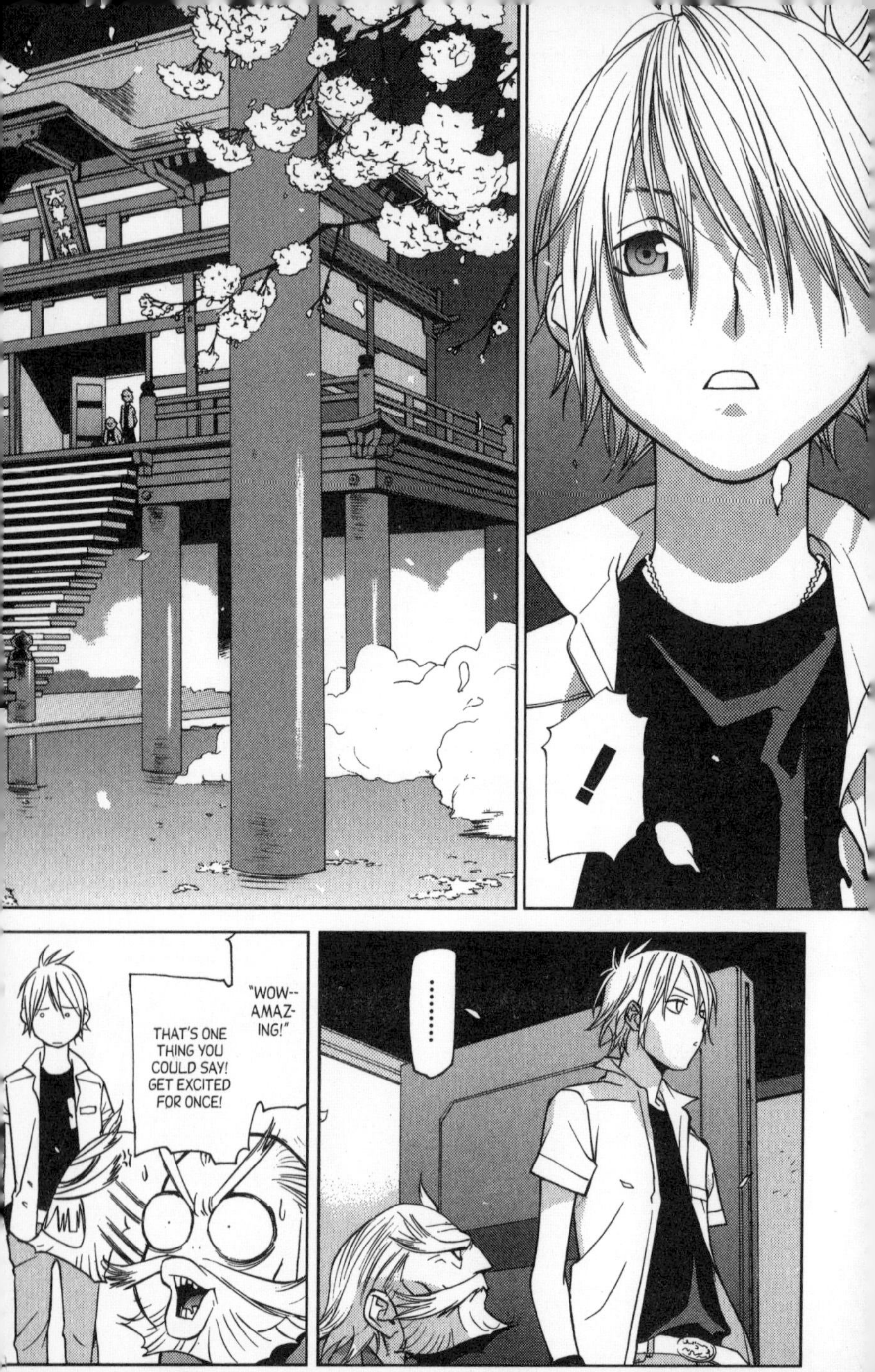
!
......
"WOW--AMAZING!"
THAT'S ONE THING YOU COULD SAY! GET EXCITED FOR ONCE!

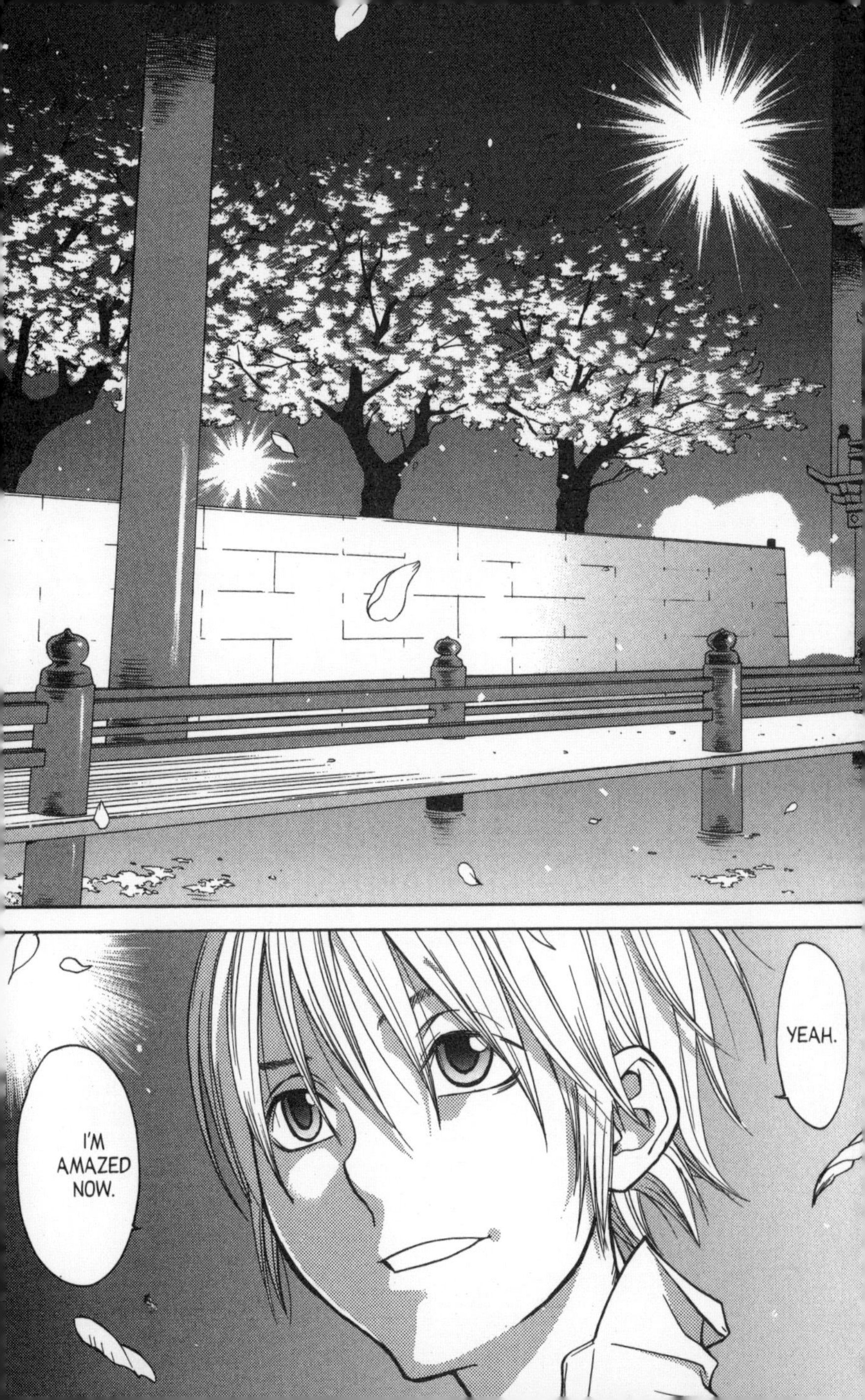
YEAH.
I'M AMAZED NOW.

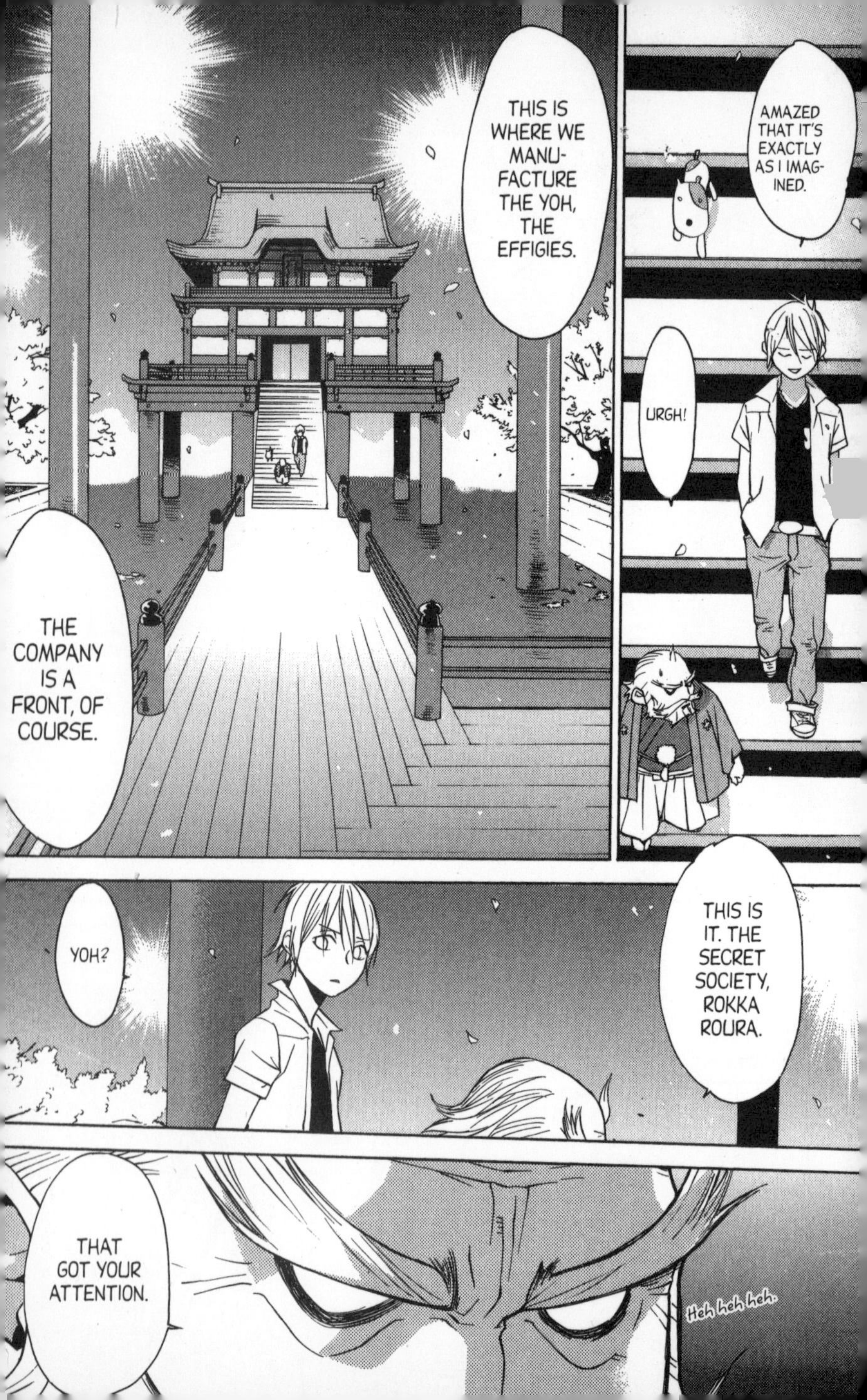
AMAZED THAT IT'S EXACTLY AS I IMAG-INED.
URGH!
THIS IS WHERE WE MANU-FACTURE THE YOH, THE EFFIGIES.
THE COMPANY IS A FRONT, OF COURSE.
THIS IS IT. THE SECRET SOCIETY, ROKKA ROURA.
YOH?
THAT GOT YOUR ATTENTION.
Heh heh heh.

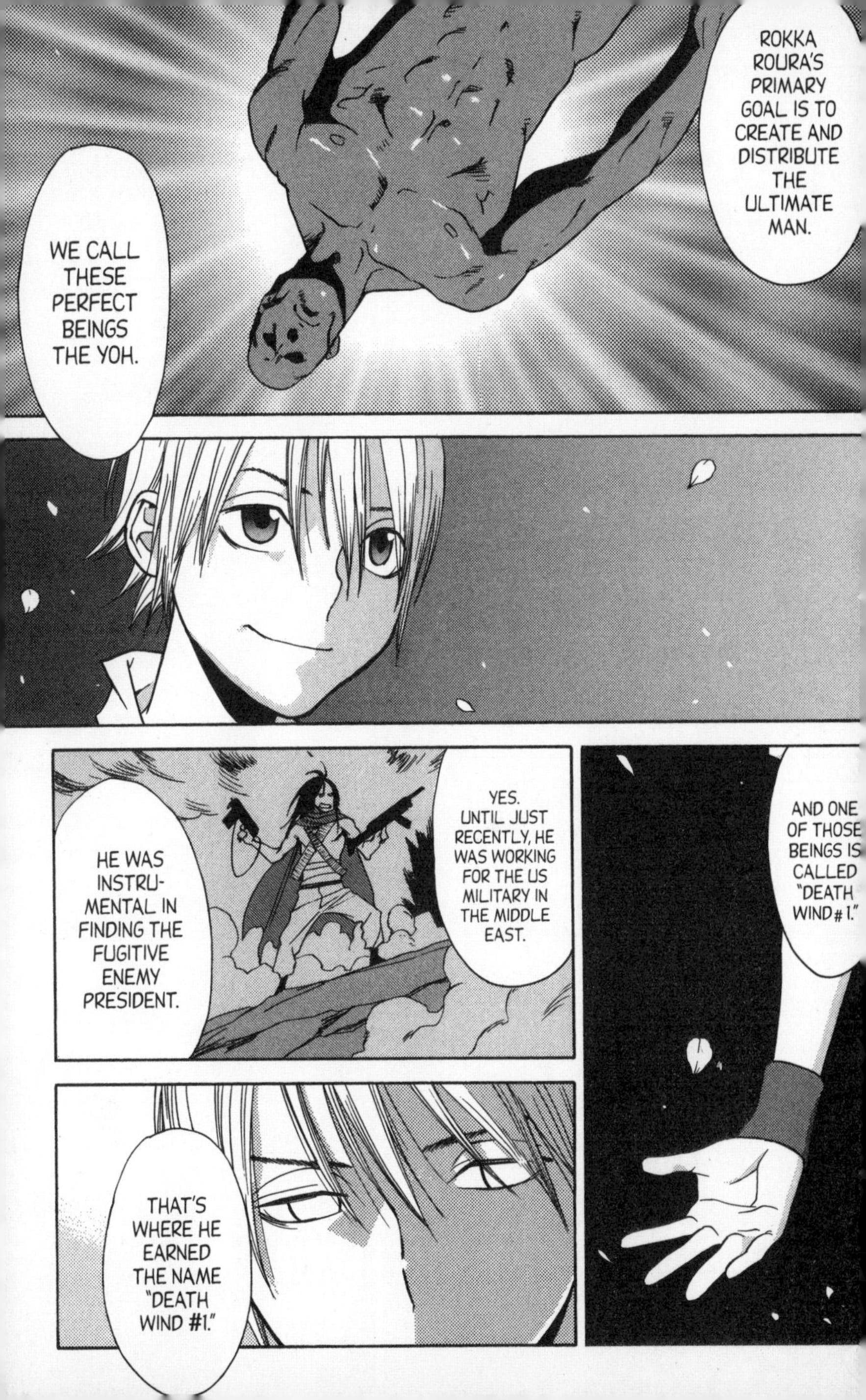
ROKKA ROURA'S PRIMARY GOAL IS TO CREATE AND DISTRIBUTE THE ULTIMATE MAN.
WE CALL THESE PERFECT BEINGS THE YOH.
AND ONE OF THOSE BEINGS IS CALLED "DEATH WIND # 1."
YES. UNTIL JUST RECENTLY, HE WAS WORKING FOR THE US MILITARY IN THE MIDDLE EAST.
HE WAS INSTRU-MENTAL IN FINDING THE FUGITIVE ENEMY PRESIDENT.
THAT'S WHERE HE EARNED THE NAME "DEATH WIND #1."

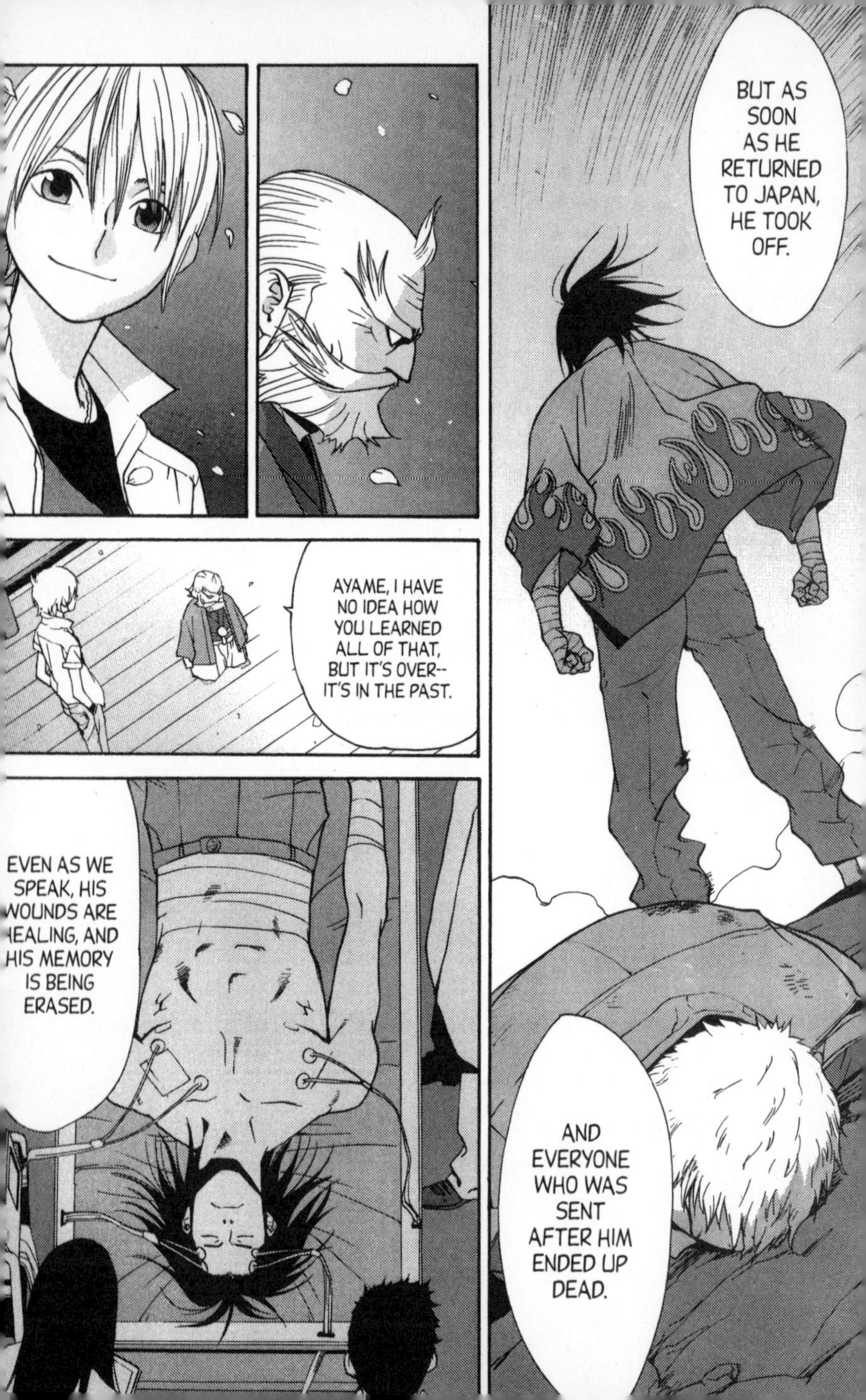
BUT AS SOON AS HE RETURNED TO JAPAN, HE TOOK OFF.
AND EVERYONE WHO WAS SENT AFTER HIM ENDED UP DEAD.
AYAME, I HAVE NO IDEA HOW YOU LEARNED ALL OF THAT, BUT IT'S OVER-- IT'S IN THE PAST.
EVEN AS WE SPEAK, HIS WOUNDS ARE HEALING, AND HIS MEMORY IS BEING ERASED.

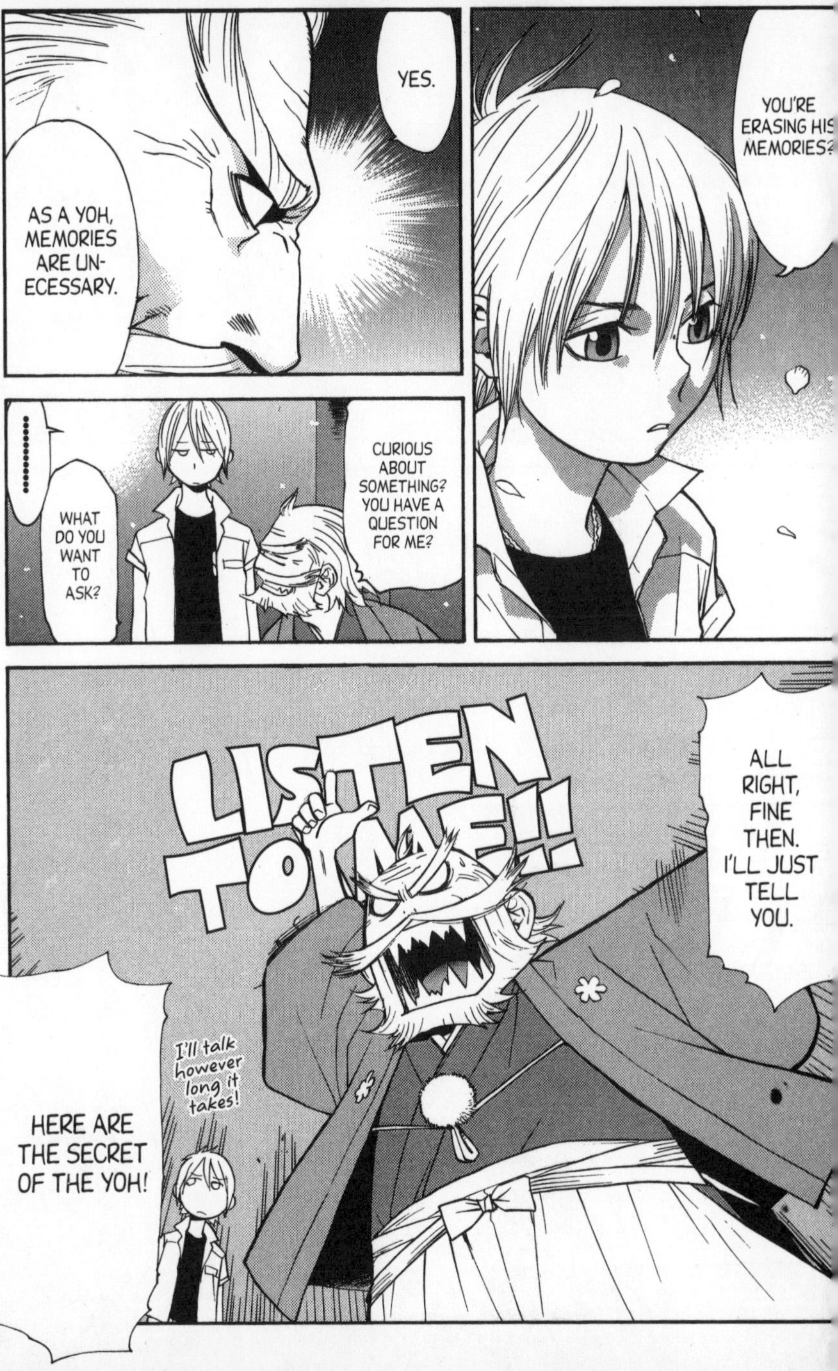
YOU'RE ERASING HIS MEMORIES?
YES.
AS A YOH, MEMORIES ARE UN-ECESSARY.
CURIOUS ABOUT SOMETHING? YOU HAVE A QUESTION FOR ME?
....
WHAT DO YOU WANT TO ASK?
ALL RIGHT, FINE THEN. I'LL JUST TELL YOU.
LISTEN TO ME!!
I'll talk however long it takes!
HERE ARE THE SECRET OF THE YOH!

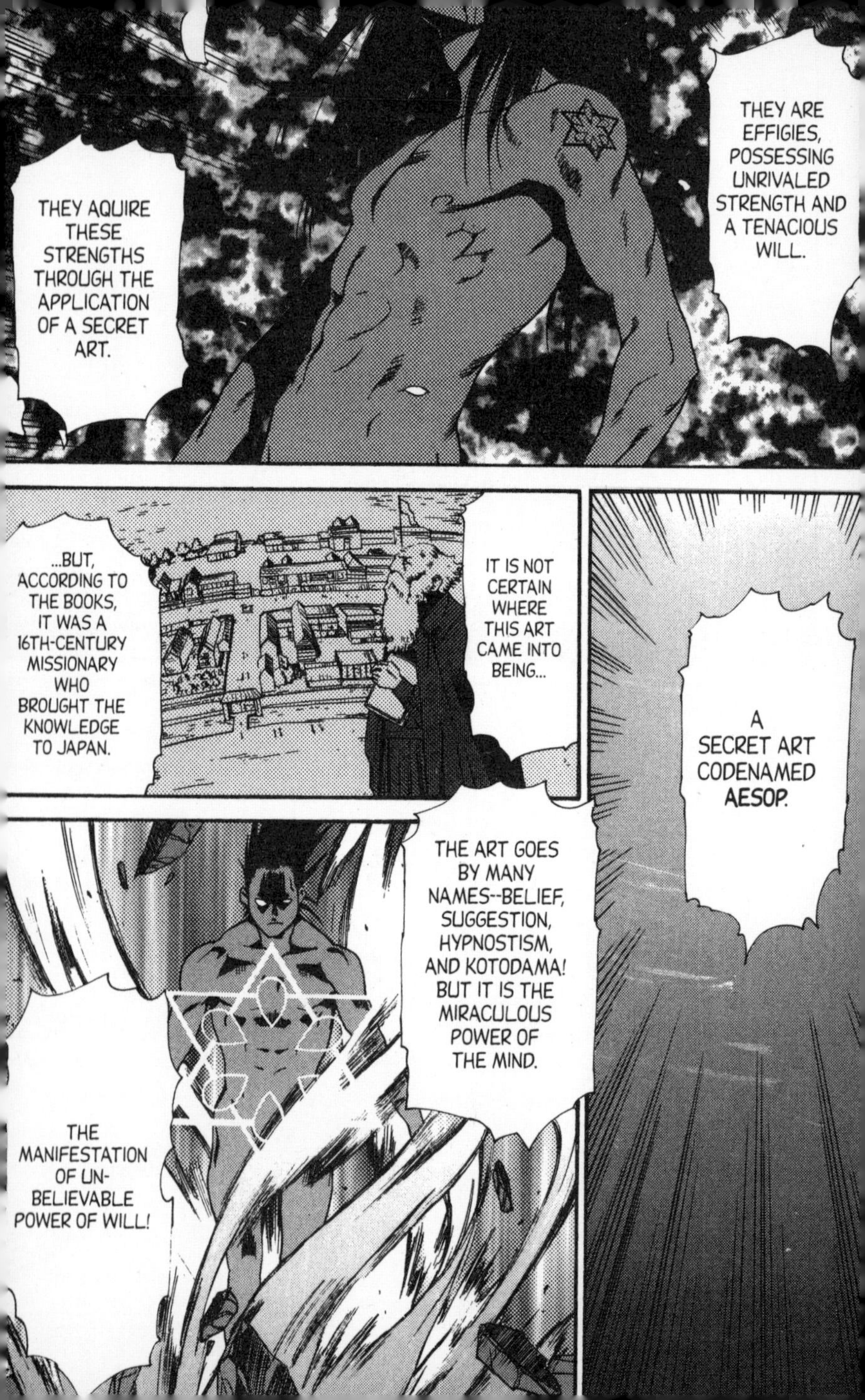
THEY ARE EFFIGIES, POSSESSING UNRIVALED STRENGTH AND A TENACIOUS WILL.
THEY AQUIRE THESE STRENGTHS THROUGH THE APPLICATION OF A SECRET ART.
A SECRET ART CODENAMED **AESOP**.
IT IS NOT CERTAIN WHERE THIS ART CAME INTO BEING...
...BUT, ACCORDING TO THE BOOKS, IT WAS A 16TH-CENTURY MISSIONARY WHO BROUGHT THE KNOWLEDGE TO JAPAN.
THE ART GOES BY MANY NAMES--BELIEF, SUGGESTION, HYPNOSTISM, AND KOTODAMA! BUT IT IS THE MIRACULOUS POWER OF THE MIND.
THE MANIFESTATION OF UN-BELIEVABLE POWER OF WILL!

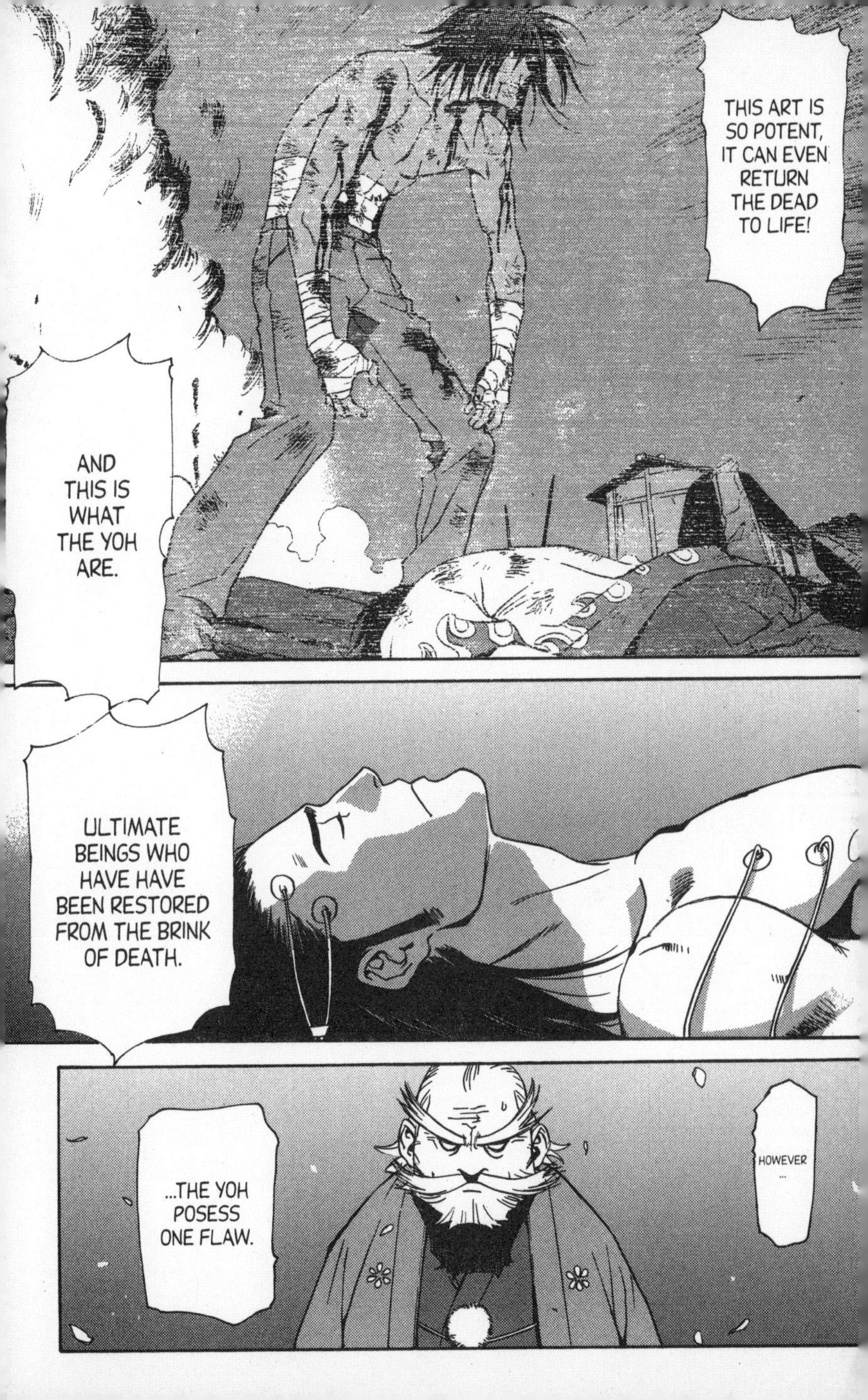
THIS ART IS SO POTENT, IT CAN EVEN RETURN THE DEAD TO LIFE!
AND THIS IS WHAT THE YOH ARE.
ULTIMATE BEINGS WHO HAVE HAVE BEEN RESTORED FROM THE BRINK OF DEATH.
HOWEVER ...
...THE YOH POSESS ONE FLAW.

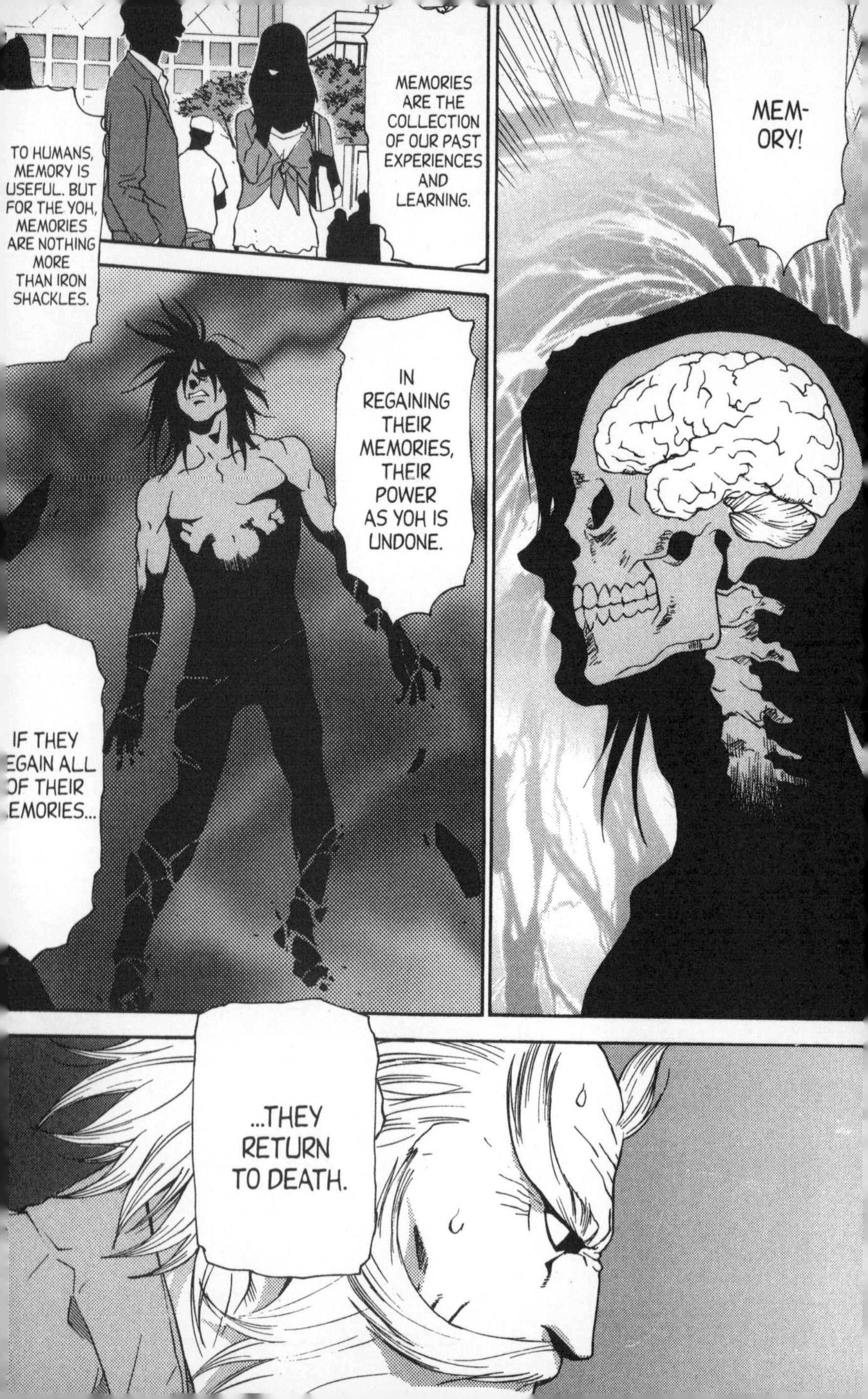

MEM-ORY!
MEMORIES ARE THE COLLECTION OF OUR PAST EXPERIENCES AND LEARNING.
TO HUMANS, MEMORY IS USEFUL. BUT FOR THE YOH, MEMORIES ARE NOTHING MORE THAN IRON SHACKLES.
IN REGAINING THEIR MEMORIES, THEIR POWER AS YOH IS UNDONE.
IF THEY EGAIN ALL OF THEIR EMORIES...
...THEY RETURN TO DEATH.

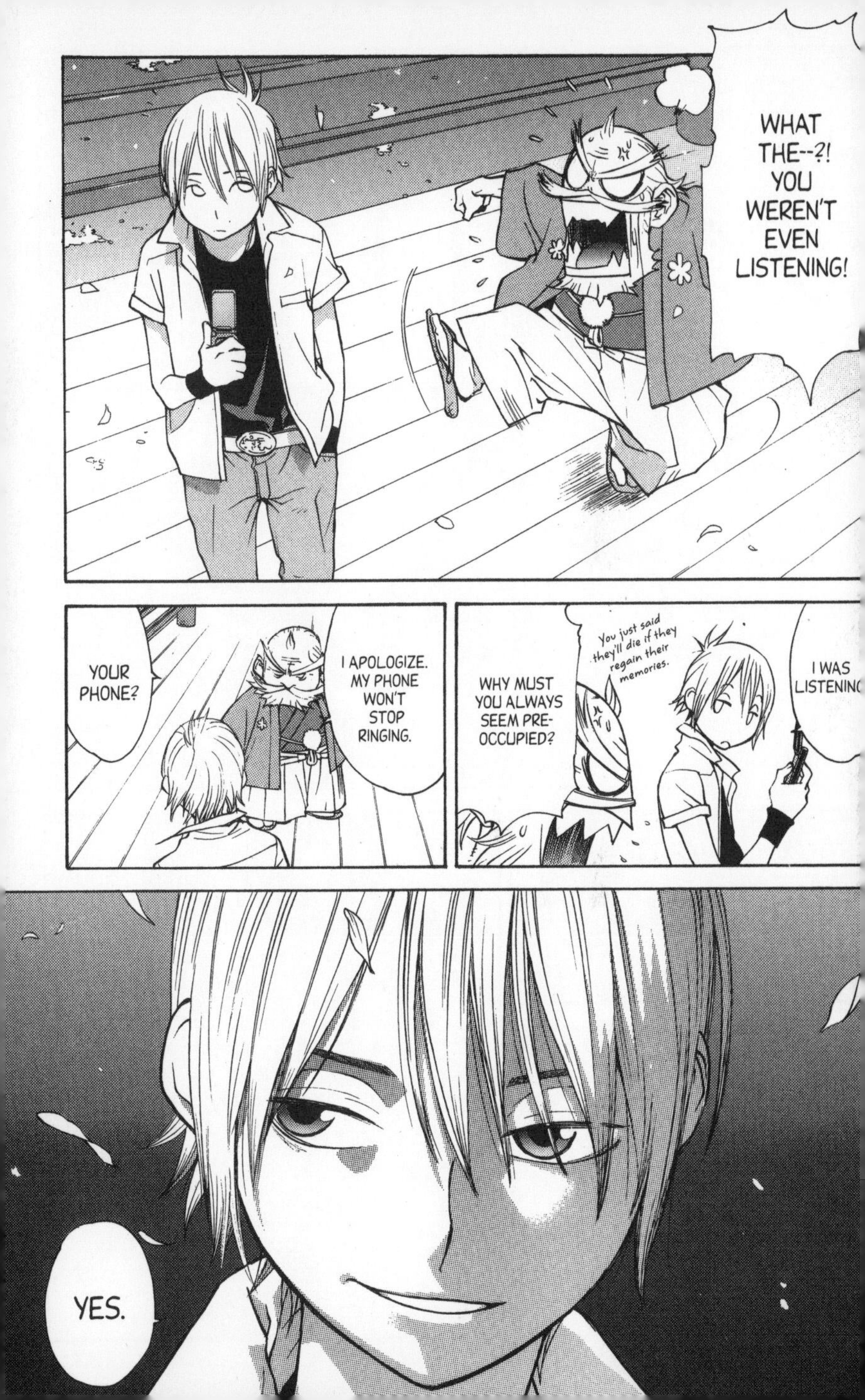
WHAT THE--?! YOU WEREN'T EVEN LISTENING!
I WAS LISTENIN
You just said they'll die if they regain their memories.
WHY MUST YOU ALWAYS SEEM PRE-OCCUPIED?
I APOLOGIZE. MY PHONE WON'T STOP RINGING.
YOUR PHONE?
YES.

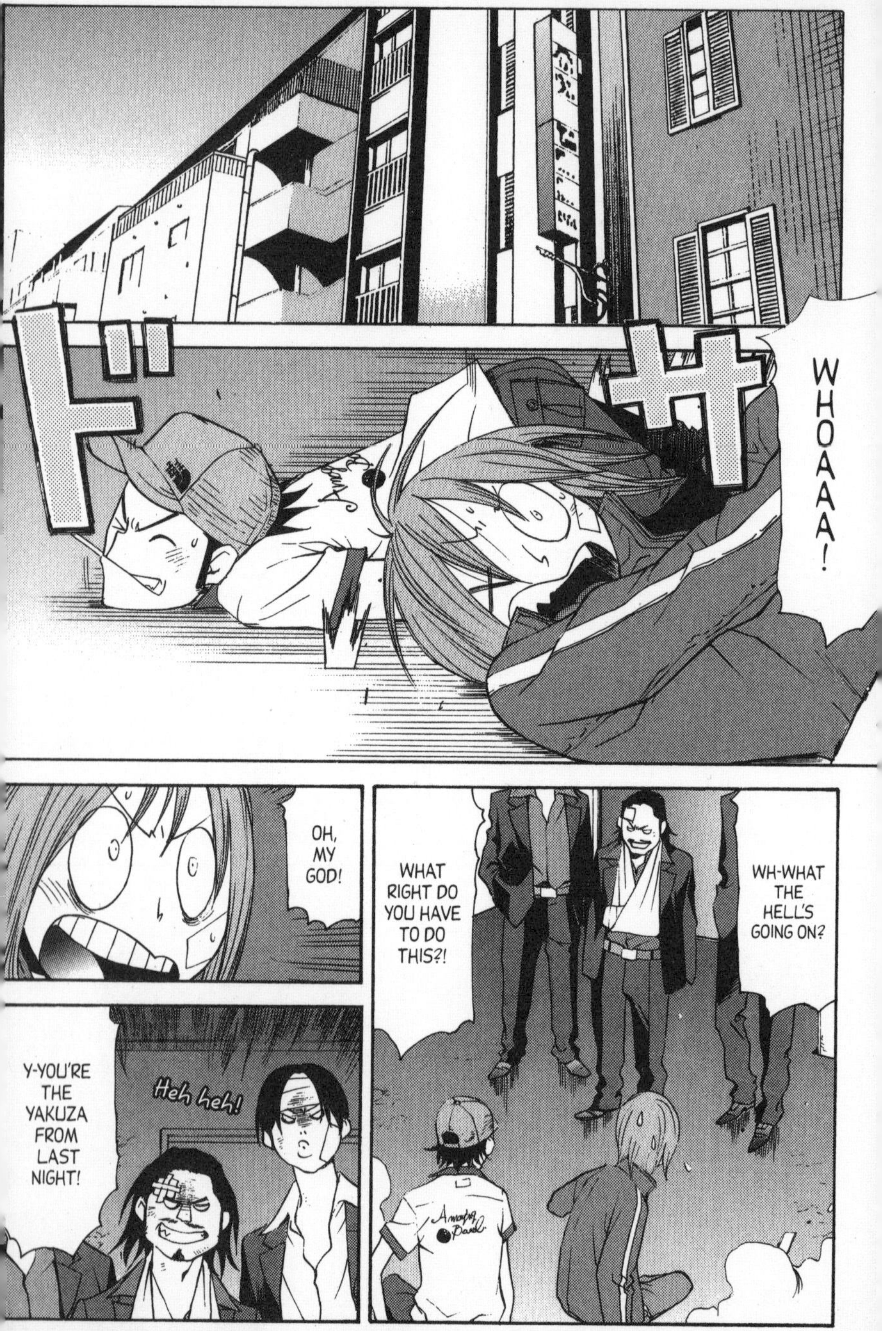
ドサ
WHOAAAA!
WH-WHAT THE HELL'S GOING ON?
WHAT RIGHT DO YOU HAVE TO DO THIS?!
OH, MY GOD!
Y-YOU'RE THE YAKUZA FROM LAST NIGHT!
Heh heh!

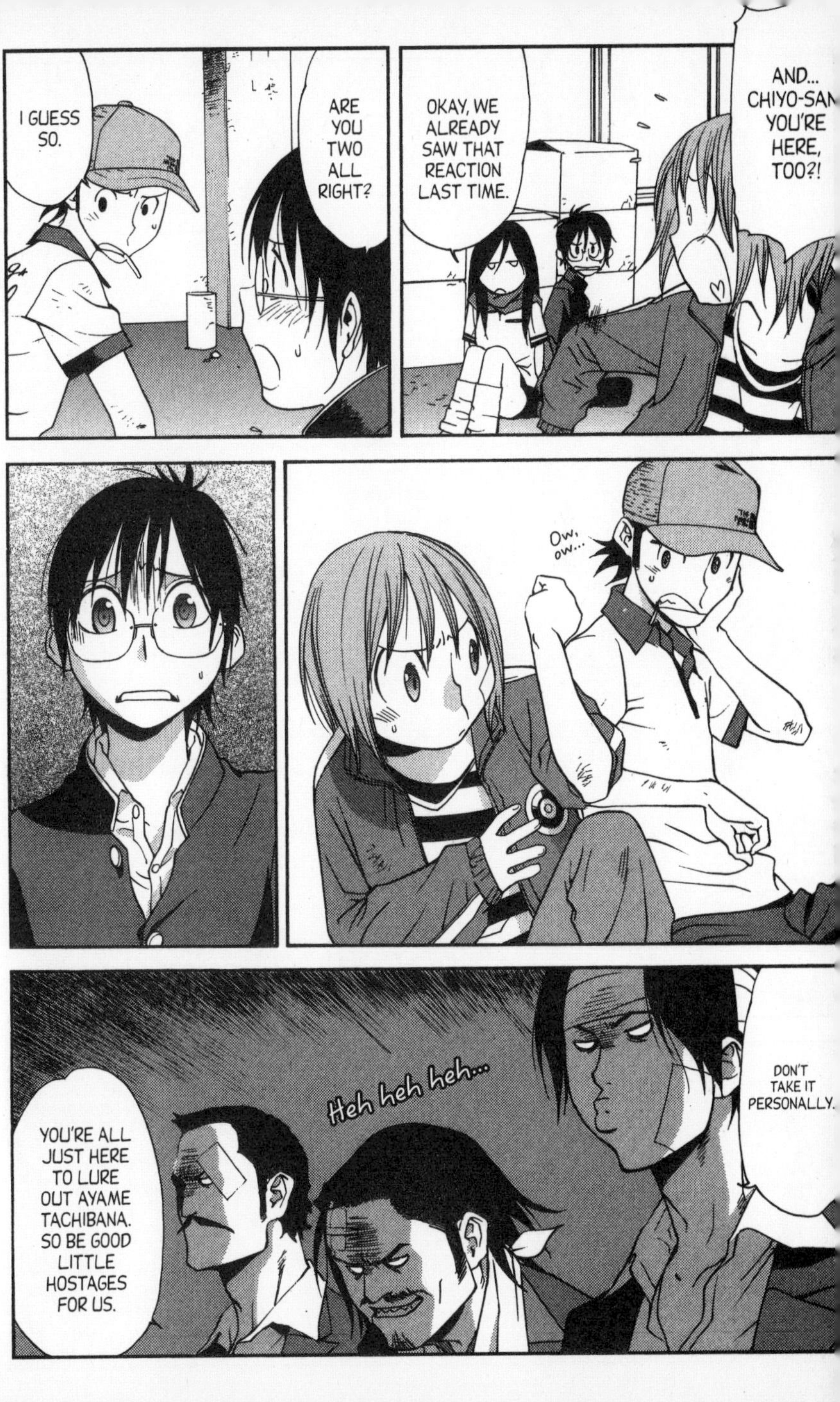
AND... CHIYO-SAN YOU'RE HERE, TOO?!
OKAY, WE ALREADY SAW THAT REACTION LAST TIME.
ARE YOU TWO ALL RIGHT?
I GUESS SO.
Ow, ow...
DON'T TAKE IT PERSONALLY.
Heh heh heh...
YOU'RE ALL JUST HERE TO LURE OUT AYAME TACHIBANA. SO BE GOOD LITTLE HOSTAGES FOR US.

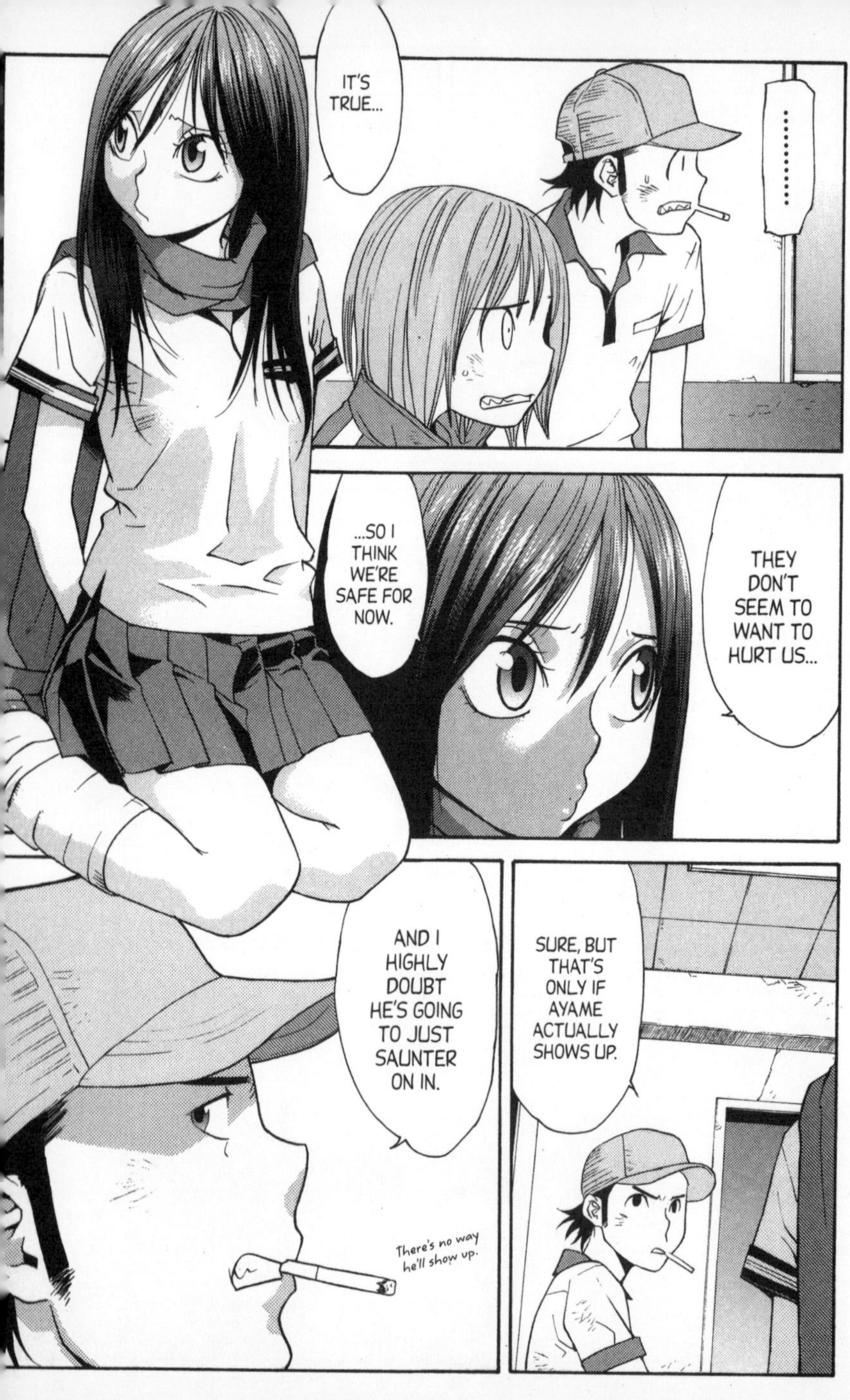
……
IT'S TRUE...
THEY DON'T SEEM TO WANT TO HURT US...
...SO I THINK WE'RE SAFE FOR NOW.
SURE, BUT THAT'S ONLY IF AYAME ACTUALLY SHOWS UP.
AND I HIGHLY DOUBT HE'S GOING TO JUST SAUNTER ON IN.
There's no way he'll show up.

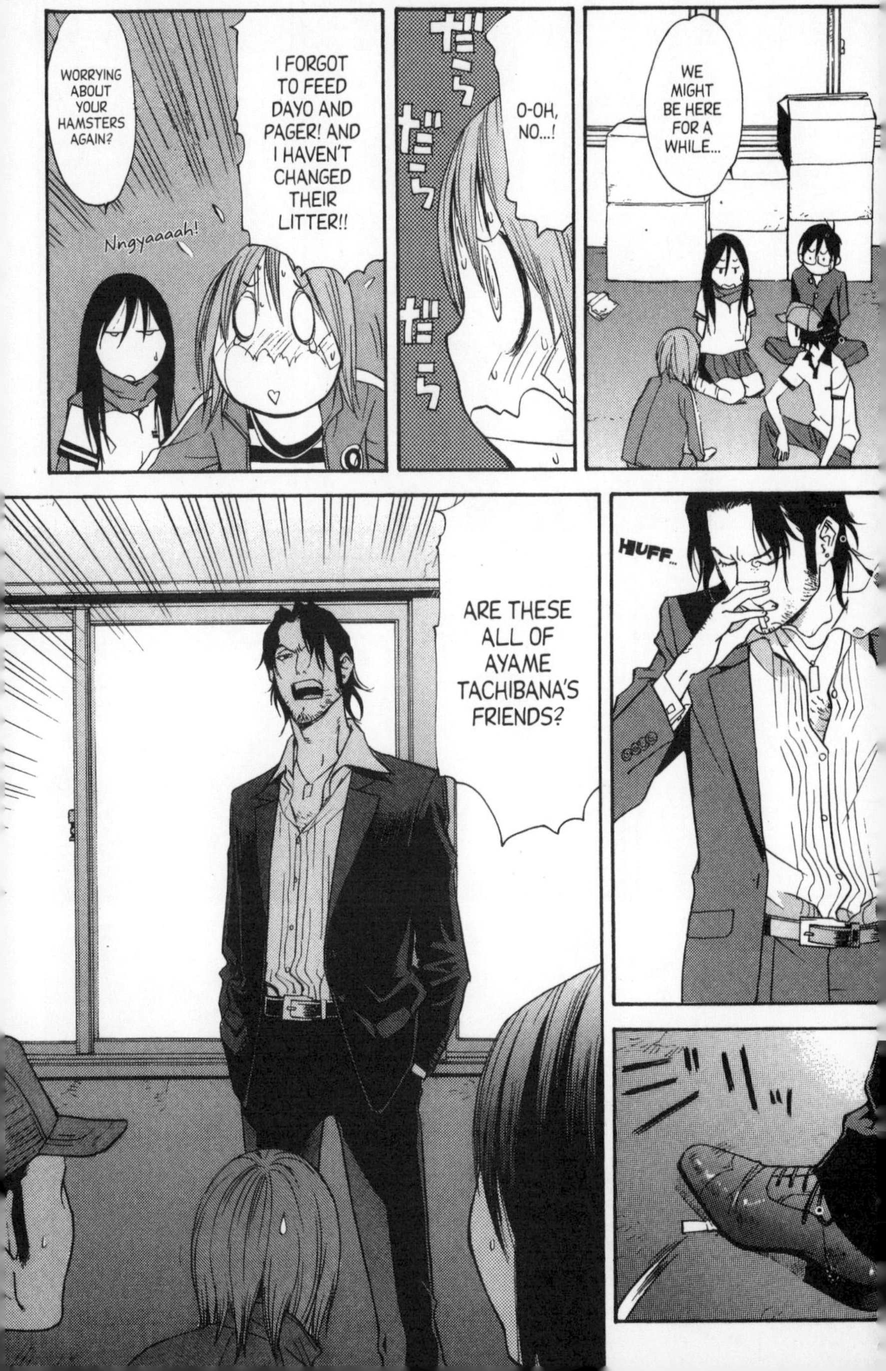
WE MIGHT BE HERE FOR A WHILE...
だらだらだら
O-OH, NO...!
I FORGOT TO FEED DAYO AND PAGER! AND I HAVEN'T CHANGED THEIR LITTER!!
WORRYING ABOUT YOUR HAMSTERS AGAIN?
Nngyaaaah!
HUFF...
ジリッ
ARE THESE ALL OF AYAME TACHIBANA'S FRIENDS?

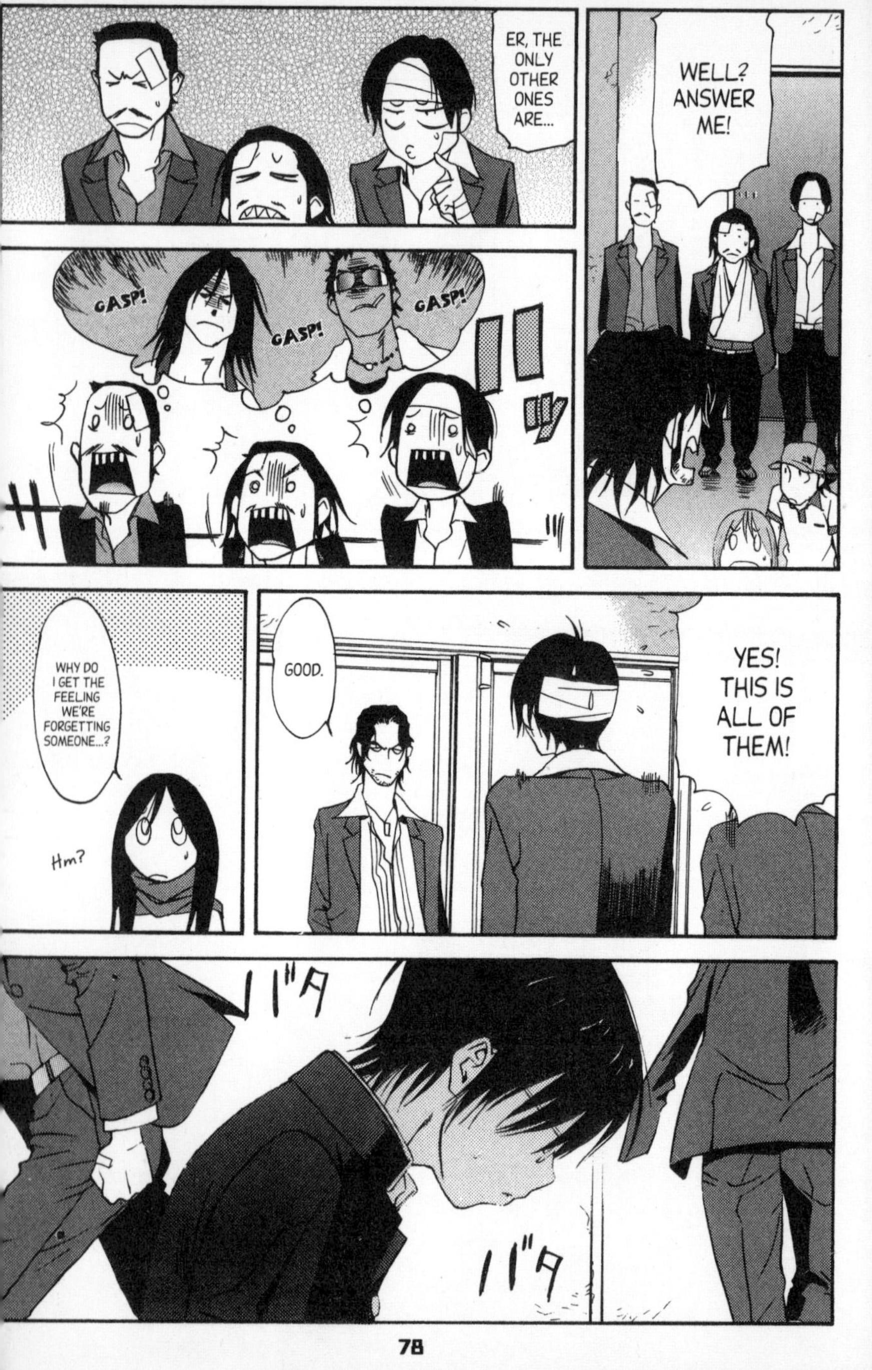
WELL? ANSWER ME!
ER, THE ONLY OTHER ONES ARE...
GASP!
GASP!
GASP!
YES! THIS IS ALL OF THEM!
GOOD.
WHY DO I GET THE FEELING WE'RE FORGETTING SOMEONE...?
Hm?
バタ
バタ

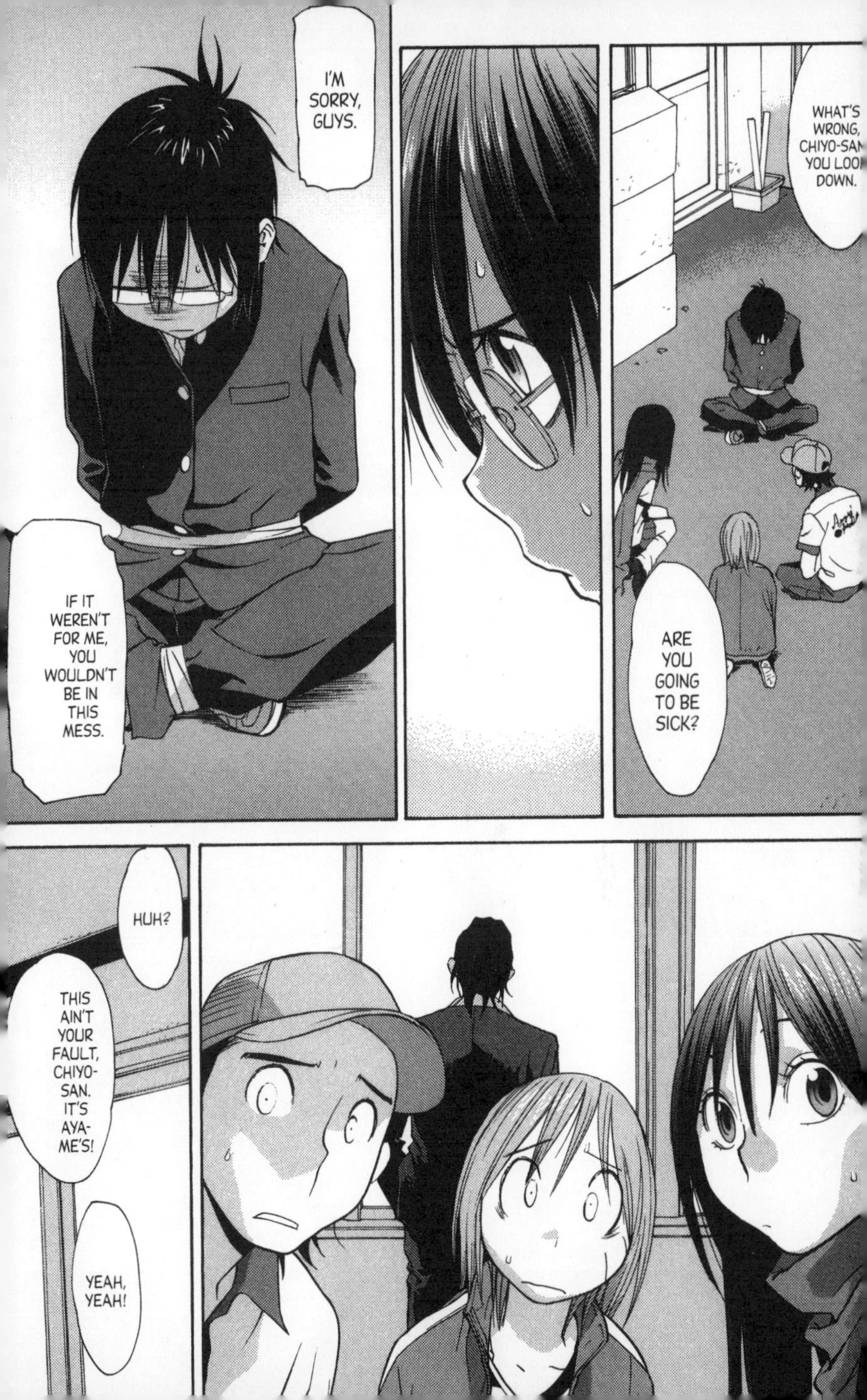
WHAT'S WRONG, CHIYO-SAN, YOU LOOK DOWN.
ARE YOU GOING TO BE SICK?
I'M SORRY, GUYS.
IF IT WEREN'T FOR ME, YOU WOULDN'T BE IN THIS MESS.
HUH?
THIS AIN'T YOUR FAULT, CHIYO-SAN. IT'S AYA-ME'S!
YEAH, YEAH!

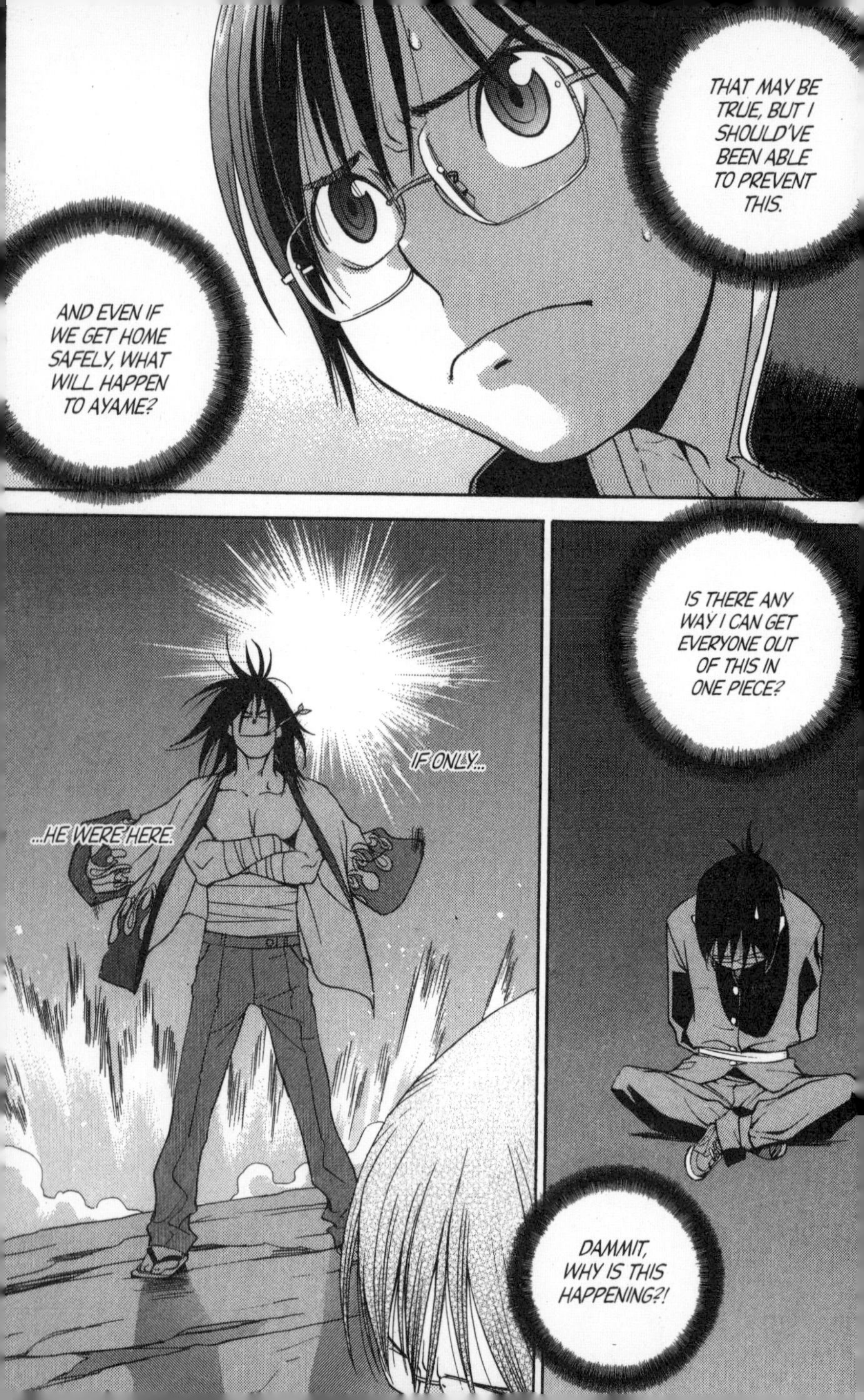
THAT MAY BE TRUE, BUT I SHOULD'VE BEEN ABLE TO PREVENT THIS.
AND EVEN IF WE GET HOME SAFELY, WHAT WILL HAPPEN TO AYAME?
IS THERE ANY WAY I CAN GET EVERYONE OUT OF THIS IN ONE PIECE?
DAMMIT, WHY IS THIS HAPPENING?!
IF ONLY...
...HE WERE HERE.

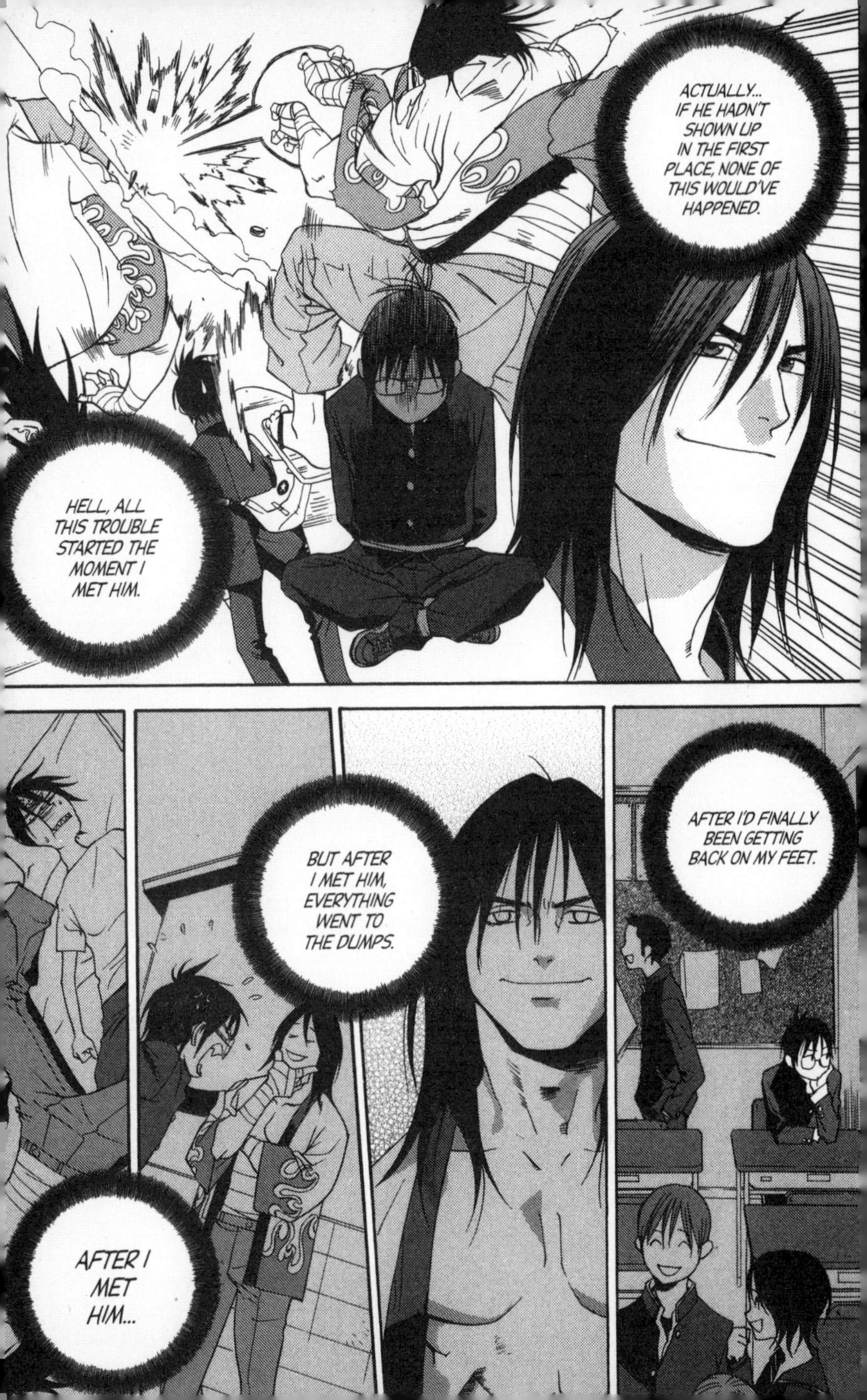
ACTUALLY... IF HE HADN'T SHOWN UP IN THE FIRST PLACE, NONE OF THIS WOULD'VE HAPPENED.
HELL, ALL THIS TROUBLE STARTED THE MOMENT I MET HIM.
AFTER I'D FINALLY BEEN GETTING BACK ON MY FEET.
BUT AFTER I MET HIM, EVERYTHING WENT TO THE DUMPS.
AFTER I MET HIM...

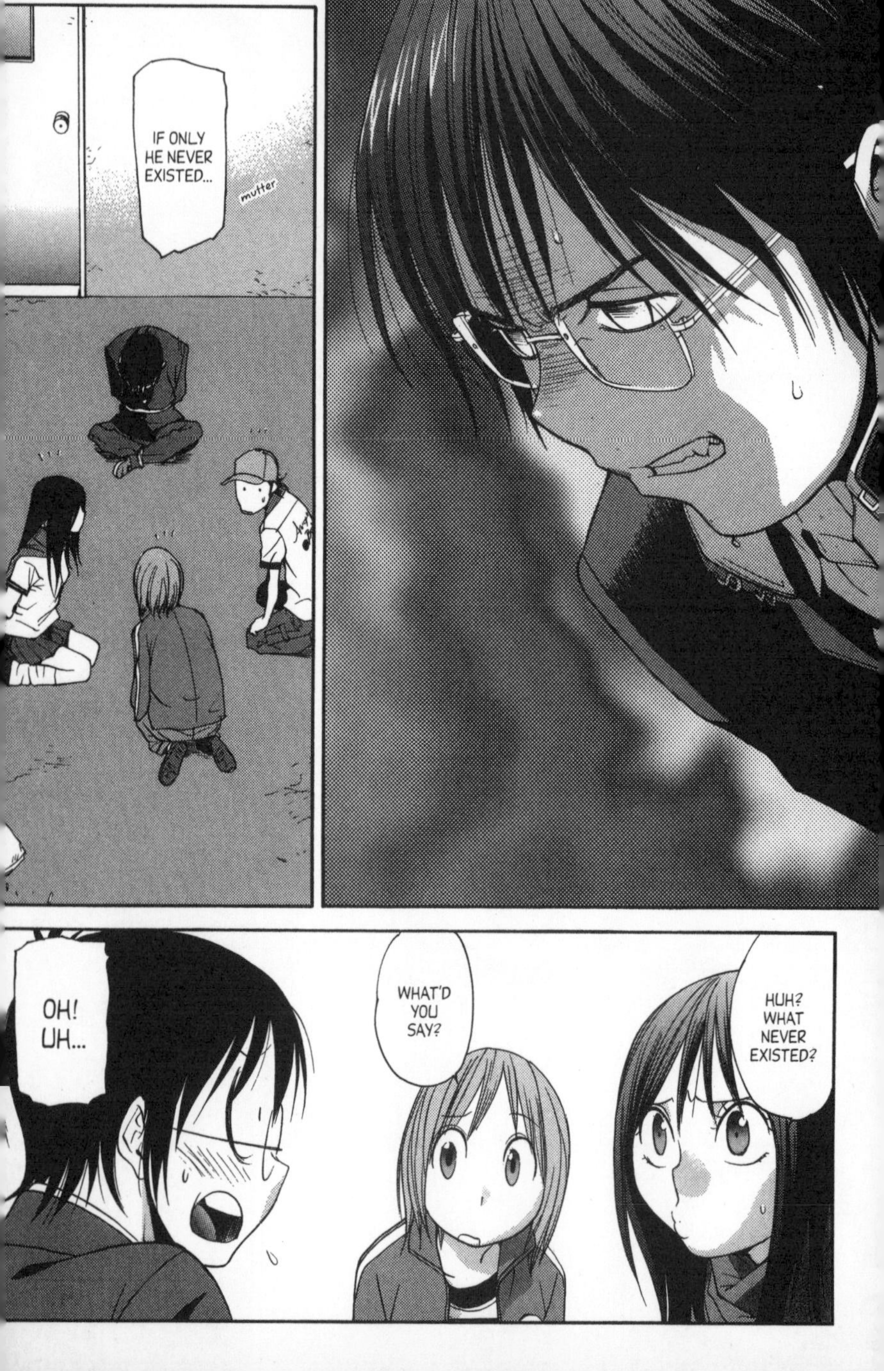
IF ONLY HE NEVER EXISTED...
mutter
HUH? WHAT NEVER EXISTED?
WHAT'D YOU SAY?
OH! UH...

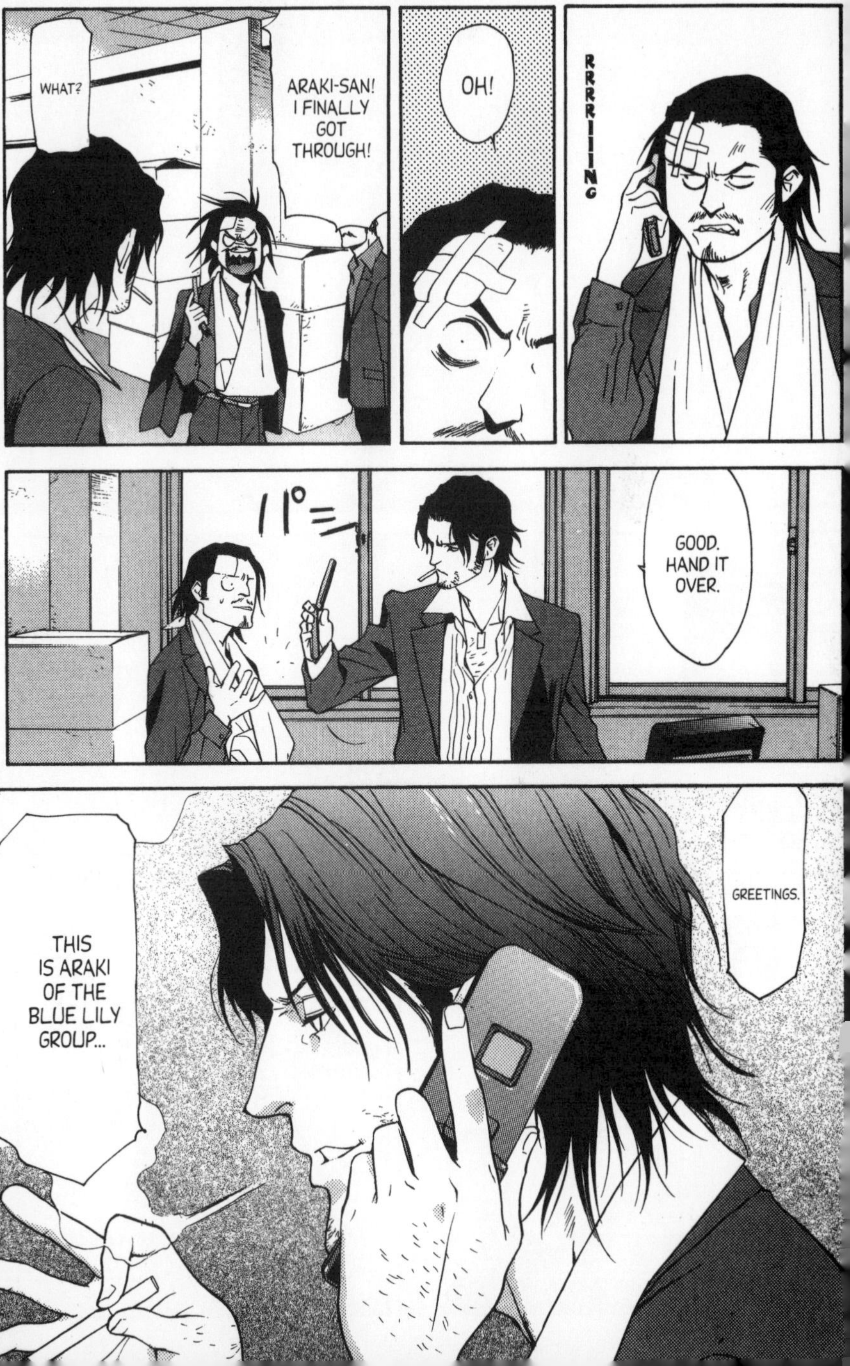
RRRRIIIING
OH!
ARAKI-SAN! I FINALLY GOT THROUGH!
WHAT?
GOOD. HAND IT OVER.
パ
GREETINGS.
THIS IS ARAKI OF THE BLUE LILY GROUP...

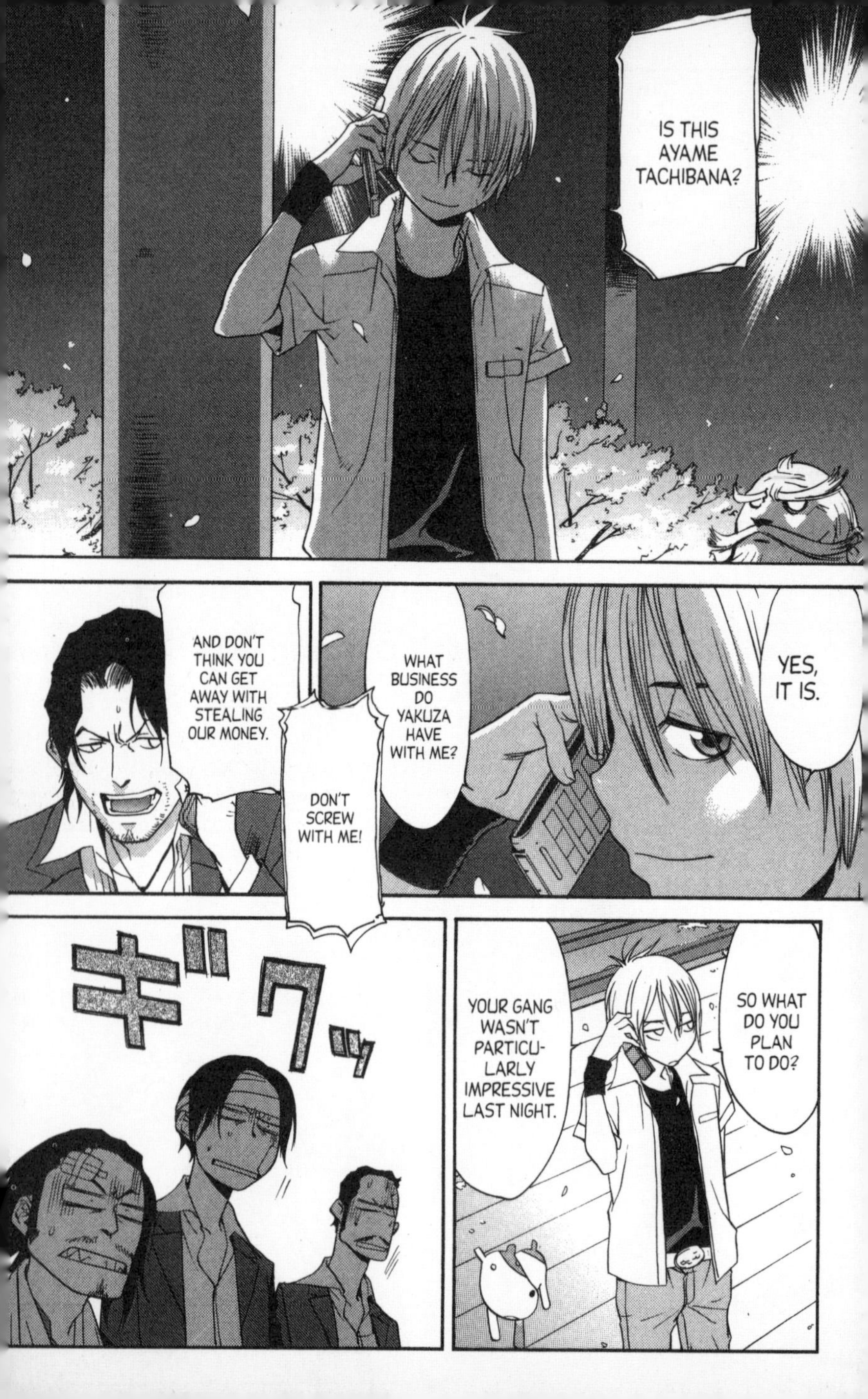
IS THIS AYAME TACHIBANA?
YES, IT IS.
WHAT BUSINESS DO YAKUZA HAVE WITH ME?
DON'T SCREW WITH ME!
AND DON'T THINK YOU CAN GET AWAY WITH STEALING OUR MONEY.
SO WHAT DO YOU PLAN TO DO?
YOUR GANG WASN'T PARTICU-LARLY IMPRESSIVE LAST NIGHT.
ギクッ

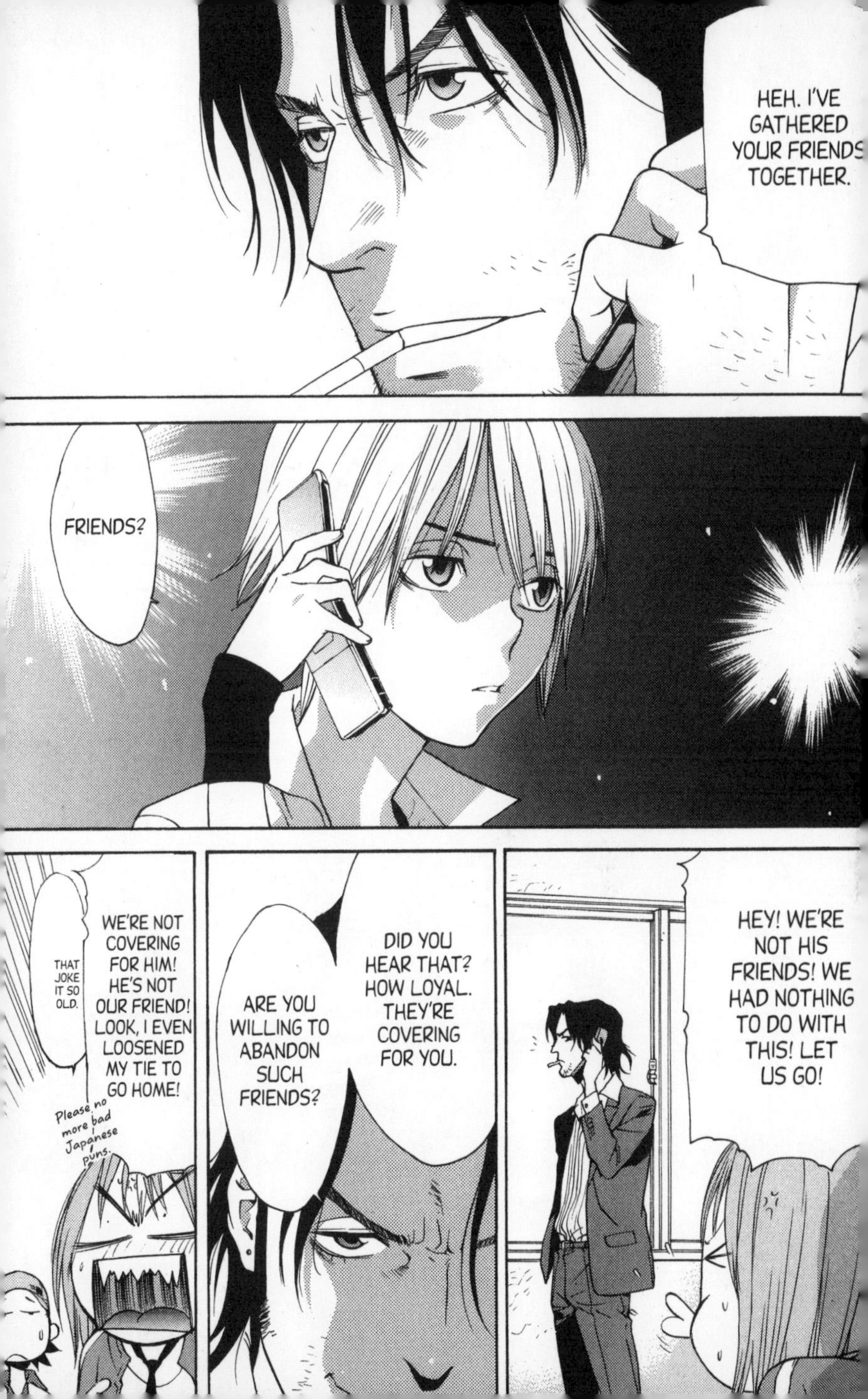
HEH. I'VE GATHERED YOUR FRIENDS TOGETHER.
FRIENDS?
HEY! WE'RE NOT HIS FRIENDS! WE HAD NOTHING TO DO WITH THIS! LET US GO!
DID YOU HEAR THAT? HOW LOYAL. THEY'RE COVERING FOR YOU.
ARE YOU WILLING TO ABANDON SUCH FRIENDS?
WE'RE NOT COVERING FOR HIM! HE'S NOT OUR FRIEND! LOOK, I EVEN LOOSENED MY TIE TO GO HOME!
THAT JOKE IT SO OLD.
Please no more bad Japanese puns.

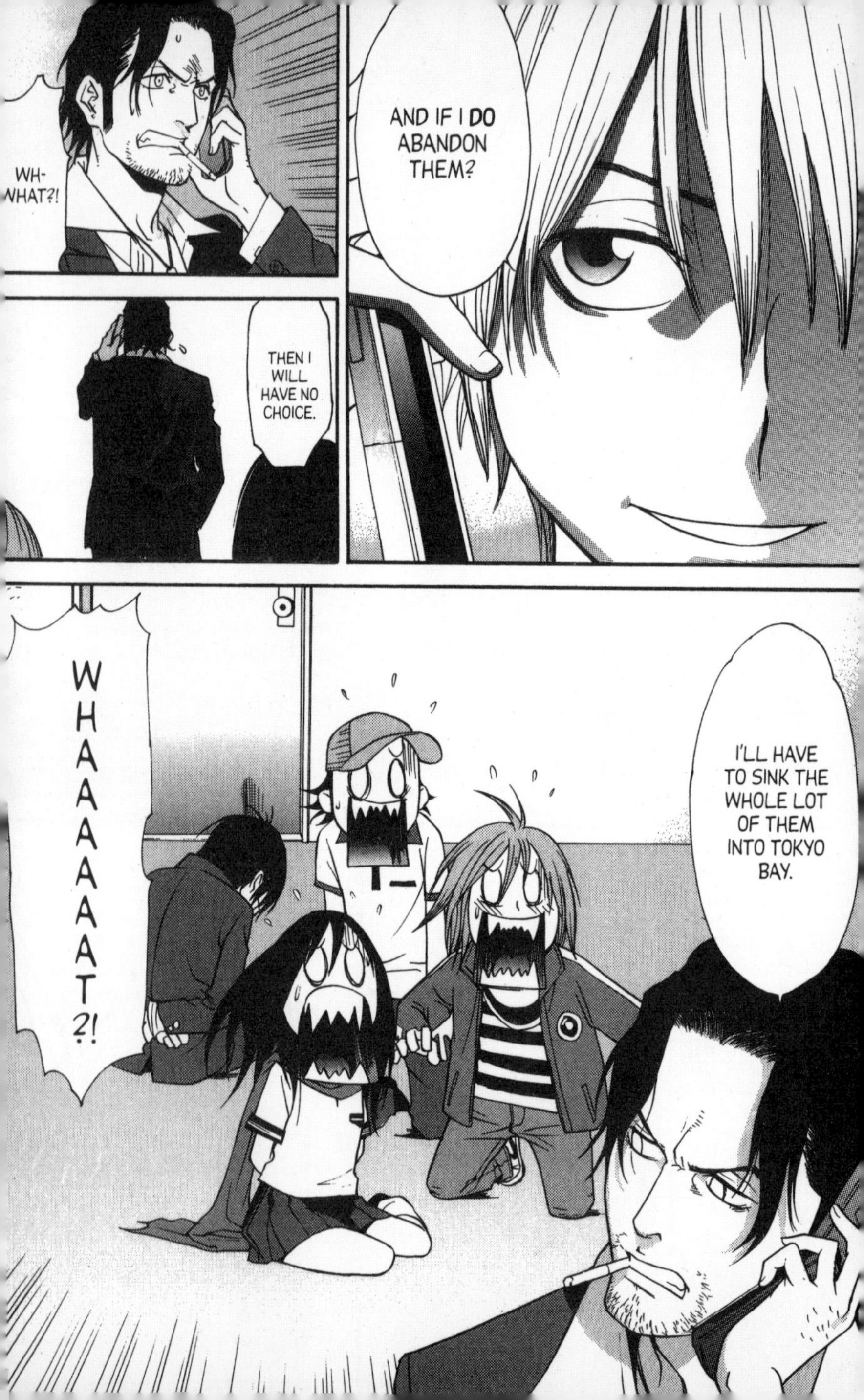
AND IF I DO ABANDON THEM?
WH- WHAT?!
THEN I WILL HAVE NO CHOICE.
I'LL HAVE TO SINK THE WHOLE LOT OF THEM INTO TOKYO BAY.
WHAAAAAAAT?!

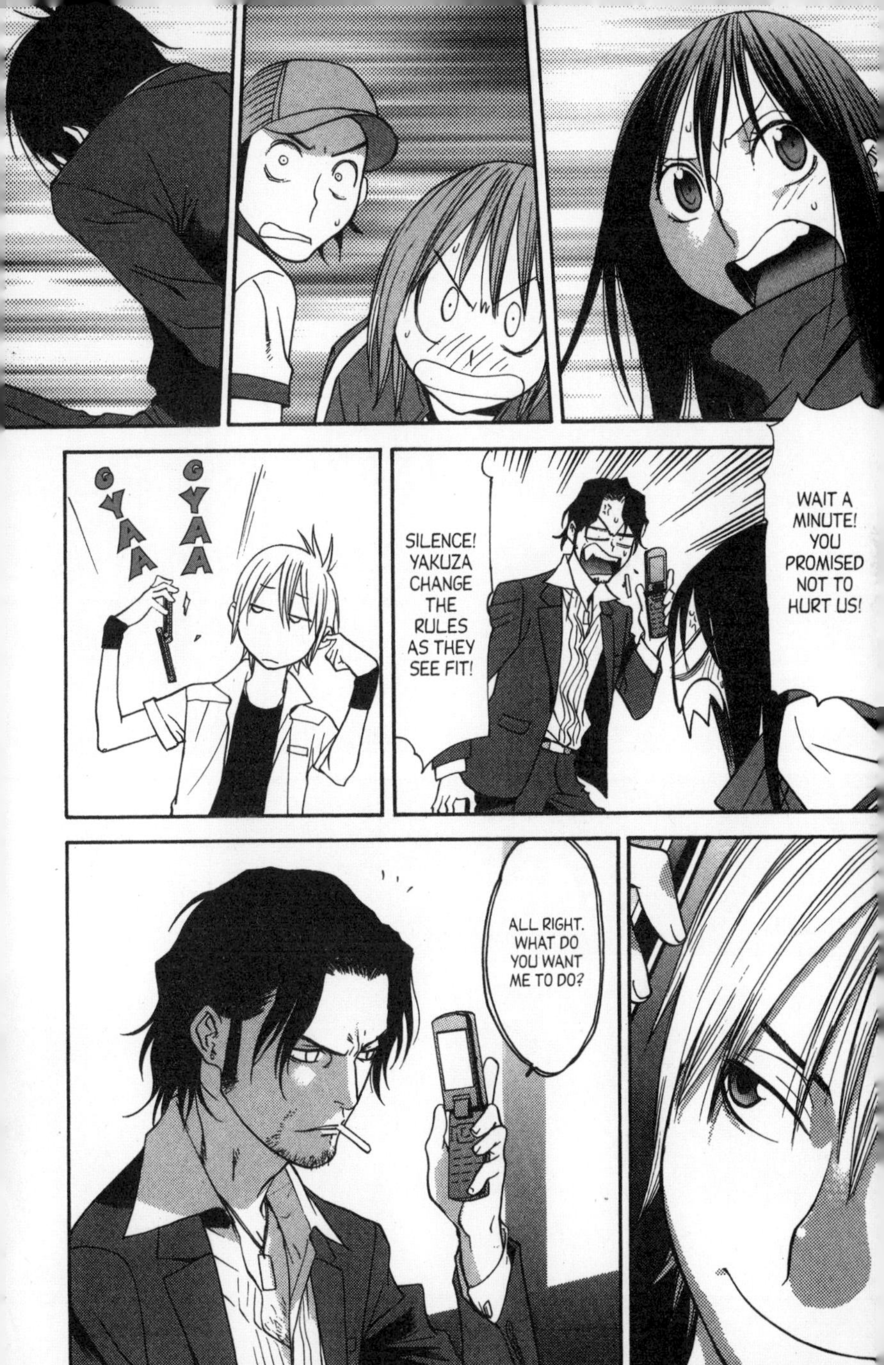
WAIT A MINUTE! YOU PROMISED NOT TO HURT US!
SILENCE! YAKUZA CHANGE THE RULES AS THEY SEE FIT!
GYAA GYAA
ALL RIGHT. WHAT DO YOU WANT ME TO DO?

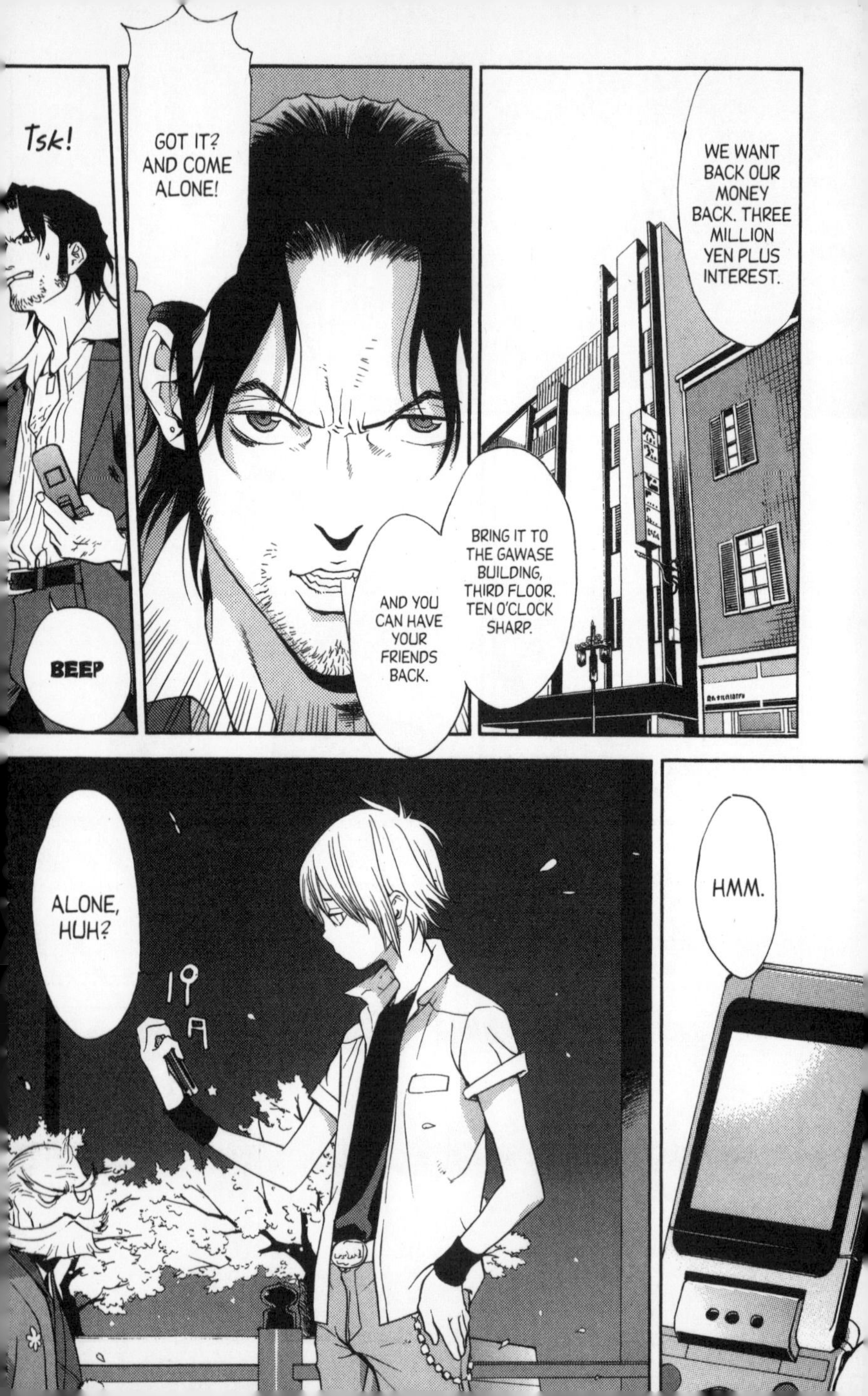
WE WANT BACK OUR MONEY BACK. THREE MILLION YEN PLUS INTEREST.
BRING IT TO THE GAWASE BUILDING, THIRD FLOOR. TEN O'CLOCK SHARP.
AND YOU CAN HAVE YOUR FRIENDS BACK.
GOT IT? AND COME ALONE!
Tsk!
BEEP
HMM.
ALONE, HUH?

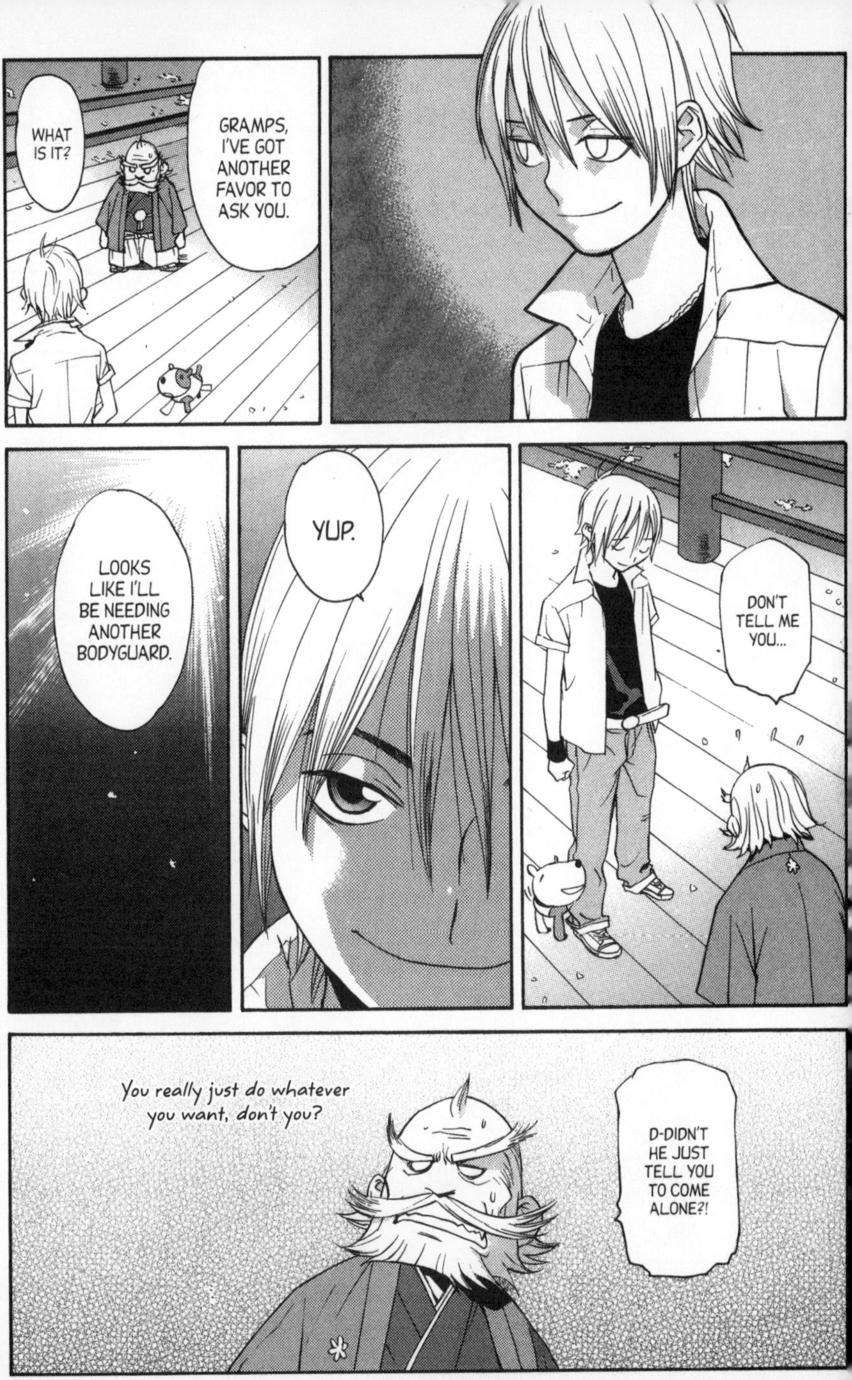
GRAMPS, I'VE GOT ANOTHER FAVOR TO ASK YOU.
WHAT IS IT?
DON'T TELL ME YOU...
YUP.
LOOKS LIKE I'LL BE NEEDING ANOTHER BODYGUARD.
D-DIDN'T HE JUST TELL YOU TO COME ALONE?!
You really just do whatever you want, don't you?

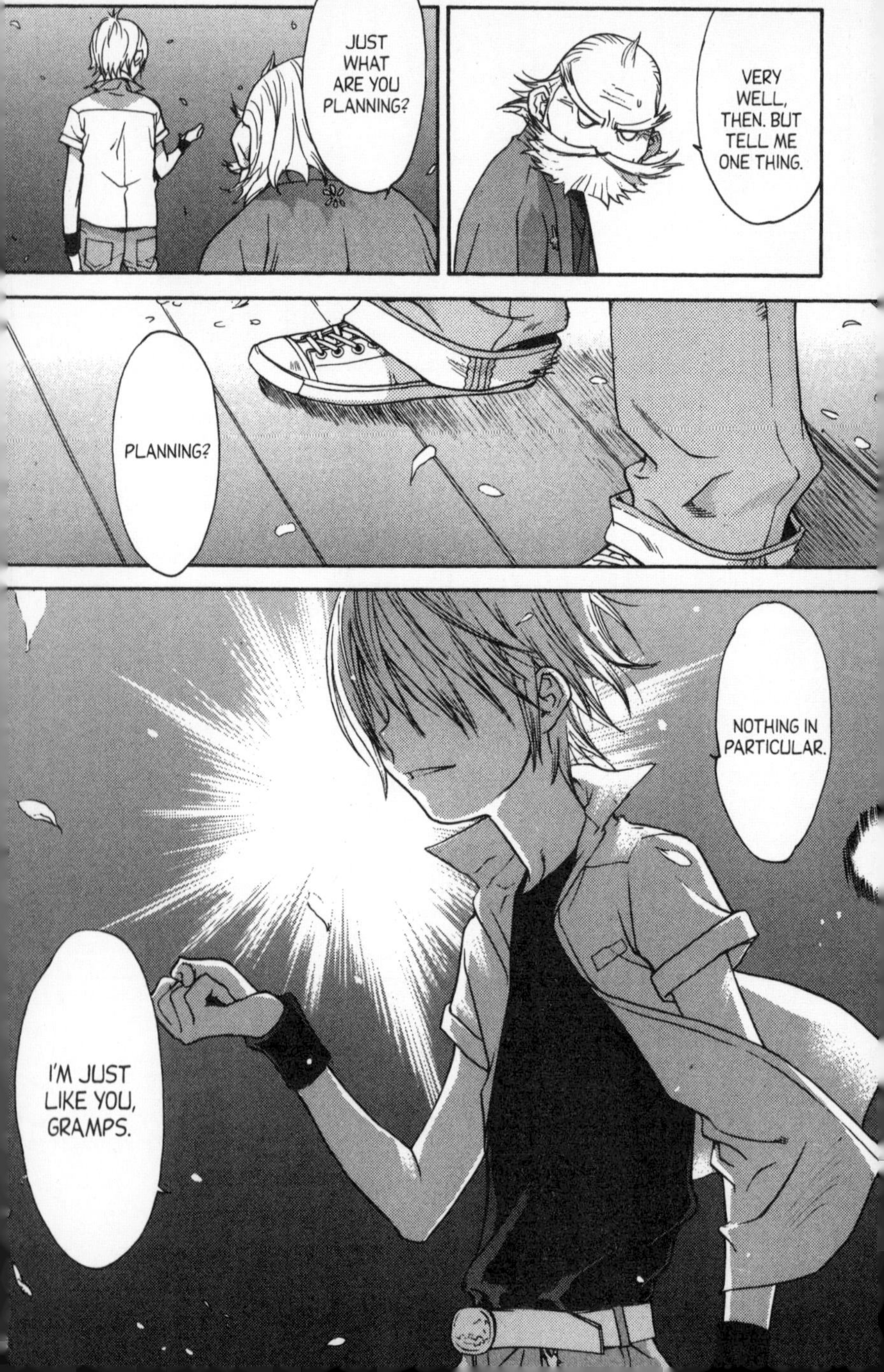
VERY WELL, THEN. BUT TELL ME ONE THING.
JUST WHAT ARE YOU PLANNING?
PLANNING?
NOTHING IN PARTICULAR.
I'M JUST LIKE YOU, GRAMPS.

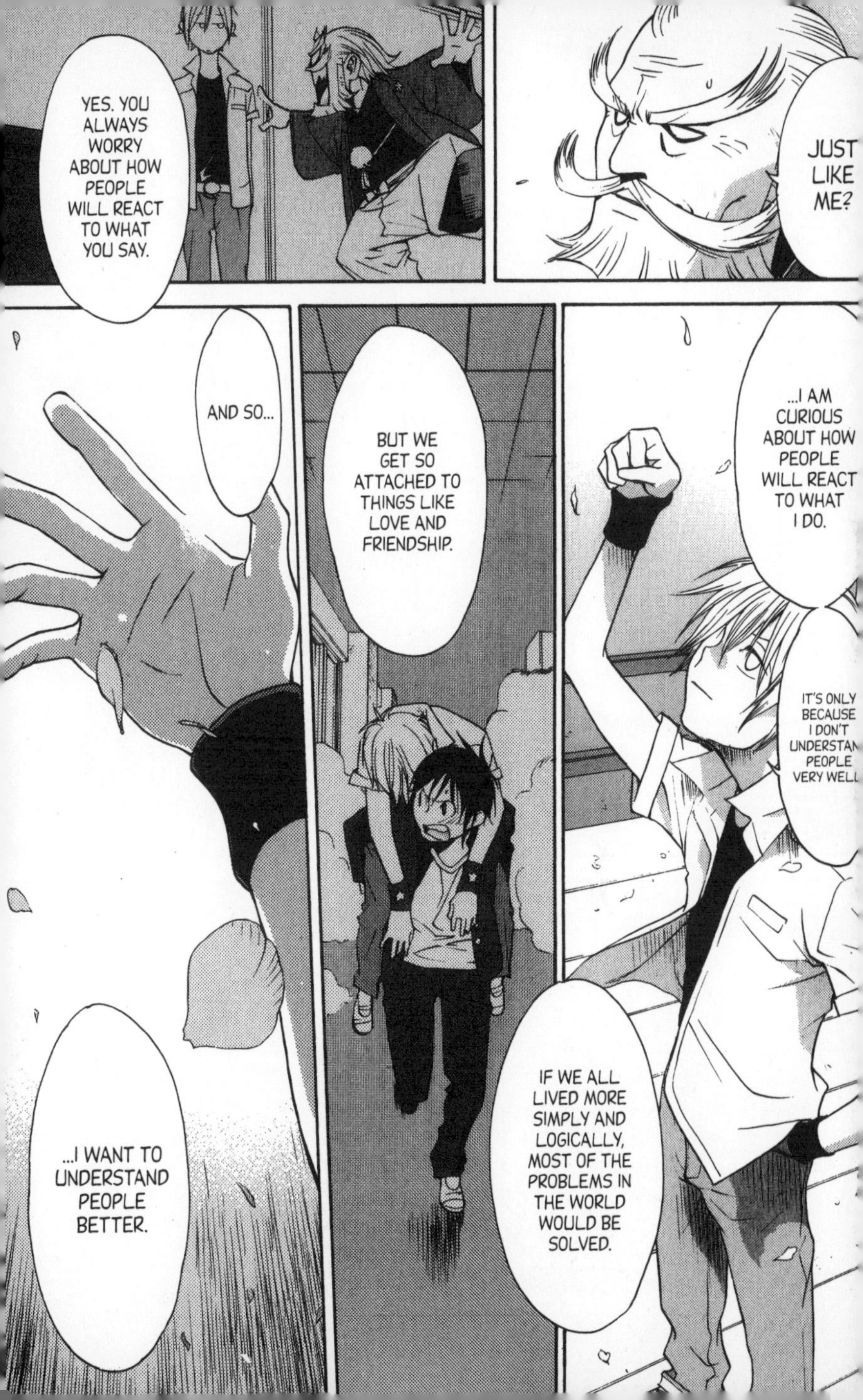
JUST LIKE ME?
YES. YOU ALWAYS WORRY ABOUT HOW PEOPLE WILL REACT TO WHAT YOU SAY.
...I AM CURIOUS ABOUT HOW PEOPLE WILL REACT TO WHAT I DO.
IT'S ONLY BECAUSE I DON'T UNDERSTAN PEOPLE VERY WELL
IF WE ALL LIVED MORE SIMPLY AND LOGICALLY, MOST OF THE PROBLEMS IN THE WORLD WOULD BE SOLVED.
BUT WE GET SO ATTACHED TO THINGS LIKE LOVE AND FRIENDSHIP.
AND SO...
...I WANT TO UNDERSTAND PEOPLE BETTER.

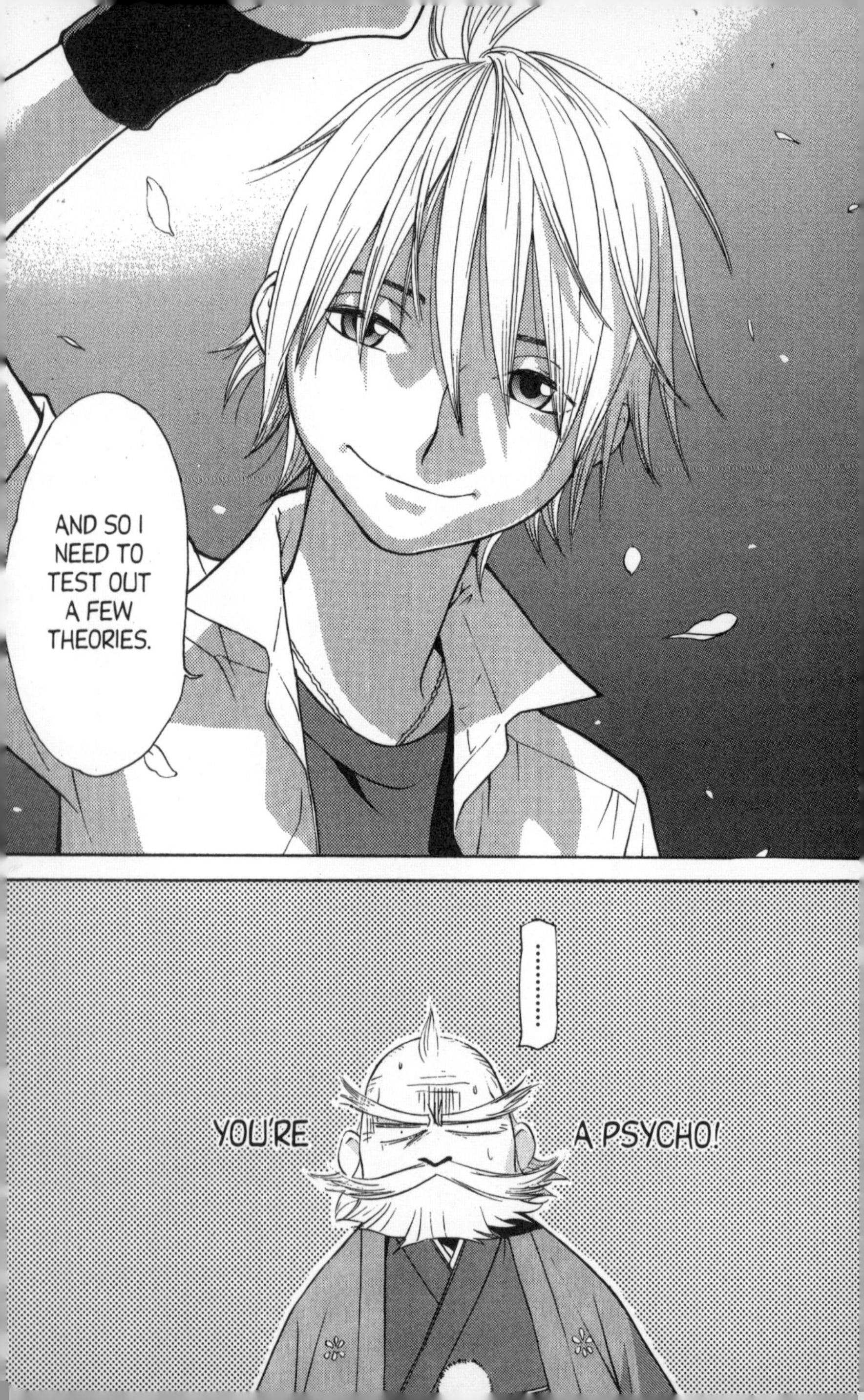
AND SO I NEED TO TEST OUT A FEW THEORIES.
......
YOU'RE
A PSYCHO!

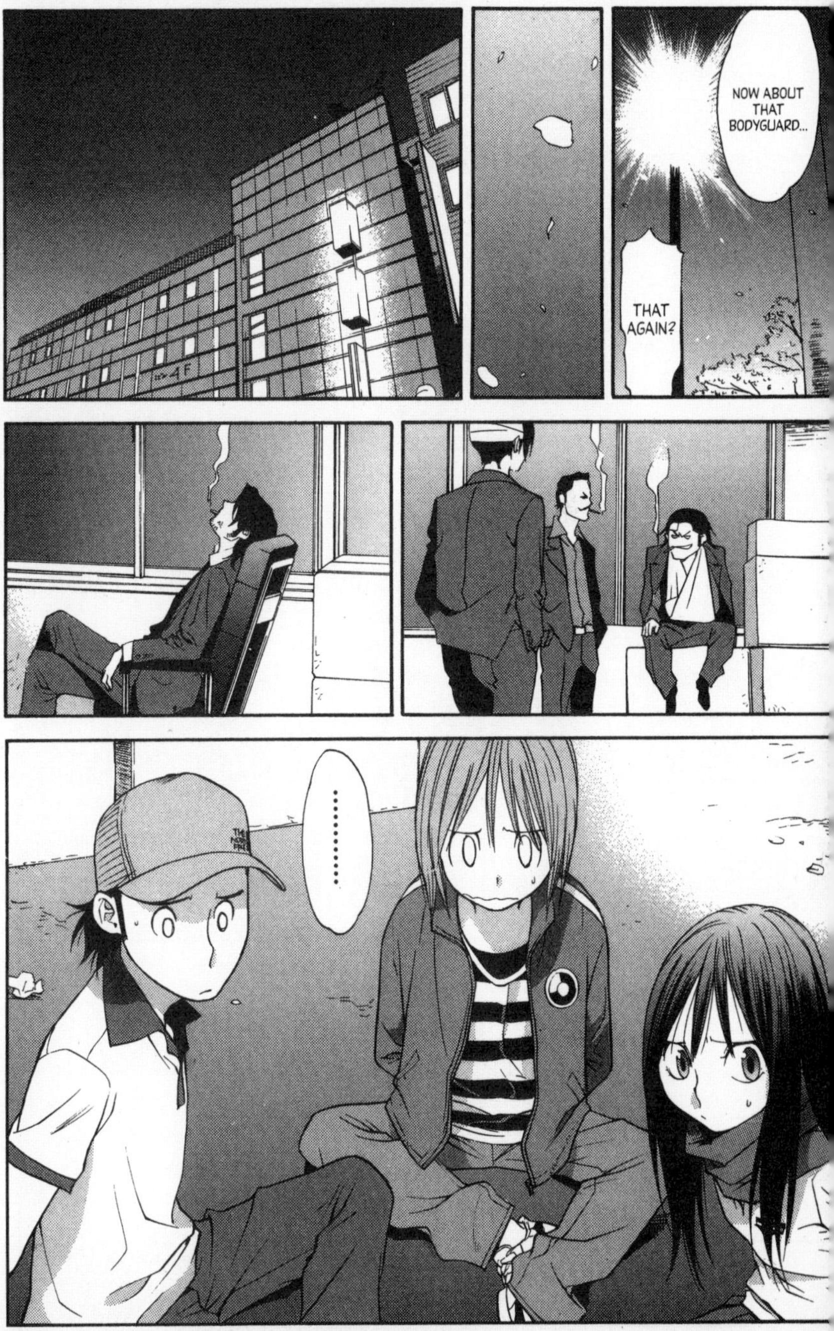
NOW ABOUT THAT BODYGUARD...
THAT AGAIN?
....

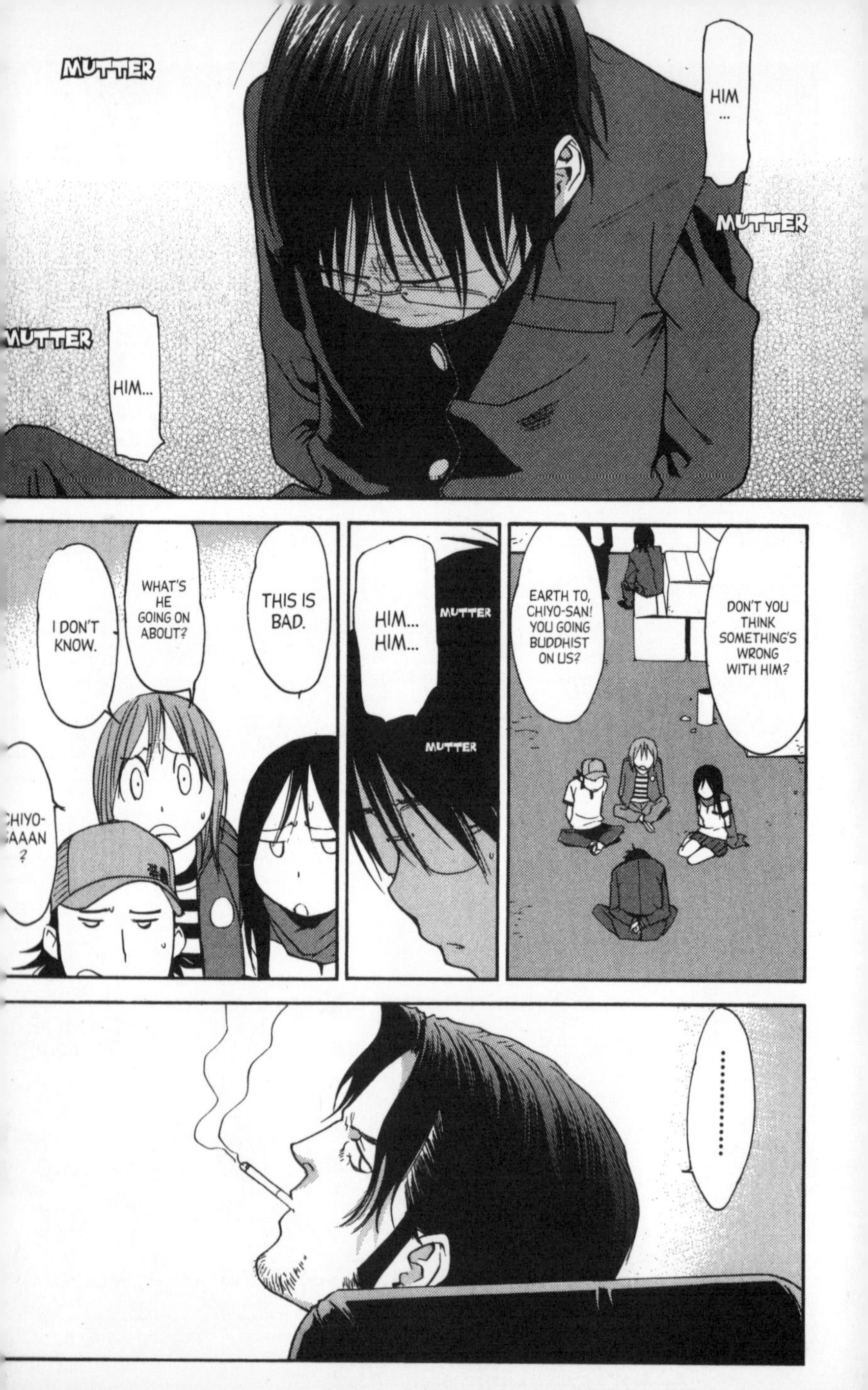
HIM ...
MUTTER
MUTTER
MUTTER
HIM...
DON'T YOU THINK SOMETHING'S WRONG WITH HIM?
EARTH TO, CHIYO-SAN! YOU GOING BUDDHIST ON US?
MUTTER
HIM... HIM...
MUTTER
THIS IS BAD.
WHAT'S HE GOING ON ABOUT?
I DON'T KNOW.
CHIYO-AAAN?
....

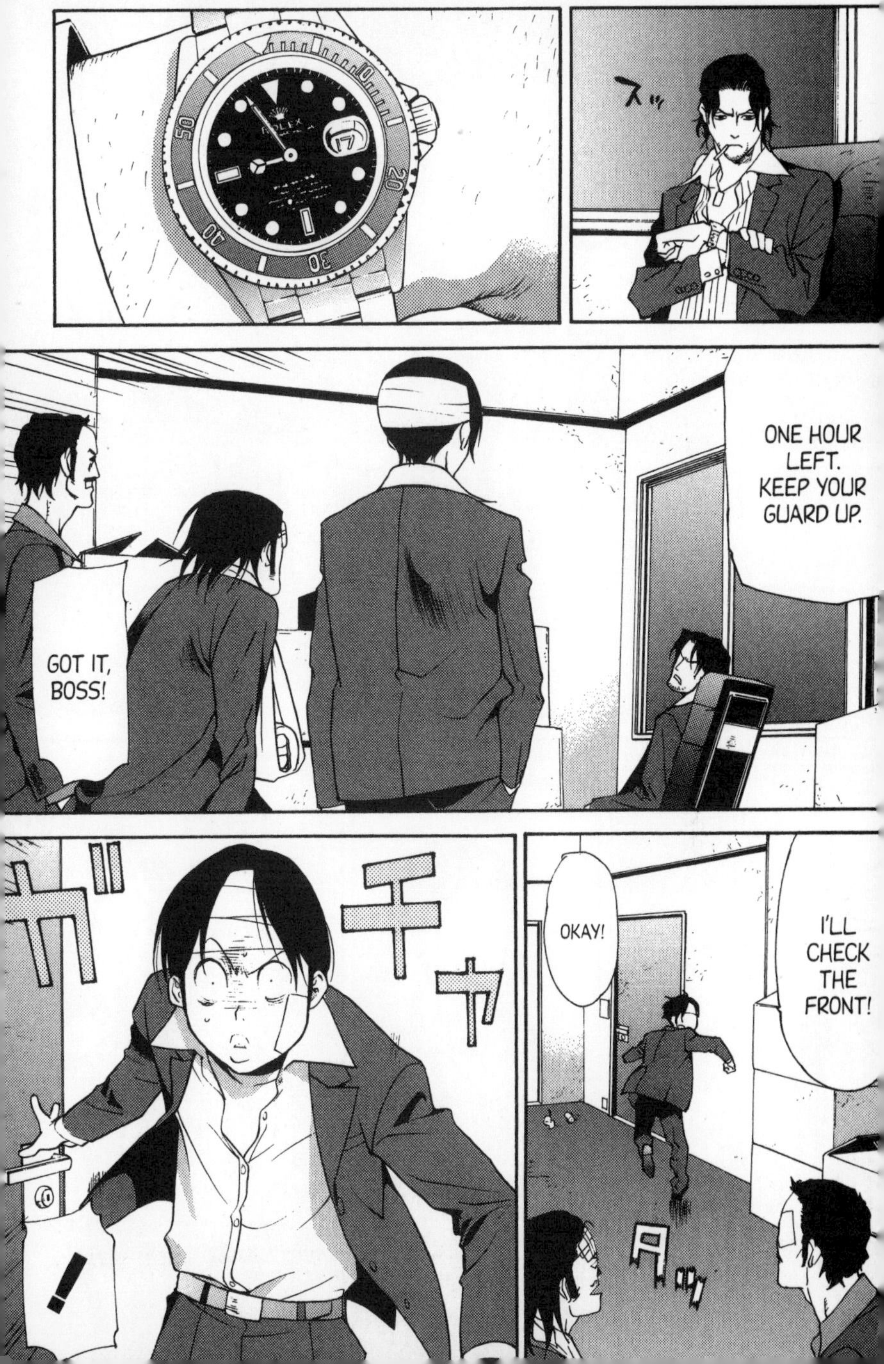
スッ
ROLEX
ONE HOUR LEFT. KEEP YOUR GUARD UP.
GOT IT, BOSS!
I'LL CHECK THE FRONT!
OKAY!
ガチャ
!

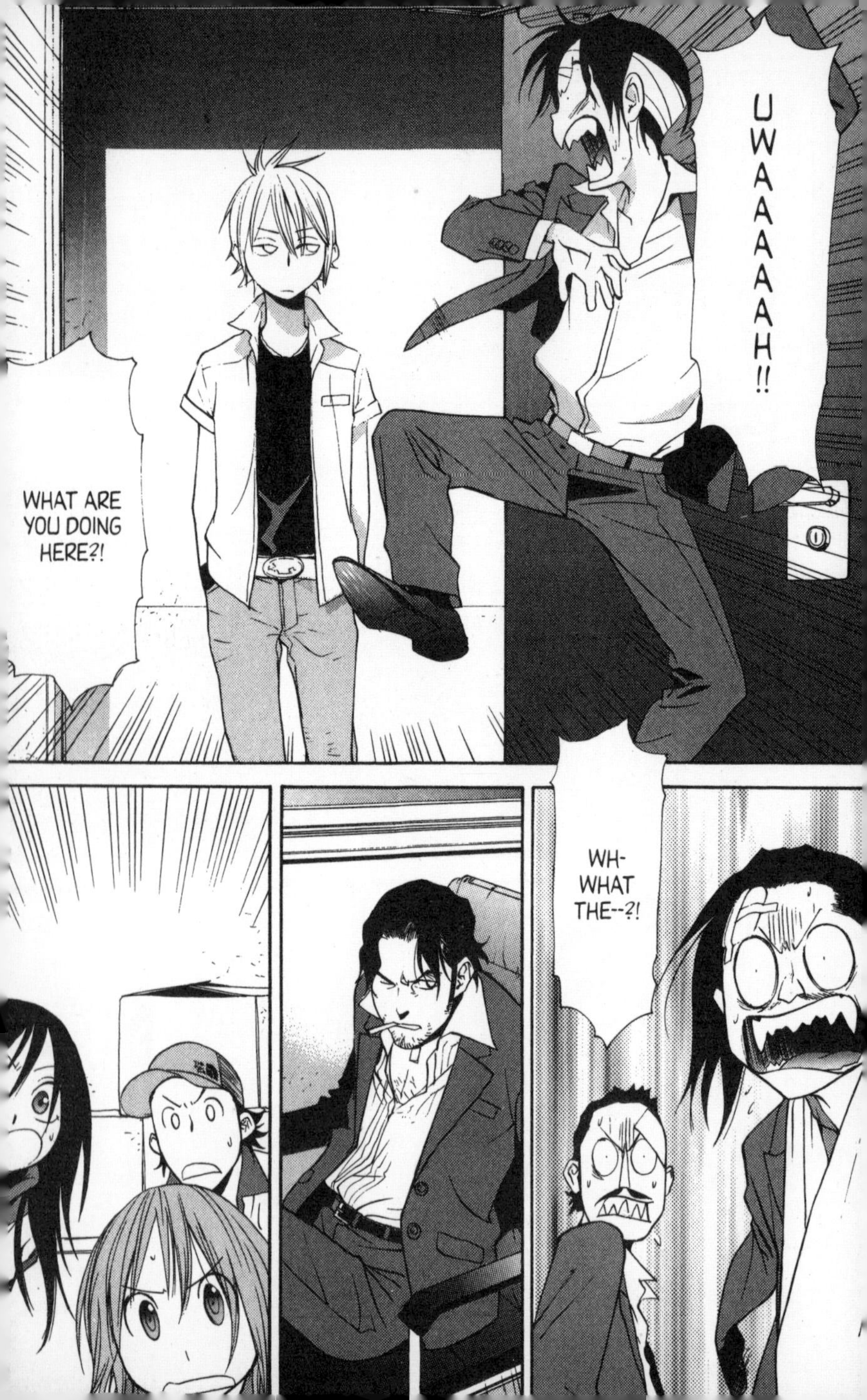
UWAAAAAAH!!
WHAT ARE YOU DOING HERE?!
WH-WHAT THE--?!

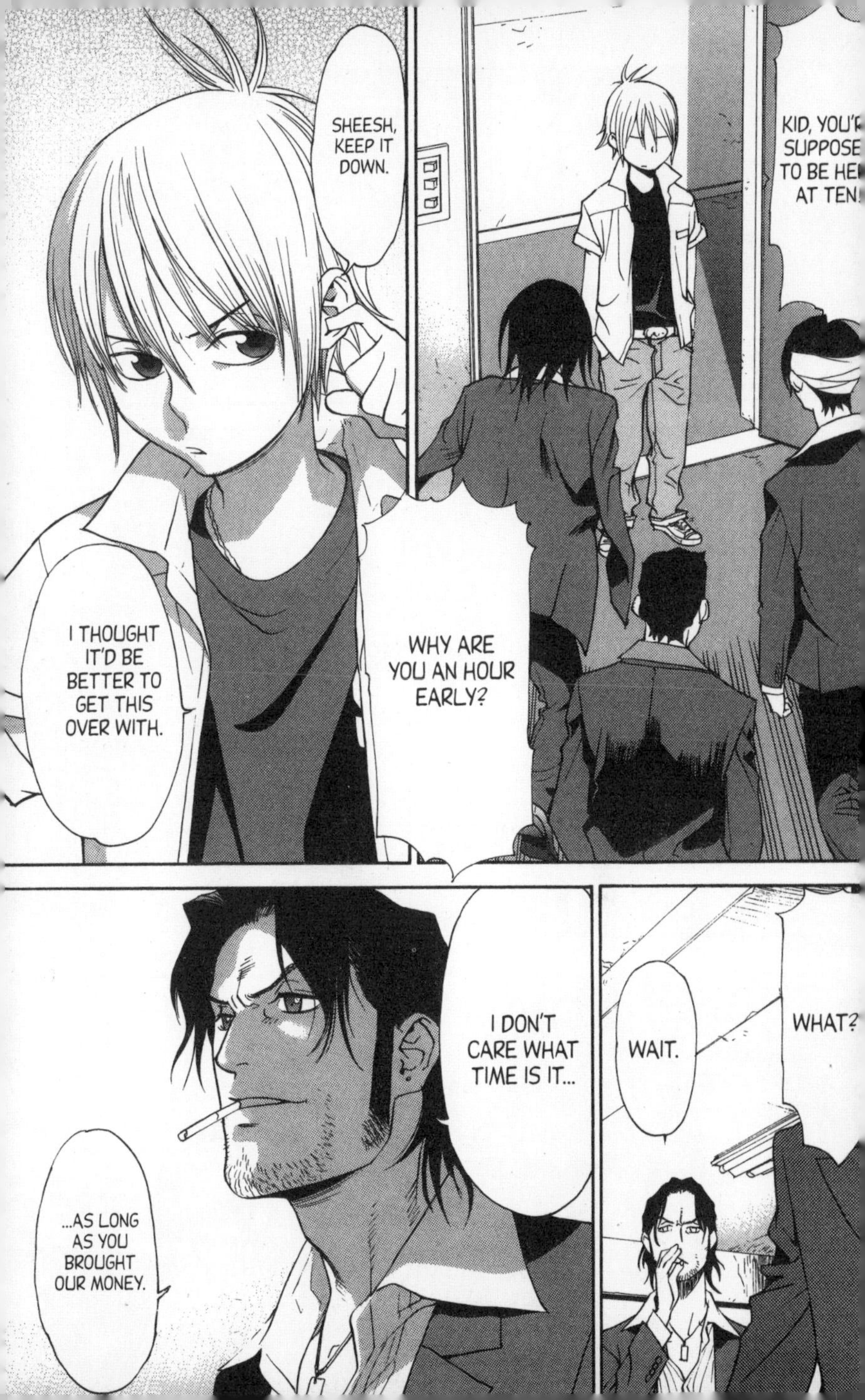
KID, YOU' SUPPOSE TO BE HE AT TEN
WHY ARE YOU AN HOUR EARLY?
SHEESH, KEEP IT DOWN.
I THOUGHT IT'D BE BETTER TO GET THIS OVER WITH.
WHAT?
WAIT.
I DON'T CARE WHAT TIME IS IT...
...AS LONG AS YOU BROUGHT OUR MONEY.

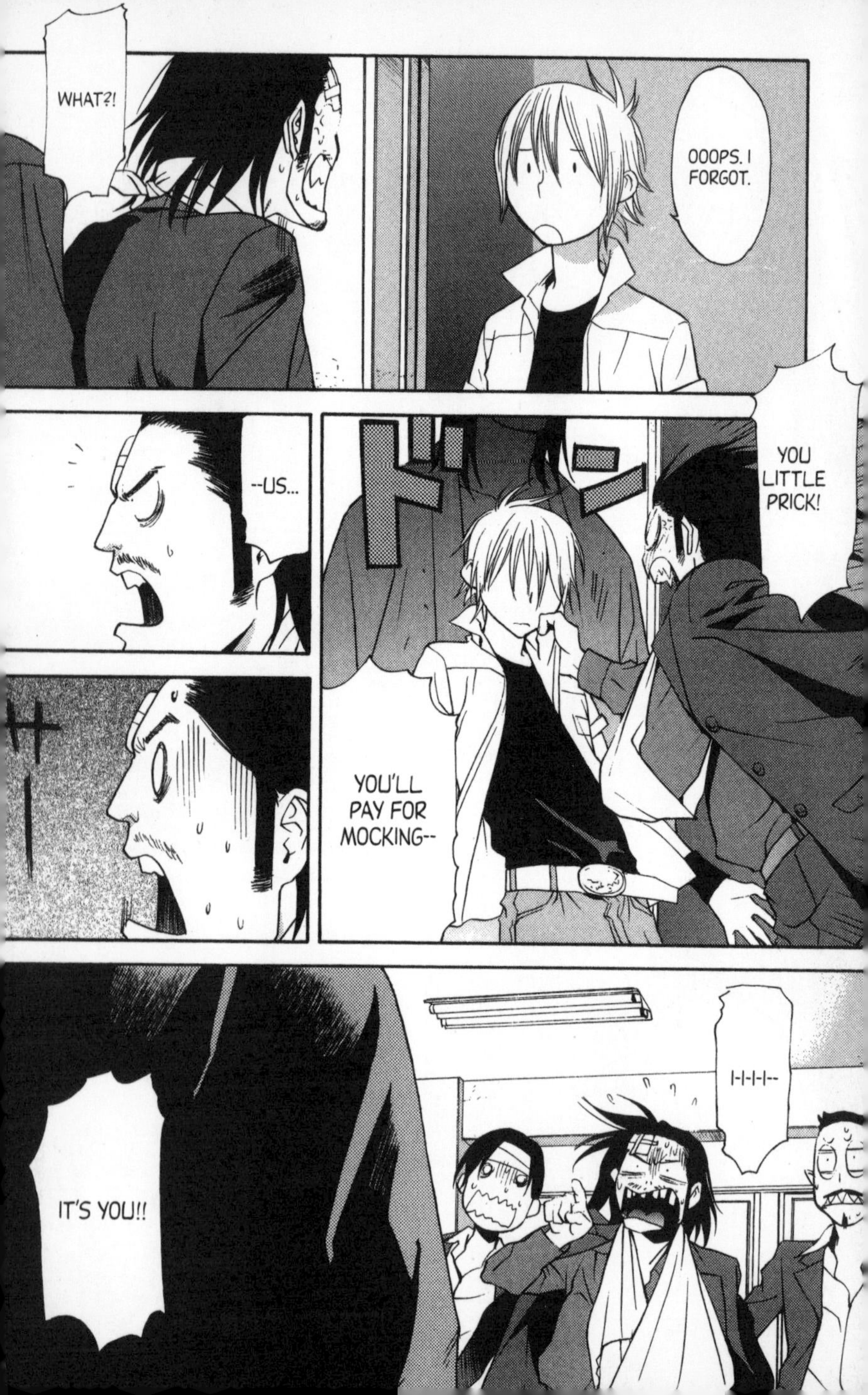
OOOPS. I FORGOT.
WHAT?!
YOU LITTLE PRICK!
YOU'LL PAY FOR MOCKING--
--US...
I-I-I-I--
IT'S YOU!!

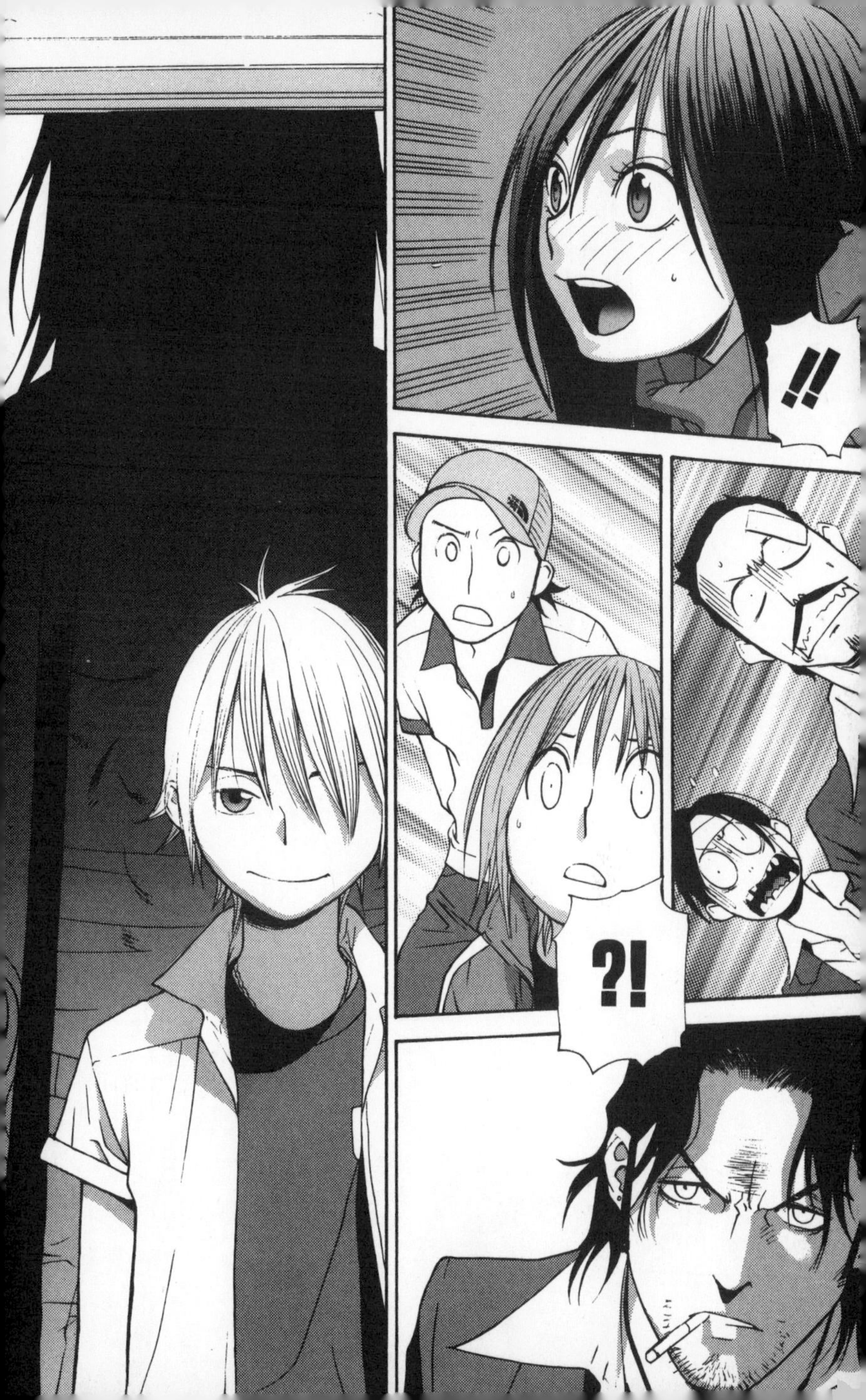
!!
?!

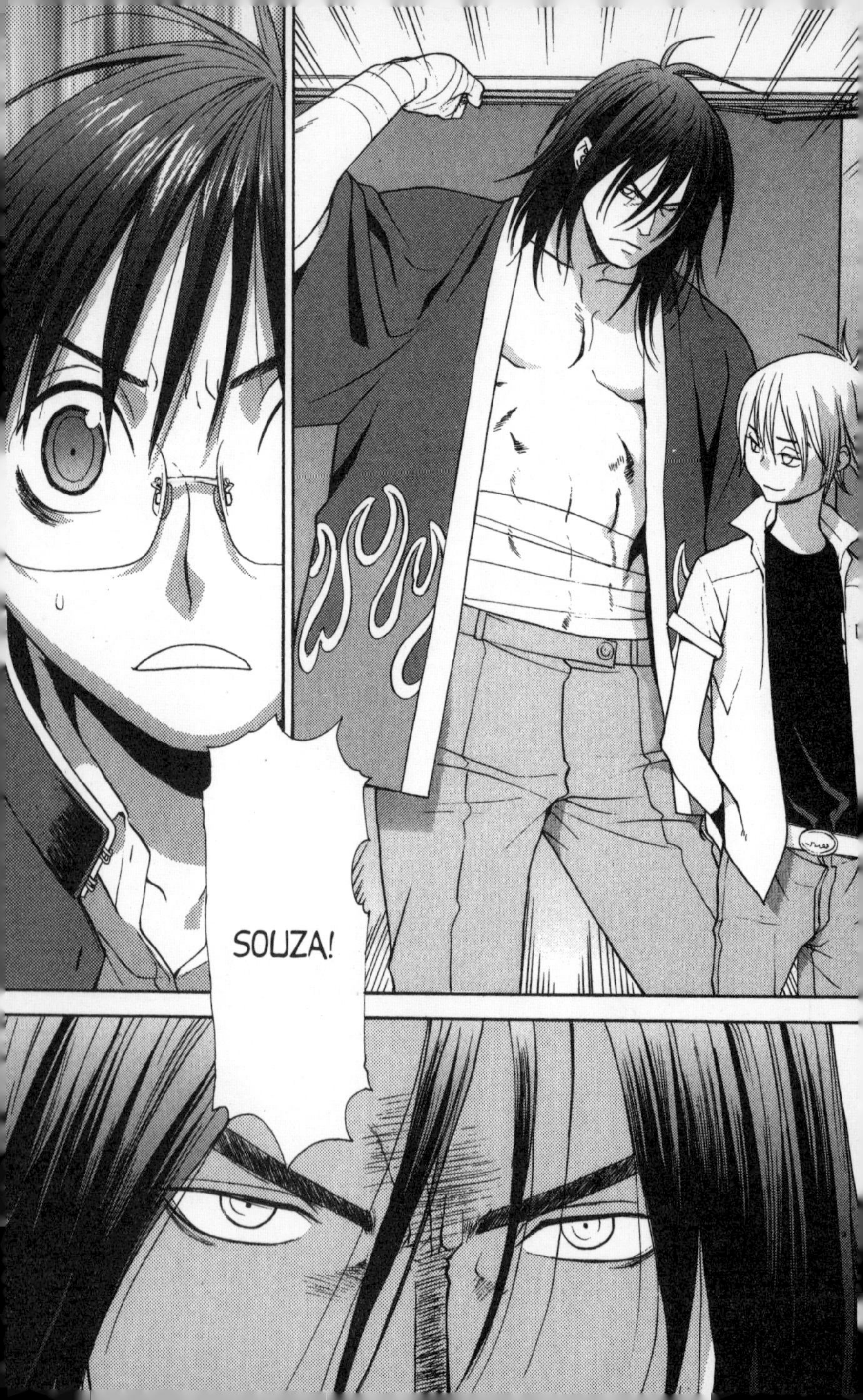
SOUZA!

Bonus Manga (3) The Mystery of Tomason

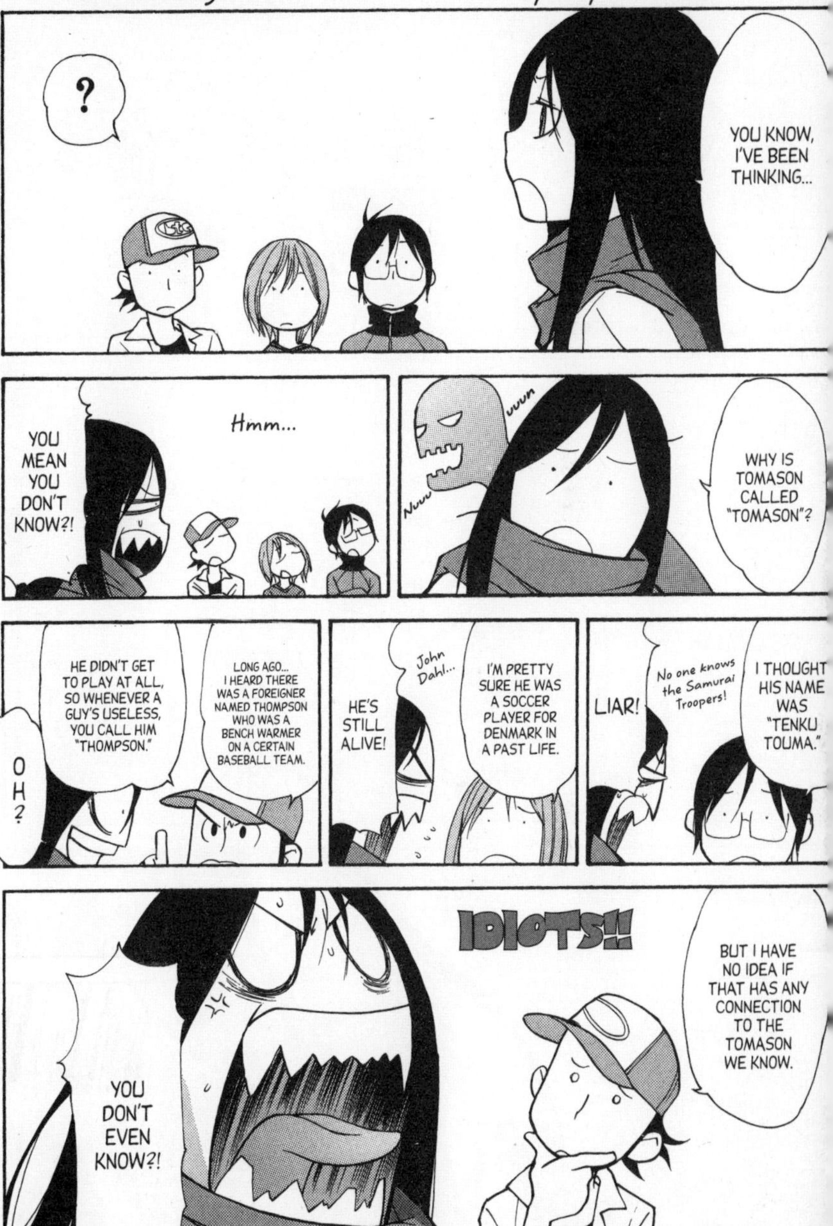
YOU KNOW, I'VE BEEN THINKING...
?
WHY IS TOMASON CALLED "TOMASON"?
uuun
Nuuu
Hmm...
YOU MEAN YOU DON'T KNOW?!
I THOUGHT HIS NAME WAS "TENKU TOUMA."
No one knows the Samurai Troopers!
LIAR!
I'M PRETTY SURE HE WAS A SOCCER PLAYER FOR DENMARK IN A PAST LIFE.
John Dahl...
HE'S STILL ALIVE!
LONG AGO... I HEARD THERE WAS A FOREIGNER NAMED THOMPSON WHO WAS A BENCH WARMER ON A CERTAIN BASEBALL TEAM.
HE DIDN'T GET TO PLAY AT ALL, SO WHENEVER A GUY'S USELESS, YOU CALL HIM "THOMPSON."
OH?
BUT I HAVE NO IDEA IF THAT HAS ANY CONNECTION TO THE TOMASON WE KNOW.
IDIOTS!!
YOU DON'T EVEN KNOW?!

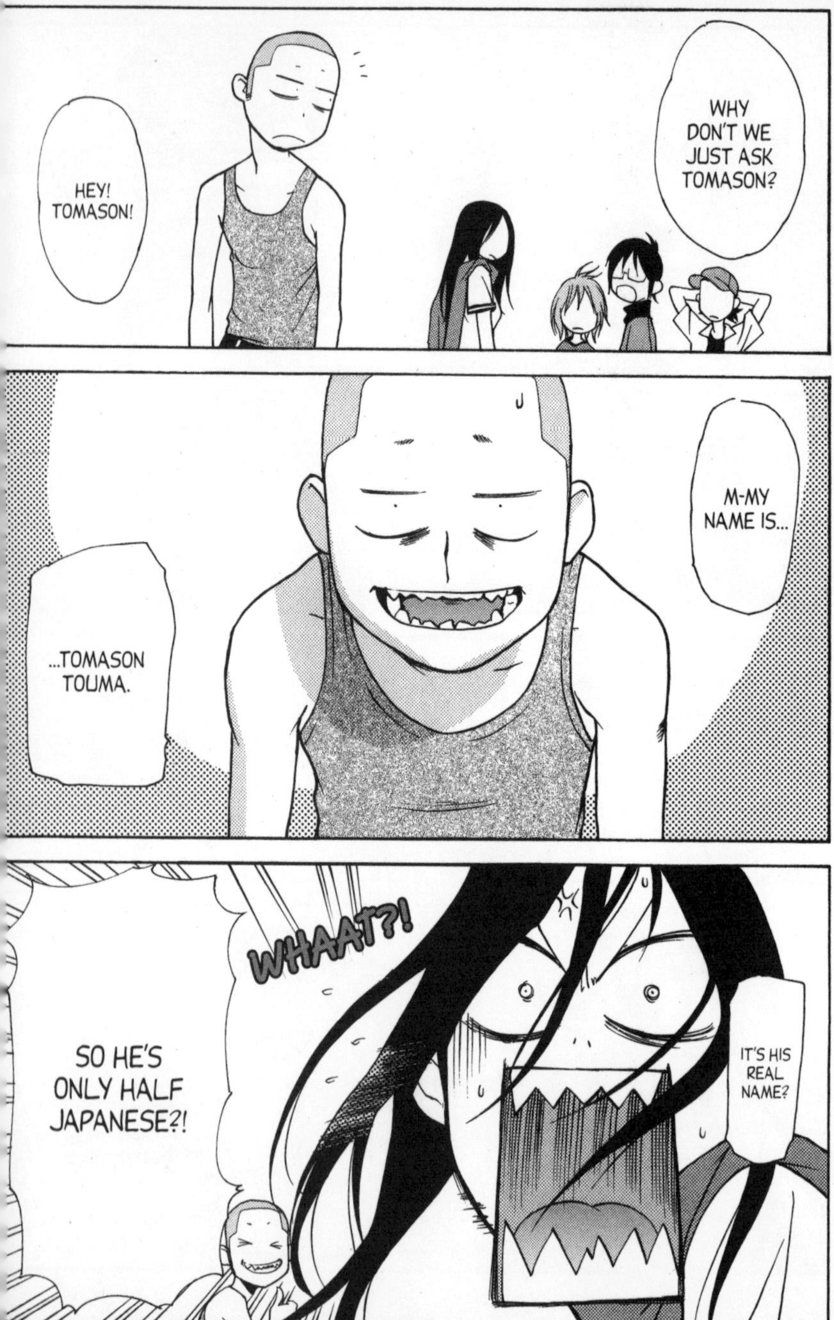
WHY DON'T WE JUST ASK TOMASON?
HEY! TOMASON!
M-MY NAME IS...
...TOMASON TOUMA.
WHAAT?!
IT'S HIS REAL NAME?
SO HE'S ONLY HALF JAPANESE?!

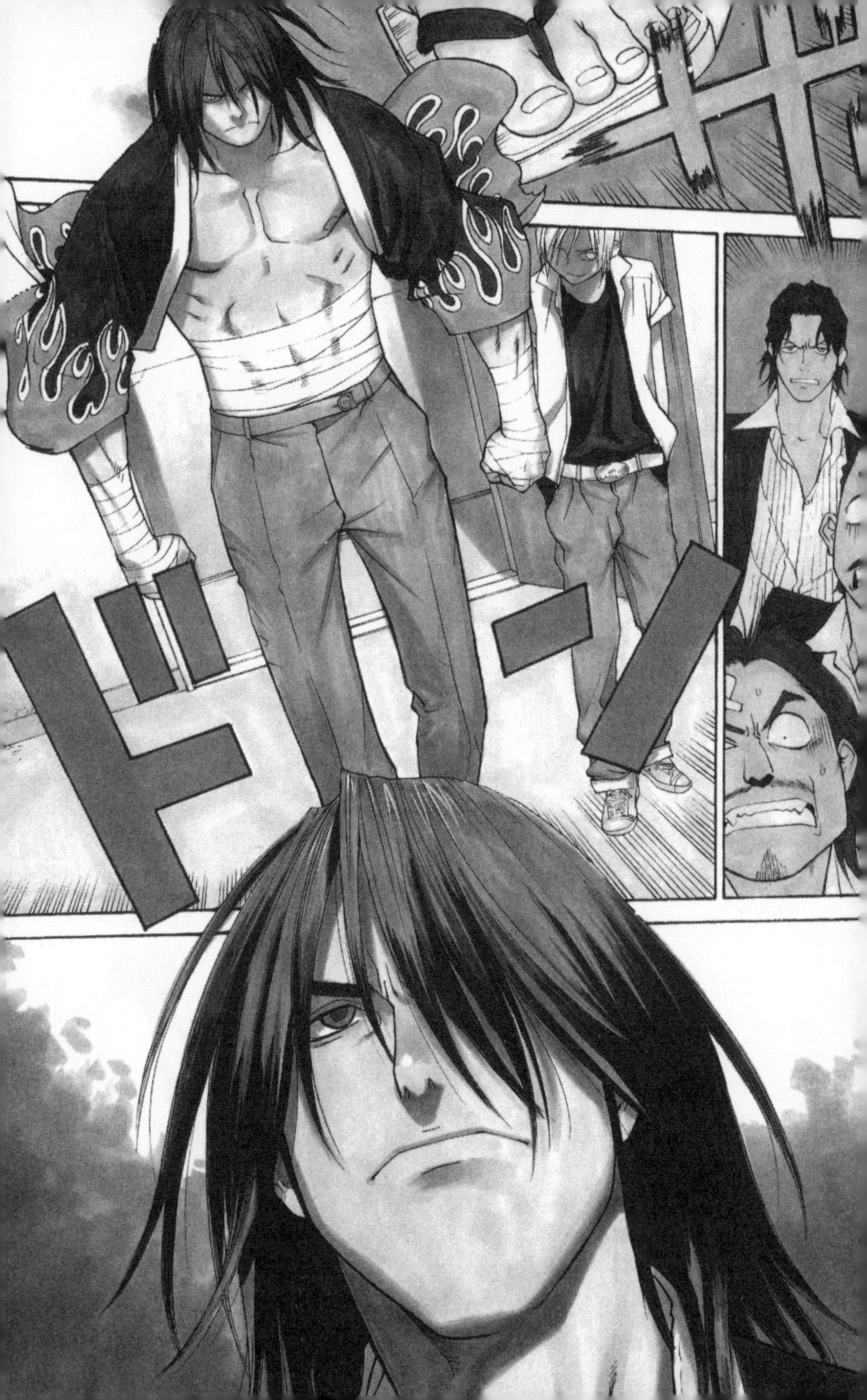
ドーン

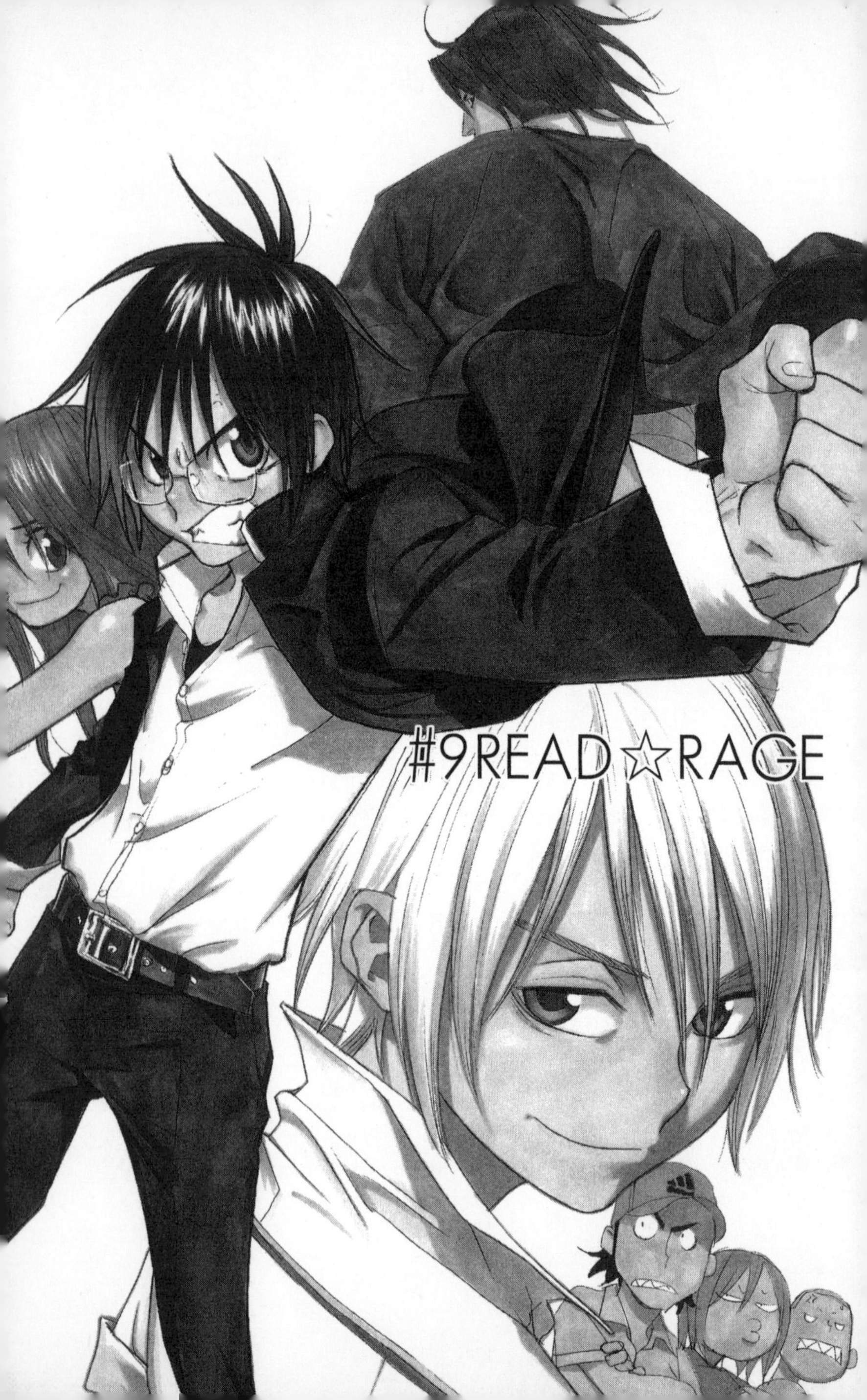
#9 READ☆RAGE

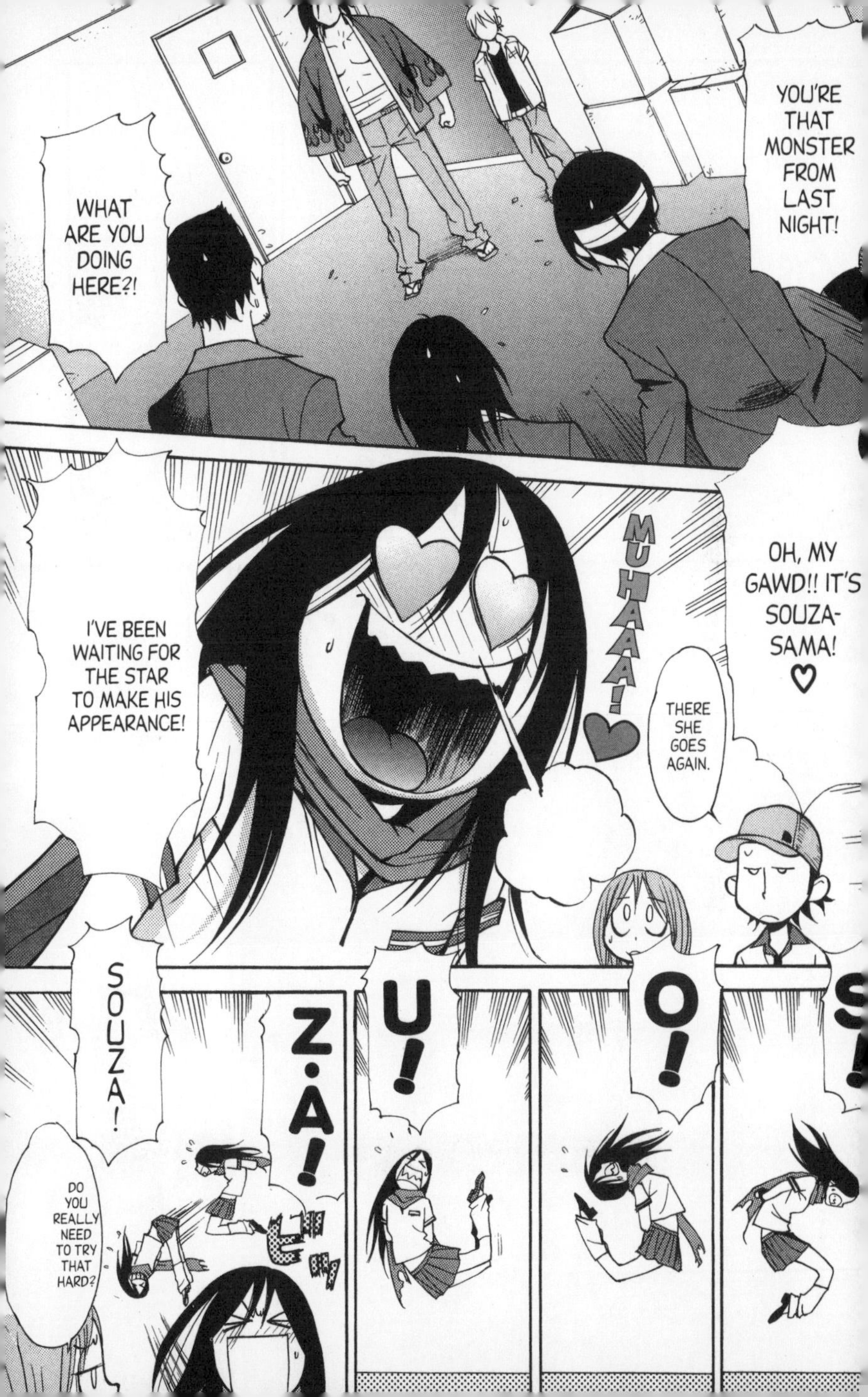
YOU'RE THAT MONSTER FROM LAST NIGHT!
WHAT ARE YOU DOING HERE?!
OH, MY GAWD!! IT'S SOUZA-SAMA! ♡
MUHAAAA!
THERE SHE GOES AGAIN.
I'VE BEEN WAITING FOR THE STAR TO MAKE HIS APPEARANCE!
S!
O!
U!
Z·A!
SOUZA!
DO YOU REALLY NEED TO TRY THAT HARD?

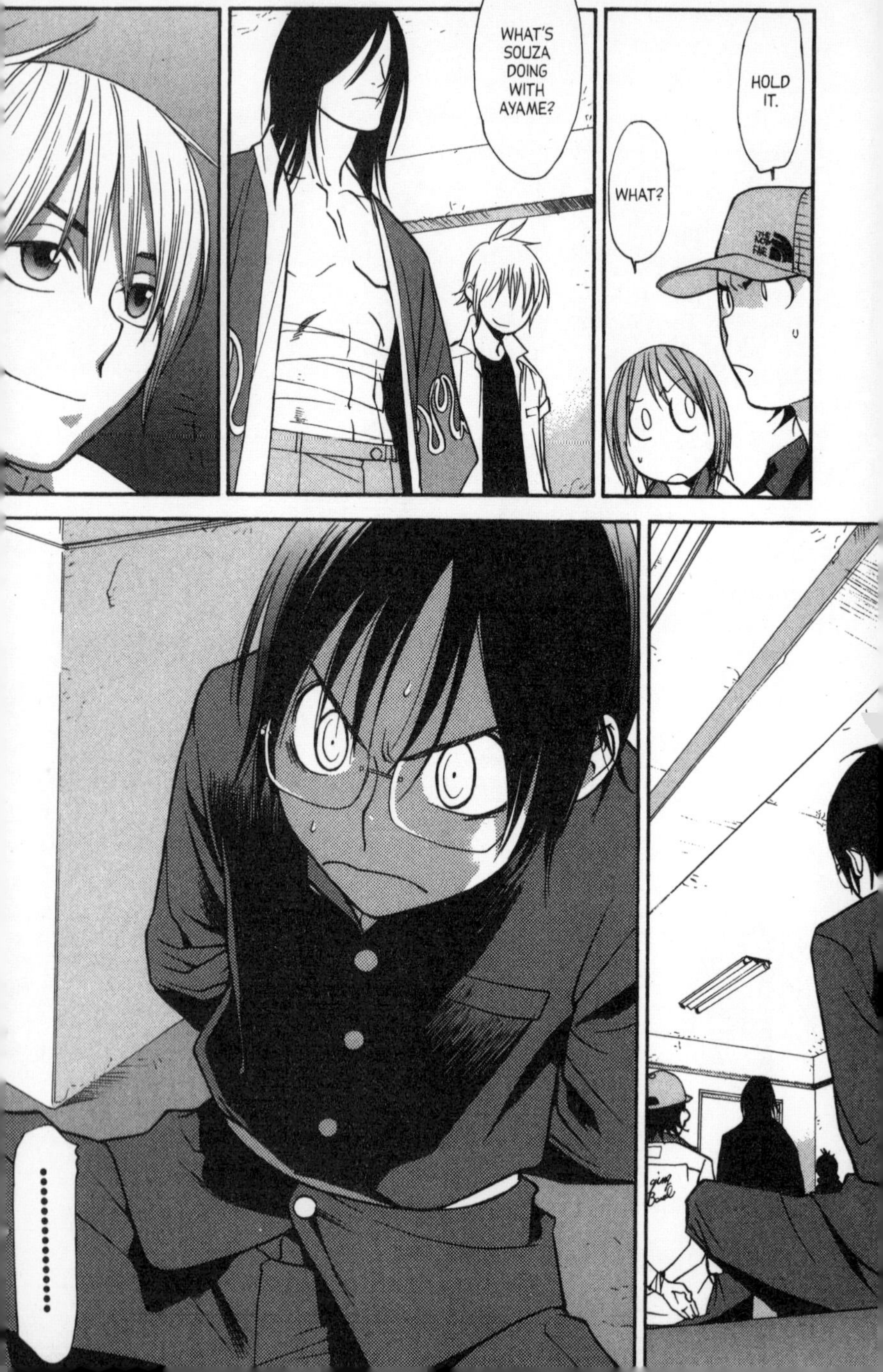
HOLD IT.
WHAT?
WHAT'S SOUZA DOING WITH AYAME?
....

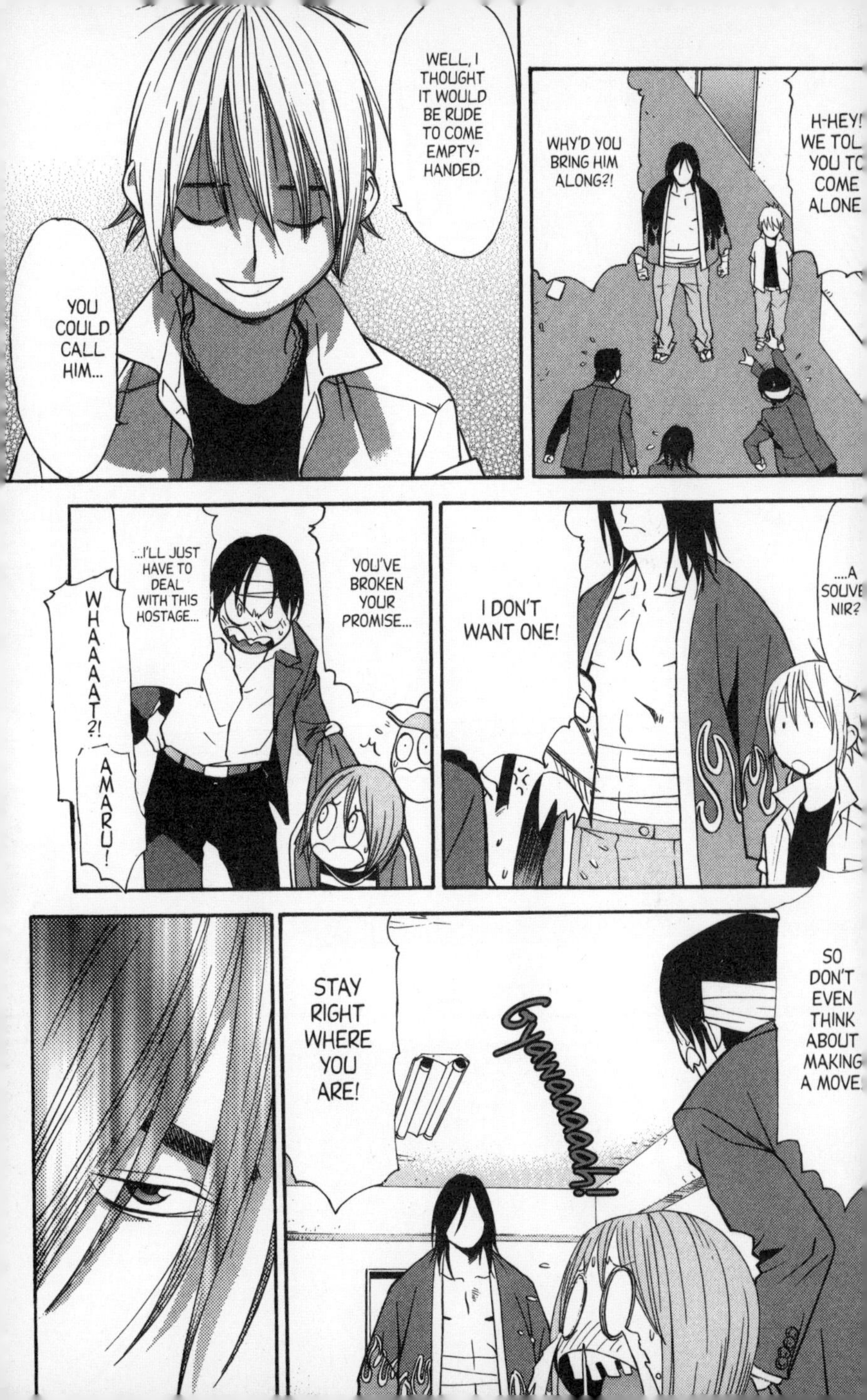
H-HEY! WE TOL YOU TC COME ALONE
WHY'D YOU BRING HIM ALONG?!
WELL, I THOUGHT IT WOULD BE RUDE TO COME EMPTY-HANDED.
YOU COULD CALL HIM...
....A SOUVE NIR?
I DON'T WANT ONE!
YOU'VE BROKEN YOUR PROMISE...
...I'LL JUST HAVE TO DEAL WITH THIS HOSTAGE...
WHAAAAT?!
AMARU!
SO DON'T EVEN THINK ABOUT MAKING A MOVE.
Gyaaaaah!
STAY RIGHT WHERE YOU ARE!

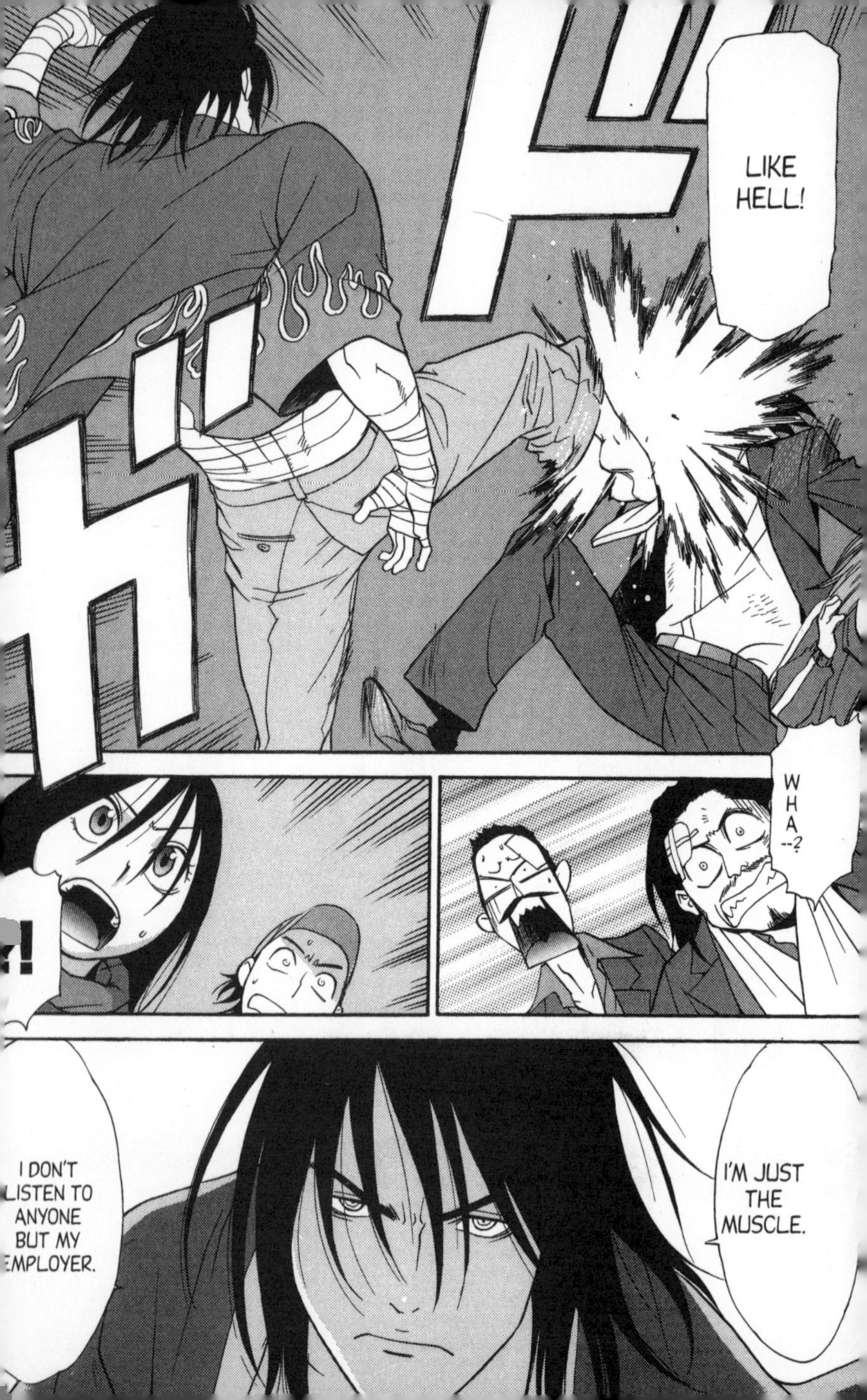
LIKE HELL!
WHA--?
?!
I'M JUST THE MUSCLE.
I DON'T LISTEN TO ANYONE BUT MY EMPLOYER.

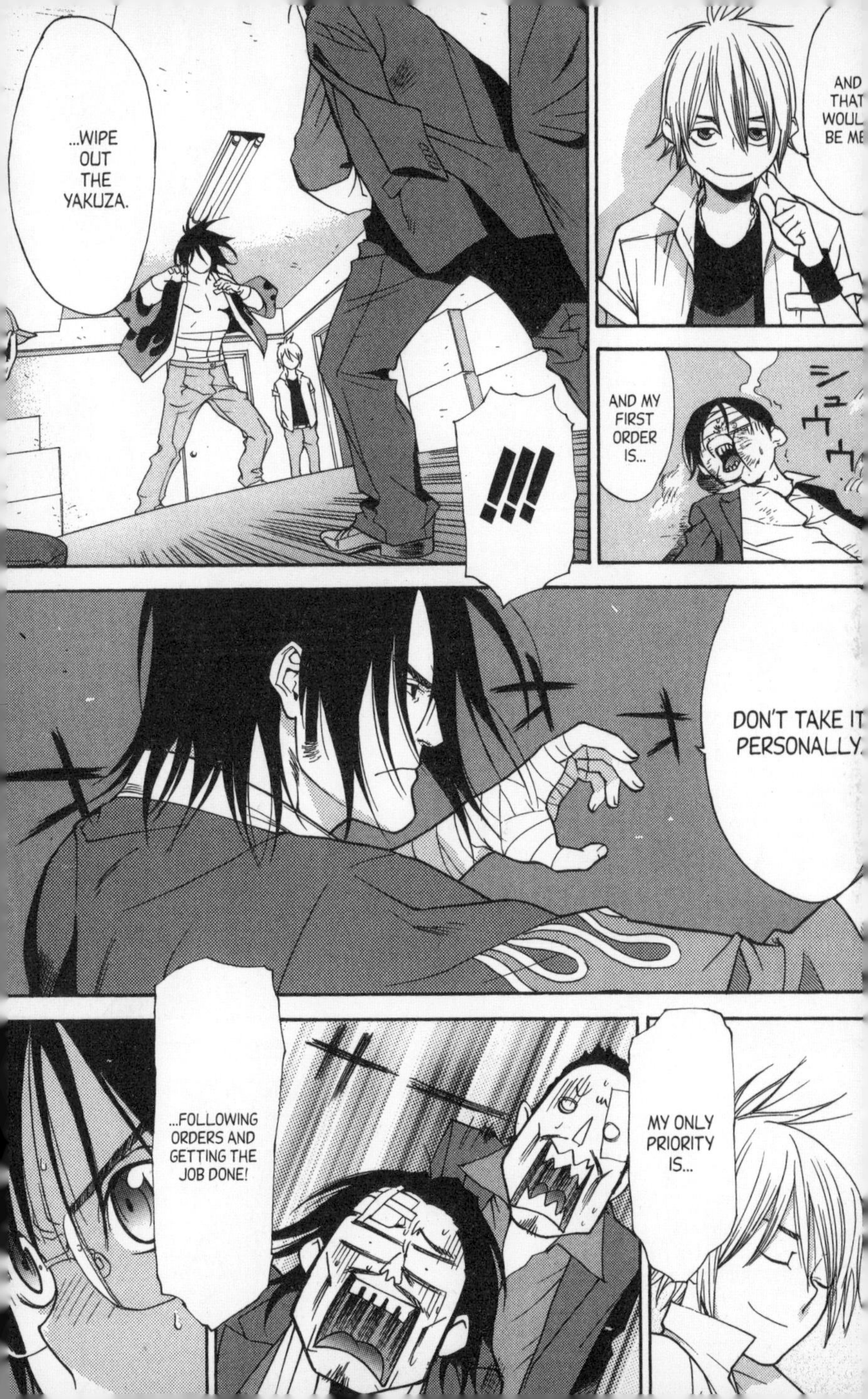
AND THAT WOUL BE ME
AND MY FIRST ORDER IS...
シュウウ
...WIPE OUT THE YAKUZA.
!!!!
DON'T TAKE IT PERSONALLY.
MY ONLY PRIORITY IS...
...FOLLOWING ORDERS AND GETTING THE JOB DONE!

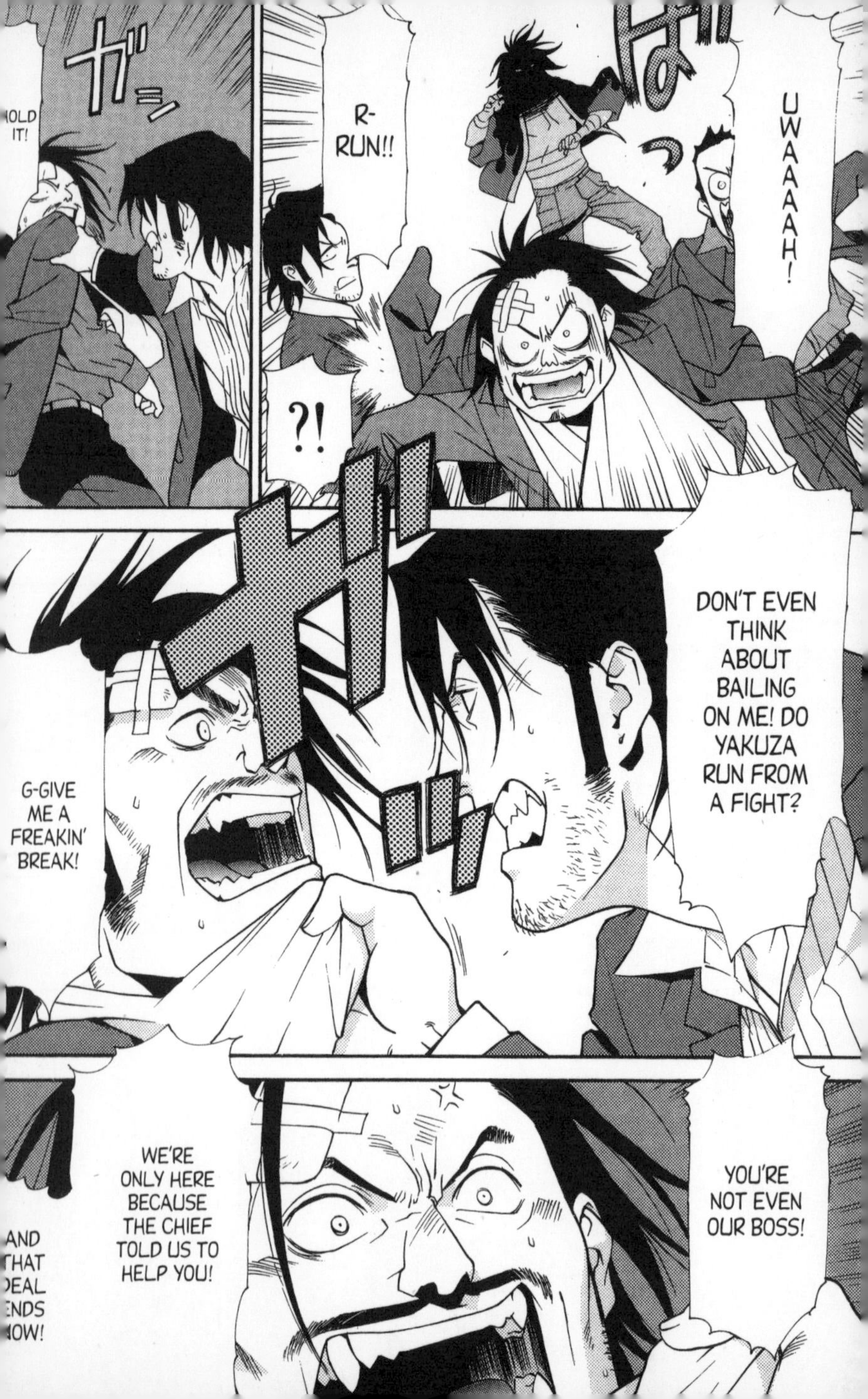
ばっ
UWAAAAAH!
R-RUN!!
?!
ガッ
HOLD IT!
DON'T EVEN THINK ABOUT BAILING ON ME! DO YAKUZA RUN FROM A FIGHT?
G-GIVE ME A FREAKIN' BREAK!
YOU'RE NOT EVEN OUR BOSS!
WE'RE ONLY HERE BECAUSE THE CHIEF TOLD US TO HELP YOU!
AND THAT DEAL ENDS NOW!

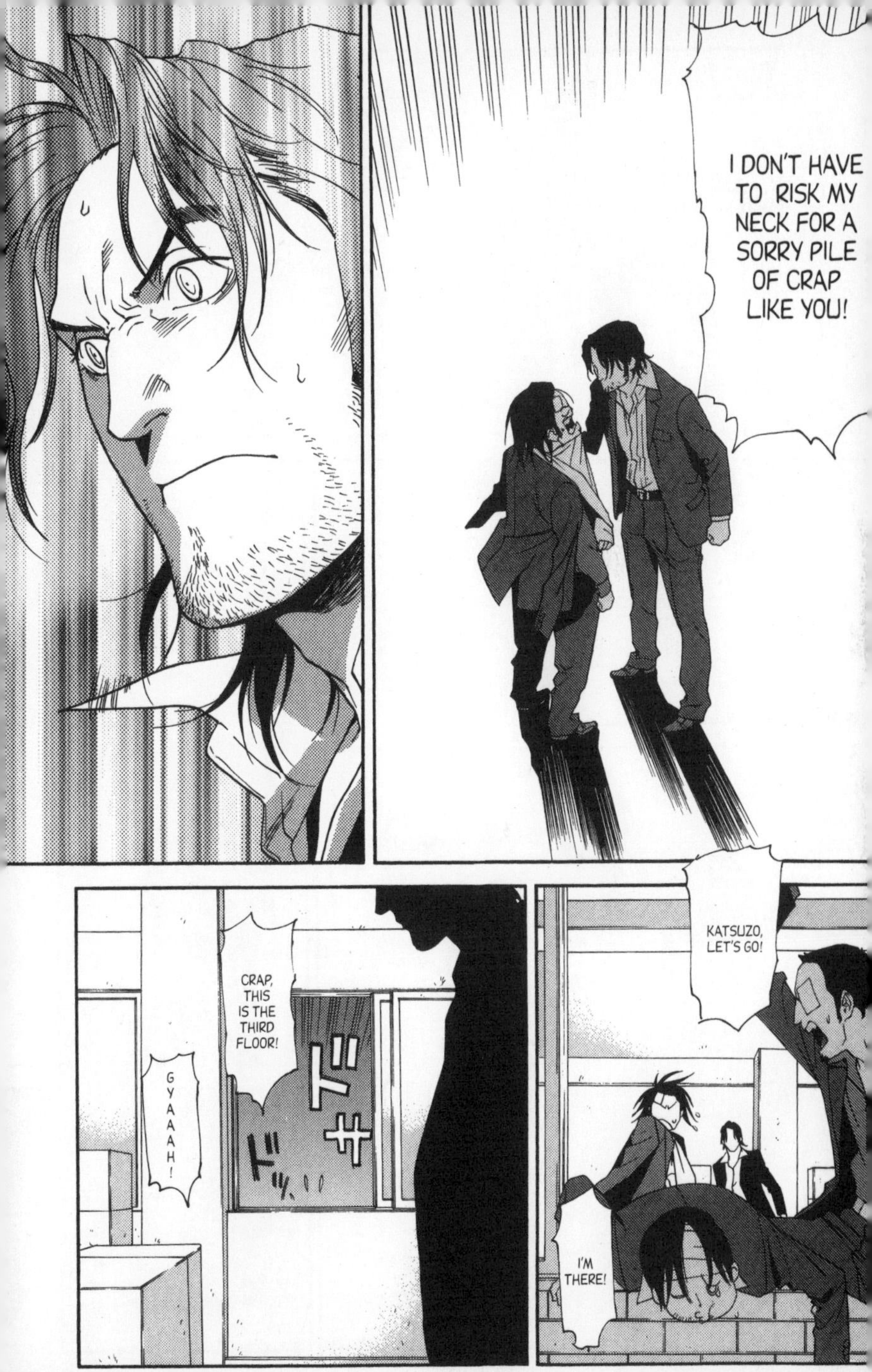
I DON'T HAVE TO RISK MY NECK FOR A SORRY PILE OF CRAP LIKE YOU!
KATSUZO, LET'S GO!
I'M THERE!
CRAP, THIS IS THE THIRD FLOOR!
ドサ
ドッ
GYAAAH!

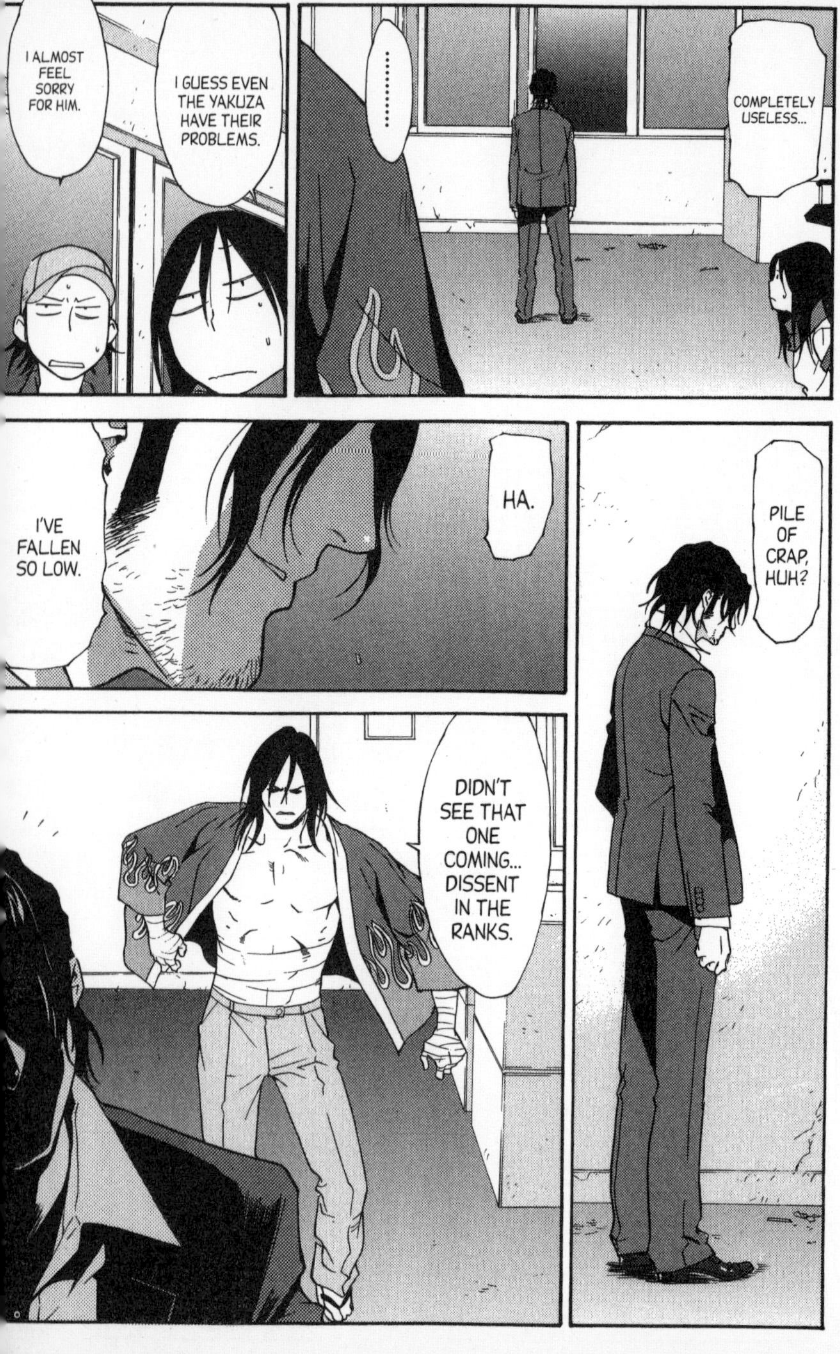
COMPLETELY USELESS...
......
I GUESS EVEN THE YAKUZA HAVE THEIR PROBLEMS.
I ALMOST FEEL SORRY FOR HIM.
PILE OF CRAP, HUH?
HA.
I'VE FALLEN SO LOW.
DIDN'T SEE THAT ONE COMING... DISSENT IN THE RANKS.

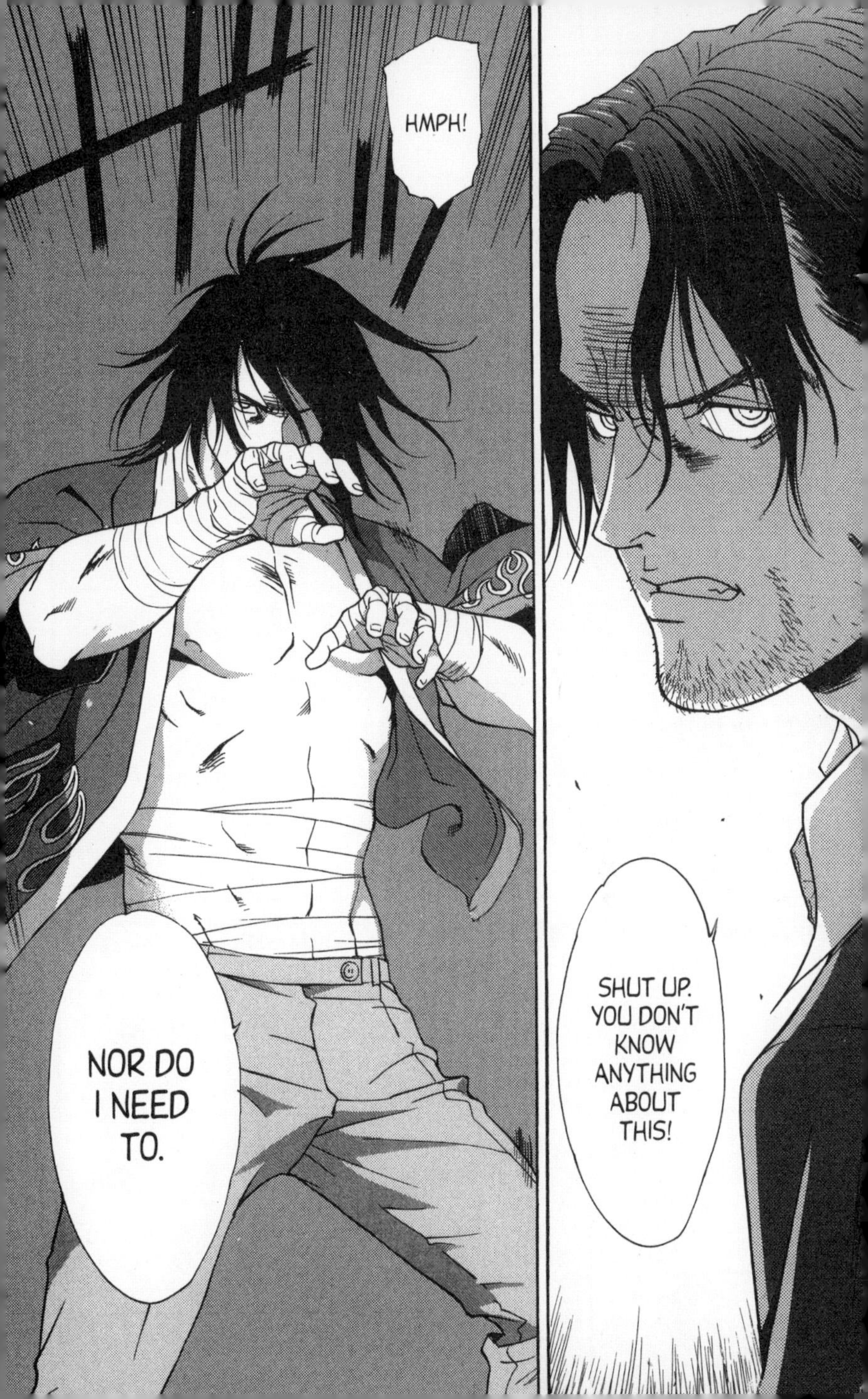
SHUT UP. YOU DON'T KNOW ANYTHING ABOUT THIS!
HMPH!
NOR DO I NEED TO.

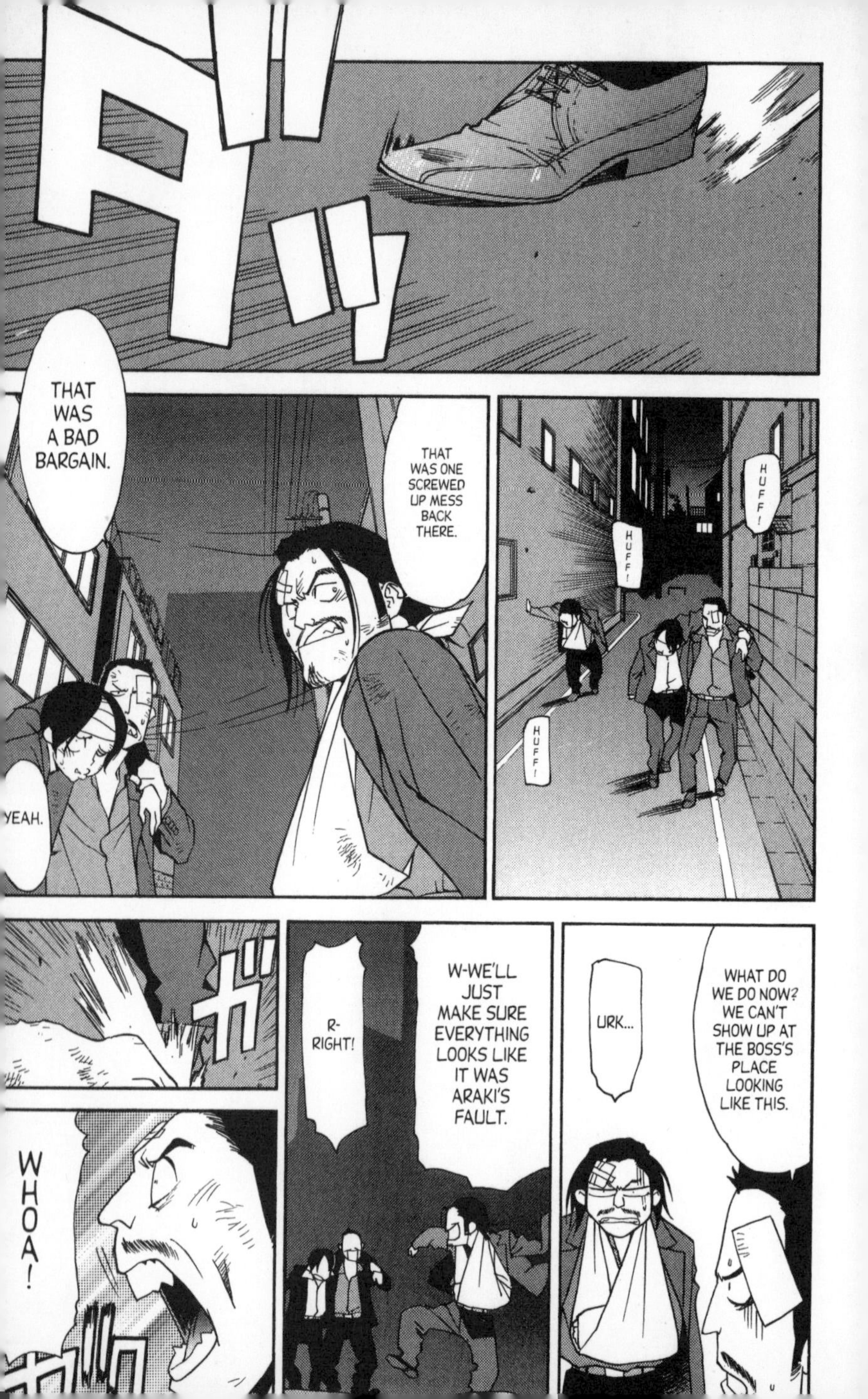
ダッ
HUFF!
HUFF!
HUFF!
THAT WAS ONE SCREWED UP MESS BACK THERE.
THAT WAS A BAD BARGAIN.
YEAH.
WHAT DO WE DO NOW? WE CAN'T SHOW UP AT THE BOSS'S PLACE LOOKING LIKE THIS.
URK...
W-WE'LL JUST MAKE SURE EVERYTHING LOOKS LIKE IT WAS ARAKI'S FAULT.
R-RIGHT!
ガッ
WHOA!

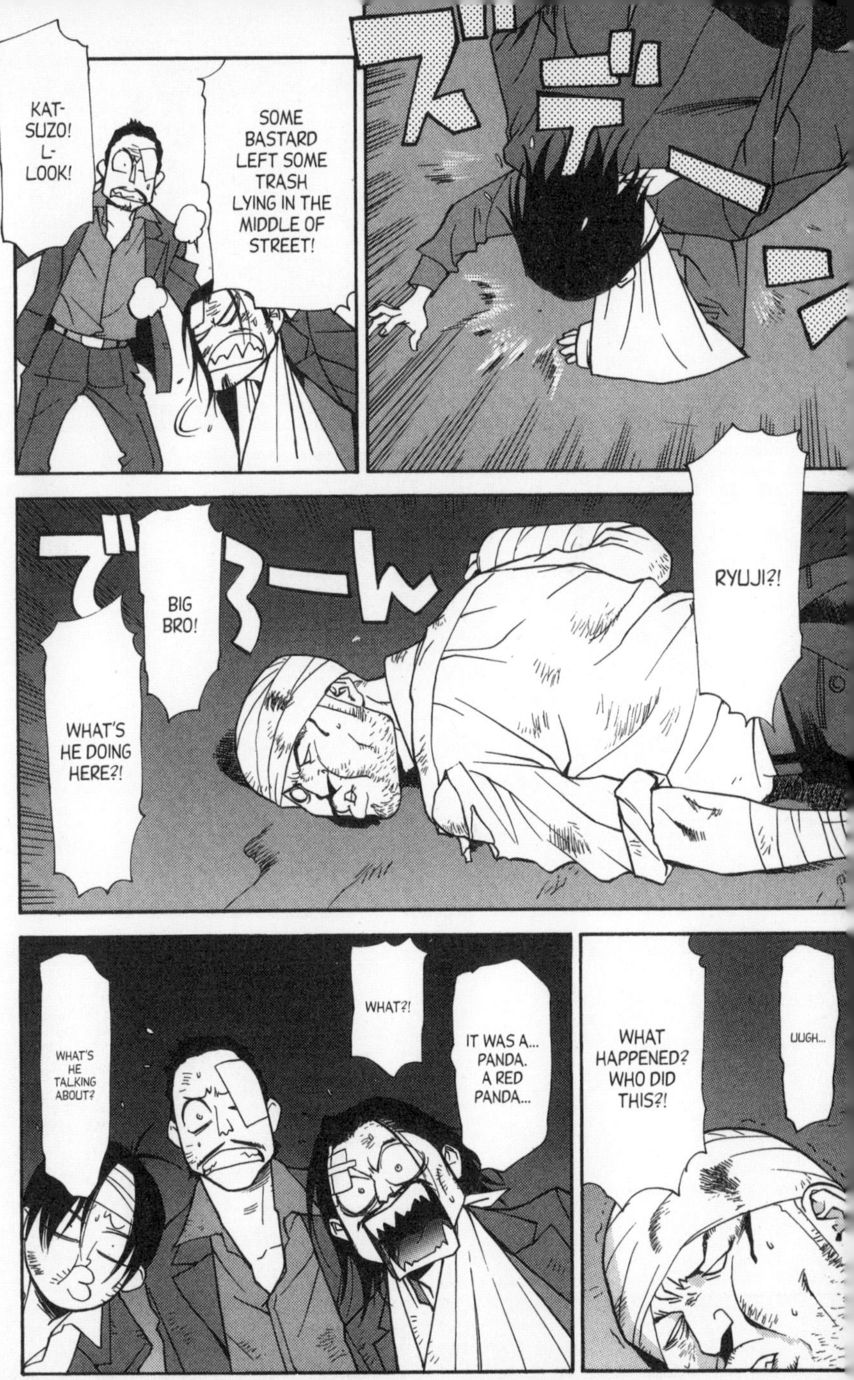
SOME BASTARD LEFT SOME TRASH LYING IN THE MIDDLE OF STREET!
KAT-SUZO! L-LOOK!
RYUJI?!
でろーん
BIG BRO!
WHAT'S HE DOING HERE?!
UUGH...
WHAT HAPPENED? WHO DID THIS?!
IT WAS A... PANDA. A RED PANDA...
WHAT?!
WHAT'S HE TALKING ABOUT?

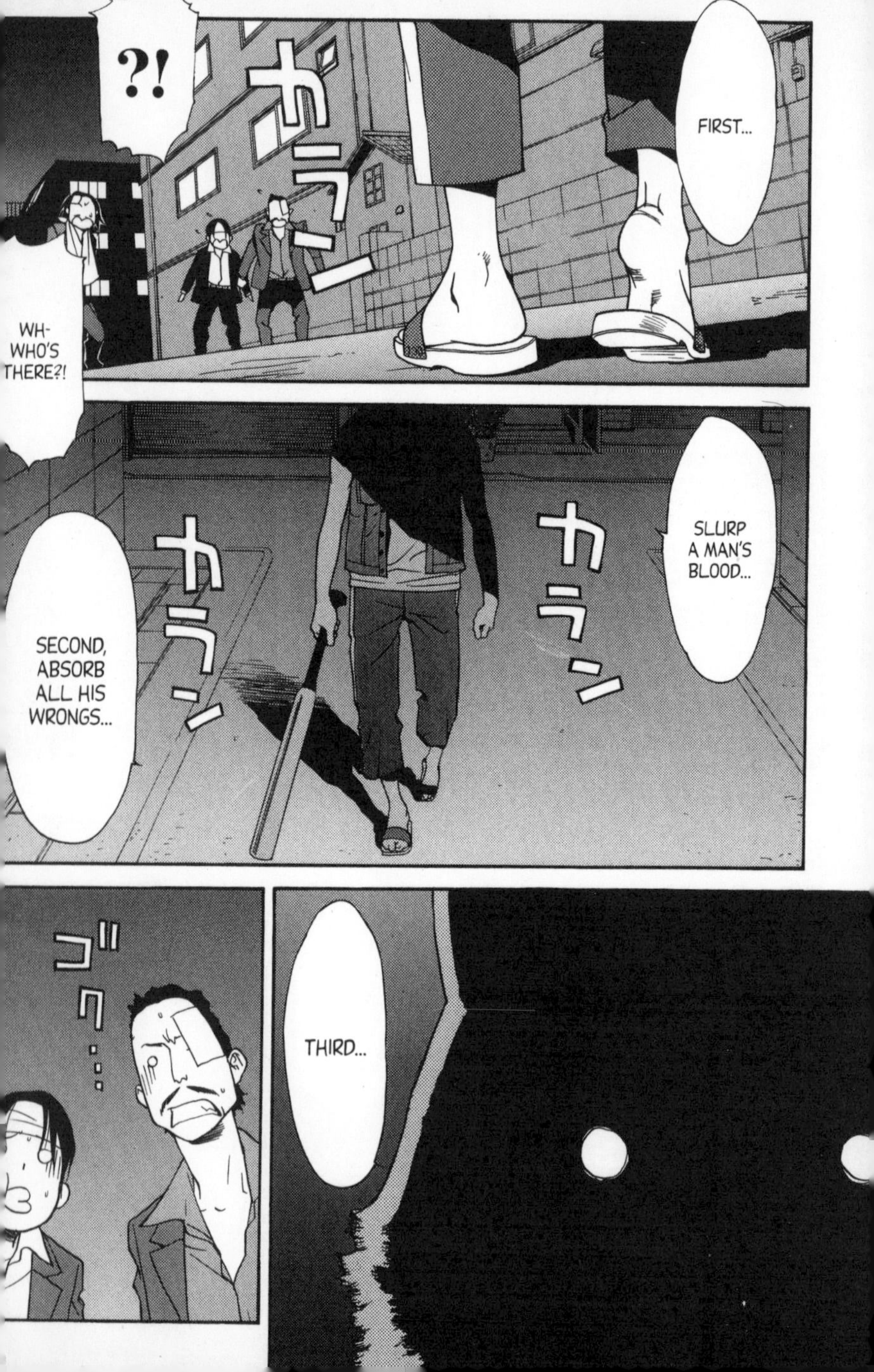
FIRST...
カラー
?!
WH-WHO'S THERE?!
SLURP A MAN'S BLOOD...
カラン
カラン
SECOND, ABSORB ALL HIS WRONGS...
THIRD...
ゴク...

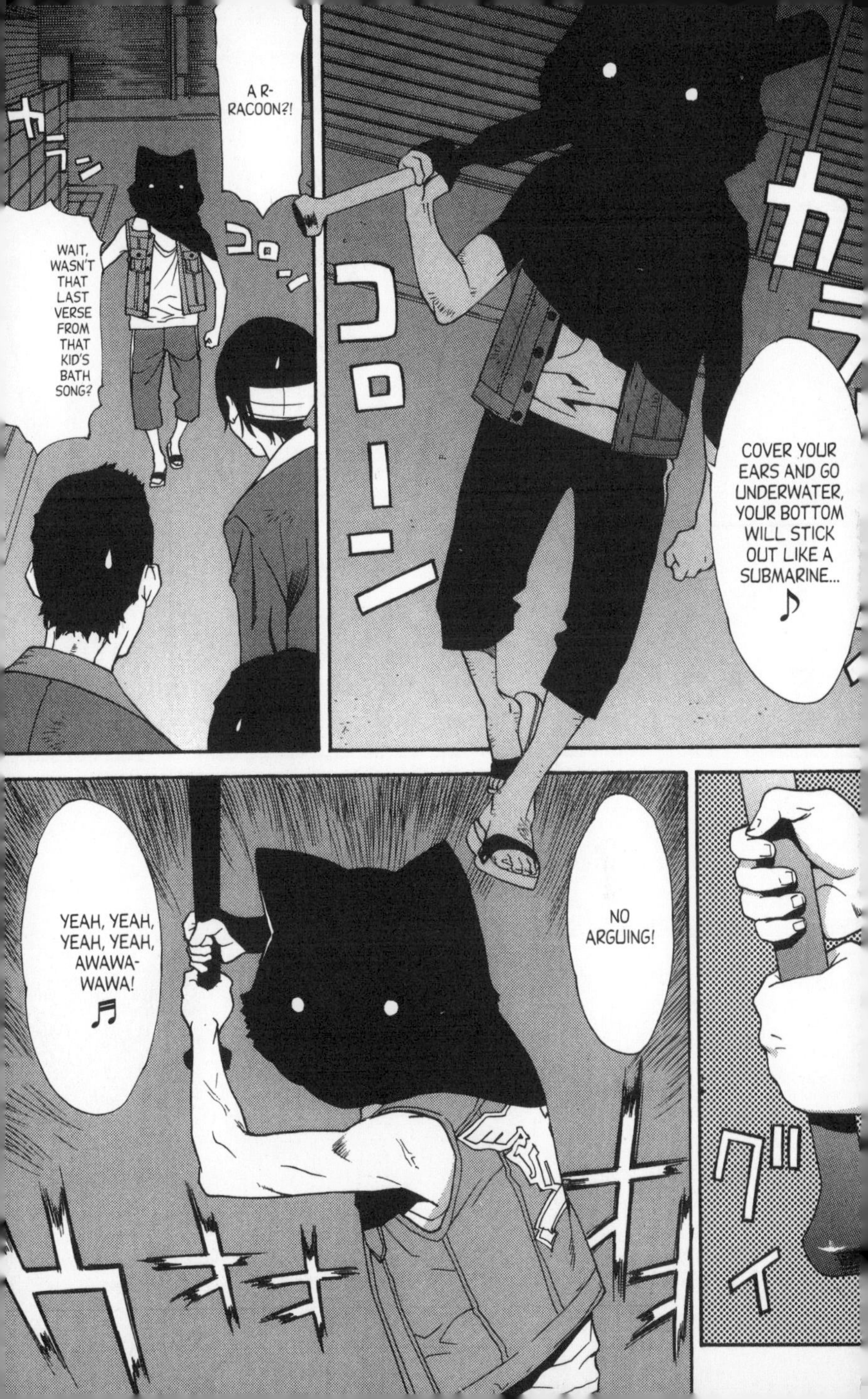
COVER YOUR EARS AND GO UNDERWATER, YOUR BOTTOM WILL STICK OUT LIKE A SUBMARINE... ♪
A R- RACOON?!
WAIT, WASN'T THAT LAST VERSE FROM THAT KID'S BATH SONG?
NO ARGUING!
YEAH, YEAH, YEAH, YEAH, AWAWA-WAWA! ♬

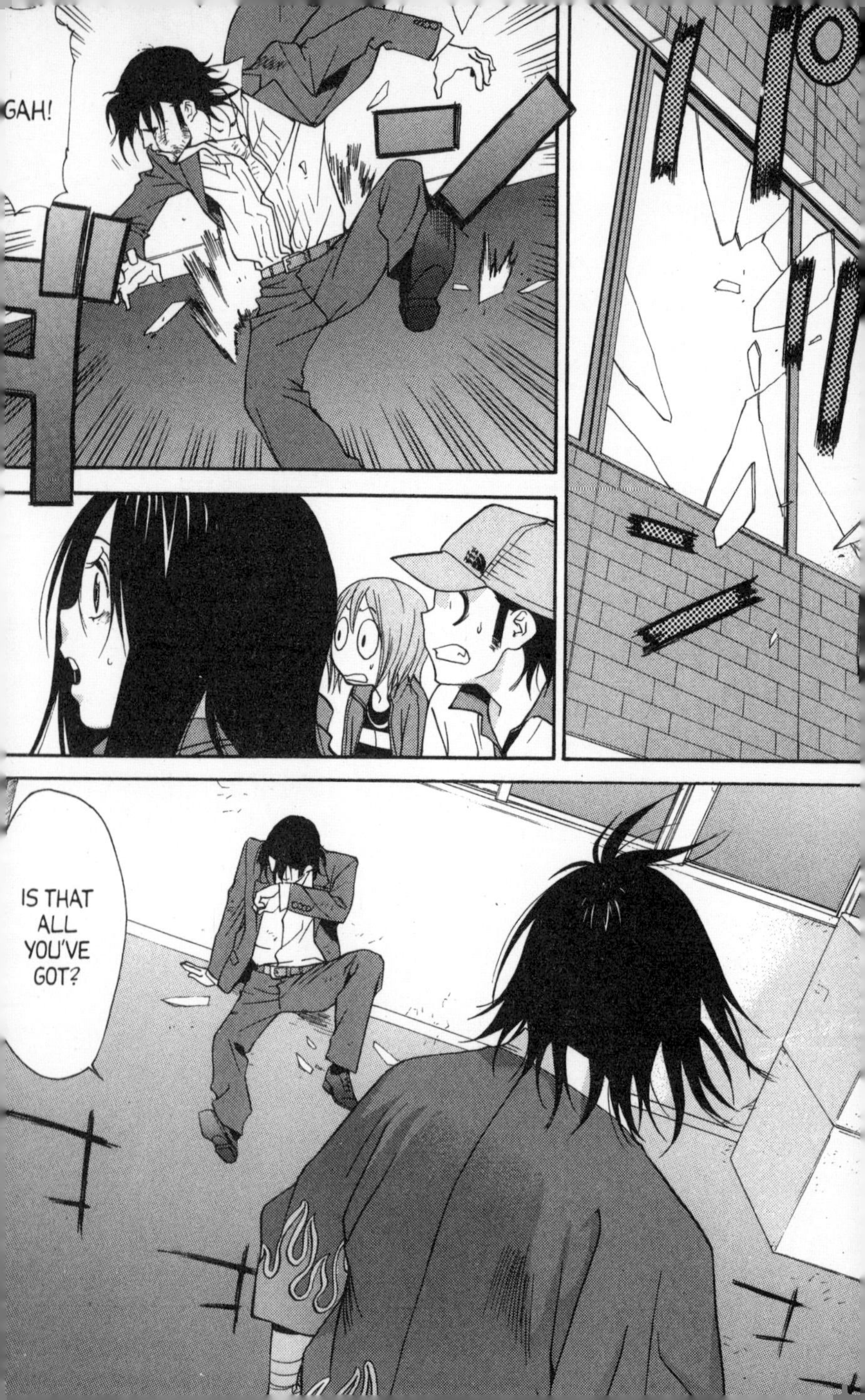
GAH!
IS THAT ALL YOU'VE GOT?

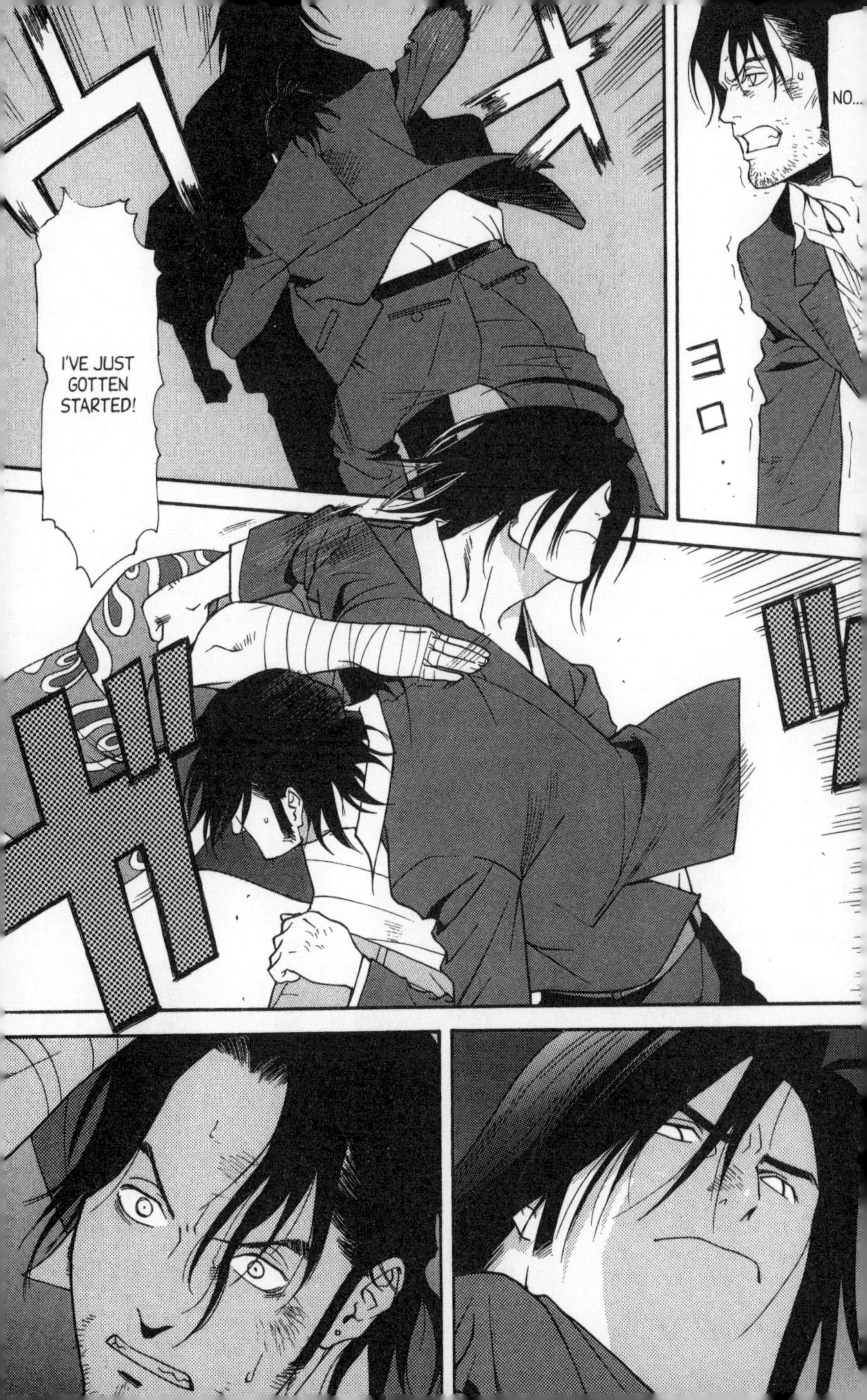
NO...
I'VE JUST GOTTEN STARTED!

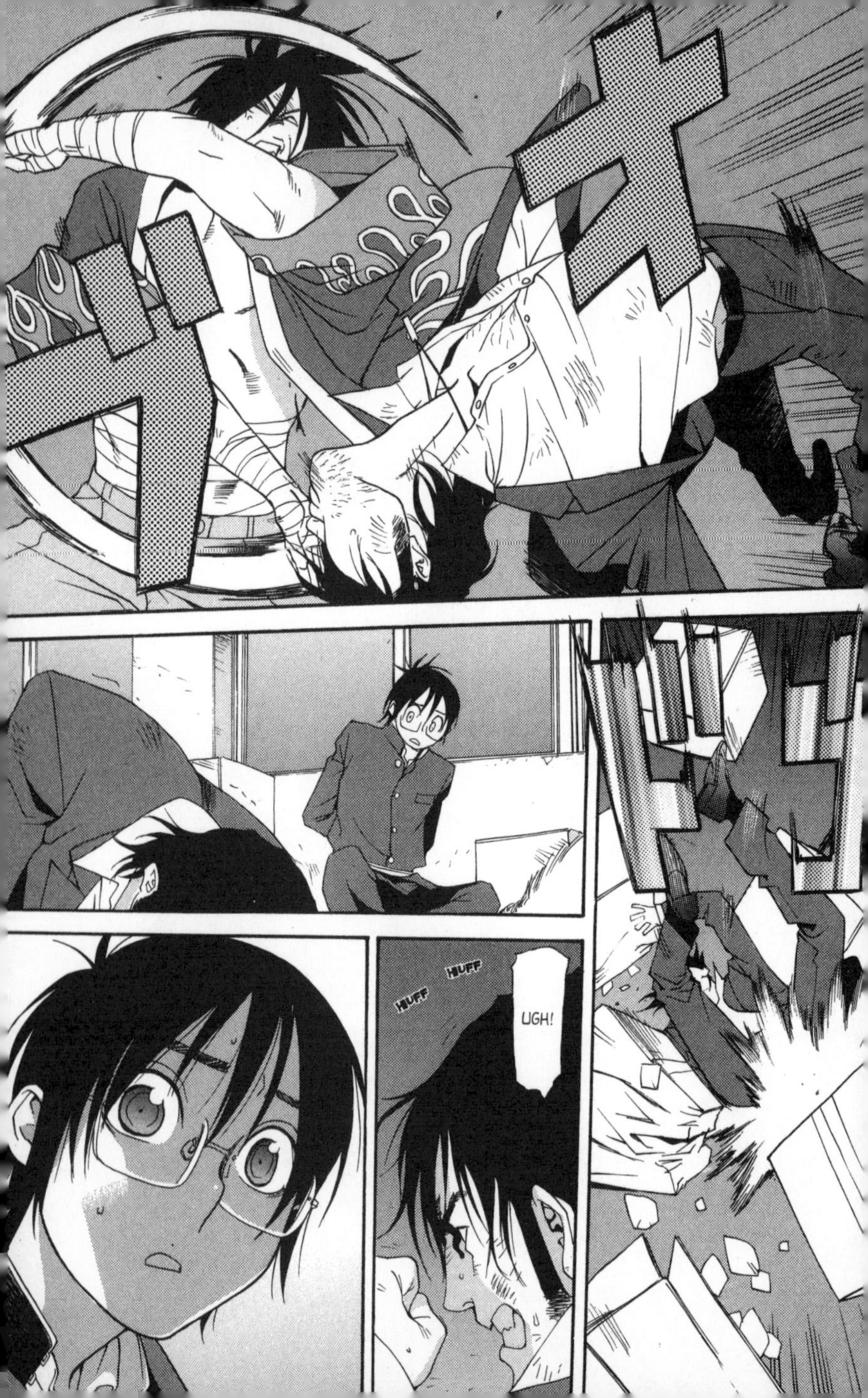
HUFF
HUFF
UGH!

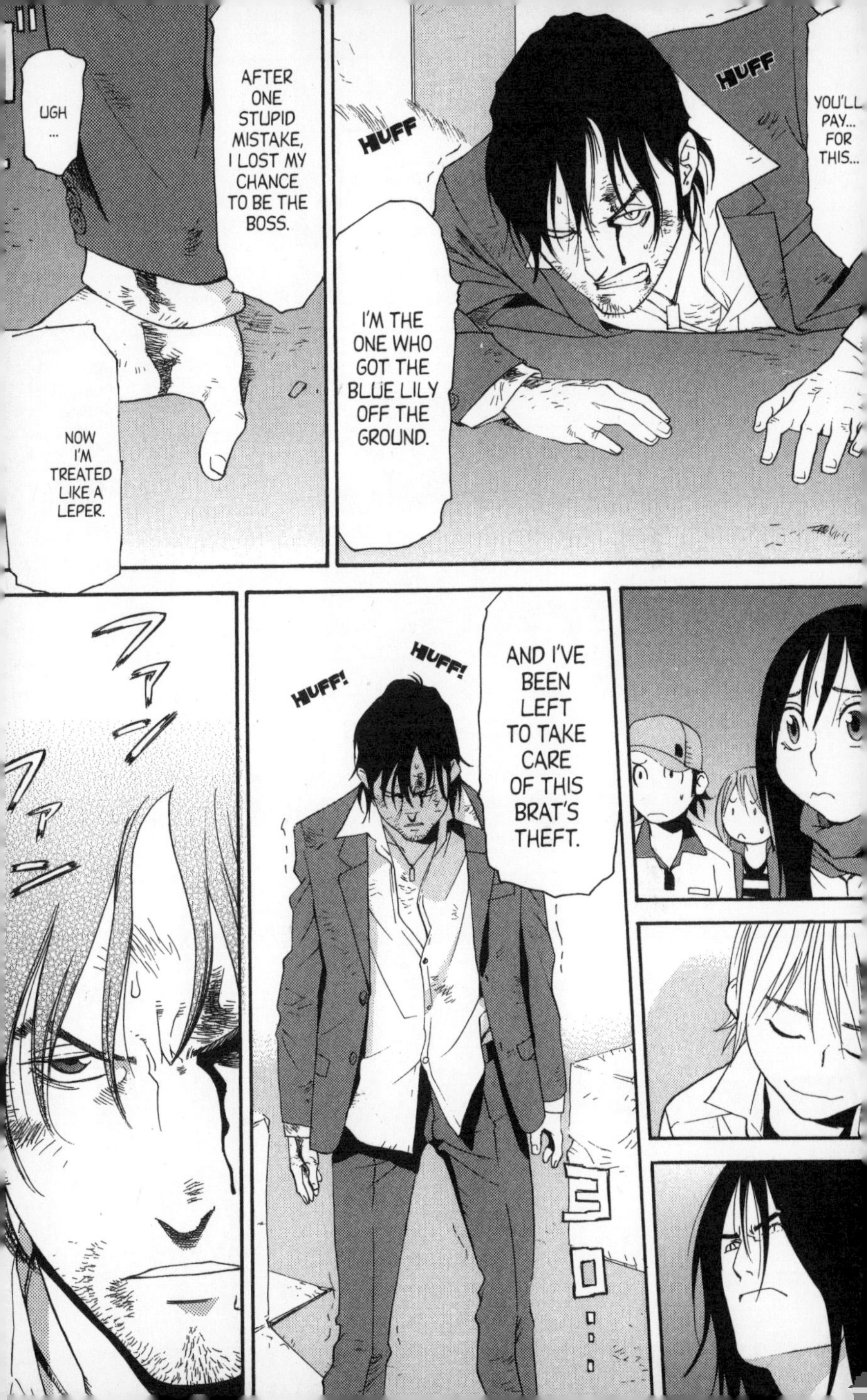
HUFF
YOU'LL PAY... FOR THIS...
HUFF
I'M THE ONE WHO GOT THE BLUE LILY OFF THE GROUND.
AFTER ONE STUPID MISTAKE, I LOST MY CHANCE TO BE THE BOSS.
UGH ...
NOW I'M TREATED LIKE A LEPER.
HUFF!
HUFF!
AND I'VE BEEN LEFT TO TAKE CARE OF THIS BRAT'S THEFT.
ヨロ...
ファン
ファン

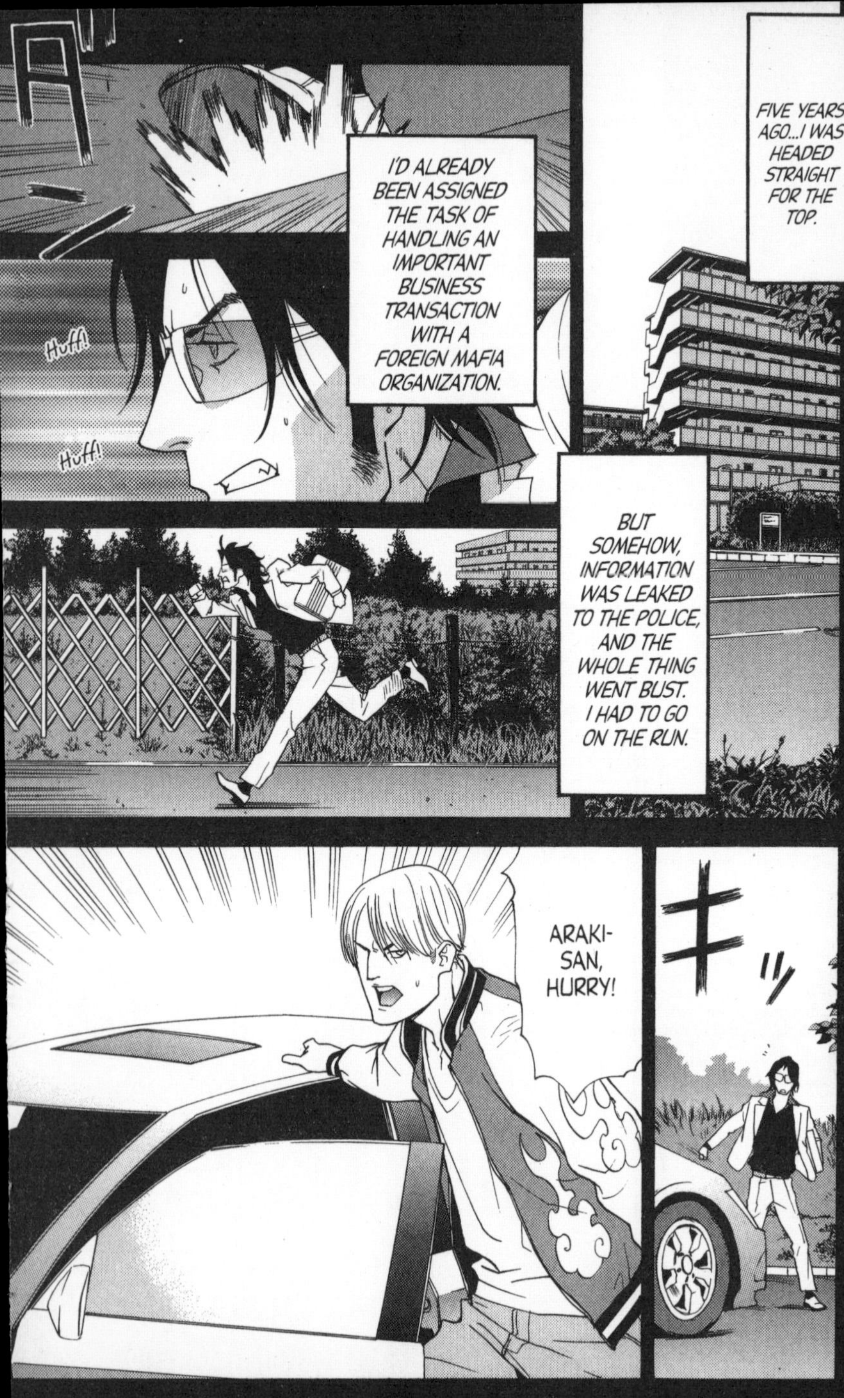
FIVE YEARS AGO...I WAS HEADED STRAIGHT FOR THE TOP.
I'D ALREADY BEEN ASSIGNED THE TASK OF HANDLING AN IMPORTANT BUSINESS TRANSACTION WITH A FOREIGN MAFIA ORGANIZATION.
Huff!
Huff!
BUT SOMEHOW, INFORMATION WAS LEAKED TO THE POLICE, AND THE WHOLE THING WENT BUST. I HAD TO GO ON THE RUN.
ARAKI-SAN, HURRY!

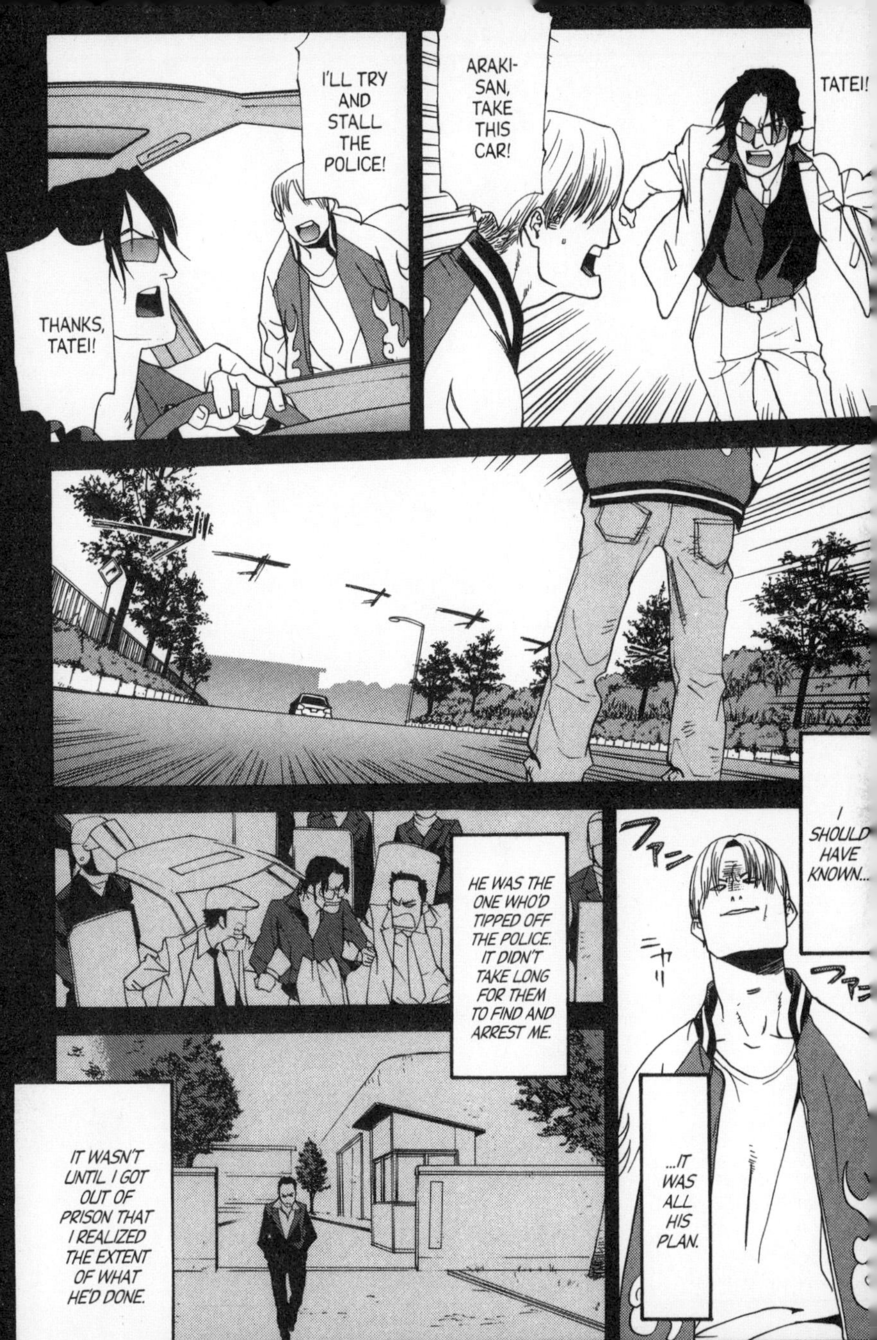
TATEI!
ARAKI-SAN, TAKE THIS CAR!
I'LL TRY AND STALL THE POLICE!
THANKS, TATEI!
I SHOULD HAVE KNOWN...
ファン
ファン
ニヤリ
...IT WAS ALL HIS PLAN.
HE WAS THE ONE WHO'D TIPPED OFF THE POLICE. IT DIDN'T TAKE LONG FOR THEM TO FIND AND ARREST ME.
IT WASN'T UNTIL I GOT OUT OF PRISON THAT I REALIZED THE EXTENT OF WHAT HE'D DONE.

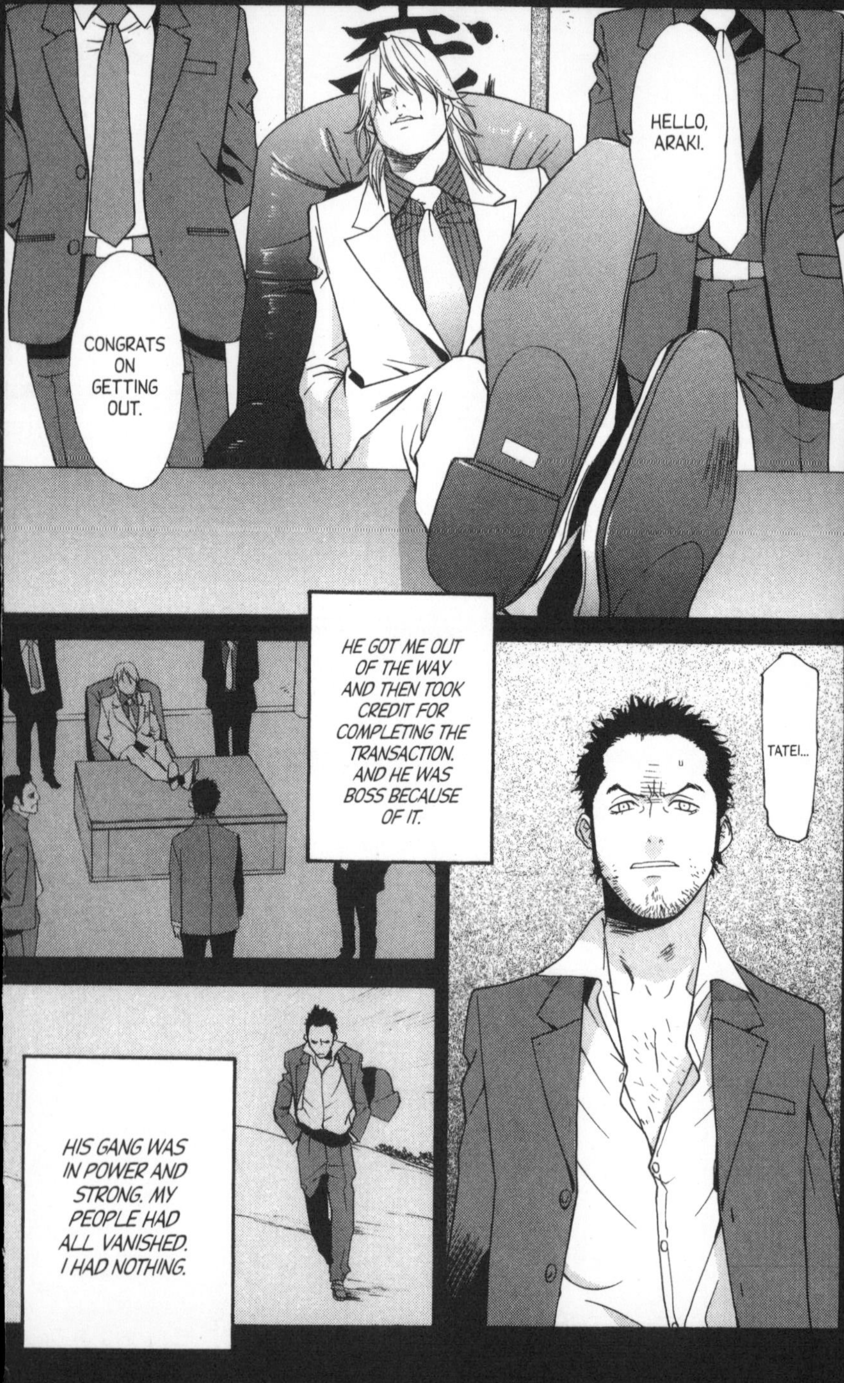
HELLO, ARAKI.
CONGRATS ON GETTING OUT.
TATEI...
HE GOT ME OUT OF THE WAY AND THEN TOOK CREDIT FOR COMPLETING THE TRANSACTION. AND HE WAS BOSS BECAUSE OF IT.
HIS GANG WAS IN POWER AND STRONG. MY PEOPLE HAD ALL VANISHED. I HAD NOTHING.

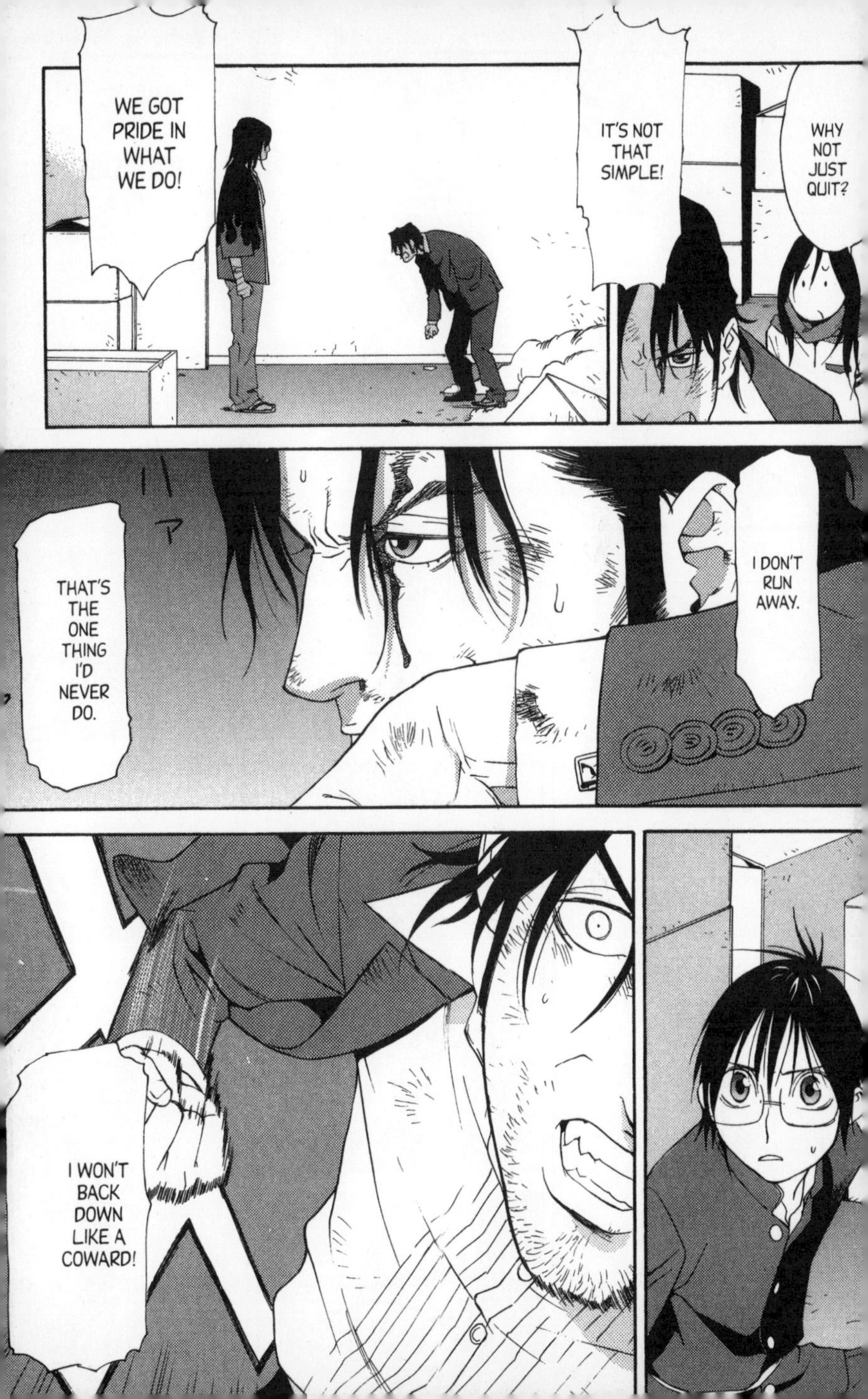
WHY NOT JUST QUIT?
IT'S NOT THAT SIMPLE!
WE GOT PRIDE IN WHAT WE DO!
I DON'T RUN AWAY.
THAT'S THE ONE THING I'D NEVER DO.
I WON'T BACK DOWN LIKE A COWARD!

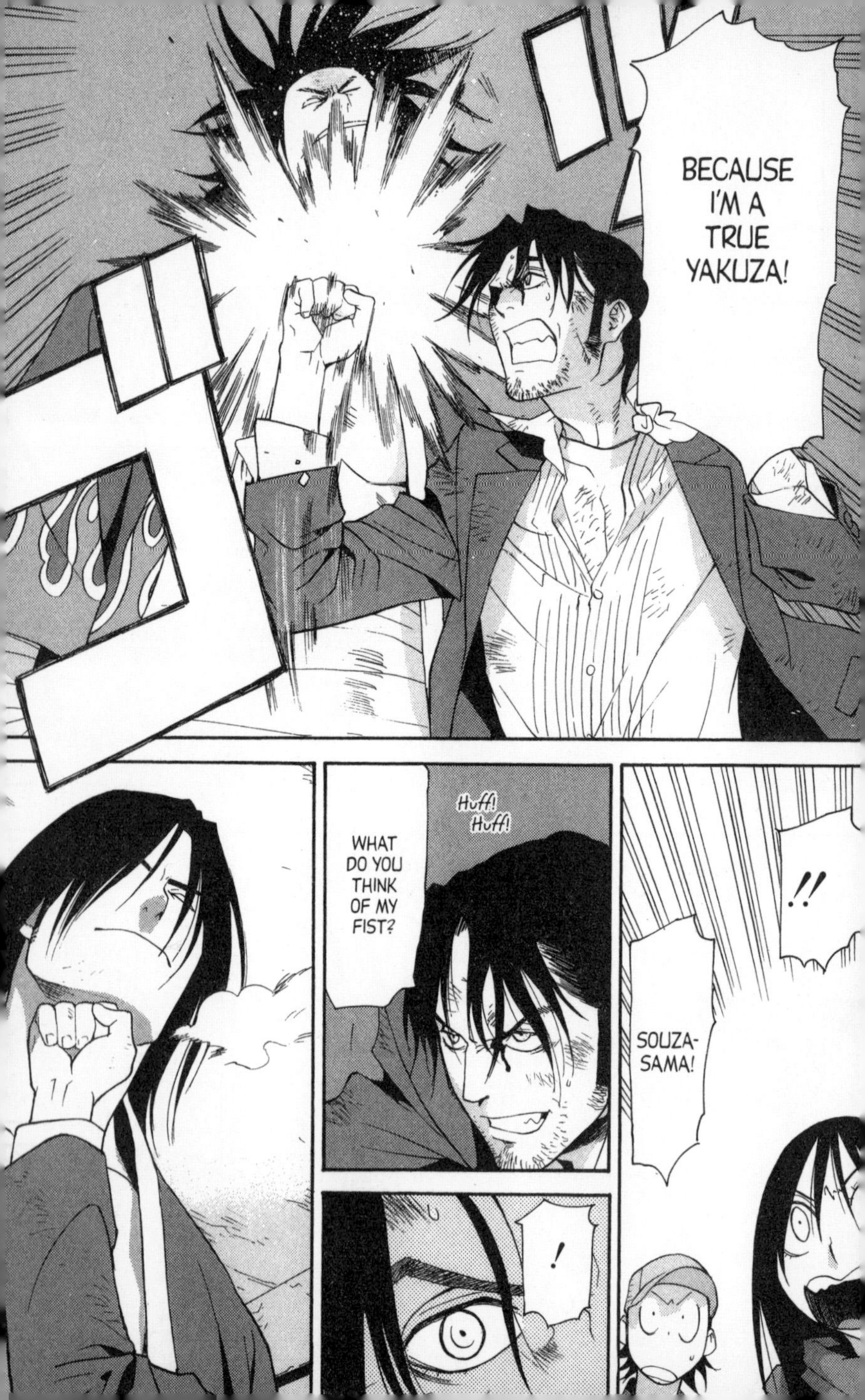
BECAUSE I'M A TRUE YAKUZA!
!!
SOUZA-SAMA!
Huff! Huff!
WHAT DO YOU THINK OF MY FIST?
!

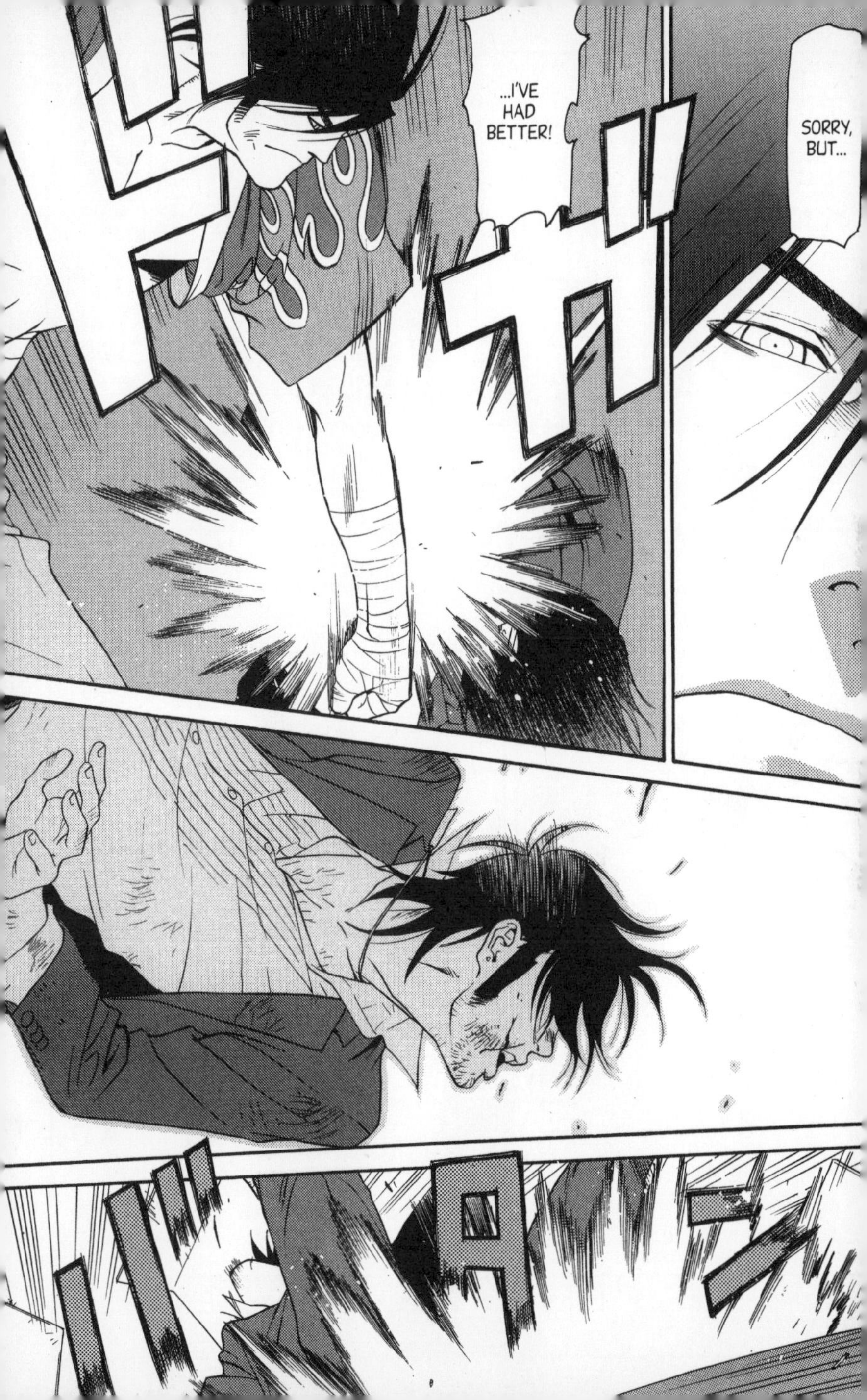
SORRY, BUT...
...I'VE HAD BETTER!

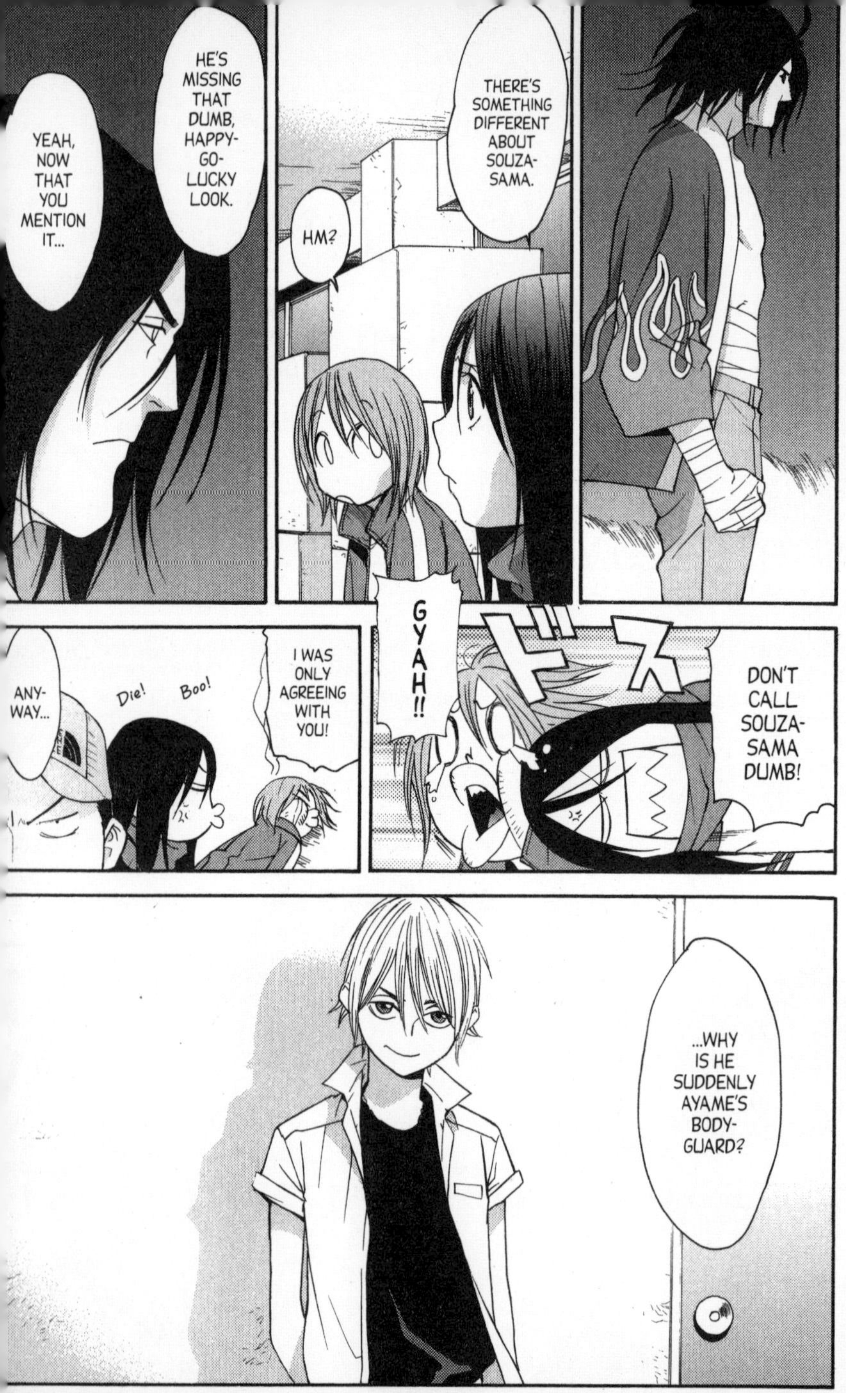
THERE'S SOMETHING DIFFERENT ABOUT SOUZA-SAMA.
HM?
HE'S MISSING THAT DUMB, HAPPY-GO-LUCKY LOOK.
YEAH, NOW THAT YOU MENTION IT...
ドス
DON'T CALL SOUZA-SAMA DUMB!
GYAH!!
I WAS ONLY AGREEING WITH YOU!
Boo!
Die!
ANY-WAY...
...WHY IS HE SUDDENLY AYAME'S BODY-GUARD?

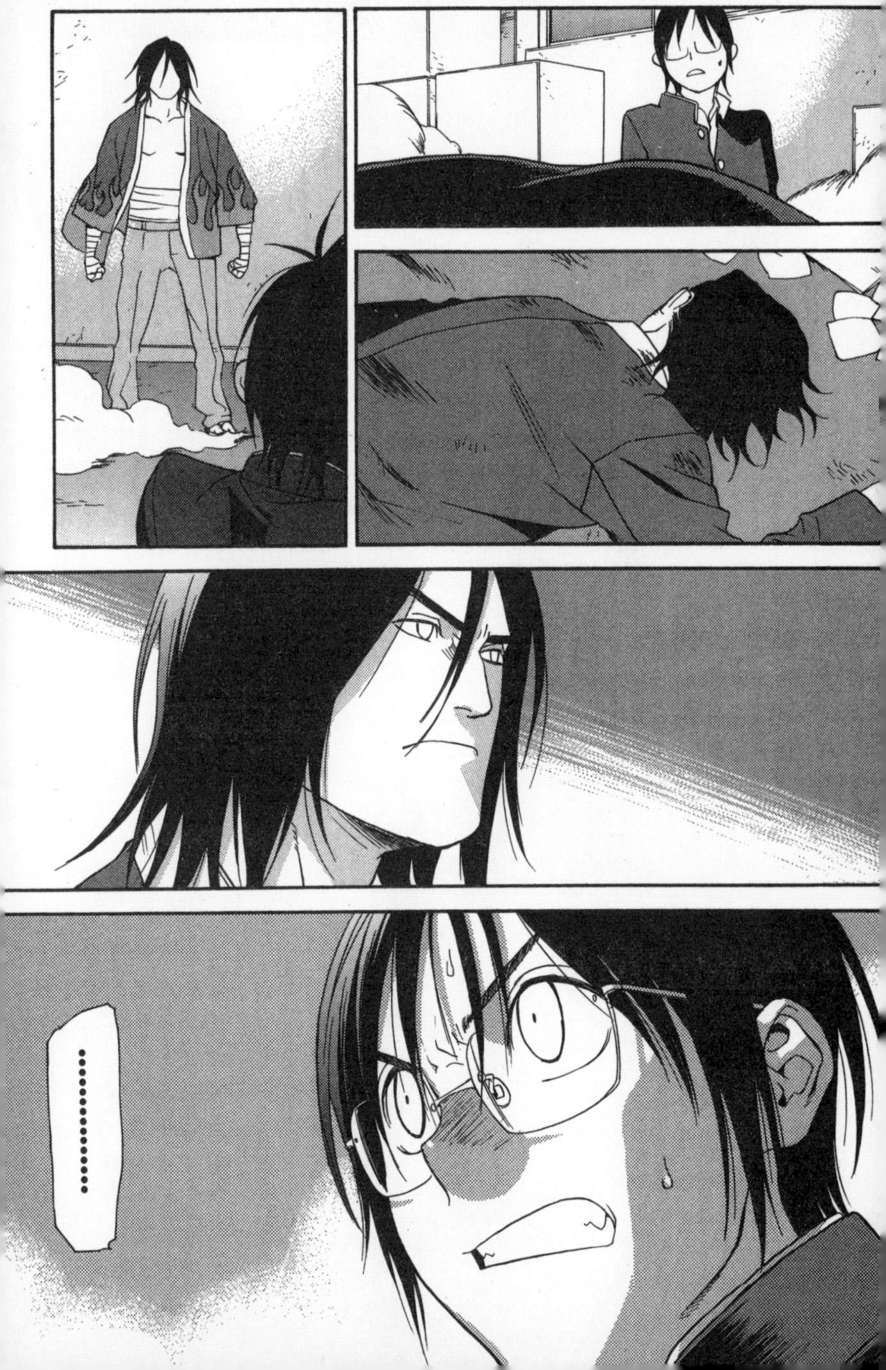
....

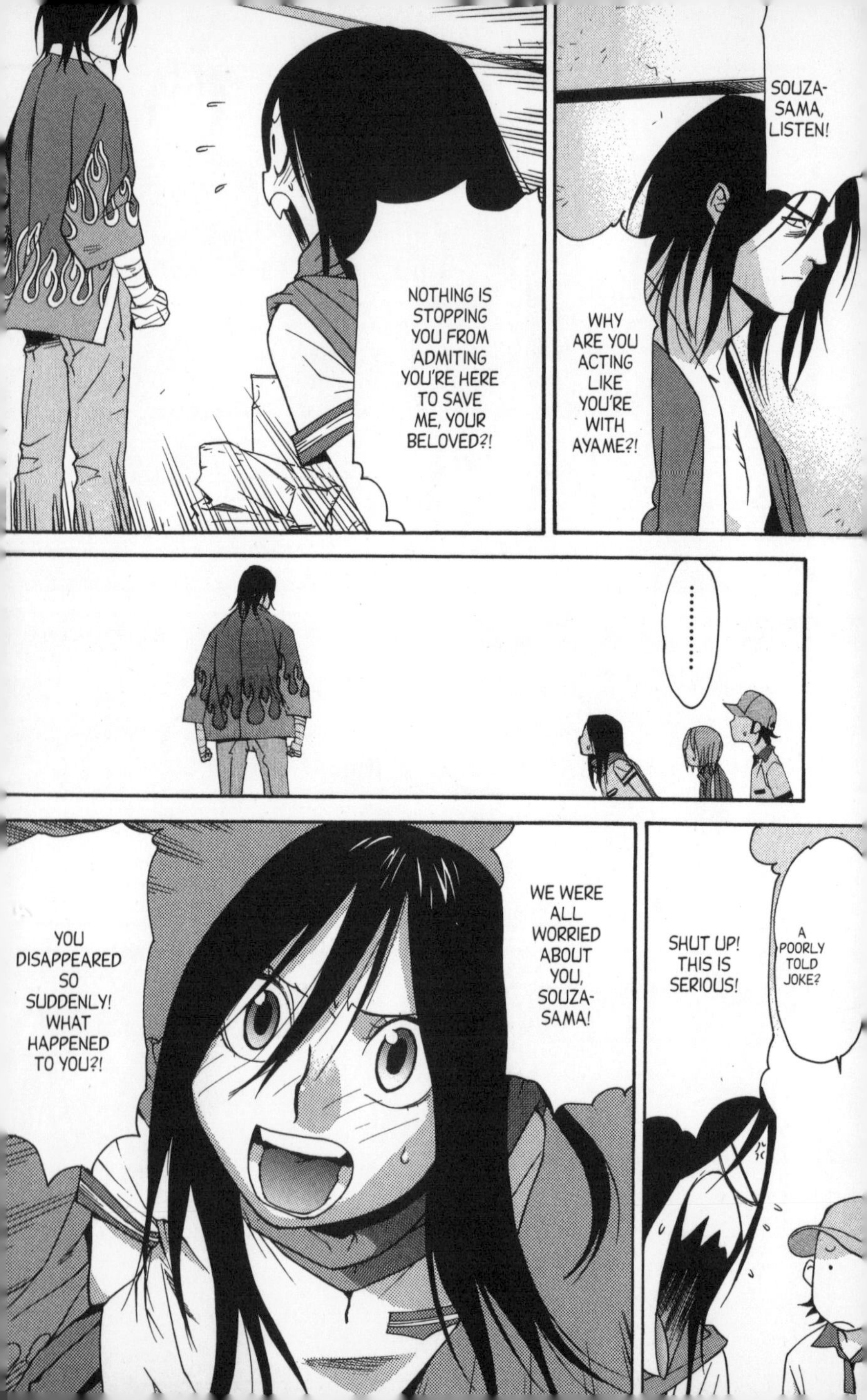
SOUZA-SAMA, LISTEN!
WHY ARE YOU ACTING LIKE YOU'RE WITH AYAME?!
NOTHING IS STOPPING YOU FROM ADMITING YOU'RE HERE TO SAVE ME, YOUR BELOVED?!
....
A POORLY TOLD JOKE?
SHUT UP! THIS IS SERIOUS!
WE WERE ALL WORRIED ABOUT YOU, SOUZA-SAMA!
YOU DISAPPEARED SO SUDDENLY! WHAT HAPPENED TO YOU?!

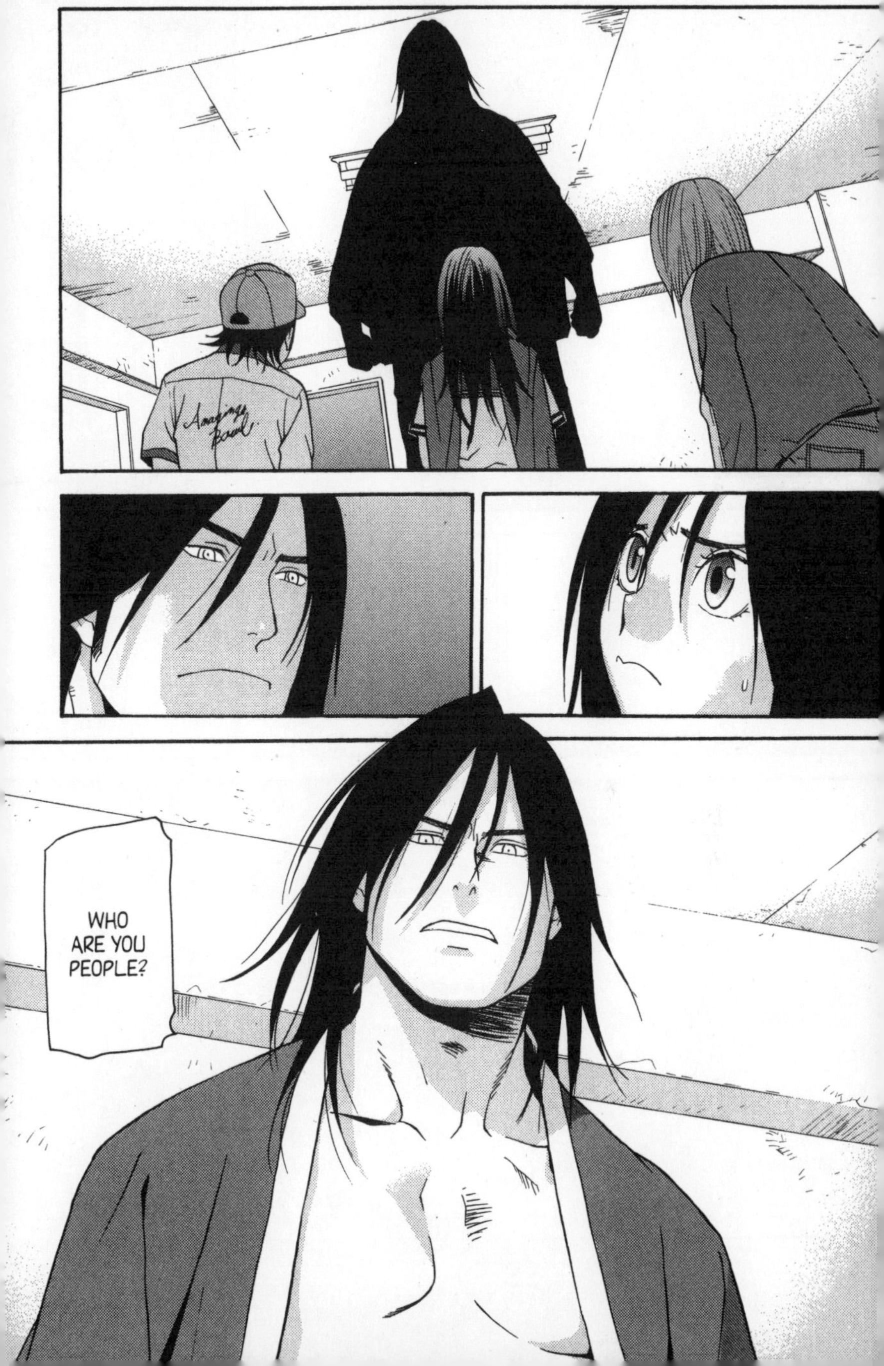
WHO ARE YOU PEOPLE?

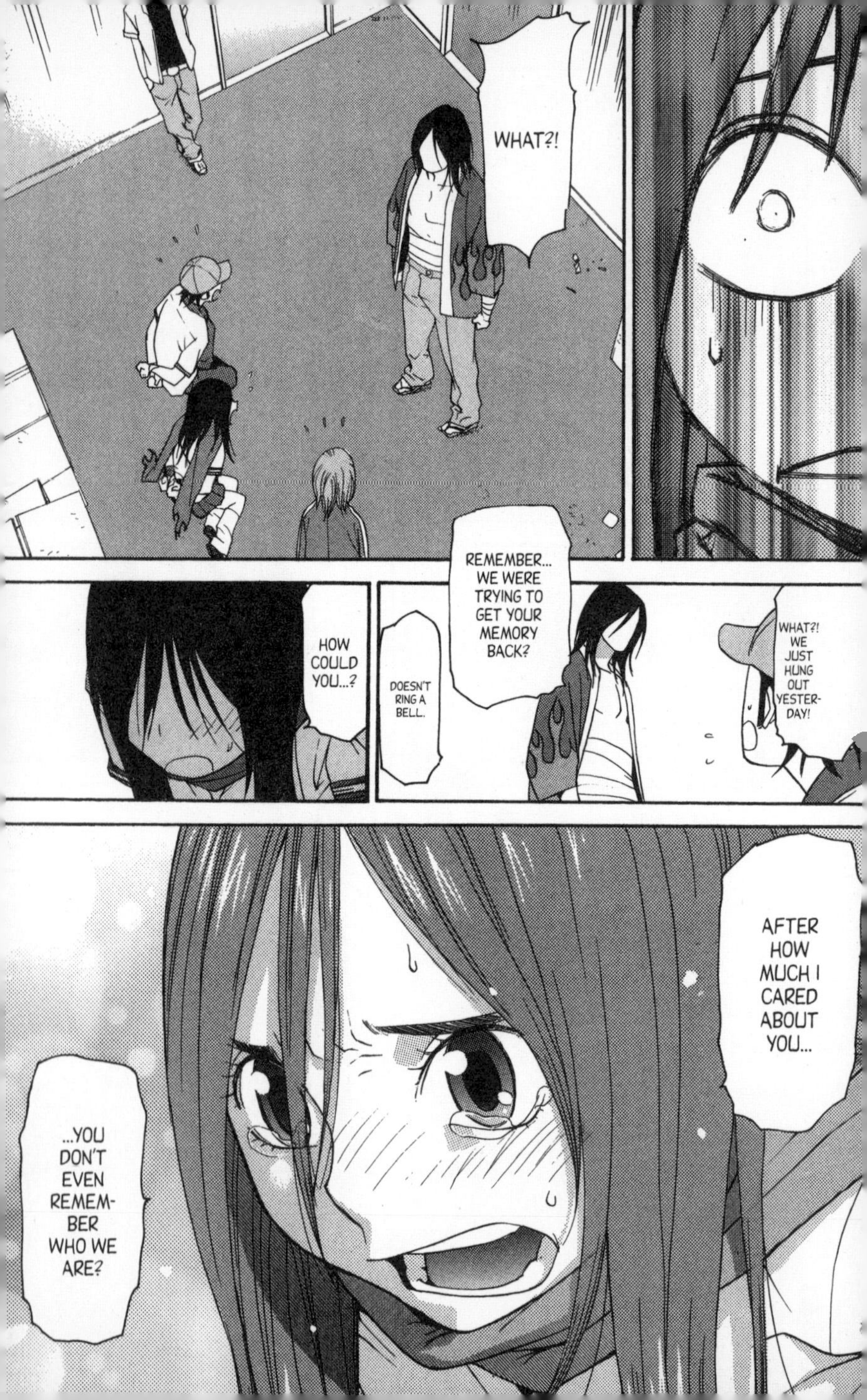
WHAT?!
WHAT?! WE JUST HUNG OUT YESTER-DAY!
REMEMBER... WE WERE TRYING TO GET YOUR MEMORY BACK?
DOESN'T RING A BELL.
HOW COULD YOU...?
AFTER HOW MUCH I CARED ABOUT YOU...
...YOU DON'T EVEN REMEM-BER WHO WE ARE?

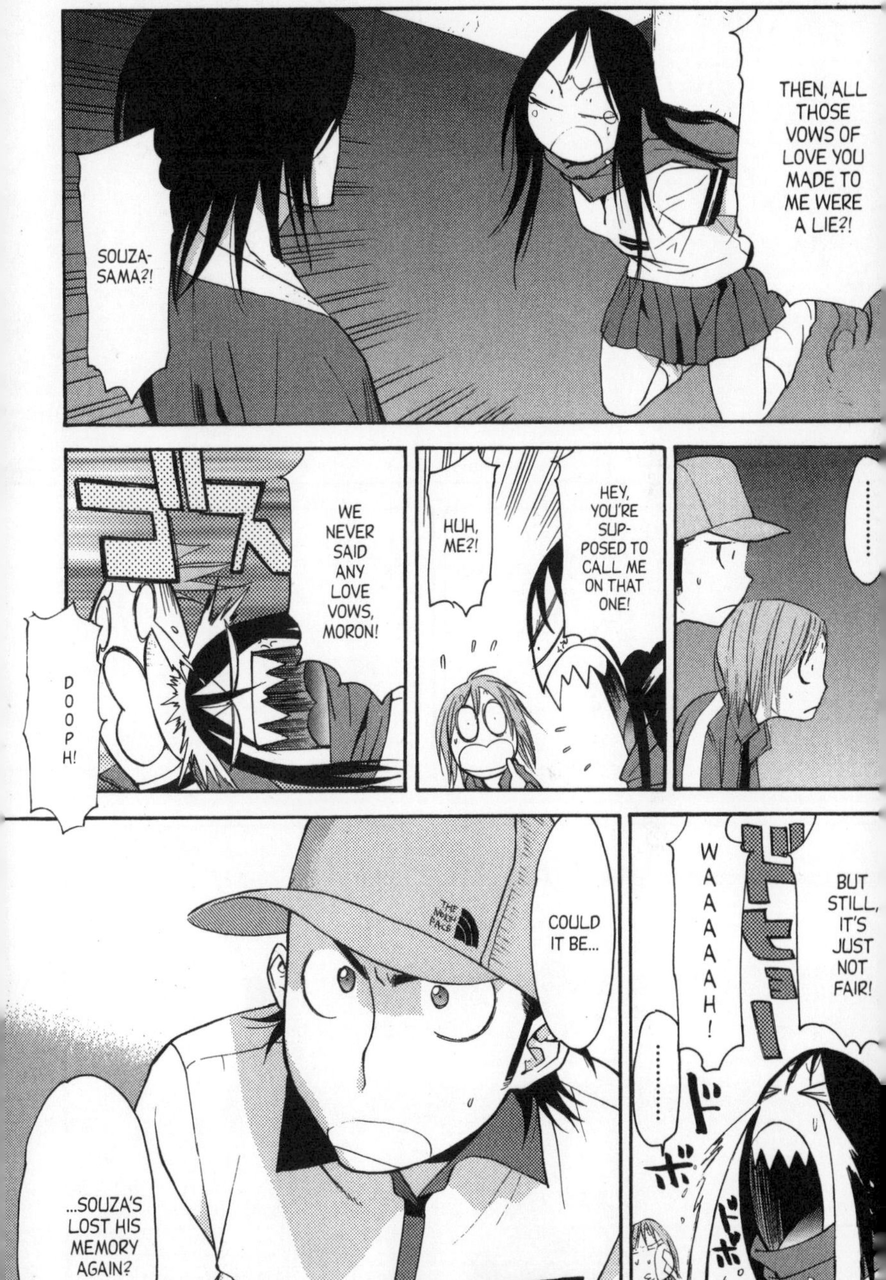
THEN, ALL THOSE VOWS OF LOVE YOU MADE TO ME WERE A LIE?!
SOUZA-SAMA?!
....
HEY, YOU'RE SUP-POSED TO CALL ME ON THAT ONE!
HUH, ME?!
WE NEVER SAID ANY LOVE VOWS, MORON!
DOOPH!
BUT STILL, IT'S JUST NOT FAIR!
WAAAAAH!
....
COULD IT BE...
...SOUZA'S LOST HIS MEMORY AGAIN?

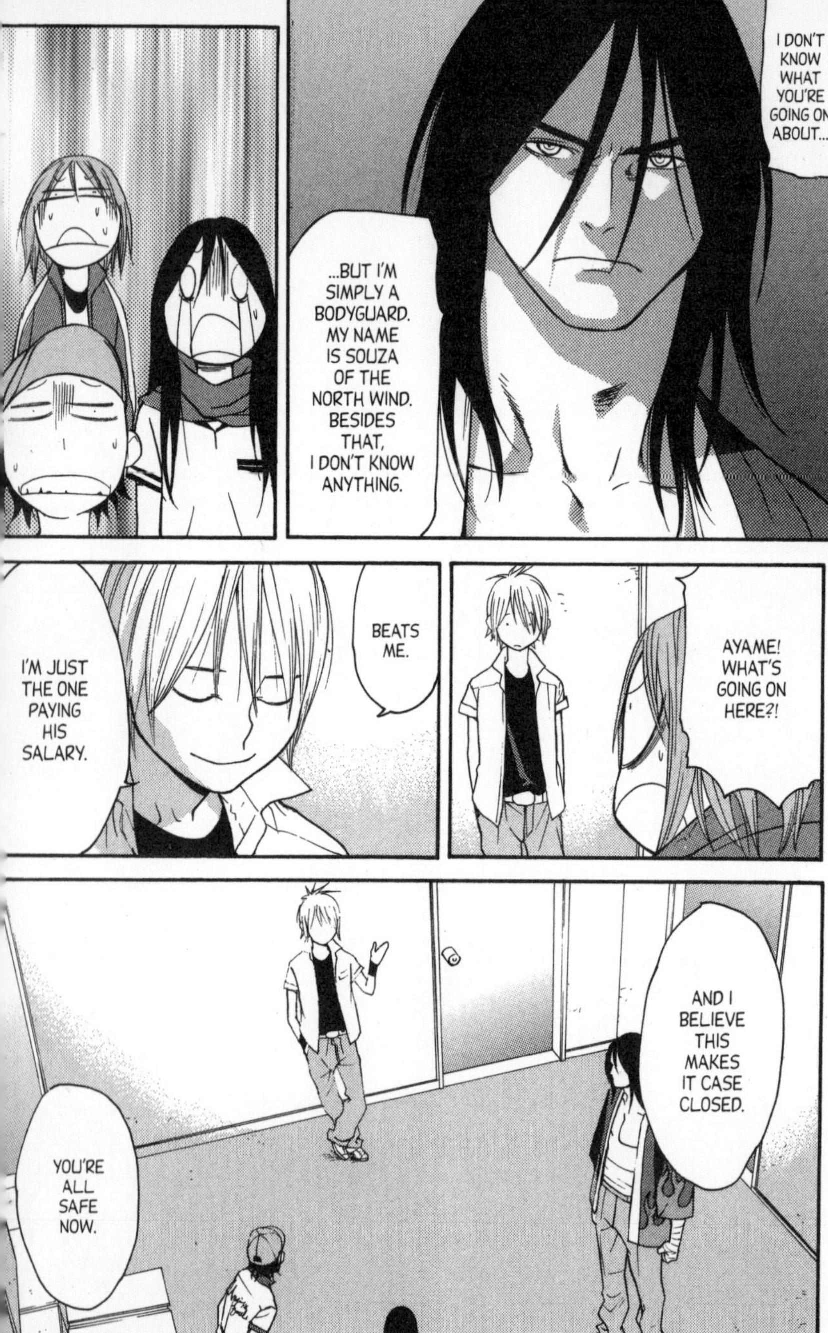
I DON'T KNOW WHAT YOU'RE GOING ON ABOUT...
...BUT I'M SIMPLY A BODYGUARD. MY NAME IS SOUZA OF THE NORTH WIND. BESIDES THAT, I DON'T KNOW ANYTHING.
AYAME! WHAT'S GOING ON HERE?!
BEATS ME.
I'M JUST THE ONE PAYING HIS SALARY.
AND I BELIEVE THIS MAKES IT CASE CLOSED.
YOU'RE ALL SAFE NOW.

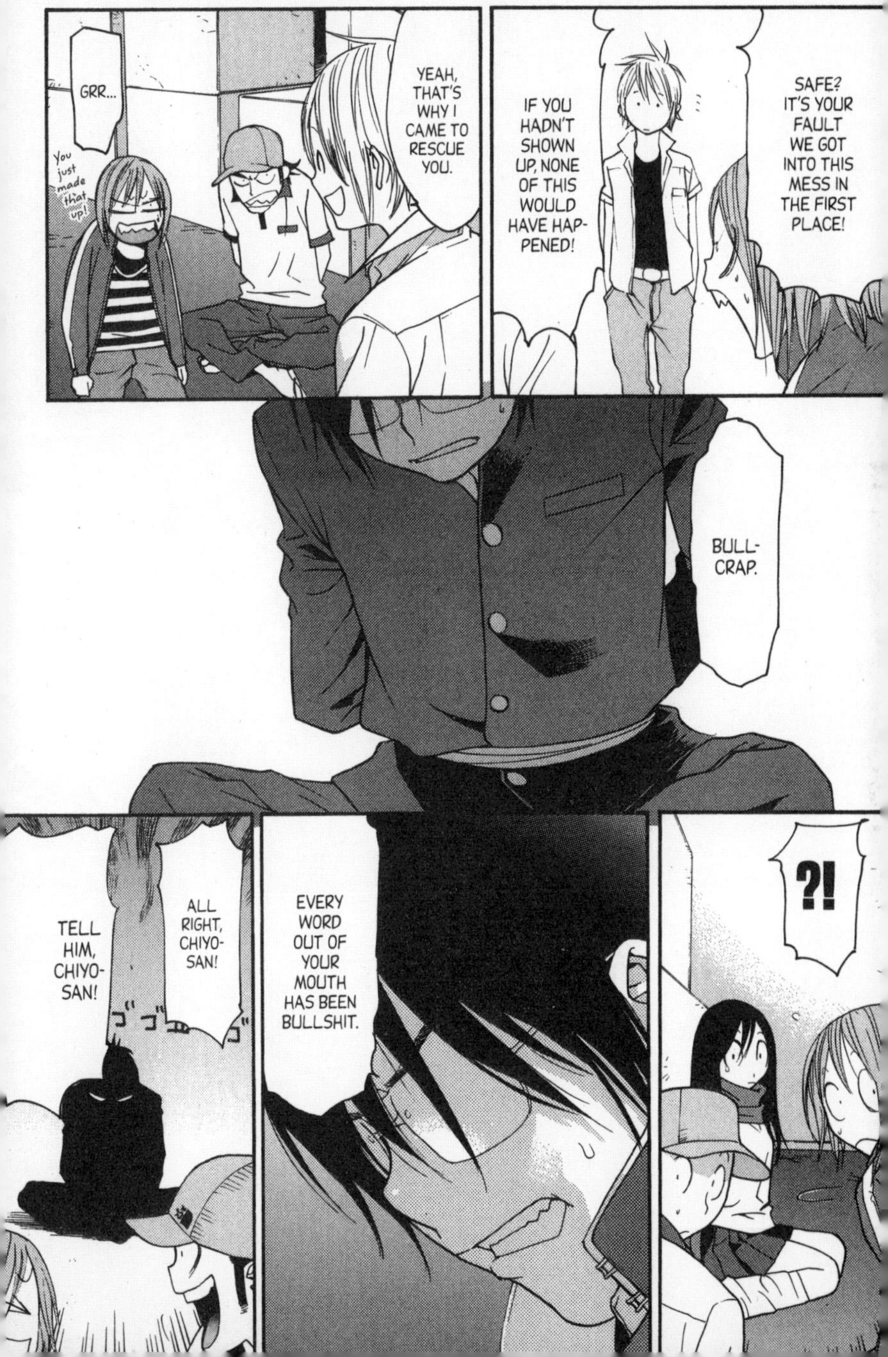
SAFE? IT'S YOUR FAULT WE GOT INTO THIS MESS IN THE FIRST PLACE!
IF YOU HADN'T SHOWN UP, NONE OF THIS WOULD HAVE HAP-PENED!
YEAH, THAT'S WHY I CAME TO RESCUE YOU.
GRR...
You just made that up!
BULL-CRAP.
?!
EVERY WORD OUT OF YOUR MOUTH HAS BEEN BULLSHIT.
ALL RIGHT, CHIYO-SAN!
TELL HIM, CHIYO-SAN!

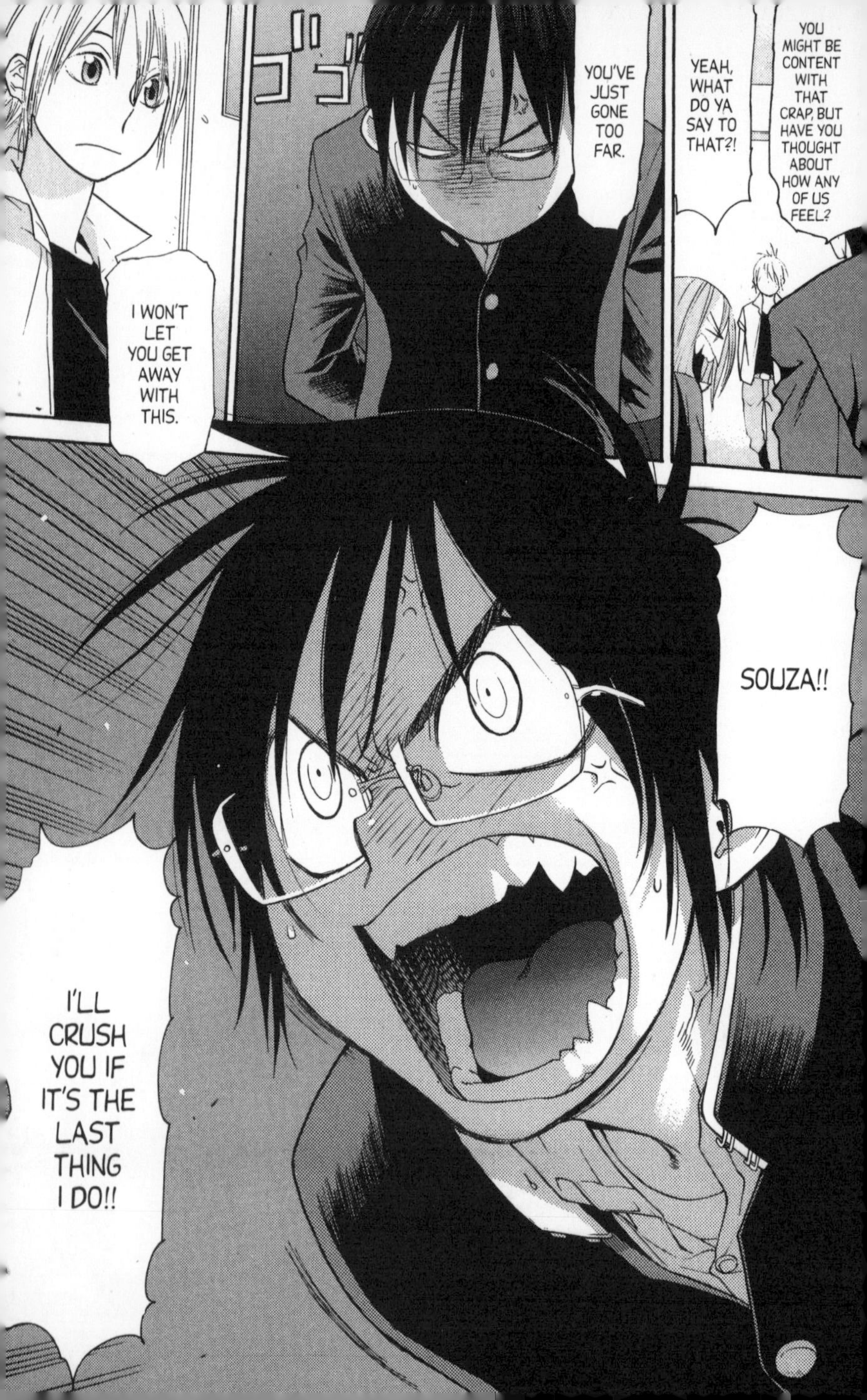
YOU MIGHT BE CONTENT WITH THAT CRAP, BUT HAVE YOU THOUGHT ABOUT HOW ANY OF US FEEL?
YEAH, WHAT DO YA SAY TO THAT?!
YOU'VE JUST GONE TOO FAR.
I WON'T LET YOU GET AWAY WITH THIS.
SOUZA!!
I'LL CRUSH YOU IF IT'S THE LAST THING I DO!!

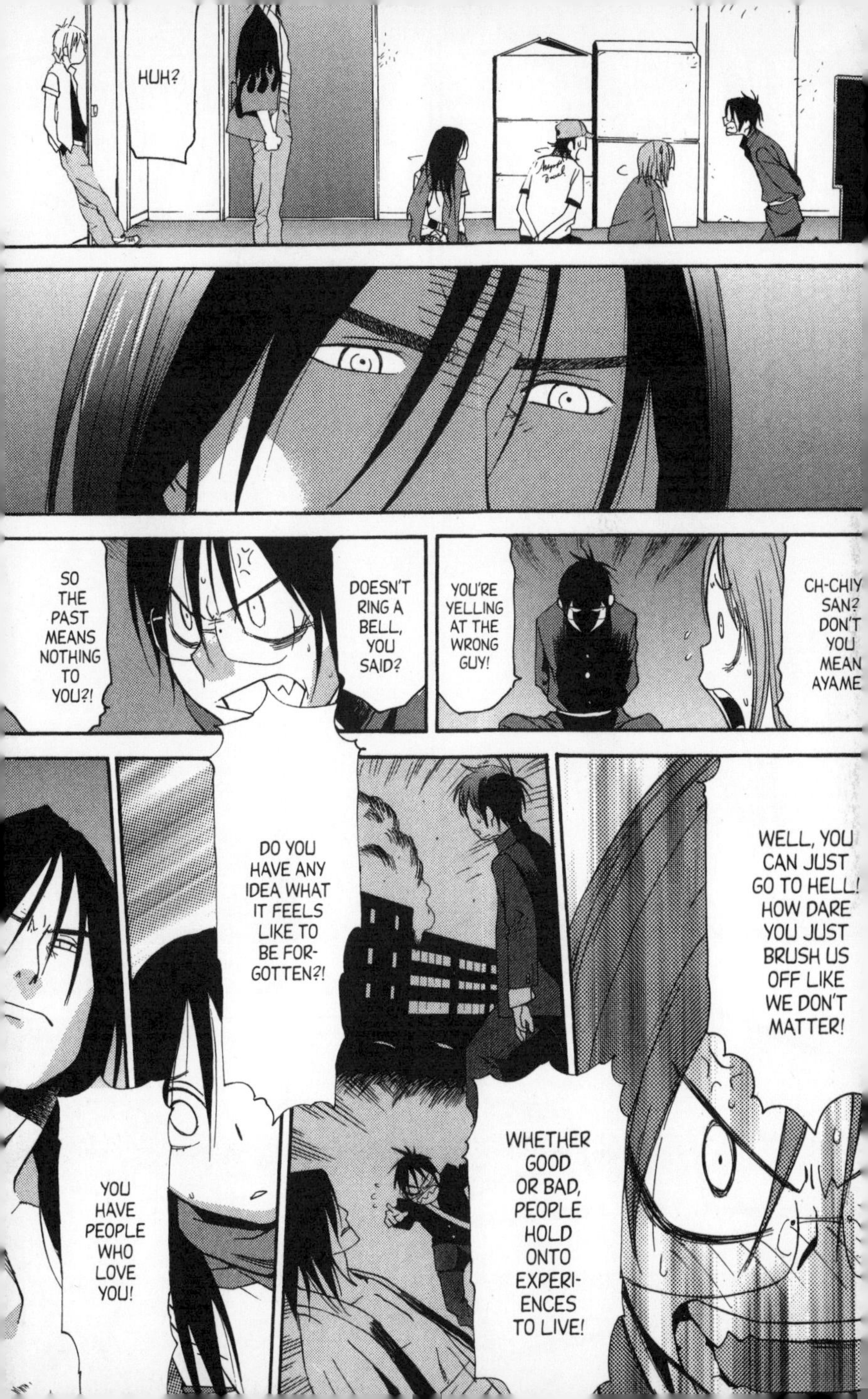
HUH?
CH-CHIY SAN? DON'T YOU MEAN AYAME
YOU'RE YELLING AT THE WRONG GUY!
DOESN'T RING A BELL, YOU SAID?
SO THE PAST MEANS NOTHING TO YOU?!
WELL, YOU CAN JUST GO TO HELL! HOW DARE YOU JUST BRUSH US OFF LIKE WE DON'T MATTER!
WHETHER GOOD OR BAD, PEOPLE HOLD ONTO EXPERI-ENCES TO LIVE!
DO YOU HAVE ANY IDEA WHAT IT FEELS LIKE TO BE FOR-GOTTEN?!
YOU HAVE PEOPLE WHO LOVE YOU!

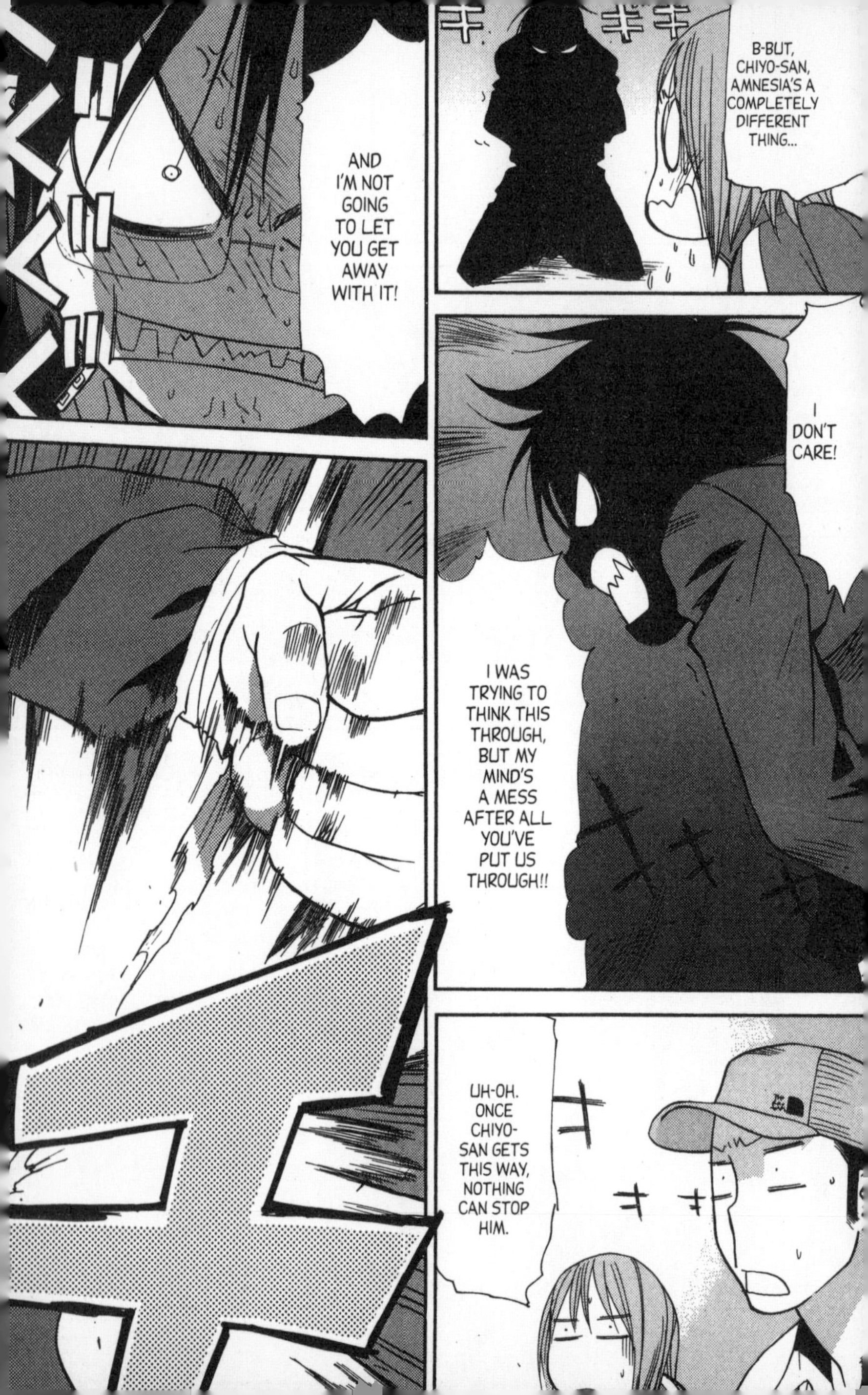
B-BUT, CHIYO-SAN, AMNESIA'S A COMPLETELY DIFFERENT THING...
I DON'T CARE!
I WAS TRYING TO THINK THIS THROUGH, BUT MY MIND'S A MESS AFTER ALL YOU'VE PUT US THROUGH!!
AND I'M NOT GOING TO LET YOU GET AWAY WITH IT!
UH-OH. ONCE CHIYO-SAN GETS THIS WAY, NOTHING CAN STOP HIM.

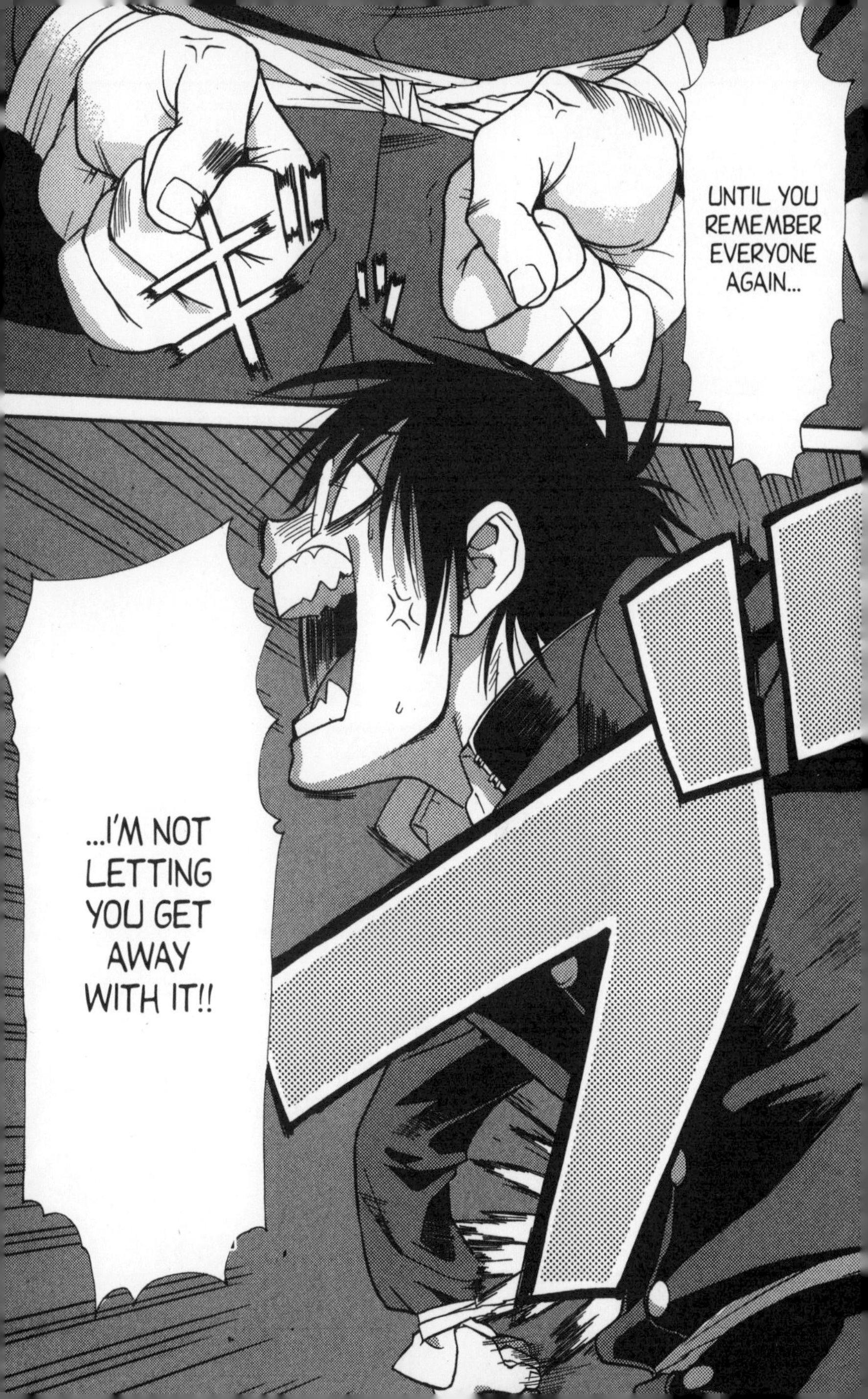
UNTIL YOU REMEMBER EVERYONE AGAIN...
...I'M NOT LETTING YOU GET AWAY WITH IT!!

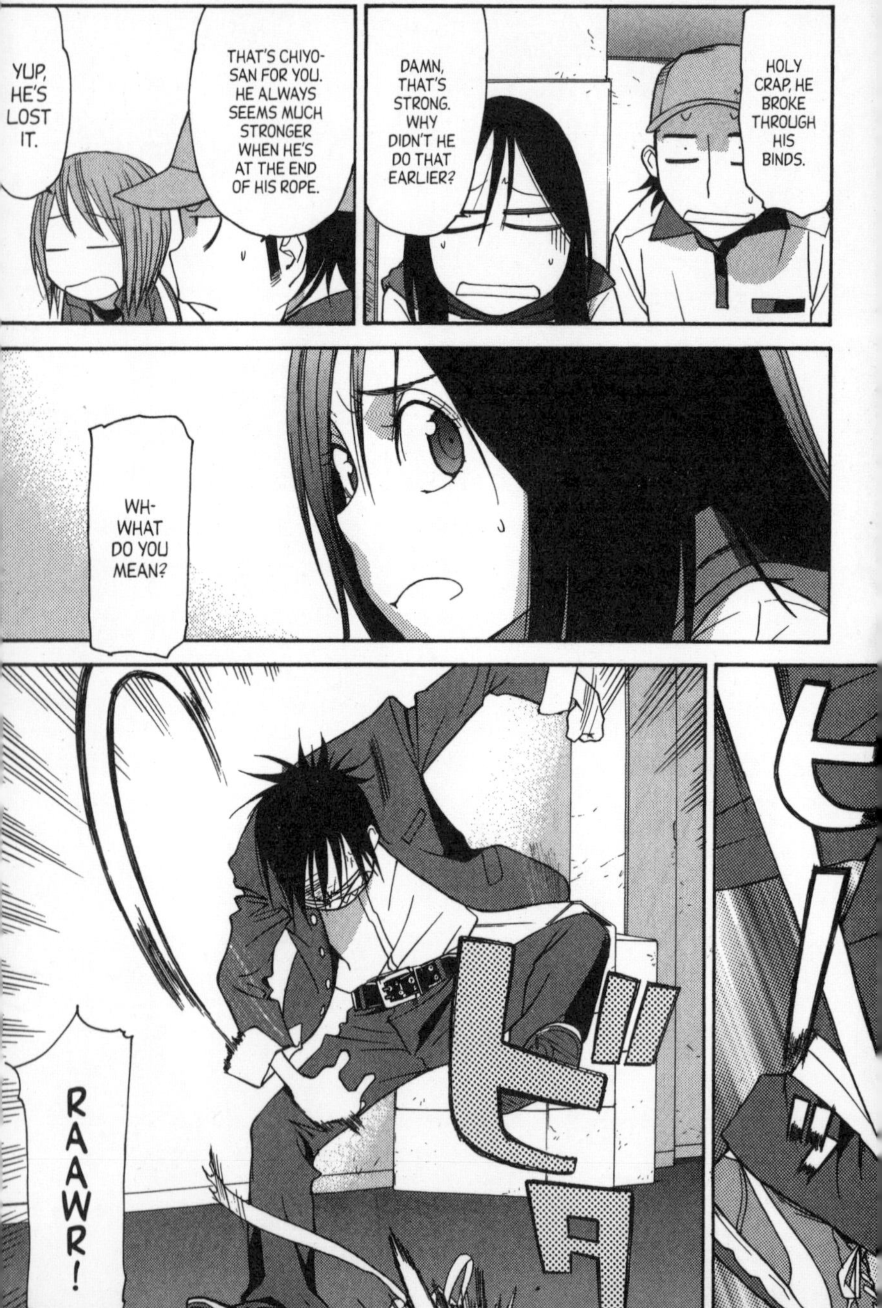
HOLY CRAP, HE BROKE THROUGH HIS BINDS.
DAMN, THAT'S STRONG. WHY DIDN'T HE DO THAT EARLIER?
THAT'S CHIYO-SAN FOR YOU. HE ALWAYS SEEMS MUCH STRONGER WHEN HE'S AT THE END OF HIS ROPE.
YUP, HE'S LOST IT.
WH-WHAT DO YOU MEAN?
RAAAWR!

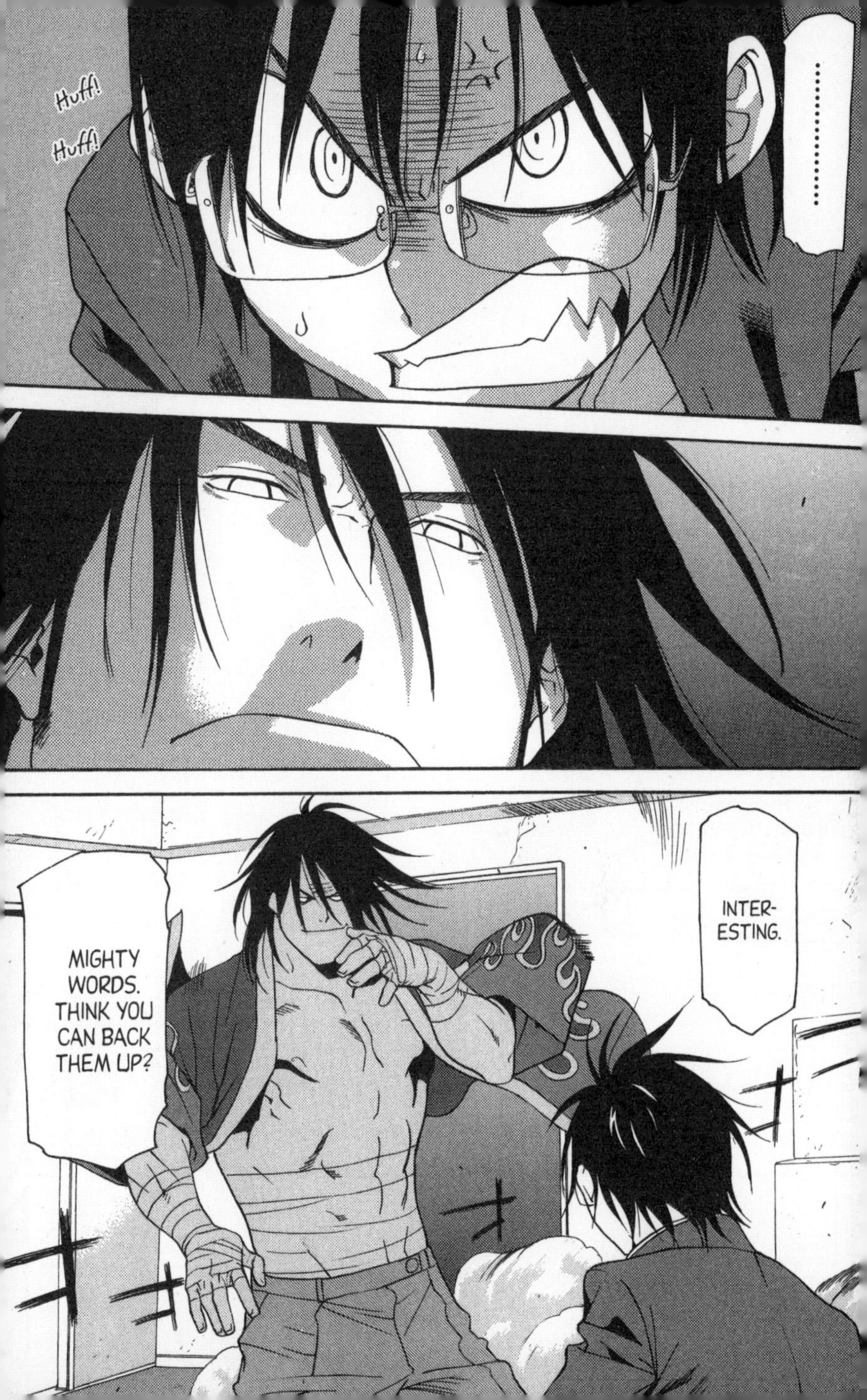

......
Huff!
Huff!
INTER-ESTING.
MIGHTY WORDS. THINK YOU CAN BACK THEM UP?

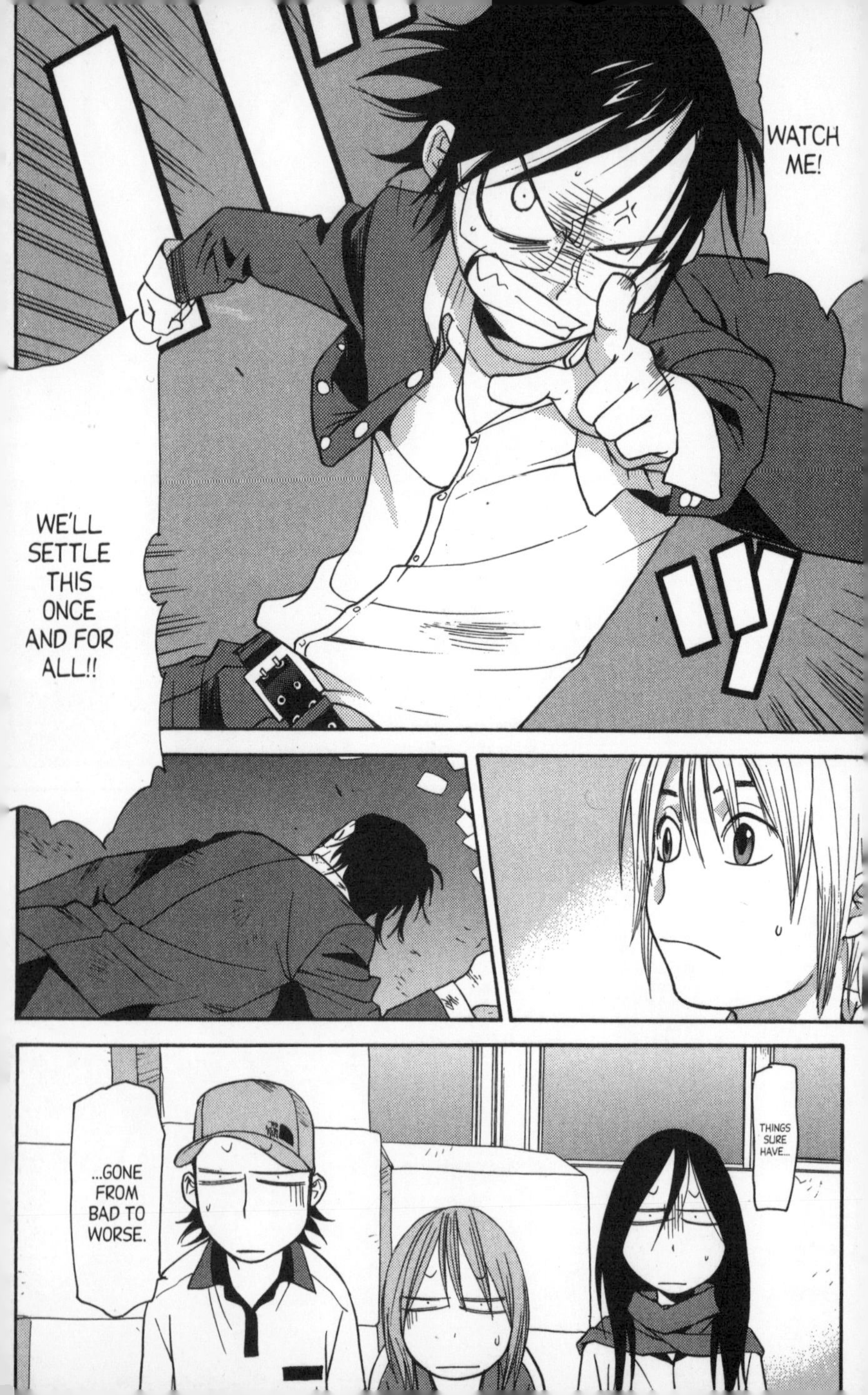
WATCH ME!
WE'LL SETTLE THIS ONCE AND FOR ALL!!
THINGS SURE HAVE...
...GONE FROM BAD TO WORSE.

Bonus Manga (4) Training the Mind Souza's UL (Useless) Training

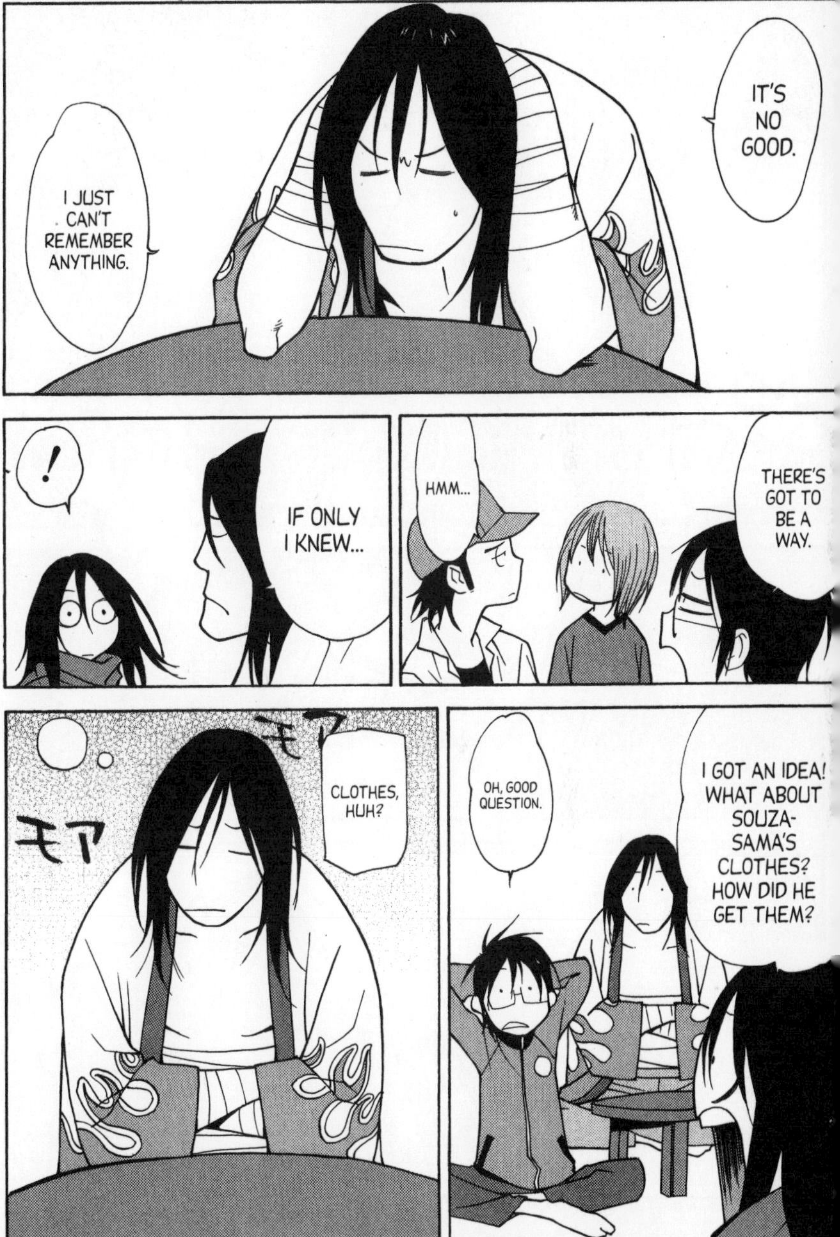
IT'S NO GOOD.
I JUST CAN'T REMEMBER ANYTHING.
THERE'S GOT TO BE A WAY.
HMM...
IF ONLY I KNEW...
!
I GOT AN IDEA! WHAT ABOUT SOUZA-SAMA'S CLOTHES? HOW DID HE GET THEM?
OH, GOOD QUESTION.
モア
CLOTHES, HUH?
モア

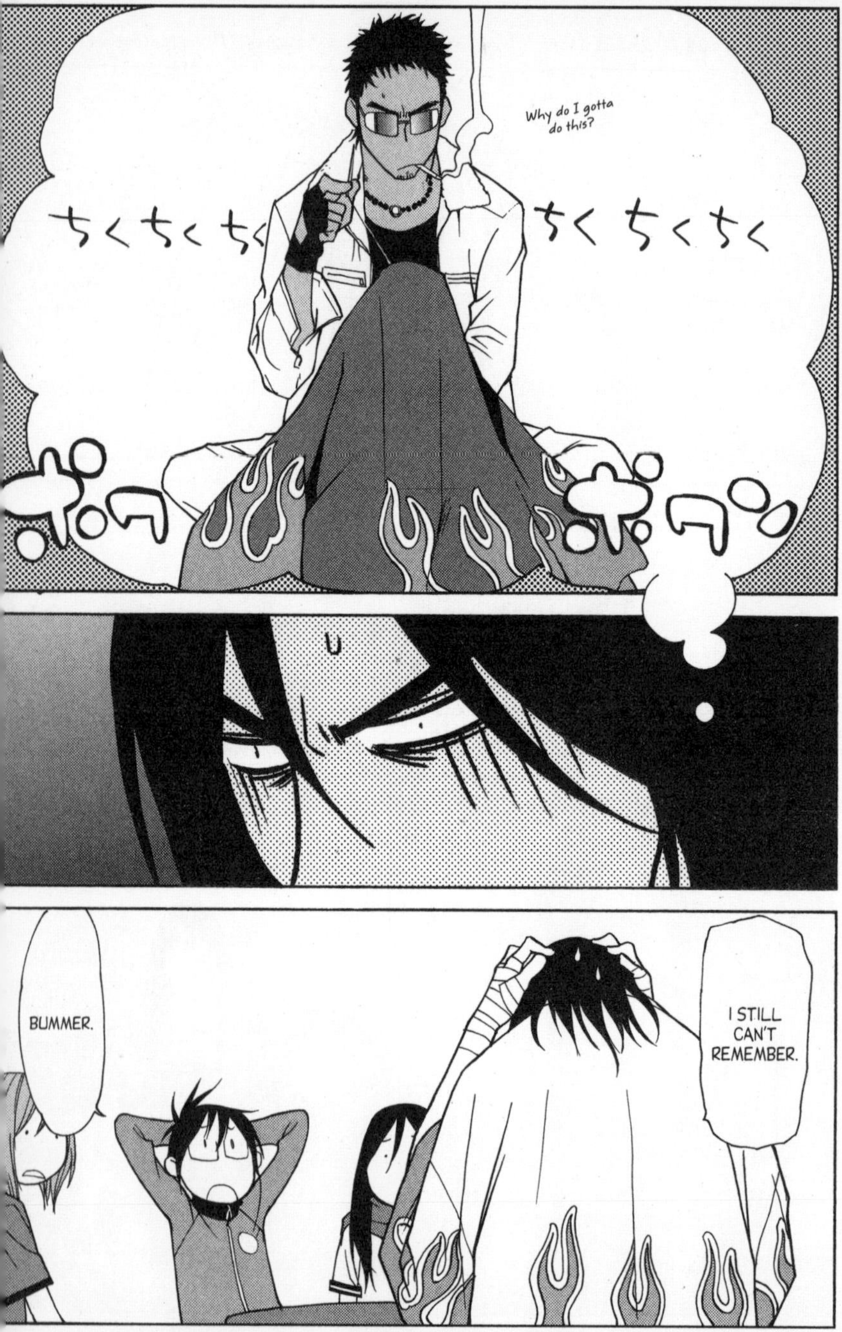
Why do I gotta do this?
ちくちくちく
ちくちくちく
I STILL CAN'T REMEMBER.
BUMMER.

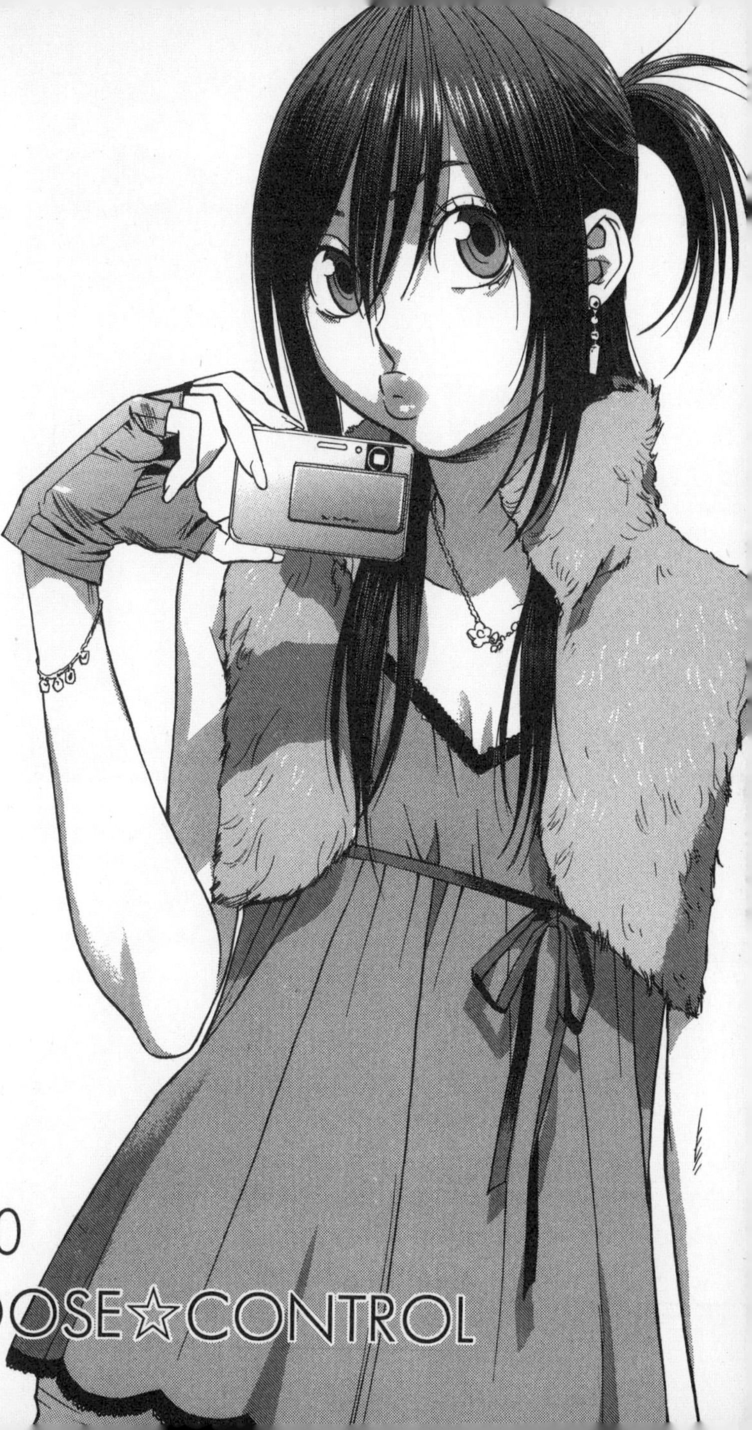

#10
LOOSE☆CONTROL

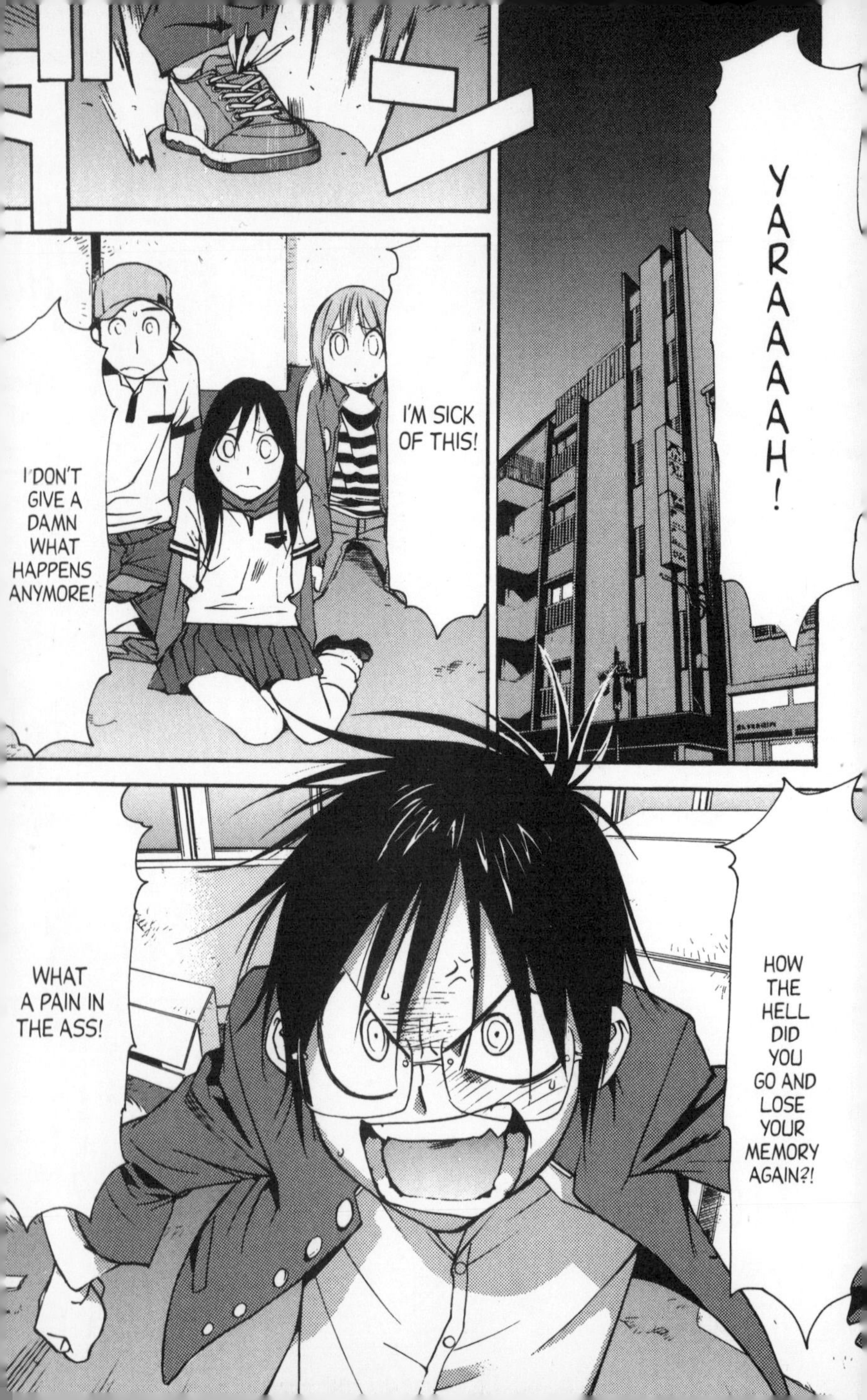
YARAAAAAH!
I'M SICK OF THIS!
I DON'T GIVE A DAMN WHAT HAPPENS ANYMORE!
HOW THE HELL DID YOU GO AND LOSE YOUR MEMORY AGAIN?!
WHAT A PAIN IN THE ASS!

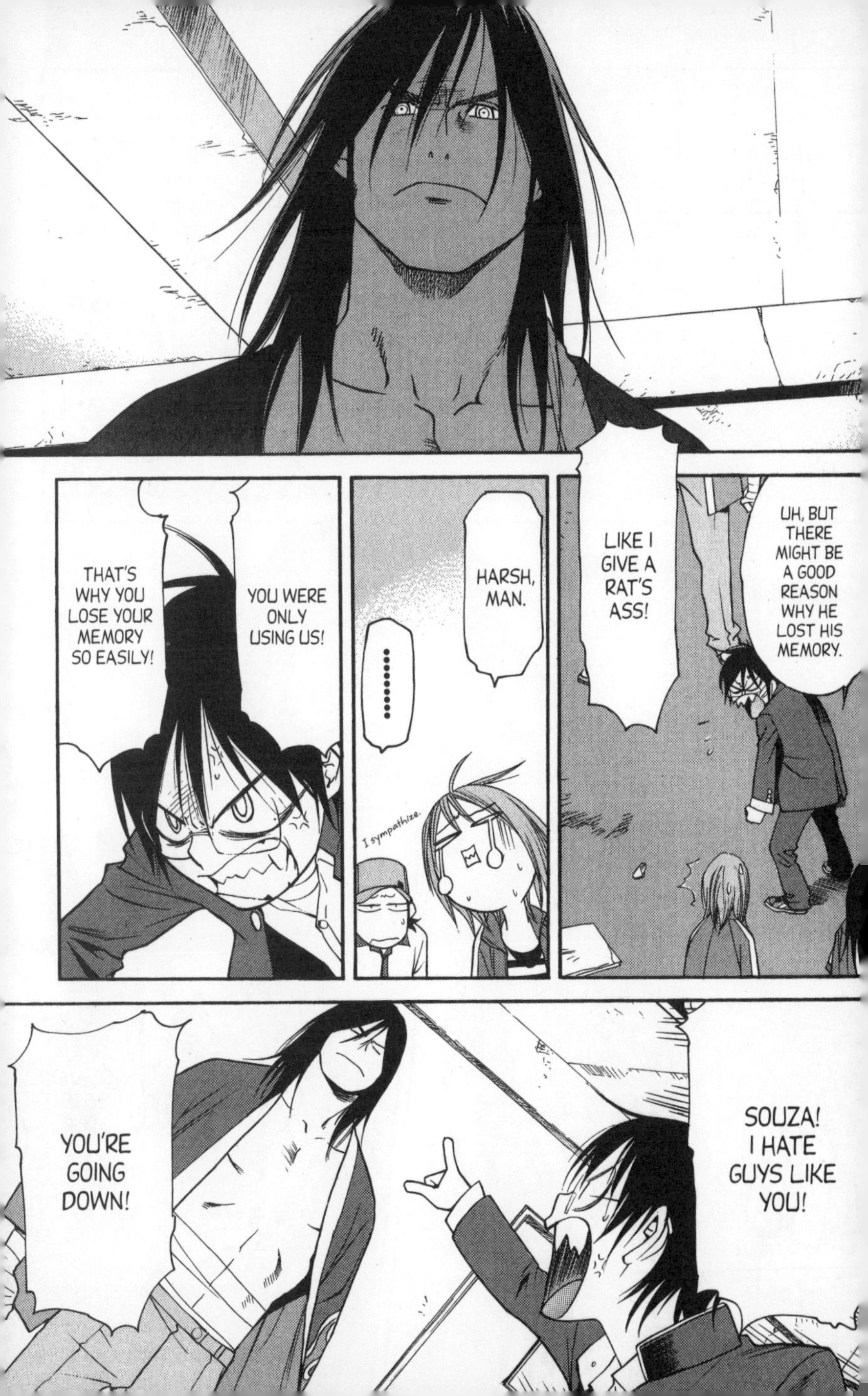
UH, BUT THERE MIGHT BE A GOOD REASON WHY HE LOST HIS MEMORY.
LIKE I GIVE A RAT'S ASS!
HARSH, MAN.
....
I sympathize.
YOU WERE ONLY USING US!
THAT'S WHY YOU LOSE YOUR MEMORY SO EASILY!
SOUZA! I HATE GUYS LIKE YOU!
YOU'RE GOING DOWN!

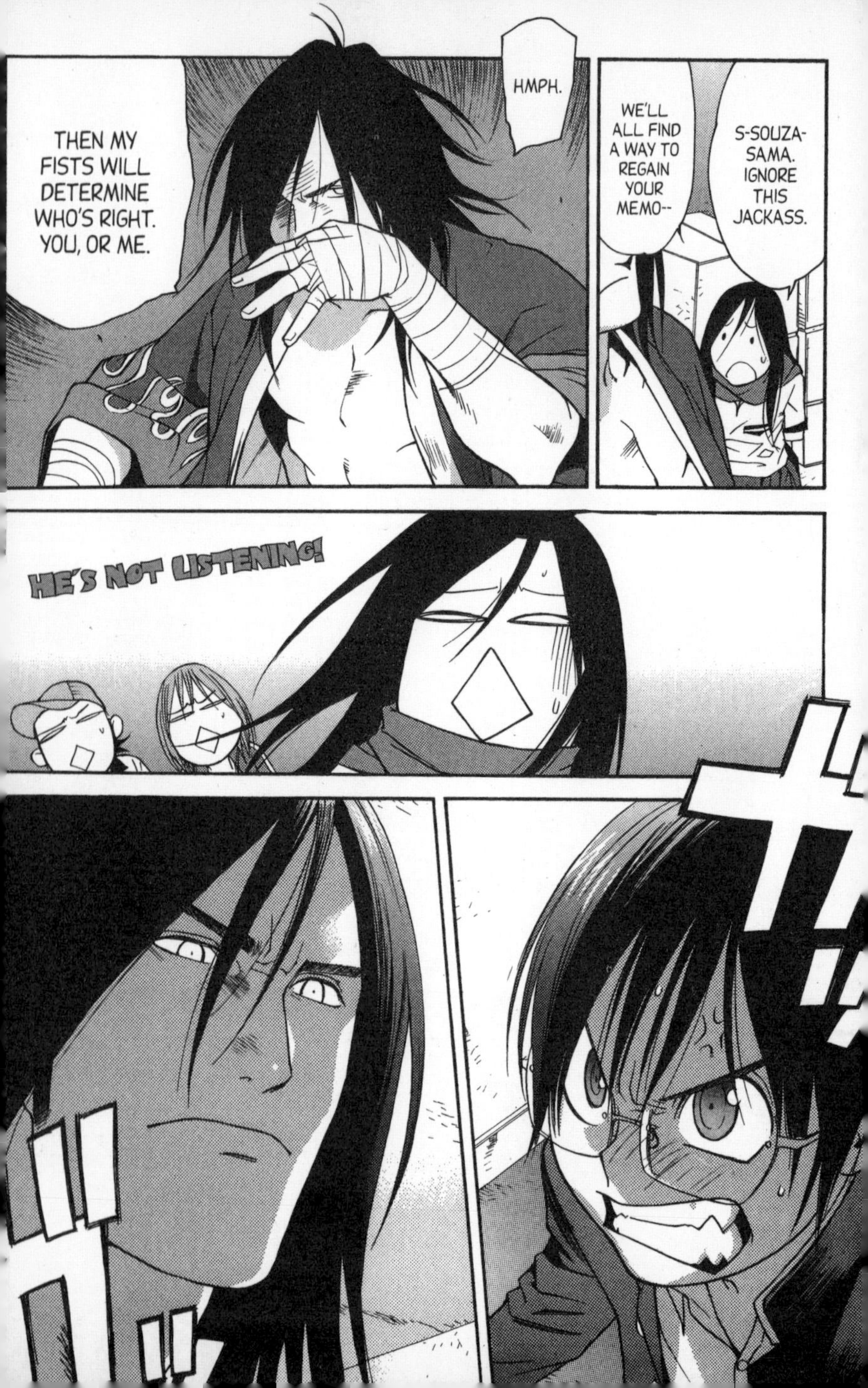
S-SOUZA-SAMA. IGNORE THIS JACKASS.
WE'LL ALL FIND A WAY TO REGAIN YOUR MEMO--
HMPH.
THEN MY FISTS WILL DETERMINE WHO'S RIGHT. YOU, OR ME.
HE'S NOT LISTENING!

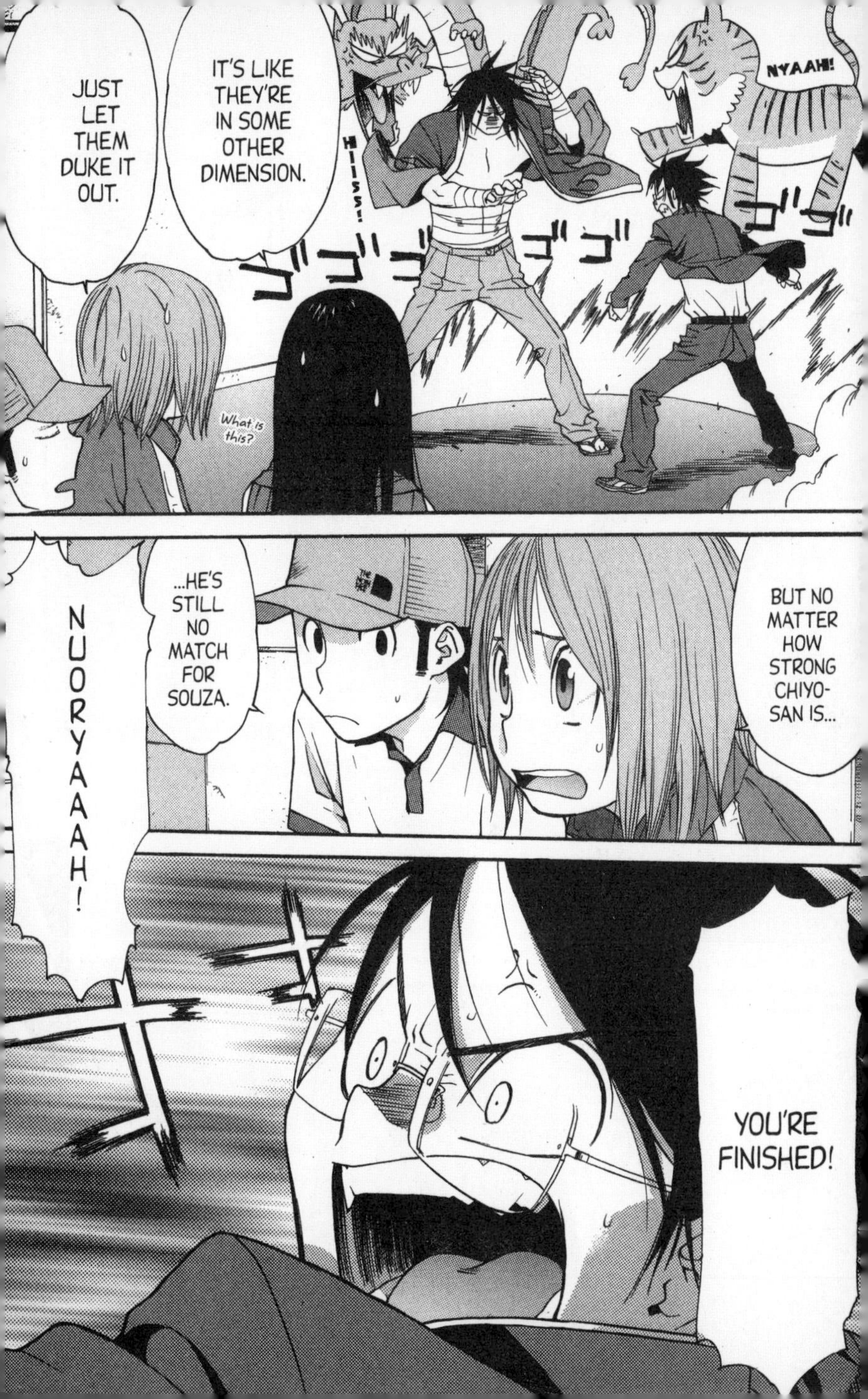
NYAAH!
HIISS!
IT'S LIKE THEY'RE IN SOME OTHER DIMENSION.
JUST LET THEM DUKE IT OUT.
What is this?
BUT NO MATTER HOW STRONG CHIYO-SAN IS...
...HE'S STILL NO MATCH FOR SOUZA.
NUORYAAAAH!
YOU'RE FINISHED!

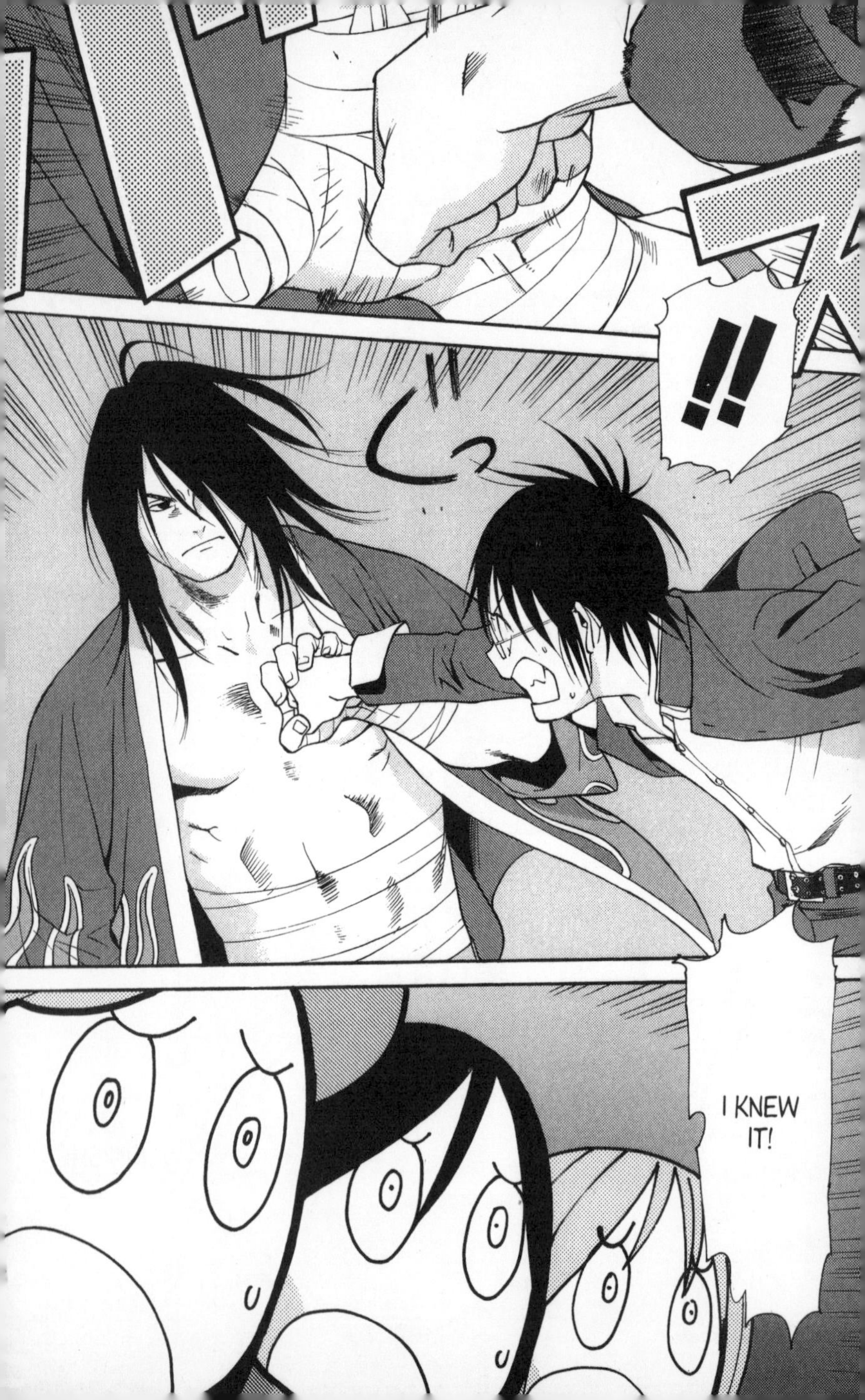
!!
I KNEW IT!

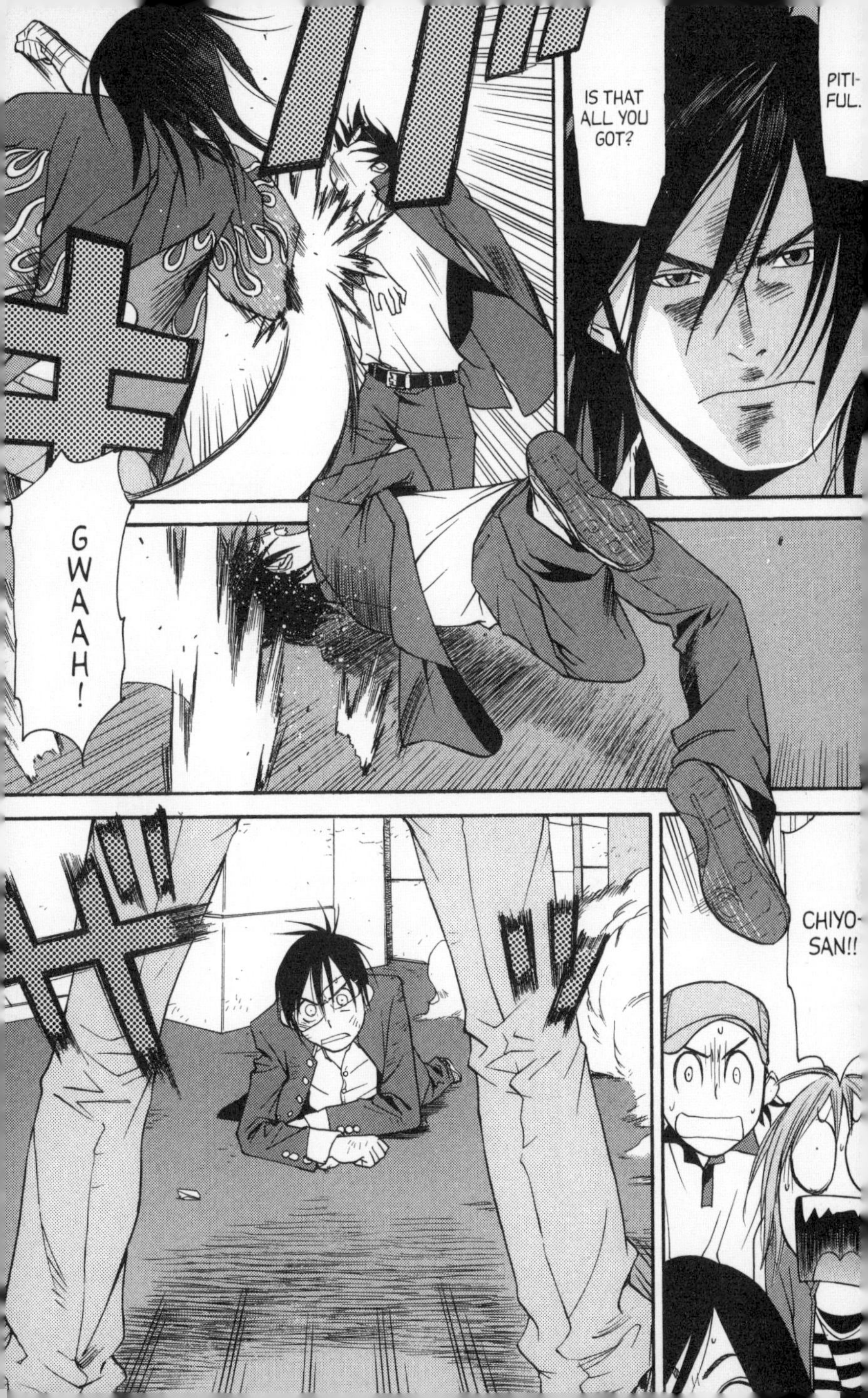
PITI-
FUL.
IS THAT ALL YOU GOT?
GWAAAH!
CHIYO-
SAN!!

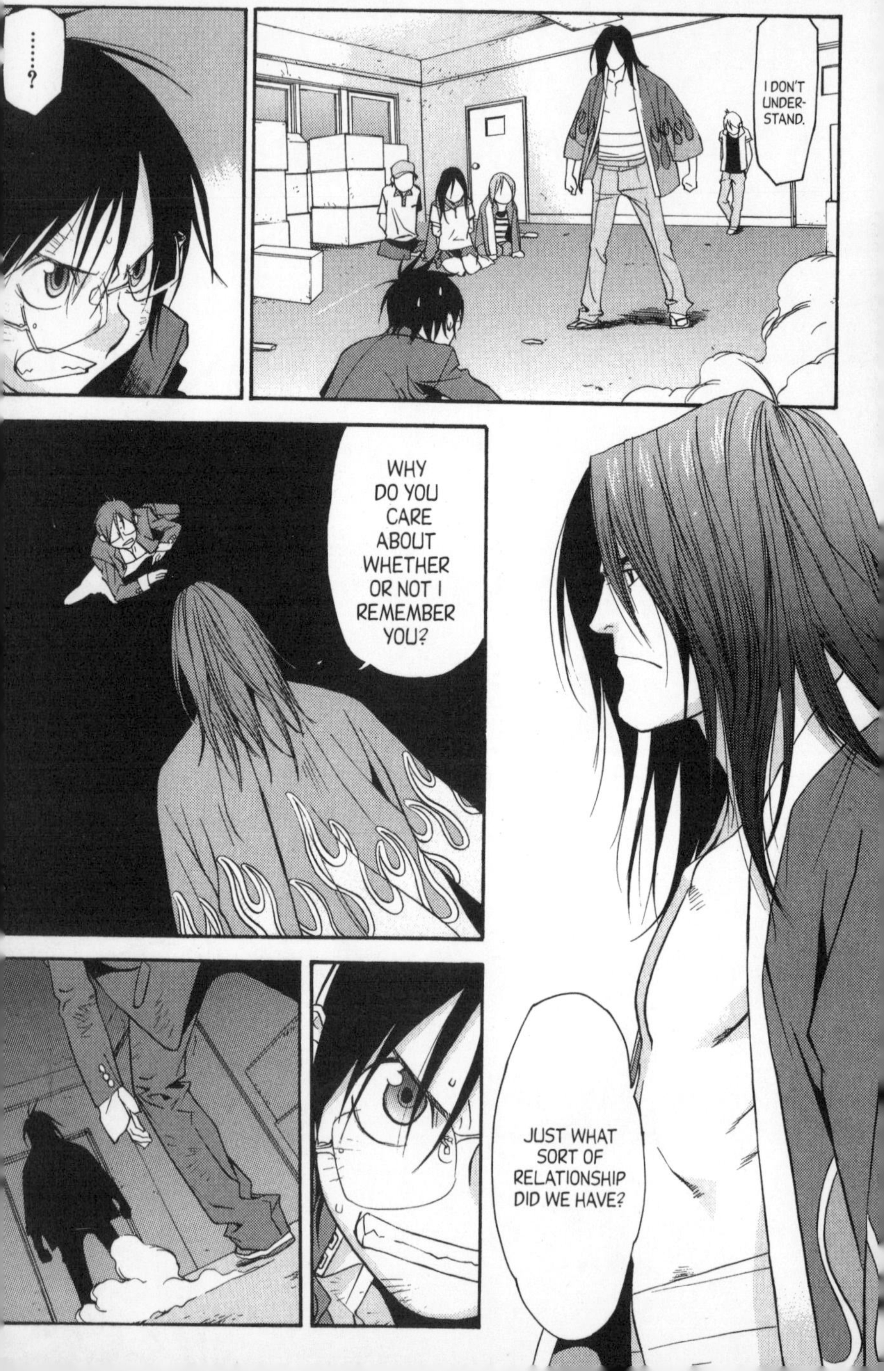
I DON'T UNDER-STAND.
……?
WHY DO YOU CARE ABOUT WHETHER OR NOT I REMEMBER YOU?
JUST WHAT SORT OF RELATIONSHIP DID WE HAVE?

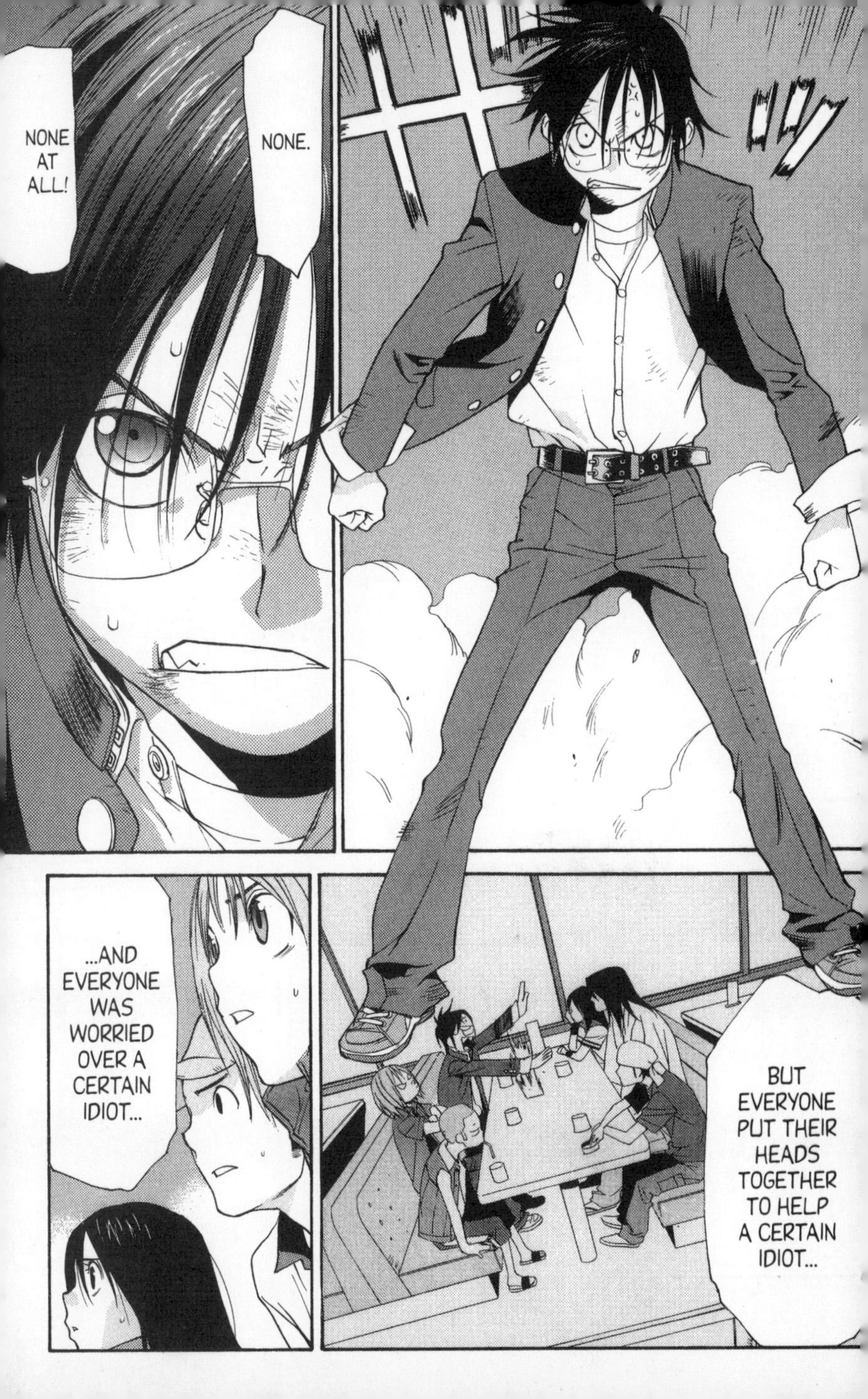
NONE.
NONE AT ALL!
BUT EVERYONE PUT THEIR HEADS TOGETHER TO HELP A CERTAIN IDIOT...
...AND EVERYONE WAS WORRIED OVER A CERTAIN IDIOT...

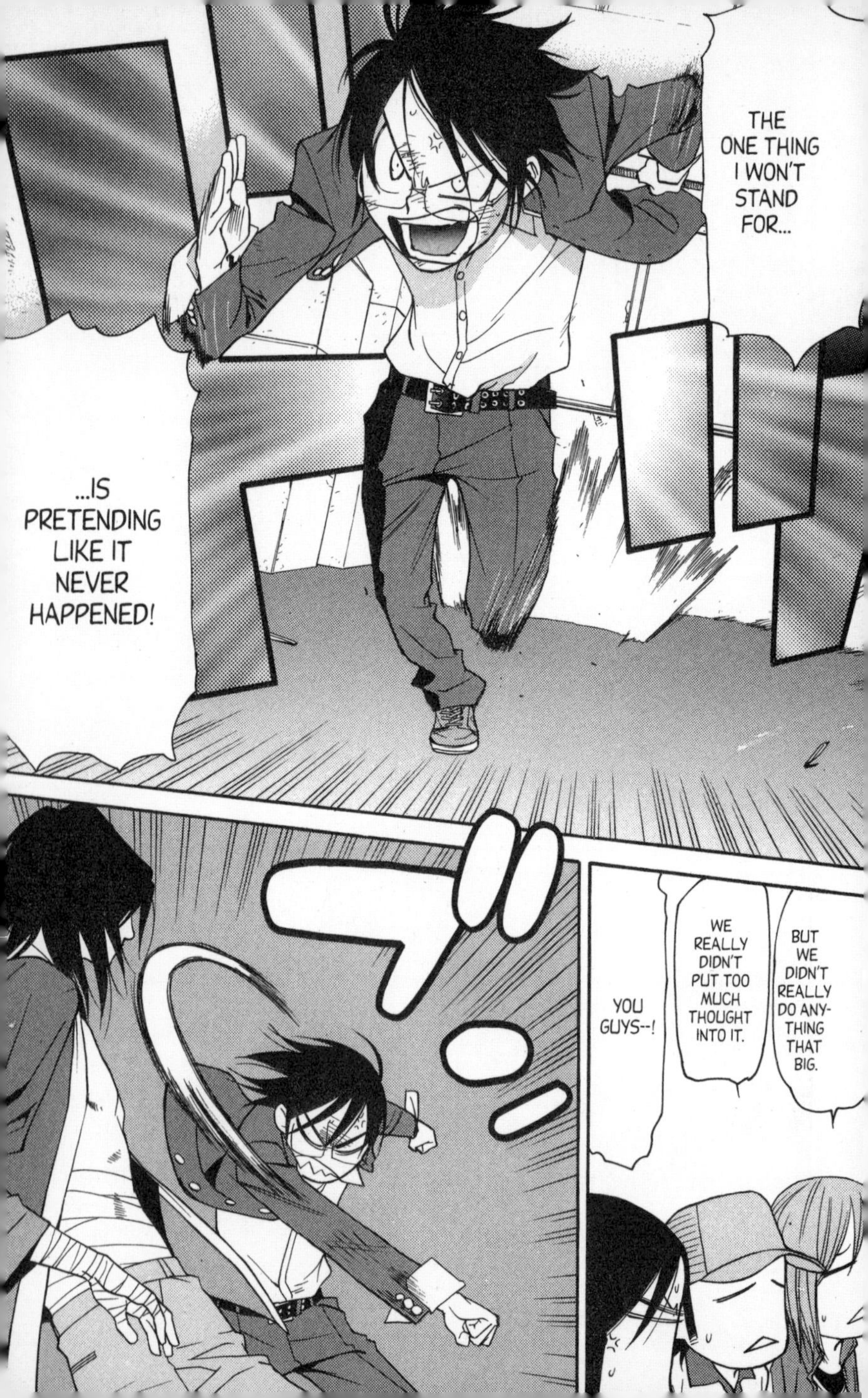
THE ONE THING I WON'T STAND FOR...
...IS PRETENDING LIKE IT NEVER HAPPENED!
BUT WE DIDN'T REALLY DO ANY-THING THAT BIG.
WE REALLY DIDN'T PUT TOO MUCH THOUGHT INTO IT.
YOU GUYS--!

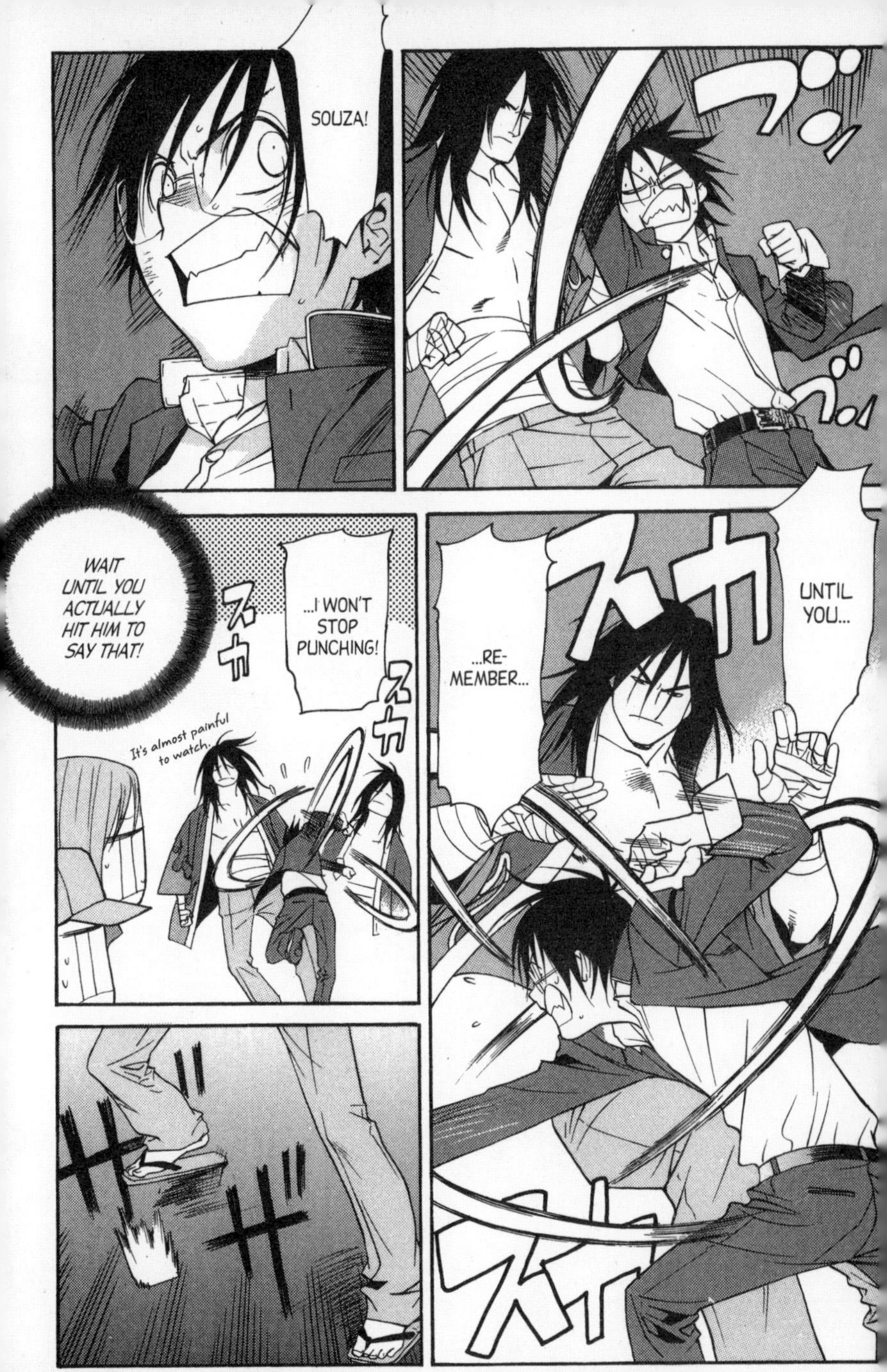
SOUZA!
UNTIL YOU...
...RE-MEMBER...
...I WON'T STOP PUNCHING!
WAIT UNTIL YOU ACTUALLY HIT HIM TO SAY THAT!
It's almost painful to watch.

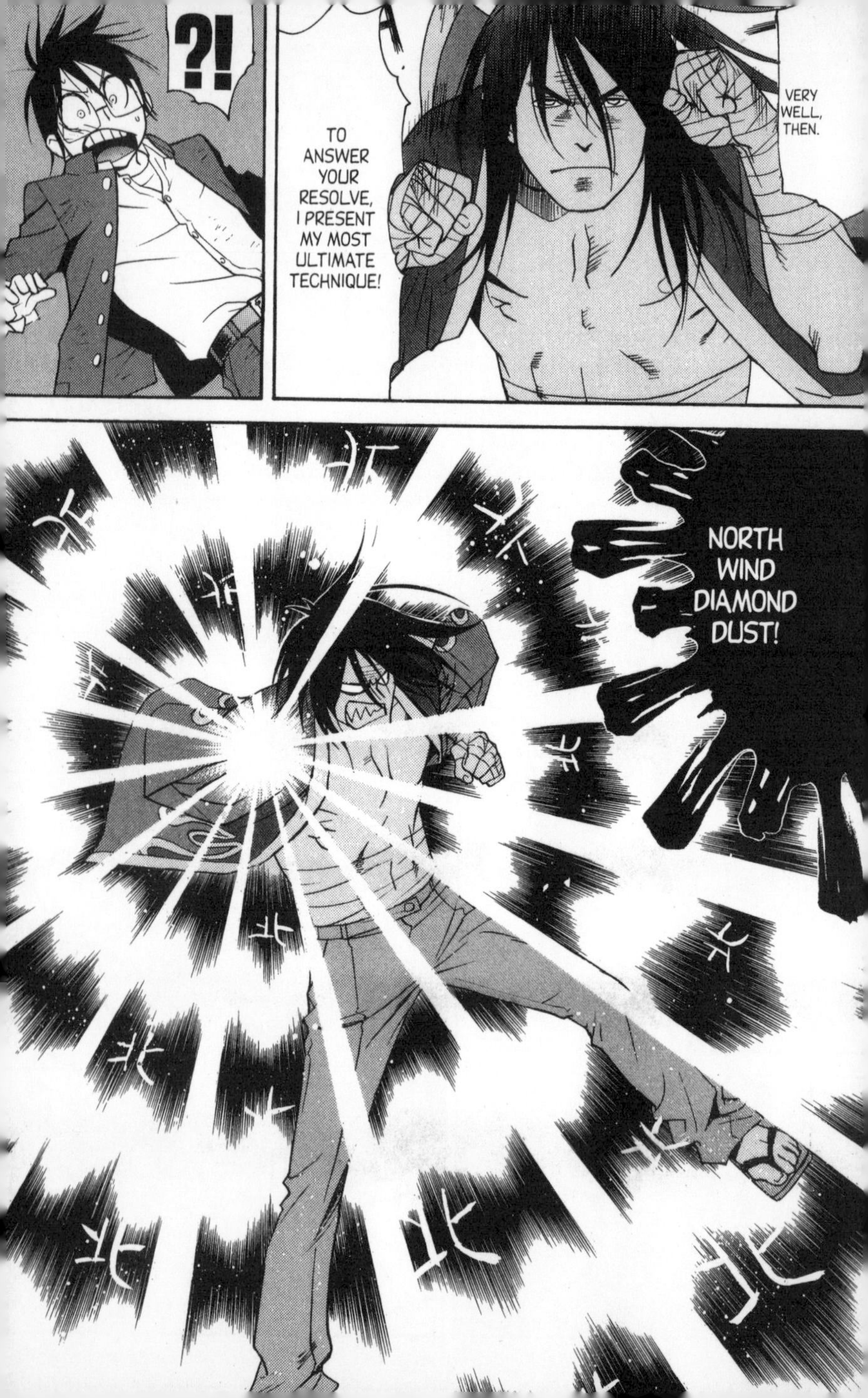
VERY WELL, THEN.
TO ANSWER YOUR RESOLVE, I PRESENT MY MOST ULTIMATE TECHNIQUE!
?!
NORTH WIND DIAMOND DUST!

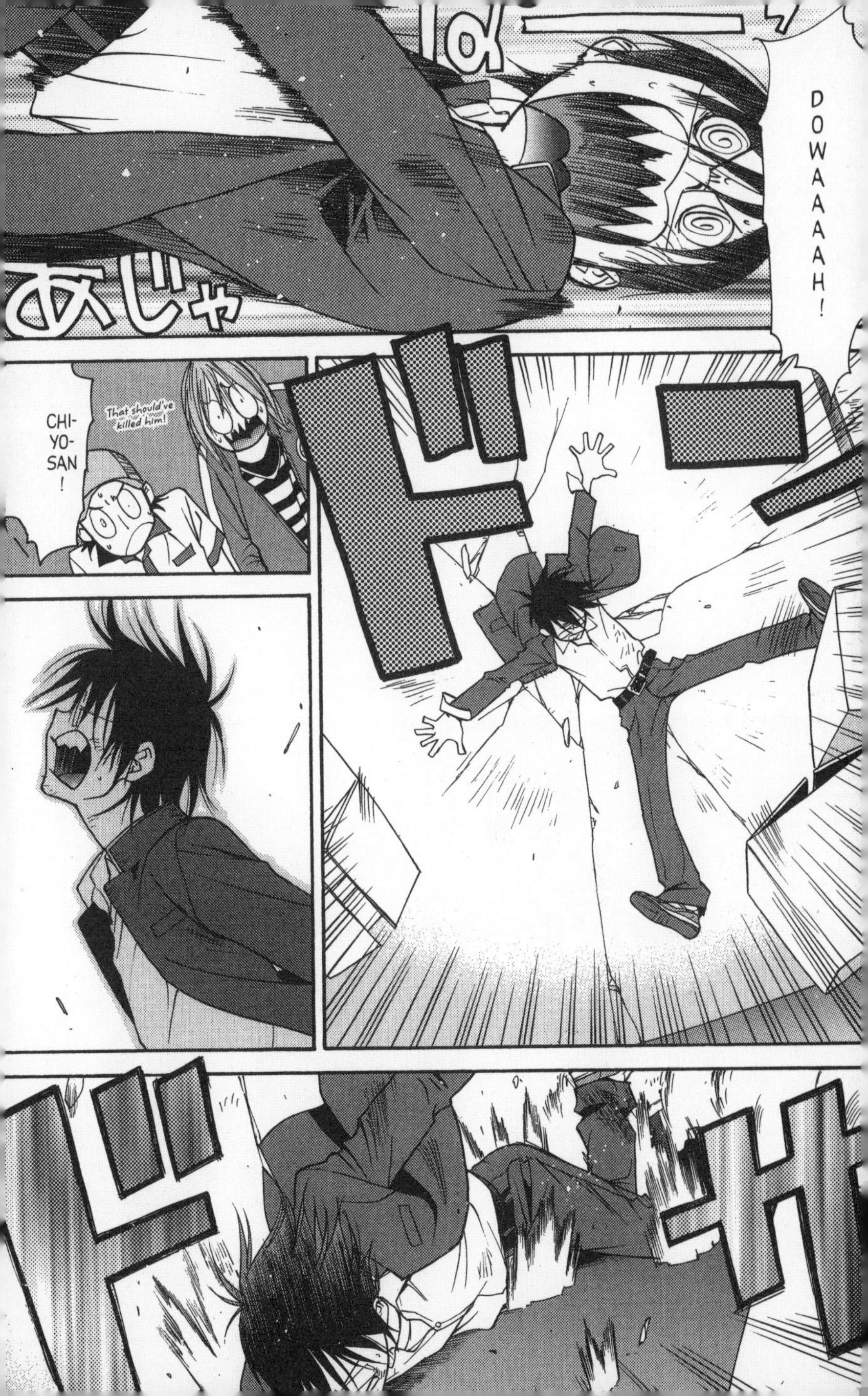

DOWAAAAAH!
はーーーっ
あじゃ
ドーン
That should've killed him!
CHI-YO-SAN!
ドザ

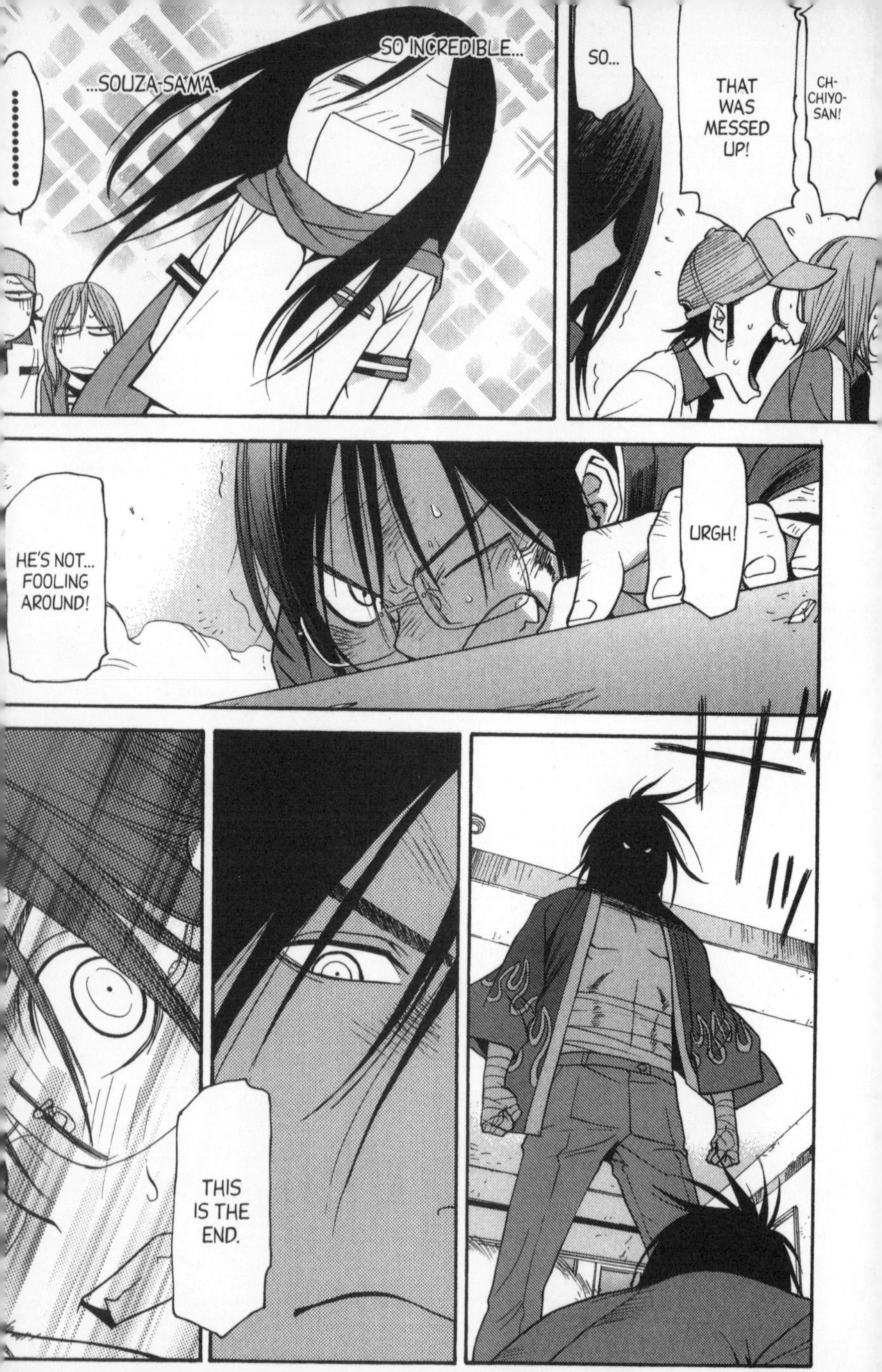
CH-CHIYO-SAN!
THAT WAS MESSED UP!
SO...
SO INCREDIBLE...
...SOUZA-SAMA.
....
URGH!
HE'S NOT... FOOLING AROUND!
THIS IS THE END.

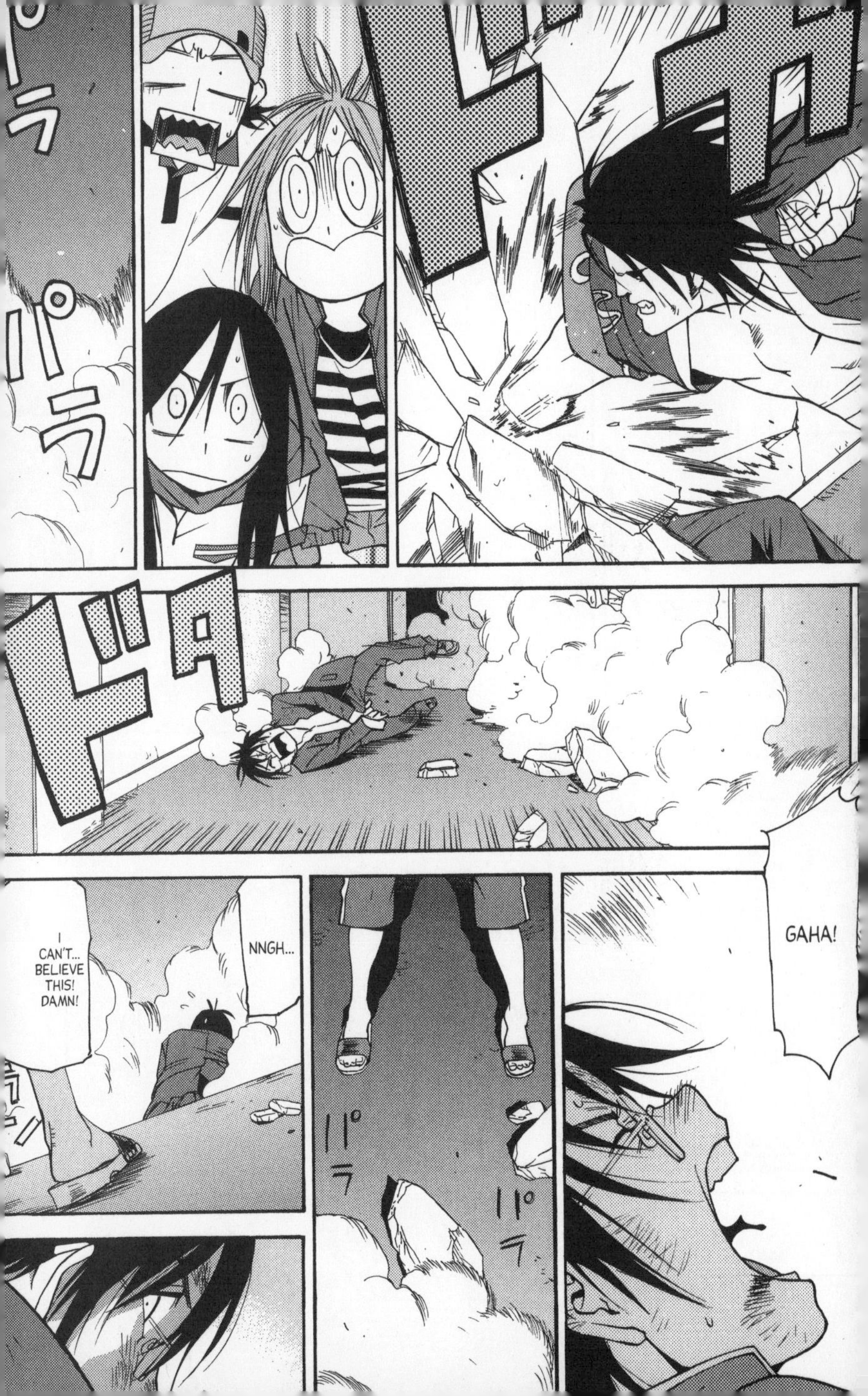
パラ
ドダ
GAHA!
パラ
パラ
NNGH...
I CAN'T... BELIEVE THIS! DAMN!

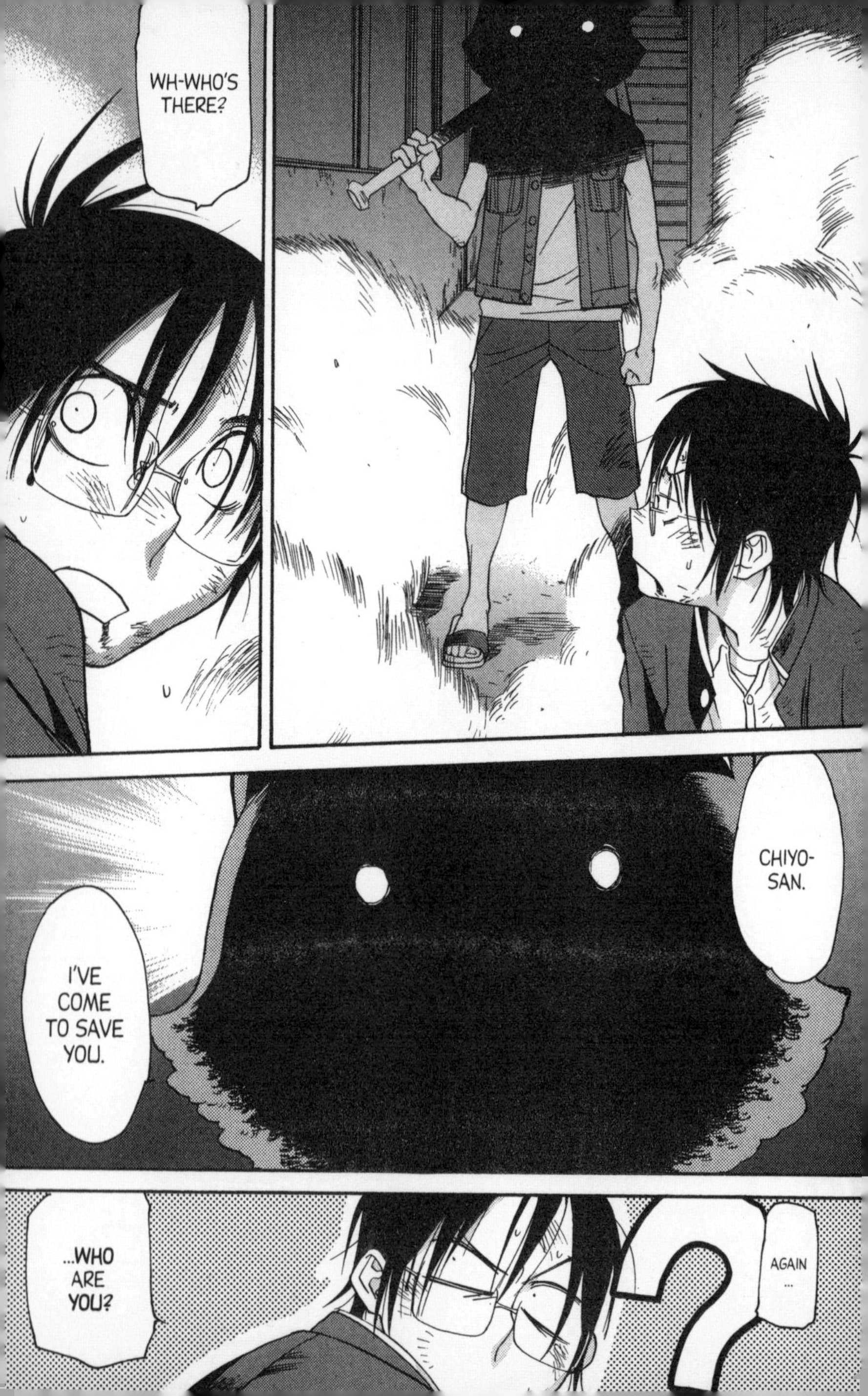
WH-WHO'S THERE?
CHIYO-SAN.
I'VE COME TO SAVE YOU.
AGAIN ...
...WHO ARE YOU?

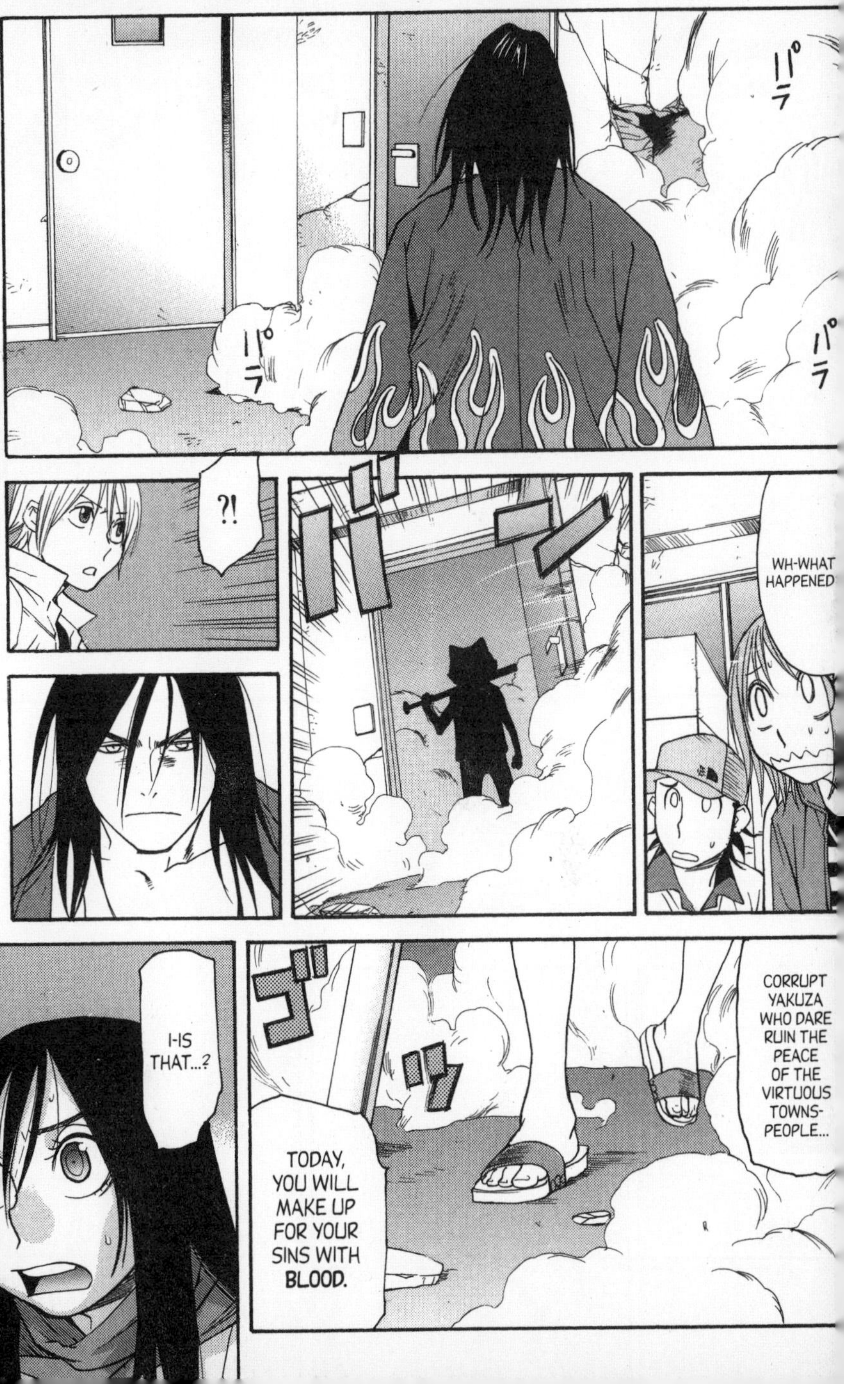
パラ
パラ
パラ
WH-WHAT HAPPENED
?!
CORRUPT YAKUZA WHO DARE RUIN THE PEACE OF THE VIRTUOUS TOWNS-PEOPLE...
ゴッ
TODAY, YOU WILL MAKE UP FOR YOUR SINS WITH **BLOOD.**
I-IS THAT...?

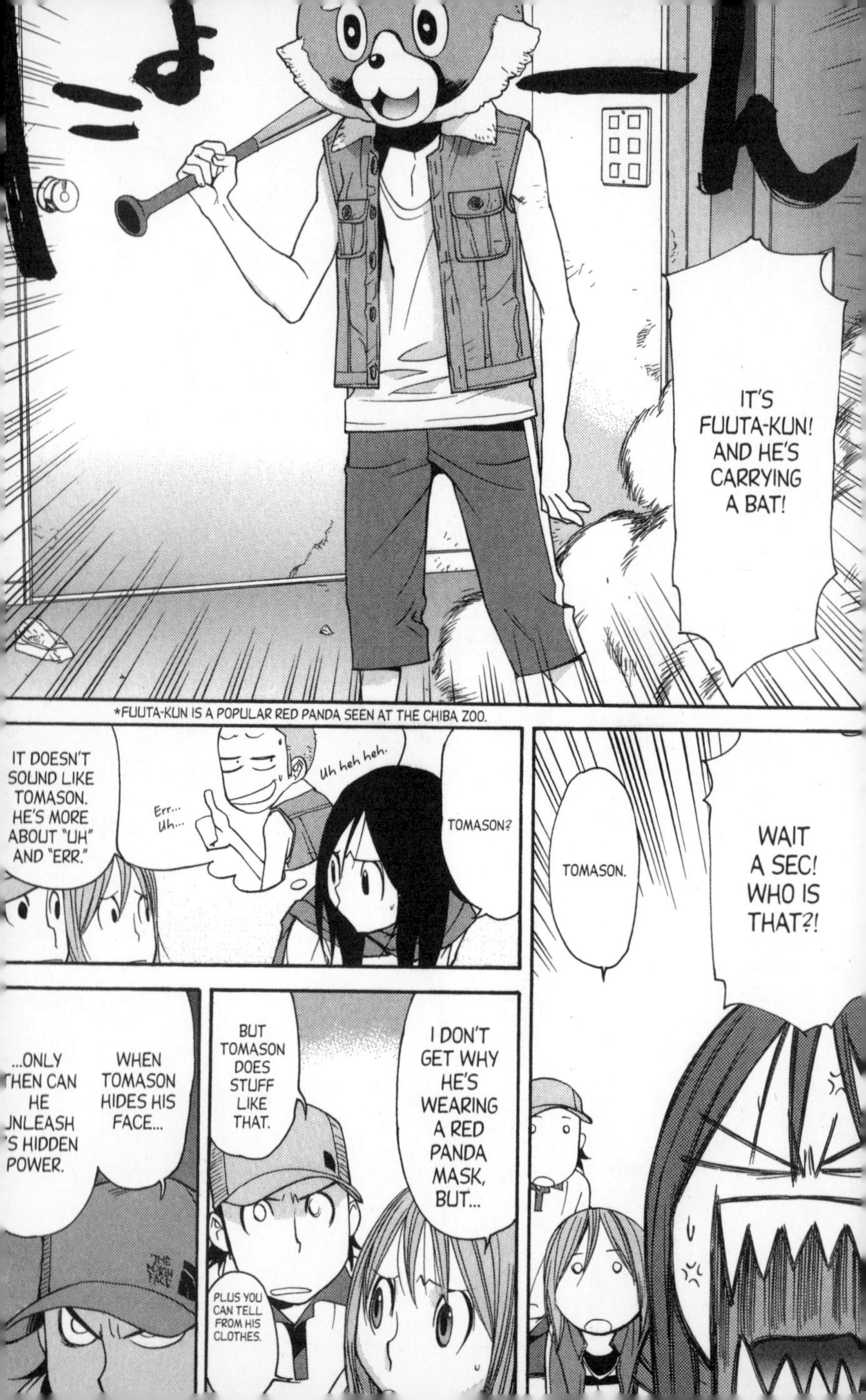
IT'S FUUTA-KUN! AND HE'S CARRYING A BAT!
*FUUTA-KUN IS A POPULAR RED PANDA SEEN AT THE CHIBA ZOO.
WAIT A SEC! WHO IS THAT?!
TOMASON.
TOMASON?
Uh heh heh.
Err... Uh...
IT DOESN'T SOUND LIKE TOMASON. HE'S MORE ABOUT "UH" AND "ERR."
I DON'T GET WHY HE'S WEARING A RED PANDA MASK, BUT...
BUT TOMASON DOES STUFF LIKE THAT.
PLUS YOU CAN TELL FROM HIS CLOTHES.
WHEN TOMASON HIDES HIS FACE...
...ONLY THEN CAN HE UNLEASH 'S HIDDEN POWER.

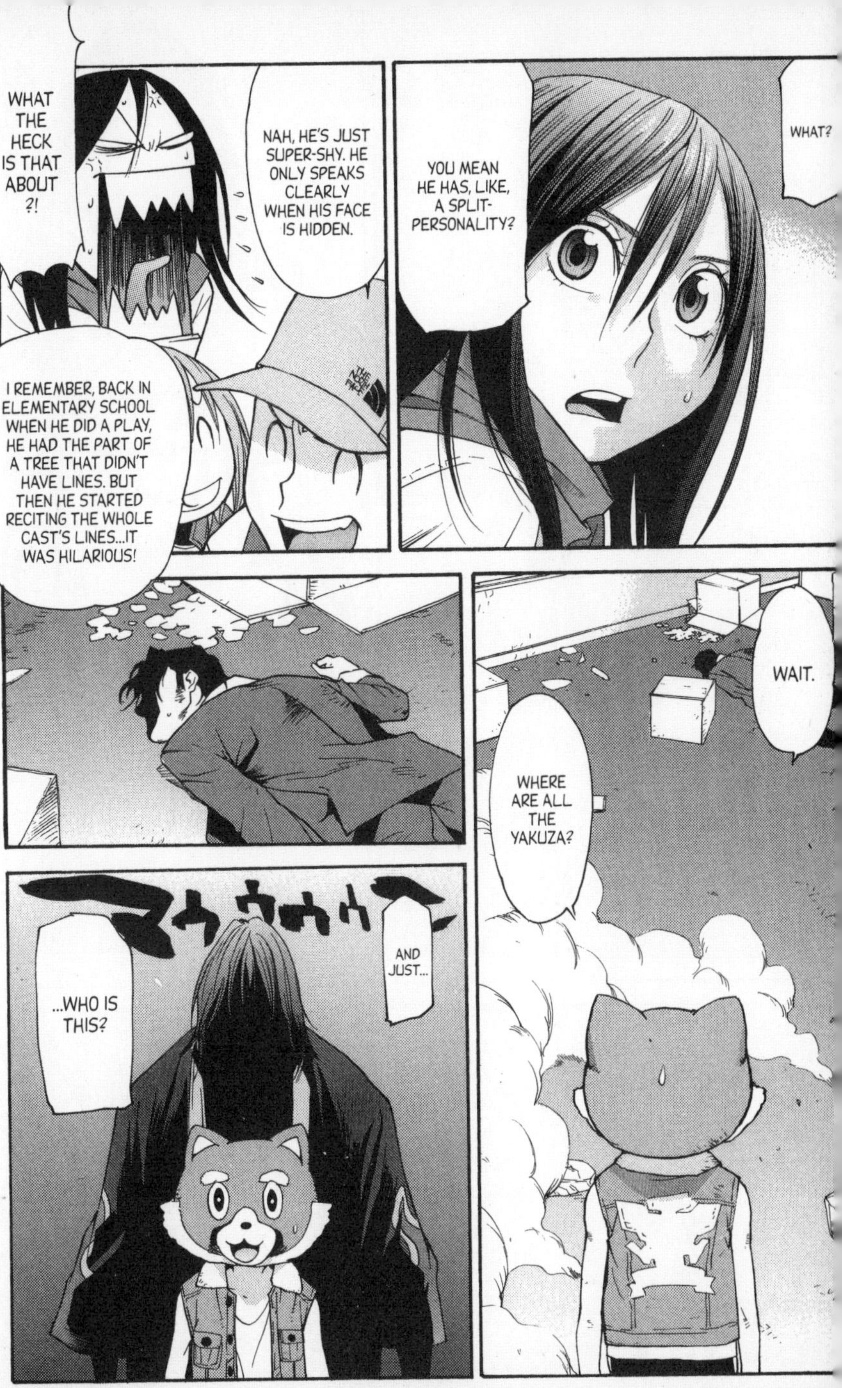
WHAT?
YOU MEAN HE HAS, LIKE, A SPLIT-PERSONALITY?
NAH, HE'S JUST SUPER-SHY. HE ONLY SPEAKS CLEARLY WHEN HIS FACE IS HIDDEN.
WHAT THE HECK IS THAT ABOUT?!
I REMEMBER, BACK IN ELEMENTARY SCHOOL WHEN HE DID A PLAY, HE HAD THE PART OF A TREE THAT DIDN'T HAVE LINES. BUT THEN HE STARTED RECITING THE WHOLE CAST'S LINES...IT WAS HILARIOUS!
WAIT.
WHERE ARE ALL THE YAKUZA?
AND JUST...
...WHO IS THIS?

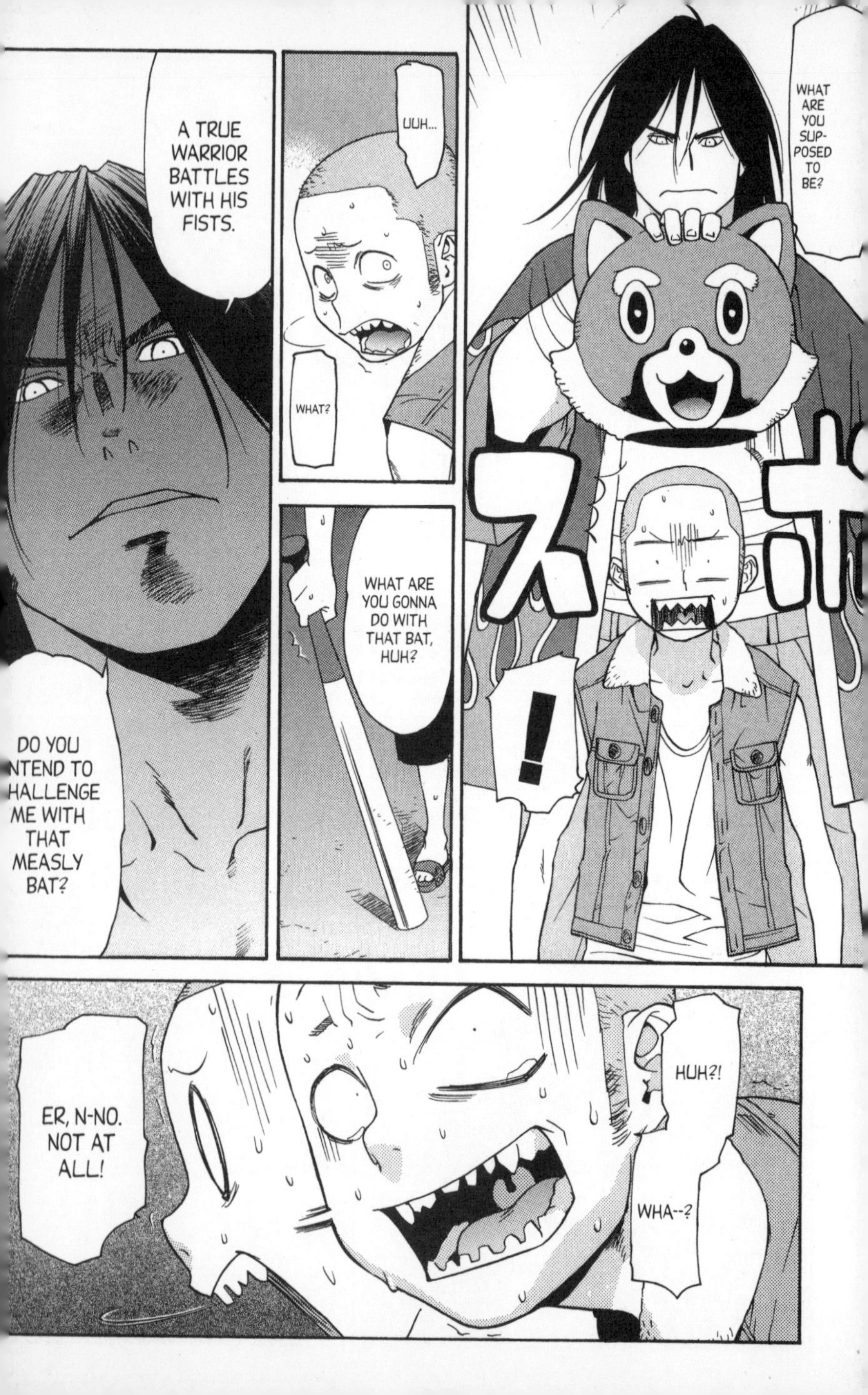
WHAT ARE YOU SUP-POSED TO BE?
スポ
!
UUH...
WHAT?
WHAT ARE YOU GONNA DO WITH THAT BAT, HUH?
A TRUE WARRIOR BATTLES WITH HIS FISTS.
DO YOU NTEND TO HALLENGE ME WITH THAT MEASLY BAT?
HUH?!
WHA--?
ER, N-NO. NOT AT ALL!

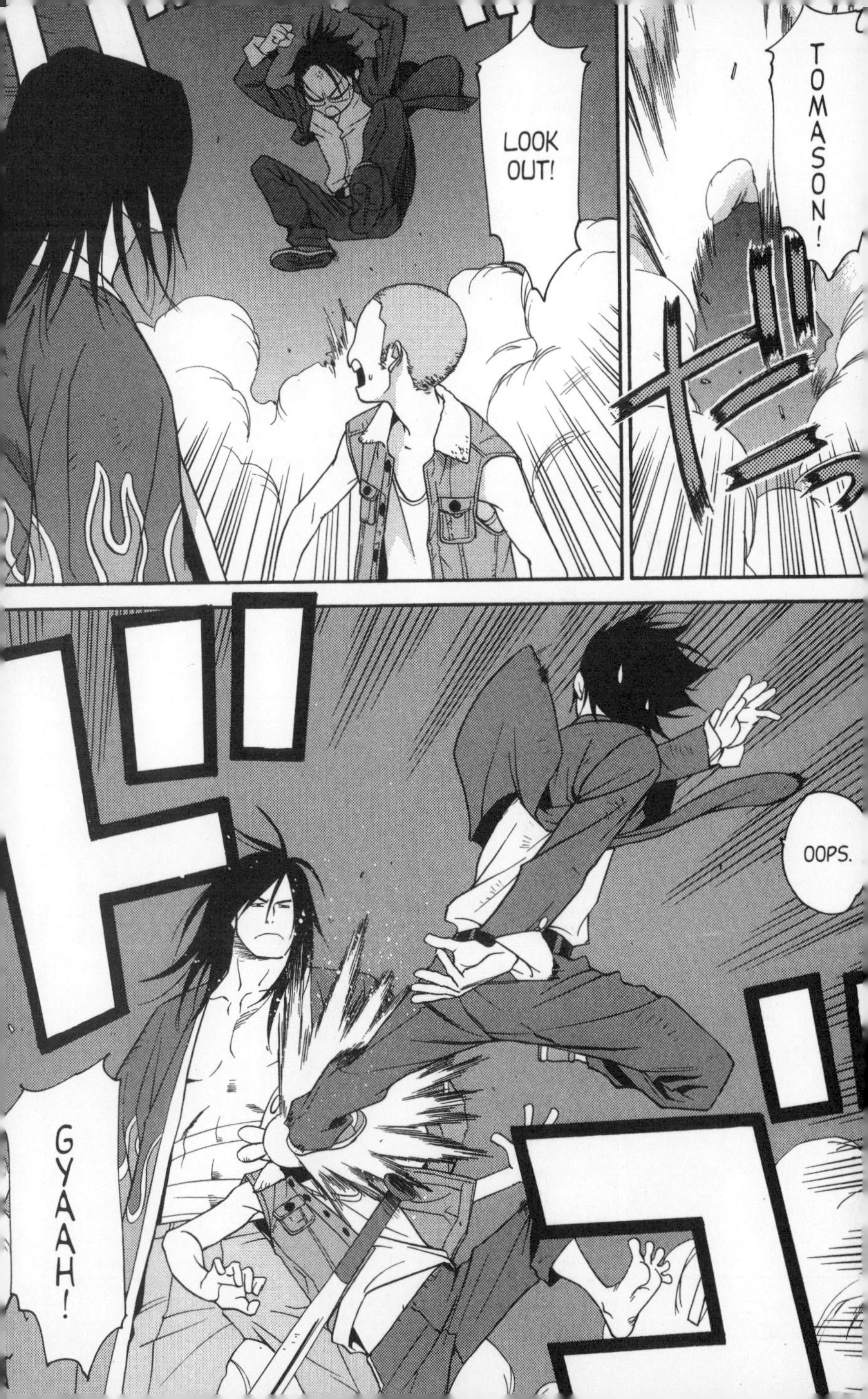
TOMASON!
LOOK OUT!
OOPS.
GYAAH!

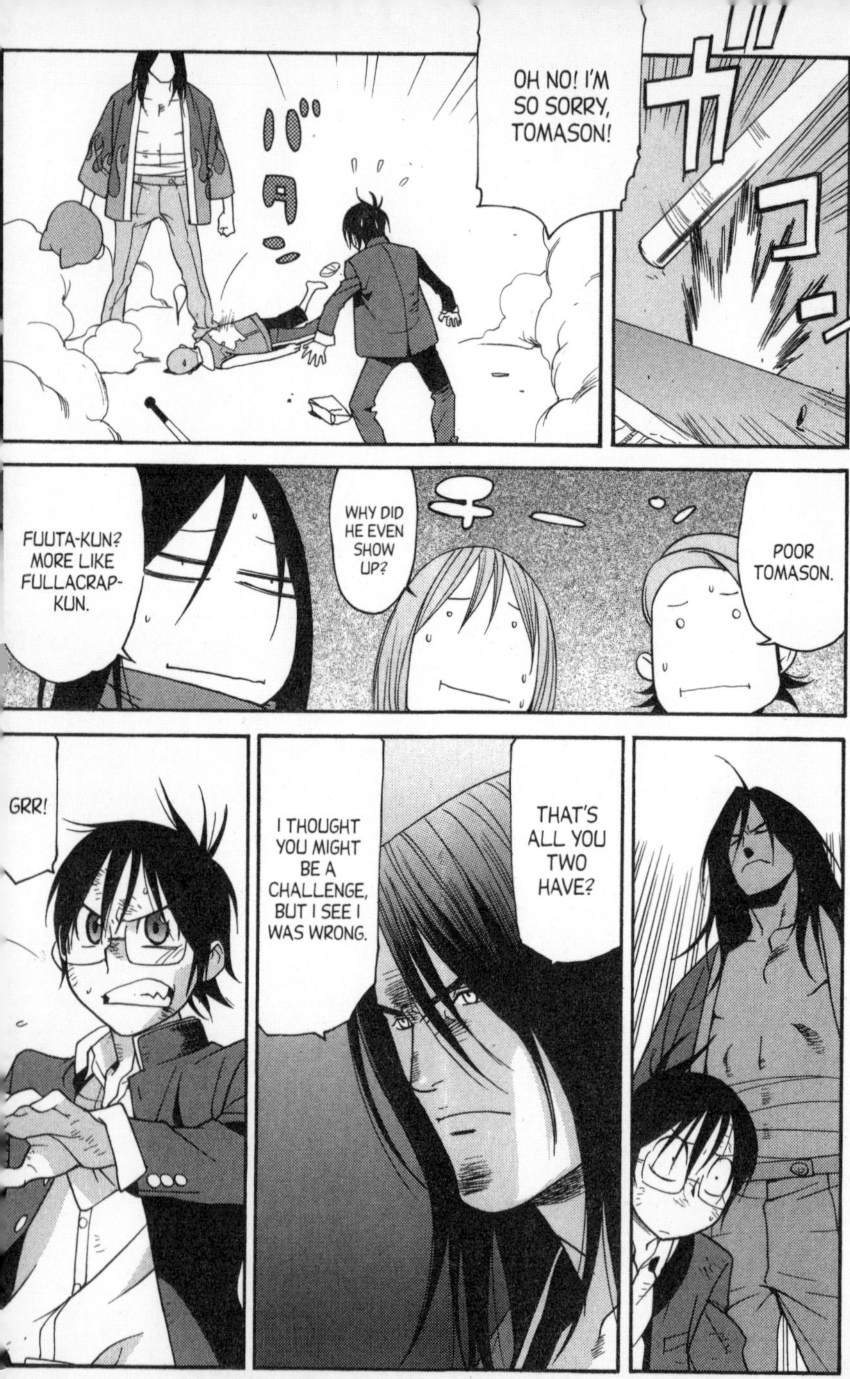
OH NO! I'M SO SORRY, TOMASON!
POOR TOMASON.
WHY DID HE EVEN SHOW UP?
FUUTA-KUN? MORE LIKE FULLACRAP-KUN.
THAT'S ALL YOU TWO HAVE?
I THOUGHT YOU MIGHT BE A CHALLENGE, BUT I SEE I WAS WRONG.
GRR!

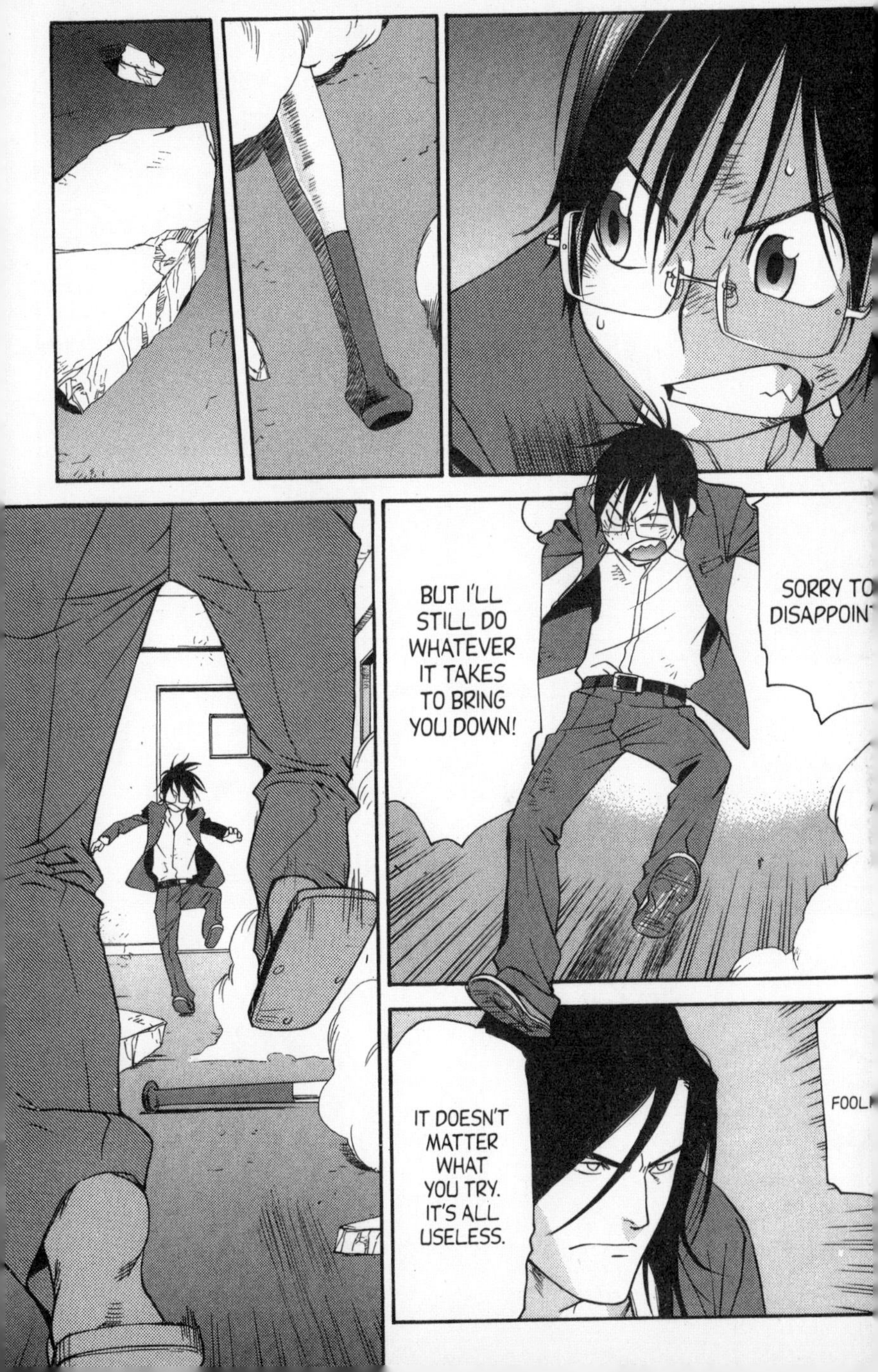
SORRY TO DISAPPOINT
BUT I'LL STILL DO WHATEVER IT TAKES TO BRING YOU DOWN!
FOOL
IT DOESN'T MATTER WHAT YOU TRY. IT'S ALL USELESS.

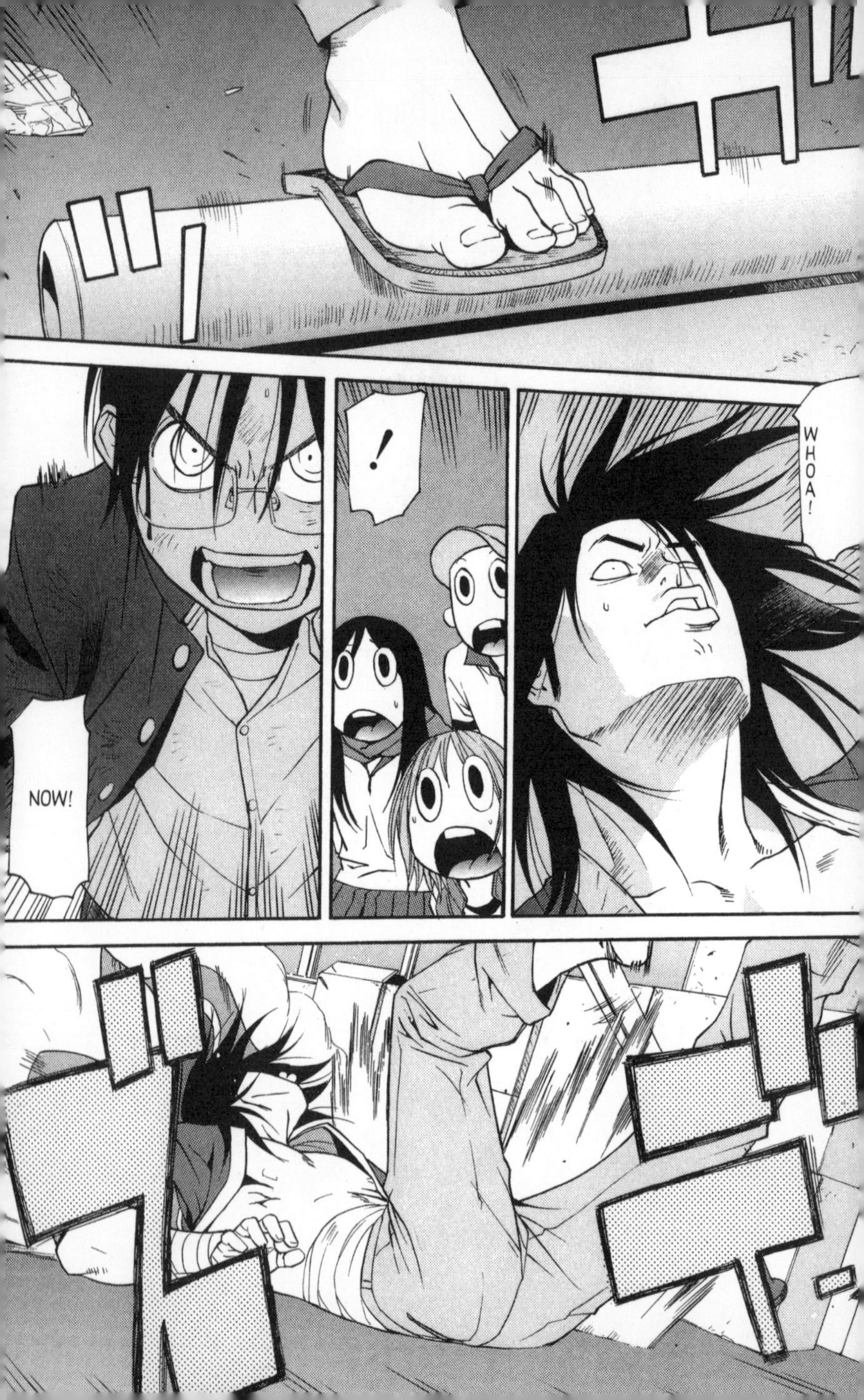
WHOA!
!
NOW!

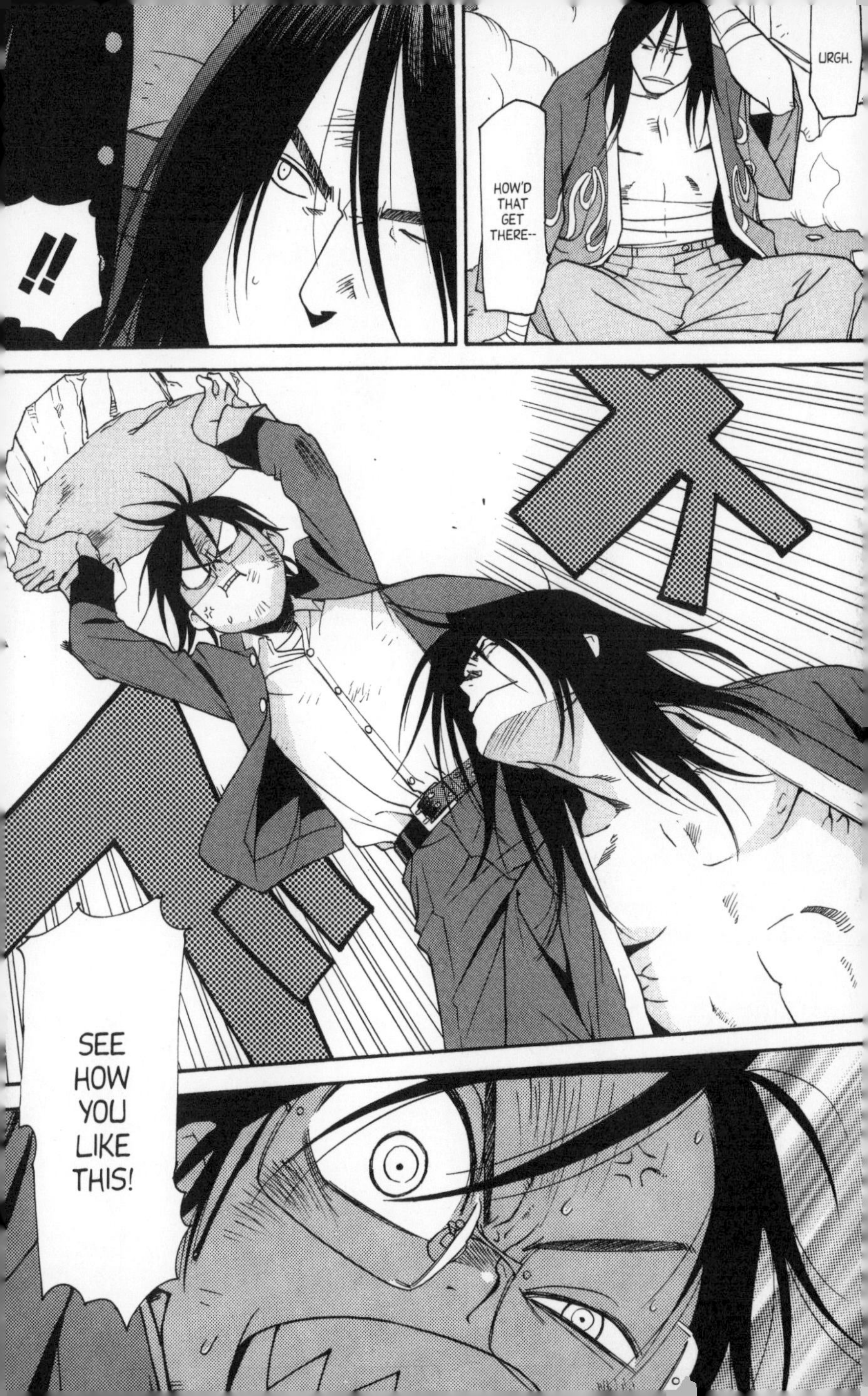
URGH.
HOW'D THAT GET THERE--
!!
SEE HOW YOU LIKE THIS!

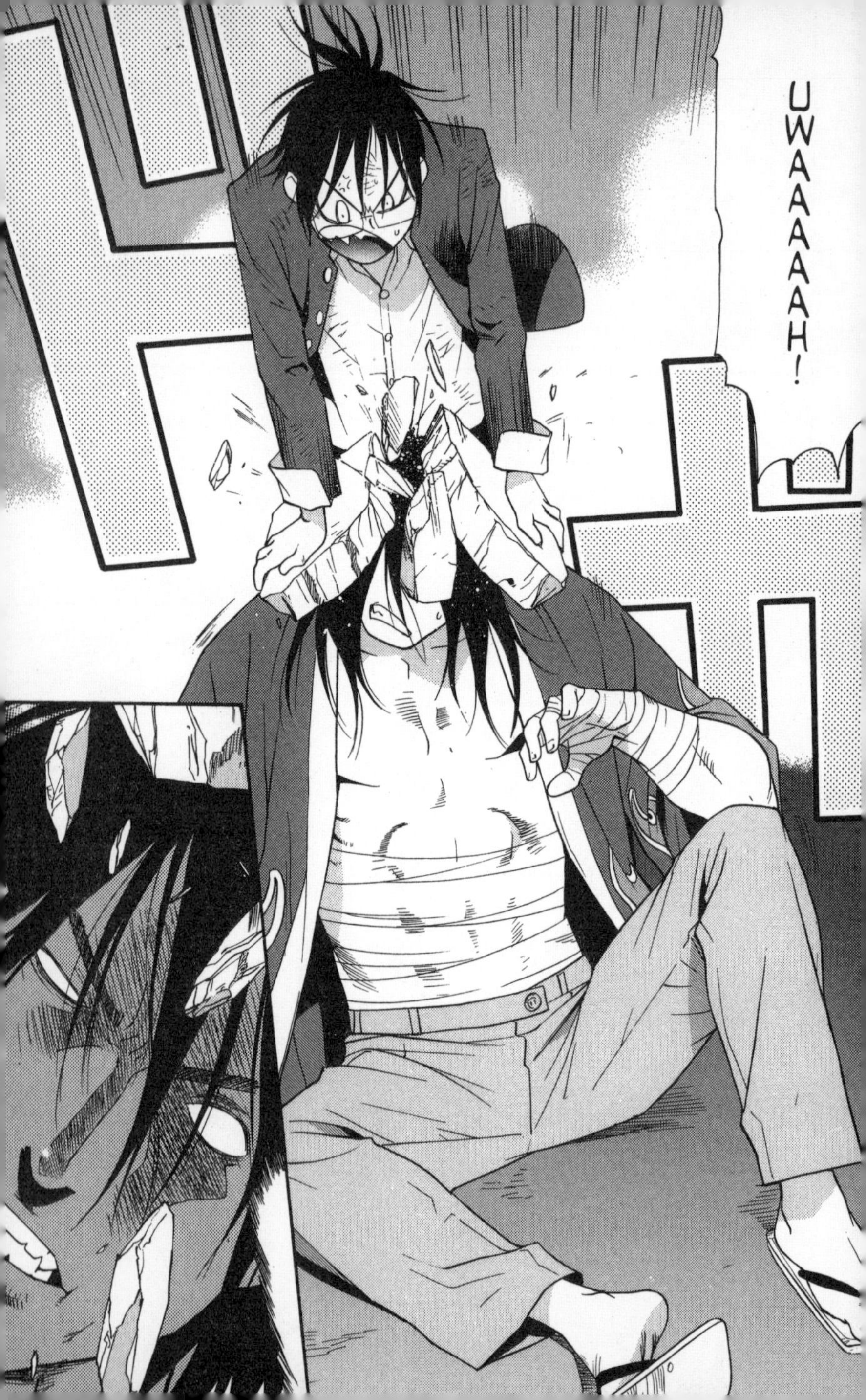
UWAAAAAAH!

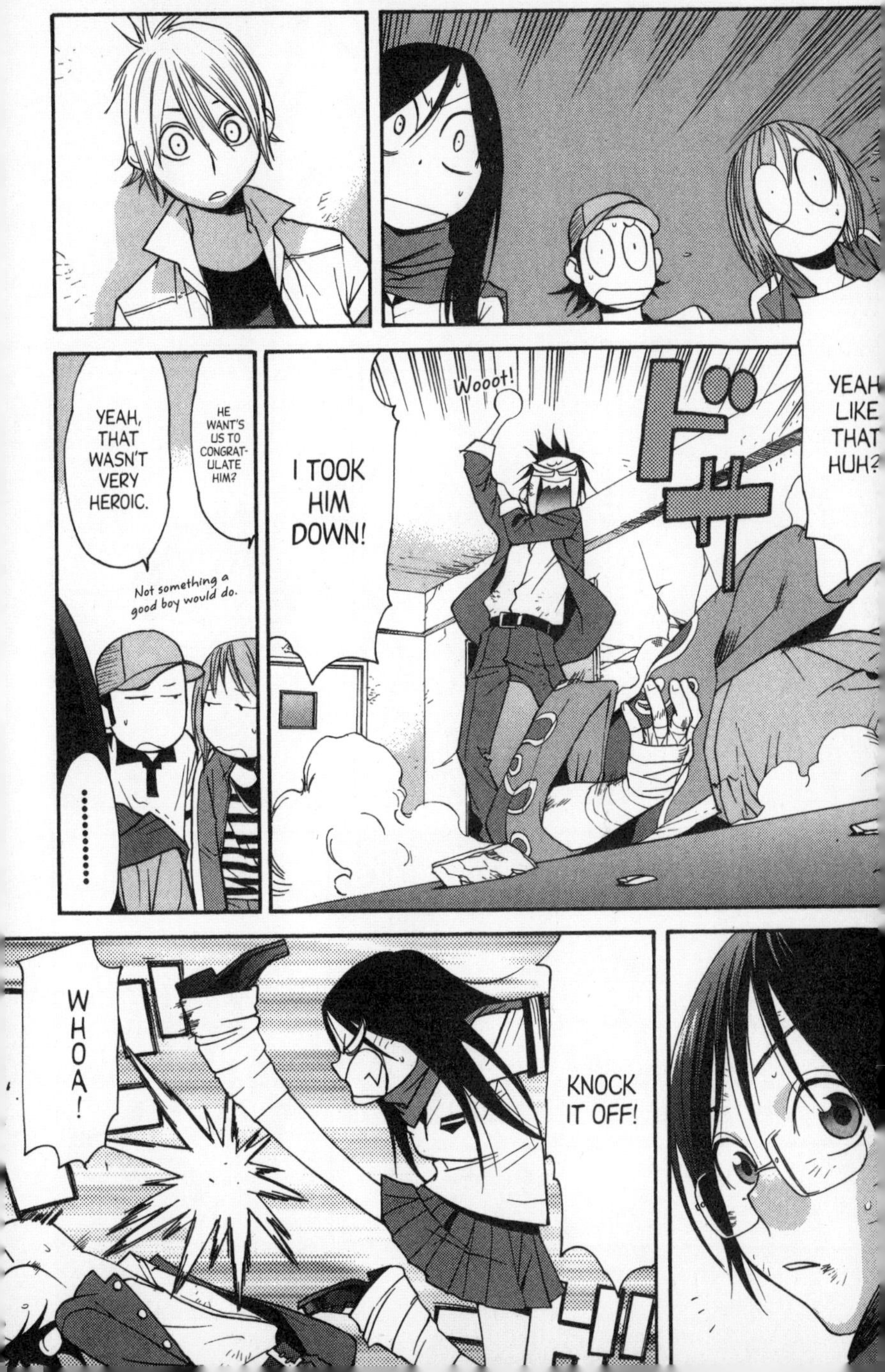
YEAH LIKE THAT HUH?
Wooot!
ドサ
I TOOK HIM DOWN!
HE WANT'S US TO CONGRAT-ULATE HIM?
YEAH, THAT WASN'T VERY HEROIC.
Not something a good boy would do.
....
KNOCK IT OFF!
WHOA!

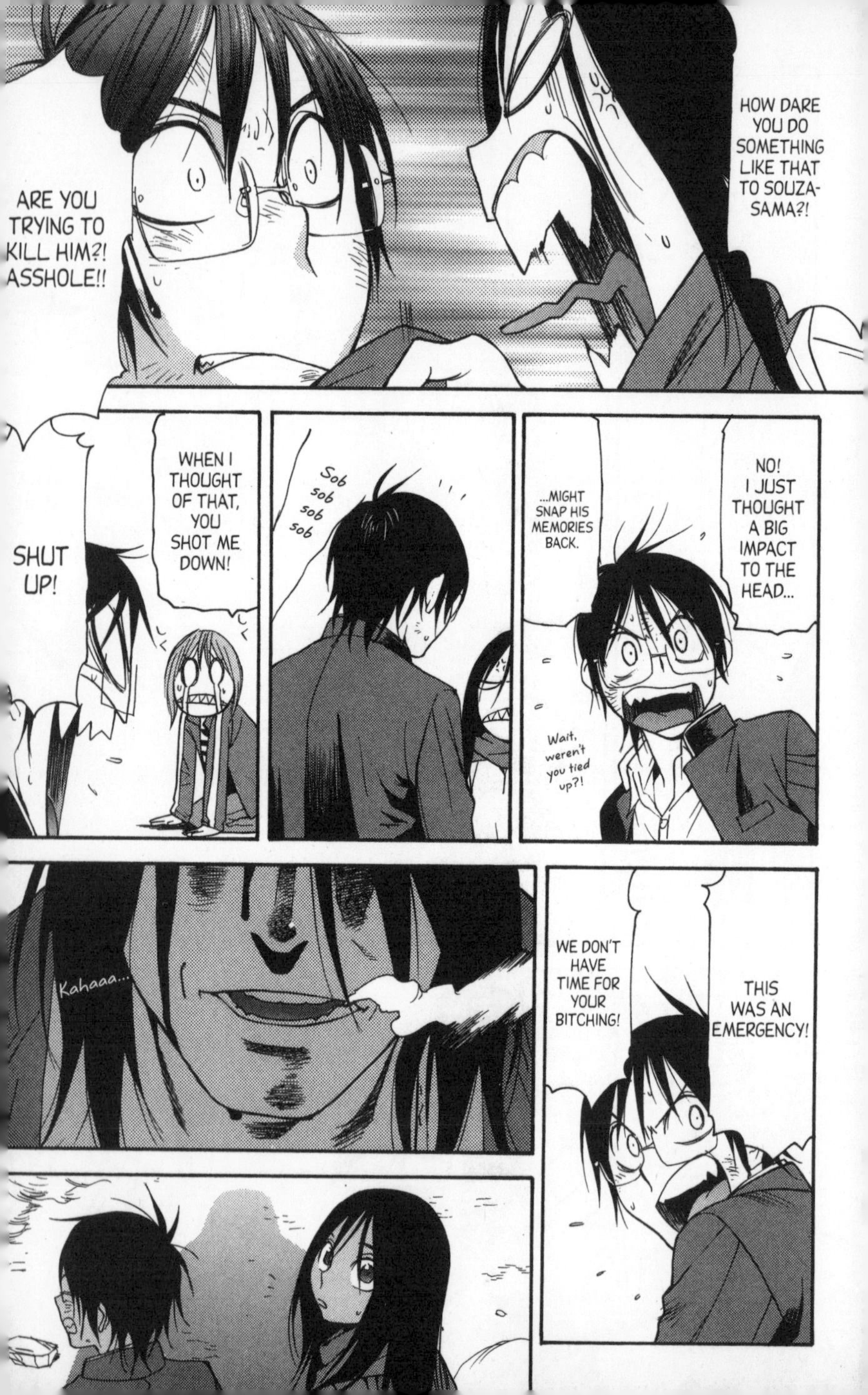
HOW DARE YOU DO SOMETHING LIKE THAT TO SOUZA-SAMA?!
ARE YOU TRYING TO KILL HIM?! ASSHOLE!!
NO! I JUST THOUGHT A BIG IMPACT TO THE HEAD...
...MIGHT SNAP HIS MEMORIES BACK.
Wait, weren't you tied up?!
Sob sob sob sob
WHEN I THOUGHT OF THAT, YOU SHOT ME DOWN!
SHUT UP!
THIS WAS AN EMERGENCY!
WE DON'T HAVE TIME FOR YOUR BITCHING!
Kahaaa...

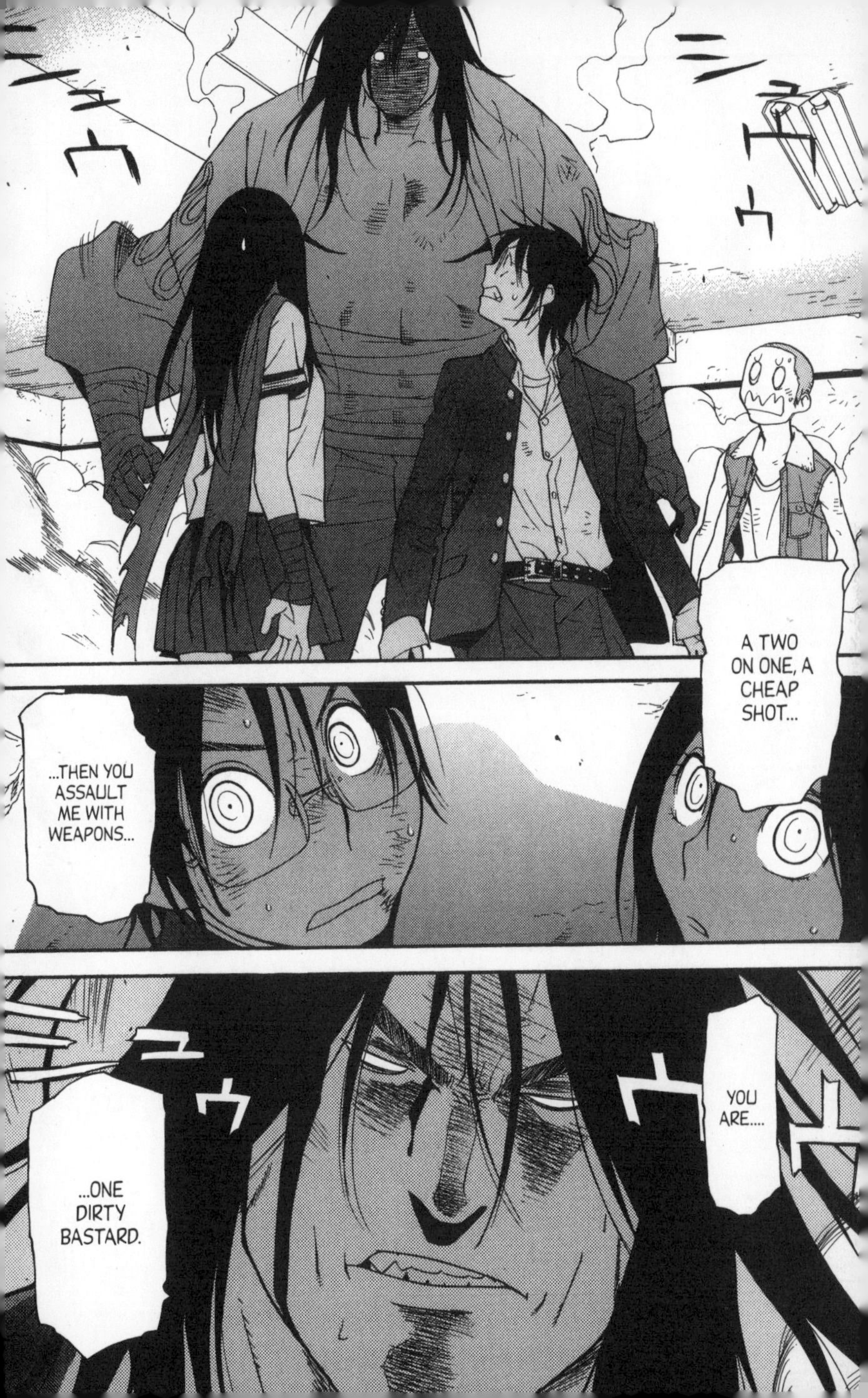
A TWO ON ONE, A CHEAP SHOT...
...THEN YOU ASSAULT ME WITH WEAPONS...
YOU ARE....
...ONE DIRTY BASTARD.

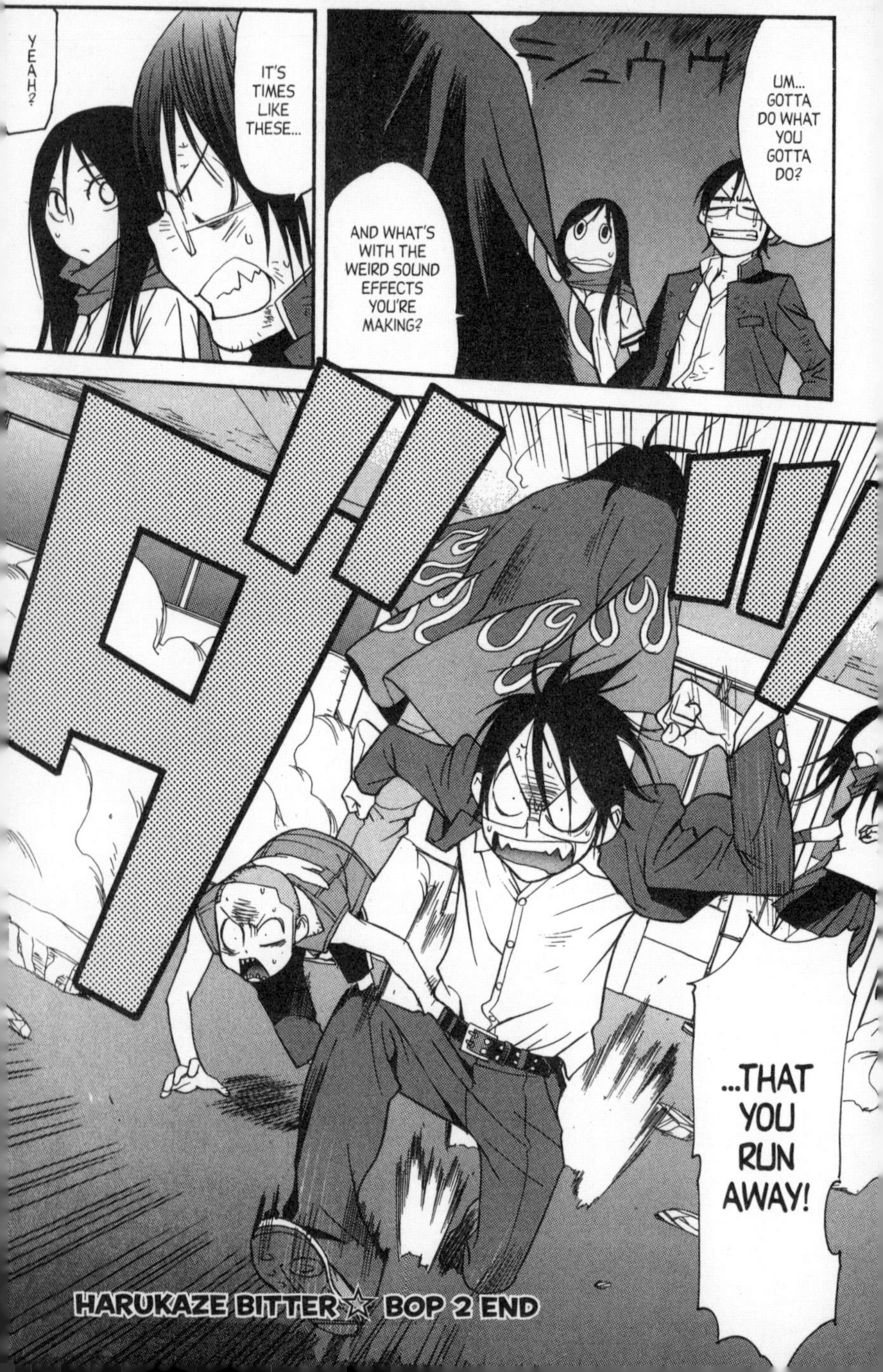
UM... GOTTA DO WHAT YOU GOTTA DO?
AND WHAT'S WITH THE WEIRD SOUND EFFECTS YOU'RE MAKING?
IT'S TIMES LIKE THESE...
YEAH?
...THAT YOU RUN AWAY!
HARUKAZE BITTER☆BOP 2 END

POSTSCRIPT SAILING☆SHIPS

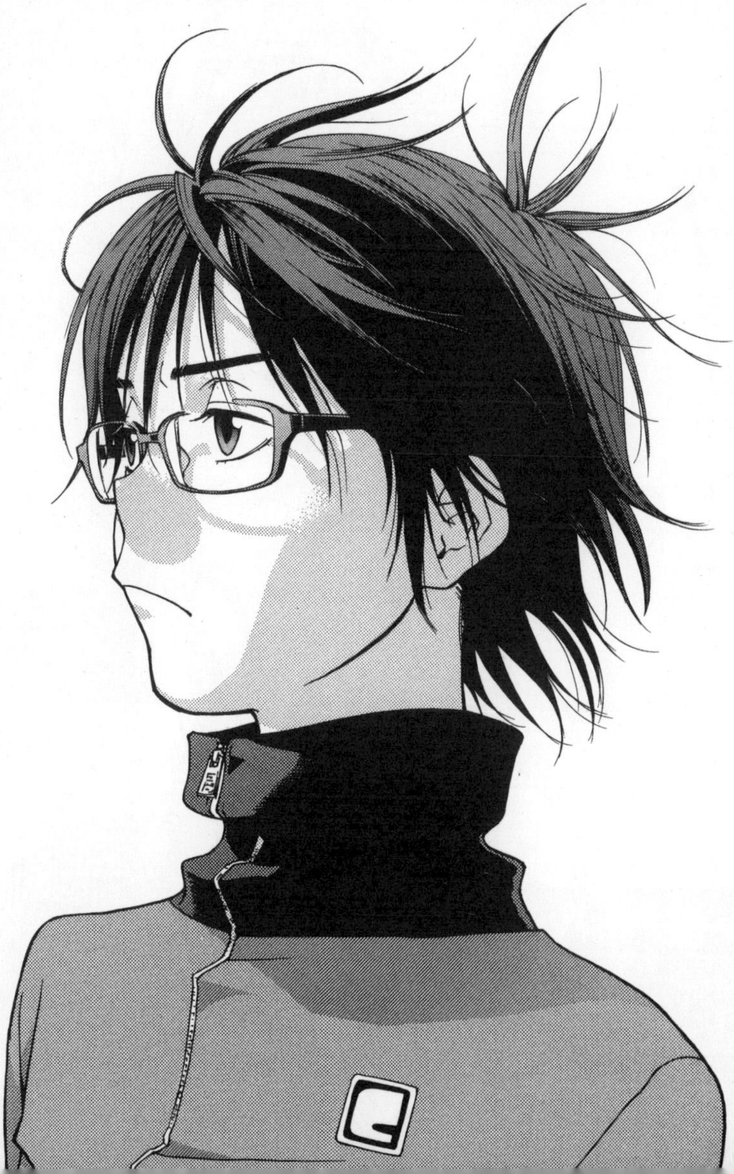

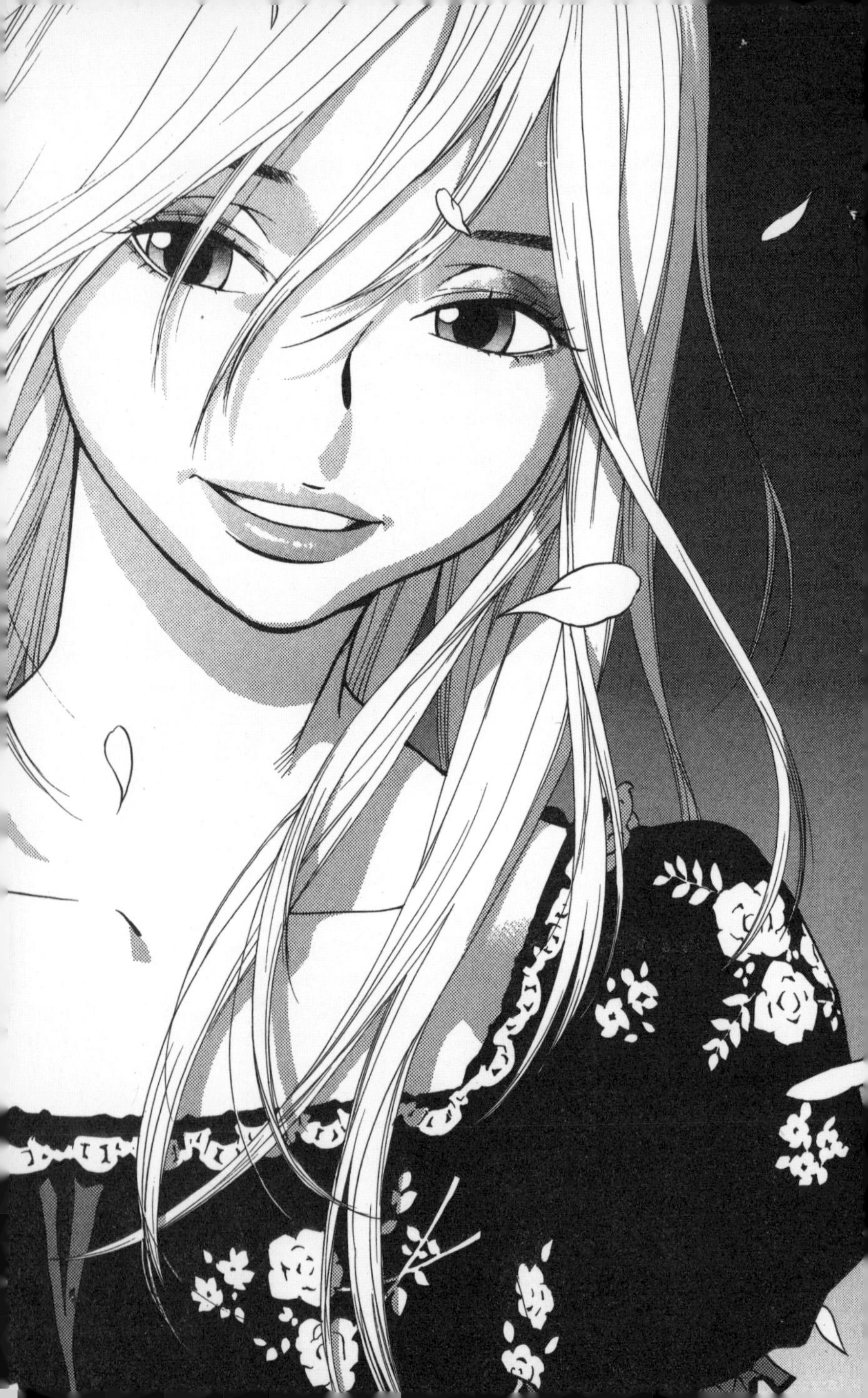

Thank you for buying Harukaze
Bitter☆Bop volume 2.
This time around, I filled the
extra pages with Bonus Manga
rather than just artwork.
I already feel like I'm running out
of material, but it's really up to all
of your input if I'll continue this
story for another volume or not.
As usual, I ask myself--Where is the
story going? Where is the end point?
Do I even know it myself? Is it going
to be a big success? Will it become
a gorgeous dancing on big boy blues
manga? Thanks for everything and I
hope you stick with me in the future.
                    Feb. XX, 2006
                    Court Betten

Next Volume

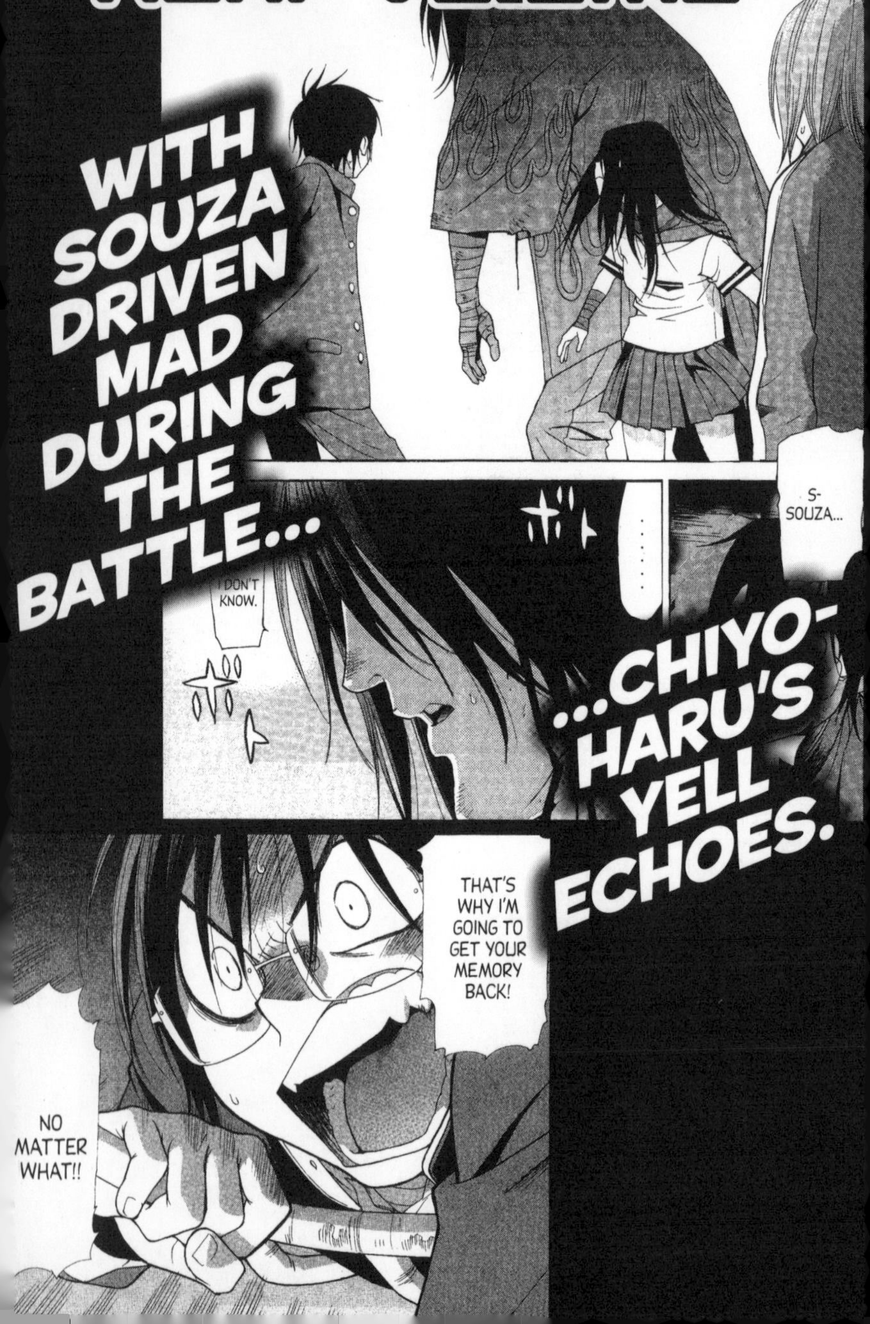
WITH SOUZA DRIVEN MAD DURING THE BATTLE...
S-SOUZA...
......
I DON'T KNOW.
...CHIYO-HARU'S YELL ECHOES.
THAT'S WHY I'M GOING TO GET YOUR MEMORY BACK!
NO MATTER WHAT!!

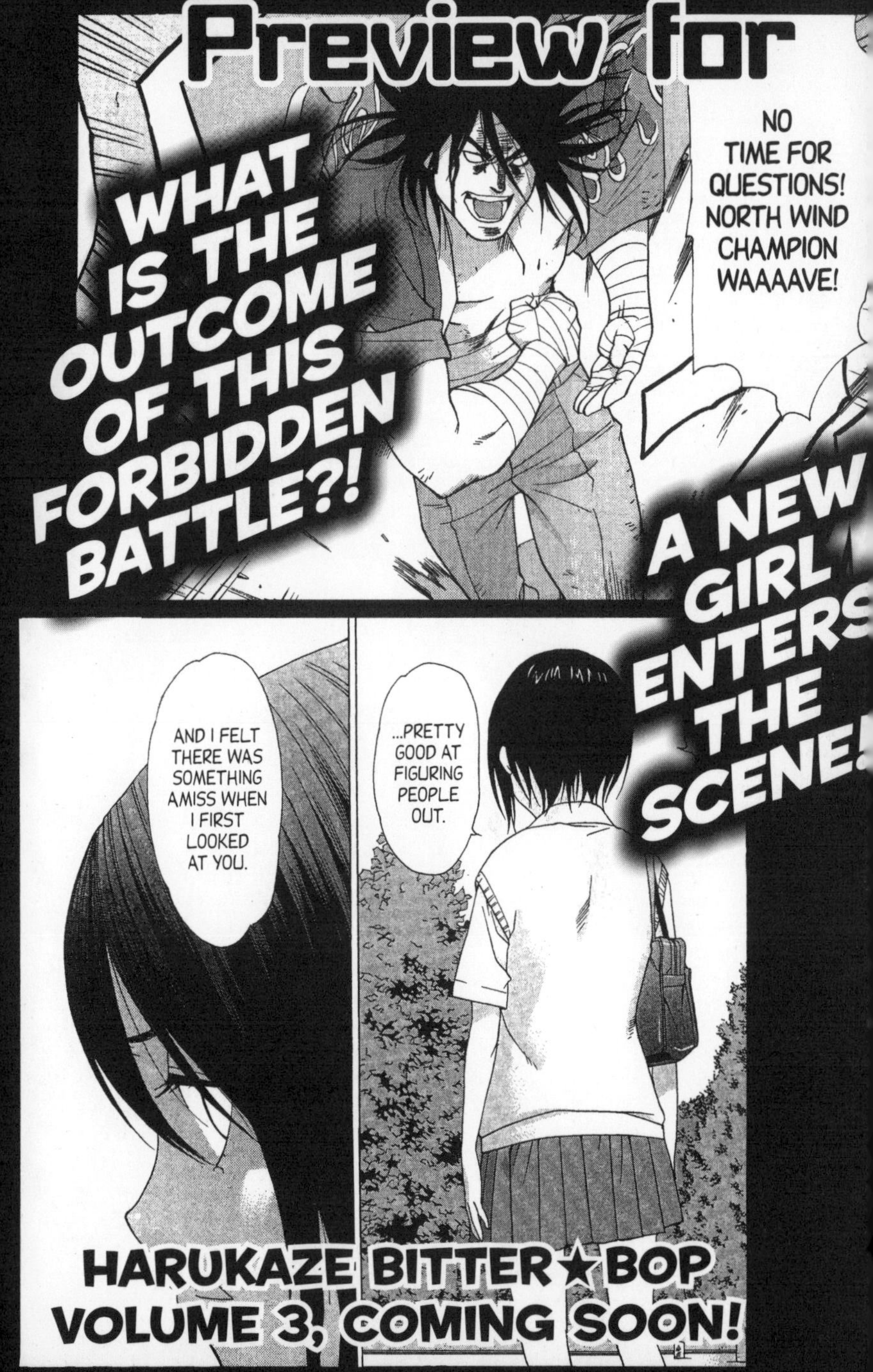
Preview for
NO TIME FOR QUESTIONS! NORTH WIND CHAMPION WAAAAVE!
WHAT IS THE OUTCOME OF THIS FORBIDDEN BATTLE?!
A NEW GIRL ENTERS THE SCENE!
...PRETTY GOOD AT FIGURING PEOPLE OUT.
AND I FELT THERE WAS SOMETHING AMISS WHEN I FIRST LOOKED AT YOU.
HARUKAZE BITTER★BOP VOLUME 3, COMING SOON!

AN INSIDE LOOK AT

STREET FIGHTER

ON PAGE 12, SOUZA USES A SPINNING ATTACK AND YELLS OUT "NORTH WIND SENPUUKYAKU!" THIS TORNADO KICK IS A PLAY OFF OF THE TATSUMAKI SENPUUKYAKU MOVE MADE FAMOUS BY KEN AND RYU IN THE *STREET FIGHTER* GAME SERIES RELEASED BY CAPCOM. MAYBE WE'LL SEE A SHORYUKEN NEXT?

SAINT SEIYA

ON PAGE 156, SOUZA DOES AN ATTACK THAT LOOKS REMARKABLY SIMILAR TO DIAMOND DUST, THE FAVORITE TECHNIQUE OF *SAINT SEIYA* CHARACTER, HYOGA. SOUZA, AGAIN, ADDS NORTH WIND INTO THE ATTACK NAME TO MAKE IT HIS OWN. SAINT SEIYA WAS AN INTERNATIONAL PHENOMENON WHEN THE ANIME WAS RELEASED IN THE LATE 80S. UNFORTUNATELY, THE SERIES WAS NOT RELEASED IN THE U.S. UNTIL 2003 AND THE DATED ANIMATION MEANT THAT IT NEVER TOOK OFF HERE. THE U.S. VERSION, RENAMED *KNIGHTS OF THE ZODIAC*, WAS ALSO UNIVERSALLY PANNED BY FANS WHO COMPLAINED OF BAD DUBBING AND EXCESSIVE EDITING. VIZ STILL RELEASES THE MANGA UNDER THE NAME *SAINT SEIYA: KNIGHTS OF THE ZODIAC*.

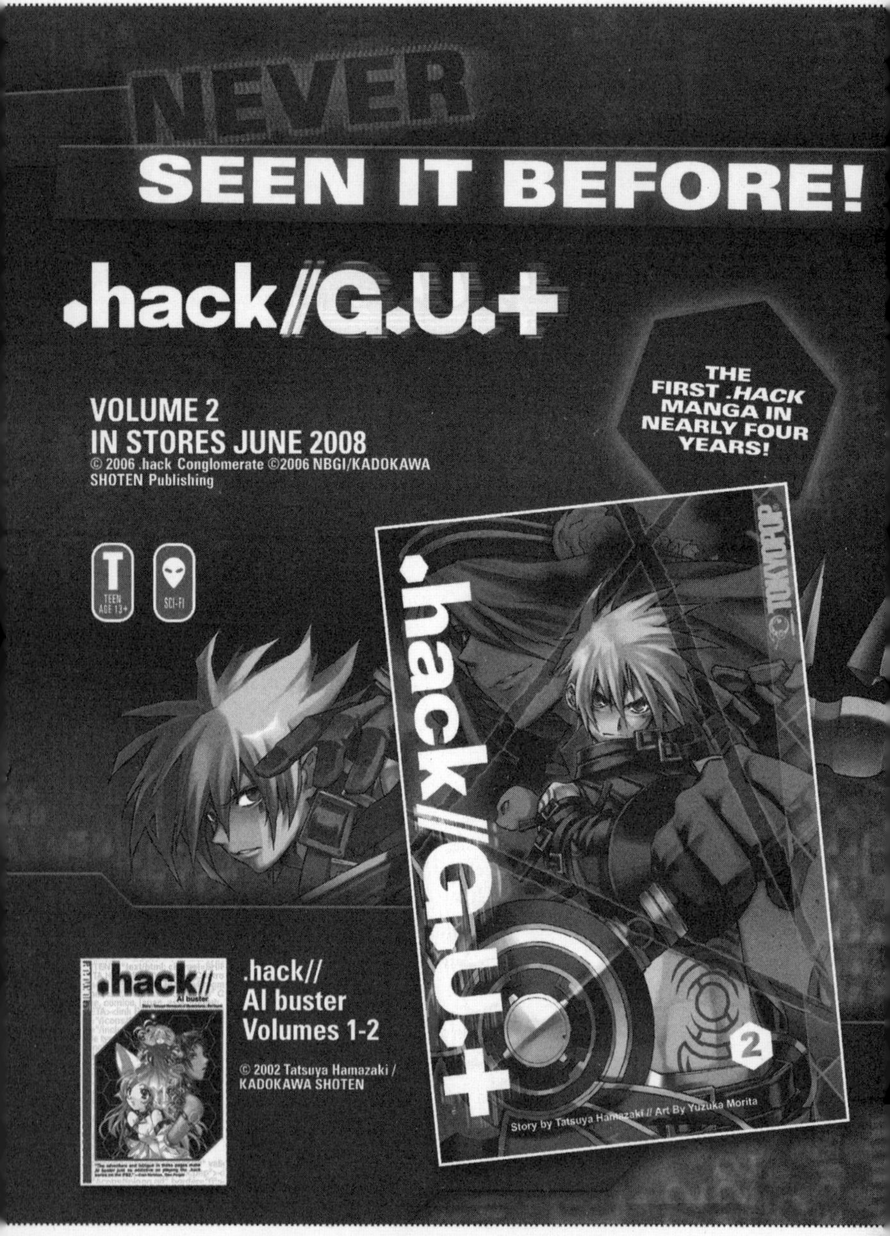
NEVER
SEEN IT BEFORE!
.hack//G.U.+
THE FIRST .HACK MANGA IN NEARLY FOUR YEARS!
VOLUME 2
IN STORES JUNE 2008
© 2006 .hack Conglomerate ©2006 NBGI/KADOKAWA SHOTEN Publishing
T TEEN AGE 13+
SCI-FI
TOKYOPOP
.hack//G.U.+
2
Story by Tatsuya Hamazaki // Art By Yuzuka Morita
.hack//
AI buster
.hack//
AI buster
Volumes 1-2
© 2002 Tatsuya Hamazaki / KADOKAWA SHOTEN

WWW.TOKYOPOP.COM

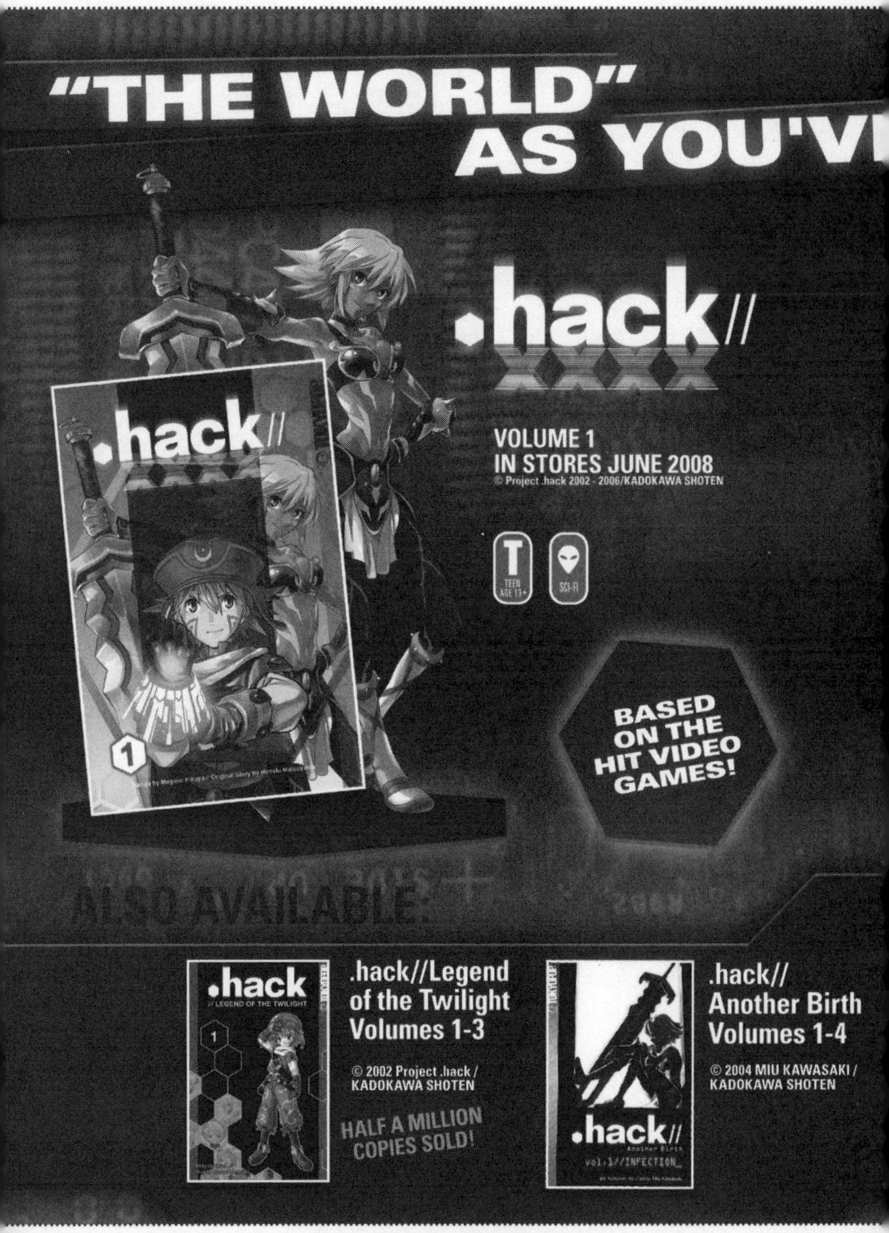
"THE WORLD"
AS YOU'VI
.hack//
VOLUME 1
IN STORES JUNE 2008
© Project .hack 2002 - 2006/KADOKAWA SHOTEN
TEEN AGE 13+
SCI-FI
BASED ON THE HIT VIDEO GAMES!
ALSO AVAILABLE:
.hack//Legend of the Twilight Volumes 1-3
© 2002 Project .hack / KADOKAWA SHOTEN
HALF A MILLION COPIES SOLD!
.hack// Another Birth Volumes 1-4
© 2004 MIU KAWASAKI / KADOKAWA SHOTEN

FOR MORE INFORMATION VISIT:

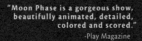

STOP!

This is the back of the book.
You wouldn't want to spoil a great ending!

This book is printed "manga-style," in the authentic Japanese right-to-left format. Since none of the artwork has been flipped or altered, readers get to experience the story just as the creator intended. You've been asking for it, so TOKYOPOP® delivered: authentic, hot-off-the-press, and far more fun!

DIRECTIONS

If this is your first time reading manga-style, here's a quick guide to help you understand how it works.

It's easy... just start in the top right panel and follow the numbers. Have fun, and look for more 100% authentic manga from TOKYOPOP®!